Russia and its Near Neighbours

Also by Maria Raquel Freire and Roger E. Kanet

RUSSIA AND EUROPEAN SECURITY *(editors)*
KEY PLAYERS AND REGIONAL DYNAMICS IN EURASIA: The Return of the 'Great Game' *(editors)*

Also by Maria Raquel Freire

PUTIN'S RUSSIA: Structuring Vectors of Foreign Policy *(in Portuguese)*
FOREIGN POLICY: Change in International Relations *(editor) (in Portuguese)*
CONFLICT AND SECURITY IN THE FORMER SOVIET UNION: The Role of the OSCE

Also by Roger E. Kanet

RUSSIAN FOREIGN POLICY IN THE 21ST CENTURY *(editor)*
THE UNITED STATES AND EUROPE IN A CHANGING WORLD *(editor)*
A RESURGENT RUSSIA AND THE WEST: The European Union, NATO and Beyond *(editor)*
IDENTITIES, NATIONS AND POLITICS AFTER COMMUNISM *(editor)*
FROM SUPERPOWER TO BESIEGED GLOBAL POWER: Restoring World Order after the Failure of the Bush Doctrine *(edited with Edward A. Kolodziej)*
RUSSIA: Re-emerging Great Power *(editor)*
POST-COMMUNIST STATES IN THE WORLD COMMUNITY: Selected Papers from the Fifth World Congress of Central and East European Studies, Warsaw, 1995 *(edited with William E. Ferry)*
THE FOREIGN POLICY OF THE RUSSIAN FEDERATION *(edited with Alexander V. Kozhemiakin)*
COPING WITH CONFLICT AFTER THE COLD WAR *(edited with Edward A. Kolodziej)*
THE COLD WAR AS COOPERATION: Superpower Cooperation in Regional Conflict Management *(edited with Edward A. Kolodziej)*
THE LIMITS OF SOVIET POWER IN THE DEVELOPING WORLD: Thermidor in the Revolutionary Struggle *(edited with Edward A. Kolodziej)*

Studies in Central and Eastern Europe
Stanislav J. Kirschbaum is general editor of the series for the International Council for Central and East European Studies

Russia and its Near Neighbours

Edited by

Maria Raquel Freire
Assistant Professor
Department of International Relations, University of Coimbra, Portugal

and

Roger E. Kanet
Professor
Department of International Studies, University of Miami, USA

First published 2012 by
PALGRAVE MACMILLAN

Palgrave Macmillan in the UK is an imprint of Macmillan Publishers Limited, registered in England, company number 785998, of Houndmills, Basingstoke, Hampshire RG21 6XS.

Palgrave Macmillan in the US is a division of St Martin's Press LLC, 175 Fifth Avenue, New York, NY 10010.

Palgrave Macmillan is the global academic imprint of the above companies and has companies and representatives throughout the world.

Palgrave® and Macmillan® are registered trademarks in the United States, the United Kingdom, Europe and other countries.

ISBN 978–0–230–39017–1

This book is printed on paper suitable for recycling and made from fully managed and sustained forest sources. Logging, pulping and manufacturing processes are expected to conform to the environmental regulations of the country of origin.

A catalogue record for this book is available from the British Library.

A catalog record for this book is available from the Library of Congress.

10 9 8 7 6 5 4 3 2 1
21 20 19 18 17 16 15 14 13 12

Printed and bound in Great Britain by
CPI Antony Rowe, Chippenham and Eastbourne

Contents

Part III   Energy in Russian–CIS Relations

List of Map and Tables

Map

Tables

Notes on Contributors

Lilia A. Arakelyan is a doctoral student and a Research Assistant at the Department of International Studies at the University of Miami. She holds a BA degree in Russian Language and Literature, with a minor in Journalism from Yerevan State University, and an MA in Russian and Slavic Studies from the University of Arizona. After graduation from Yerevan State University she worked as a journalist for major Russian–Armenian newspapers in Yerevan. In 2001, she received a state award from Armenia for a series of newspaper articles in *The Voice of Armenia*. She taught Russian at the University of Arizona in 2007–09 and also served as a Russian translator for the US Census in 2010. Her Master's thesis was devoted to a preliminary study of Armenian immigration to the United States after the Soviet Union collapsed. Her goal was to achieve an understanding of the problems of Armenian immigration to the US that will lead to changes in international laws in both the sending and receiving countries. Her current research interests focus on Soviet/Russian foreign policy, and problems of gender inequalities in post-communist Europe, different aspects of nationalism, ethno-national conflicts in the former Soviet empire and on international security more broadly. Lilia worked for the daily *New Time* in Yerevan from 1998 to 2001, covering politics, crime and socio-economic issues. She was also a reporter for *The Voice of Armenia* daily in Yerevan from 2001 to 2007, where she covered a wide range of national events, including politics, foreign affairs and socioeconomic issues.

Diana Digol gained her PhD from the European University Institute in Florence in 2007. In March 2008, she joined the Institute for Peace Research and Security Policy at the University of Hamburg. Prior to that she worked as a Teaching Fellow at the European Inter-University Centre for Human Rights and Democratisation in Venice. She is interested in foreign policy, diplomacy and democratisation. Her publications include a book on *Emerging Diplomatic Elites in Post-Communist Europe: Analysis of Diplomats* (VDM Verlag Dr Müller, 2010); a chapter on the United Nations Children's Fund (UNICEF) in H. Anheier, R. List and S. Toepler (eds), *International Encyclopedia of Civil Society* (Springer, 2009); an article 'Right or wrong: debate in Russia on conflict in Georgia' in *S+F Sicherheit und Frieden/Security and Peace* (2009, 1); and several others.

John B. Dunlop has since 1983 been a Senior Fellow at the Hoover Institution, Stanford University. He is the author, editor or co-editor of ten books, including *The Faces of Contemporary Nationalism* (Princeton University Press, 1983); *The Rise of Russia and the Fall of the Soviet Empire* (Princeton University Press, 1993, 1995); *Russia Confronts Chechnya: Roots of a Separatist Conflict* (Cambridge University Press, 1998); *The New Russian Nationalism* (Praeger Publishers, 1985); *The Faces of Contemporary Russian Nationalism* (Princeton University Press, 1983); *The New Russian Revolutionaries* (Nordland Publishing Company, 1976); and is co-editor of *Aleksandr Solzhenitsyn: Critical Essays and Documentary Materials* (Collier-Macmillan, 1975) and *Solzhenitsyn in Exile* (Hoover Institution Press, 1985). During 2008, he served as Acting Director of the Center for Russian, East European and Eurasian Studies at Stanford University.

Maria Raquel Freire is Assistant Professor at the Department of International Relations at the University of Coimbra and Researcher at the Centre for Social Studies (CES) at the University of Coimbra. She holds a PhD in International Relations from the University of Kent. Her research focuses on foreign policy, Russia and the post-Soviet space and peace studies. She has published several articles in refereed journals dealing with these topics, such as *Asian Perspective*, *Global Society* and *Journal of Conflict, Security and Development*. Recent publications include *Russian Foreign Policy under Putin* (Almedina, 2011, in Portuguese); her co-editing with Roger E. Kanet, *Key Players and Regional Dynamics in Eurasia: The Return of the 'Great Game'* (Palgrave Macmillan, 2010); a chapter on the Organization for Security and Co-operation in Europe (OSCE) in Central Asia in E. Kavalski (ed.), *The New Central Asia* (World Scientific Publishing, 2010); Russia and the EU in Roger E. Kanet (ed.), *A Resurgent Russia and the West: The European Union, NATO and Beyond* (Republic of Letters Publishing, 2009); 'Russia and the Commonwealth of Independent States (CIS)', in Edward A. Kolodziej and Roger E. Kanet (eds), *From Superpower to Besieged Global Power: Restoring World Order after the Failure of the Bush Doctrine* (University of Georgia Press, 2008); 'The European Security and Defence Policy (ESDP) history, structures and capabilities', in Michael Merlingen and Rasa Ostrauskaite (eds), *The European Security and Defence Policy: An Implementation Perspective* (Routledge, 2008). She is also the author of *Conflict and Security in the Former Soviet Union: The Role of the OSCE* (Ashgate, 2003); and *The Challenges to Democratisation in a Global World* (Afrontamento, 2004).

Graeme P. Herd is Head of the International Security Programme at the Geneva Centre for Security Policy (GCSP), as well as Co-Director of the

International Training Course in Security Policy (ITC) at the GCST. Before moving to Switzerland, he was appointed Professor of Civil–Military Relations at the George C. Marshall European Center for Security Studies, Garmisch-Partenkirchen (2002–05) and a non-resident Associate Fellow of the International Security Programme, Chatham House (2004–07). Prior to this he was Lecturer in International Relations at the University of Aberdeen (1997–2002) and at Staffordshire University (1994–97) and a Projects Officer at the Department of War Studies at King's College London (1993–94). During his doctoral archival research on seventeenth-century Russian military and diplomatic history, he studied as a British Council Scholar at the Institute of Russian History, Russian Academy of Sciences, Moscow (1991–92). Dr Herd's publications since 2006 include: editor, *Great Powers and Strategic Stability in the 21st Century: Competing Visions of World Order* (Routledge/GCSP, 2010); with Paul Dukes and Jarmo Kotilaine, *Stuarts and Romanovs: The Rise and Fall of a Special Relationship* (Dundee University Press, 2009); edited with Anne Aldis, *The Ideological War on Terror: Worldwide Strategies for Counter-Terrorism* (Routledge, 2007); and with Tuomas Forsberg, *Divided West: European Security and the Transatlantic Relationship* (Blackwell's and Chatham House, 2006). His latest publications include, 'The global puzzle: order in an age of primacy, power-shifts and interdependence', *Geneva Papers–Research Series*, No. 1 (GCSP, January 2011); and with Nayef R. F. Al-Rodhan and Lisa Watanabe, *Critical Turning Points in the Middle East: 1915–2015* (Palgrave MacMillan, 2011).

Roger E. Kanet is Professor at the Department of International Studies at the University of Miami, where he served as Dean of the School of International Studies (1997–2000). Prior to 1997, he taught at the University of Illinois at Urbana-Champaign, where he was a member of the Department of Political Science and served as Head of the Department (1984–87), and as Associate Vice Chancellor for Academic Affairs and Director of International Programs and Studies (1989–97). He has published more than 200 scholarly articles and edited over twenty-five books. Recent publications include: editor, *Russian Foreign Policy in the 21st Century* (Palgrave Macmillan, 2010); co-editor with Maria Raquel Freire, *Key Players and Regional Dynamics in Eurasia: The Return of the 'Great Game'* (Palgrave Macmillan, 2010); editor, *The United States and Europe in a Changing World* (Republic of Letters Publishing, 2009); editor, *A Resurgent Russia and the West: The European Union, NATO and Beyond* (Republic of Letters Publishing, 2009); co-editor with Edward A. Kolodziej, *From Superpower to Besieged Global Power: Restoring World Order after the Failure of the Bush*

Doctrine (University of Georgia Press, 2008); editor, *Russia: Re-emerging Great Power* (Palgrave Macmillan, 2007); and editor, *The New Security Environment: The Impact on Russia, Central and Eastern Europe* (Ashgate Publishing, 2005). He is a member of the Council on Foreign Relations, New York.

Ria Laenen is Senior Research Fellow at the Institute for International and European Policy at the University of Leuven. Dr Laenen wrote her PhD thesis on the link between Russia's search for identity and its policy towards the 'Near Abroad'. Since 2004, she is also the coordinator of the Chair InBev-Baillet Latour EU–Russia at KU Leuven. Among her publications are: the chapter, 'Ill-equipped to stop the bear: the UN Security Council and the case of the Russian–Georgian August 2008 War', in Jan Wouters, Edith Drieskens and Sven Biscop (eds), *Belgium in the UN Security Council: Reflections on the 2007–2008 Membership* (Antwerp Intersentia, 2009); and co-edited with Katlijn Malfliet, *Elusive Russia: Current Developments in Russian State Identity and Institutional Reform under President Putin* (Leuven University Press, 2008).

Luke March is Senior Lecturer in Soviet and Post-Soviet Politics at the University of Edinburgh. From 1999–2006 he was Lecturer in Soviet and Post-Soviet Politics at Edinburgh and in 1999 he was Temporary Lecturer in Russian Politics at the University of Birmingham. His main research interests are contemporary Russian and Moldovan politics, the radical left in Europe, Communism and Russian nationalism. He has published numerous articles and several books. His most recent articles include: 'Managing opposition in a hybrid regime: just Russia and parastatal opposition', *Slavic Review* (2009, 68). His books include that edited with Roland Dannreuther, *Russia and Islam: State, Society and Radicalism* (Routledge, 2010); and *The Communist Party in Post-Soviet Russia* (Manchester University Press, 2002). His most recent book is *Radical Left Parties in Europe* (Routledge, 2011).

Bertil Nygren is Associate Professor of Political Science at the Swedish National Defence College and at the Department of Political Science, Stockholm University. He has held various administrative positions at Stockholm University, including Head of Department and Deputy Head of Department (1994–2001). His most recent monograph is *The Rebuilding of Greater Russia: Putin's Foreign Policy toward the CIS Countries* (Routledge, 2008). He has also published articles and chapters in various anthologies on Russian politics, especially foreign policy. These include, 'Putin's use of natural gas to reintegreate the CIS region', *Problems of Post-Communism* (2008, 5), and chapters in Roger E. Kanet (ed.), *Russia: Re-emerging Great Power* (Palgrave Macmillan, 2007); in Kjell Engelbrekt and Jan Hallenberg (eds), *The European Union and Strategy: An Emerging Actor* (Routledge, 2008); in Charlotte Wagnsson, James Sperling and Jan Hallenberg (eds), *The EU in a Multipolar World: Security Governance Meets Great Power Gambit* (Routledge, 2009); in Roger E. Kanet (ed.), *A Resurgent Russia and the West: The European Union, NATO and Beyond* (Republic of Letters Publishing, 2009); in Kjell Engelbrekt and Bertil Nygren (eds), *Russia and Europe: Building Bridges, Digging Trenches* (Routledge, 2010); Bertil Nygren et al. (eds), *Russia on our Minds: Russian Security and Northern Europe, Strategic Yearbook 2008–2009* (Swedish National Defence College, 2010); in Maria Raquel Freire and Roger E. Kanet (eds), *Key Players and Regional Dynamics in Eurasia: The Return of the 'Great Game'* (Palgrave Macmillan, 2010); and in Roger E. Kanet (ed.), *Russian Foreign Policy in the 21st Century* (Palgrave Macmillan, 2010).

John Russell is Professor of Russian and Security Studies at the School of Social and International Studies at the University of Bradford. Author of *Chechnya: Russia's 'War on Terror'* (Routledge, 2007), he has published articles on Russia, Chechnya and terrorism in a number of international journals, including *Europe–Asia Studies, Nationalities Papers, Third World Quarterly*, as well as for *The World Today*. In recent years he has given papers and seminars at the Association for the Study of Nationalities (ASN) in Paris and New York, the International Studies Association (ISA) in New York, International Council for Central and East European Studies (ICCEES) in Stockholm, the Royal Institute of International Affairs in London, International Institute for Strategic Studies (IISS) in London and Rostov, at the University of Cambridge and University of Oxford, Stockholm International Peace Research Institute (SIPRI) in Stockholm, and the NATO Parliamentary Assembly's Political Committee in the Reichstag in Berlin. Currently he is writing a monograph on Ramzan Kadyrov, the eccentric young President of Chechnya.

Licínia Simão has a PhD in International Relations and teaches at the University of Beira Interior. Her previous positions include, among others, being a Teaching and Research Fellow at the University of Coimbra and at the OSCE Academy in Bishkek, a Junior Researcher at the Research Unit in Political Science and International Relations (NICPRI) at the University of Minho, and a Visiting Research Fellow at the Centre for European Policy Studies in Brussels. Her research interests include EU foreign policy, regional and international dynamics in the Commonwealth of Independent States (CIS), especially in the South Caucasus and Central Asia. Her publications include a chapter co-written with Sandra Fernandes, 'Competing for

Eurasia: Russian and European Union perspectives', in Maria Raquel Freire and Roger E. Kanet (eds), *Key Players and Regional Dynamics in Eurasia: The Return of the 'Great Game'* (Palgrave Macmillan, 2010); 'Are civil society organizations the missing link? Assessing EU engagement in the Nagorno-Karabakh conflict', in Nathalie Tocci (ed.), *The European Union, Civil Society and Conflict* (Routledge, 2010); 'An improbable partnership: Spanish and Kazakh efforts to bring Central Asia to the fore of European Politics', *UNISCI Discussion Papers* (2010); co-written with Maria Raquel Freire, 'The EU's neighborhood policy and the South Caucasus: unfolding new patterns of cooperation', *Caucasian Review of International Affairs* (2008, 2); co-written with Nathalie Tocci, Burcu Gültenkin-Punsmann and Nicolas Tavitian, 'The case for opening the Turkish–Armenian border', a study for the Foreign Affairs Committee of the European Parliament, Trans-European Policy Studies Association (TEPSA) (2007; available on TEPSA and European Parliament websites); co-written with Maria Raquel Freire, 'The EU's neighborhood policy towards the Southern Caucasus: searching for commonalty in a patchy scenario', in *Comparative Constitutional Review Journal* (in Russian; 2007, 57).

Hanna Smith is a Researcher at the Aleksanteri Institute and is an expert in Russian foreign policy as well as Russian domestic policy trends affecting Russia's foreign relations. She has degrees from Sweden and Great Britain in Russian Language, History and Politics as well as International Relations. In 2001–02, she was a Visiting Researcher at the University of Birmingham, and in 2006 at the Finnish Ministry of Foreign Affairs. Hanna Smith has worked on numerous academic and policy-oriented projects. Her publications include: editor, *Russia and its Foreign Policy: Influences, Interests and Issues* (Kikimora Publications, 2005); editor, *The Two-Level Game: Russia's Relations with Great Britain, Finland and the European Union* (Kikimora Publications, 2006); Osmo Kuusi, Paula Tiihonen and Hanna Smith (eds), 'Venäjä 2017-kolme skenaariota' (Russia 2017: three scenarios) (Committee of the Future, Parliament of Finland, 2007); editor, 'Haasteiden Venäjä' (Challenges of Russia) (Ministry of Defence, Finland, 2008); and 'Russian foreign policy, regional cooperation and northern relations', in Pami Aalto, Helge Blakkisrud and Hanna Smith (eds), *The New Northern Dimension of the European Neighbourhood* (Center for European Policy Studies (CEPS), 2009); as well as numerous articles.

Matthew Sussex is Senior Lecturer at the School of Government at the University of Tasmania. His PhD on contemporary Russian foreign policy (2001) was completed at the University of Melbourne. Matthew's research interests include strategic and security studies, Russian politics and foreign policy and conflict in the international system. He has been awarded grants from bodies such as the Australian Research Council and the Fulbright Commission, amongst others. His publications include *European Security after 9/11* (Ashgate, 2004) and *Conflict in the Former USSR* (Cambridge University Press, 2011), as well as articles and book chapters on globalisation and contemporary war, Russian foreign policy, the foreign policies of great powers and Australian security policy. He is a Fellow at the Contemporary Europe Research Centre, a National Executive member of the Australian Institute of International Affairs and a founding member of the Australian Council for Strategic Studies. His next book, *How States Cheat on 'Global' Human Rights Norms* (forthcoming, 2012), will be on how renovations to global human rights such as the R2P paradoxically assist 'cheating' in the arena of international justice.

General Editor's Preface

Studies in Central and Eastern Europe

This is the third world congress organised by the International Council for Central and East European Studies (ICCEES) that has the privilege of seeing congress volumes published by Palgrave Macmillan. That this is happening is an indication not only of the very fruitful relationship that ICCEES has with Palgrave Macmillan, but also of the recognition that the field of Central and East European Studies continues to enjoy not only academic excellence, but also continued pertinence as an area of study.

In their Preface to earlier volumes from the 1995 Warsaw and the 2005 Berlin Congresses, my two predecessors as General Editor, Professor Ronald Hill of Trinity College Dublin and Professor Roger E. Kanet of the University of Miami, outlined the historical conditions that not only brought about the creation of ICCEES, but above all of the importance of publishing the research that is presented at ICCEES congresses. All congresses studied Central and Eastern Europe through the lens of various disciplines, but also mirrored the changes that were taking place in the area since Western scholars came together in Banff, Canada, in 1974 in order to organise the research that they were engaged in, but which lacked an organisational structure that could coordinate their results and offer an opportunity for debate and discussion. This is why the International Committee for Soviet and East European Studies (ICSEES) was created; today it is known as the International Council for Central and East European Studies (ICCEES). The change in name reflected not only the mutations that the area was undergoing, but also the field of study.

After 1989, the societies and states of Central and Eastern Europe began experiencing major political, economic and social change. As a result, no longer were Western scholars engaged in 'Communist Studies', rather, they were focusing on an area that was undergoing redefinition as a geopolitical region. Domestic politics were in flux and interstate relations were experiencing a qualitative change that henceforth stressed cooperation rather than confrontation. ICCEES understood the need to give its congresses thematic direction. The 1990 ICCEES World Congress in Harrogate, England, celebrated the end of the Cold War; the 1995 Warsaw Congress focused on the democratic development of the former 'Communist states'; the 2000 Congress in Tampere, Finland,

stressed the divergences, convergences and uncertainties in Central
and Eastern Europe; the 2005 Berlin Congress focused on the European
Union; while the 2010 Stockholm Congress examined the prospects for
wider cooperation in Eurasia. This volume in the series reflects this last
theme.

Putting together a volume that has thematic unity from the plethora
of papers presented at a world congress is a major challenge. There was
a time when it was sufficient to bring together high-quality papers and
publish them as congress proceedings. The list of such publications,
found on the ICCEES Web page, testifies to the vitality of research in
the area. This is no longer the case. Fortunately many journals offer
a publishing outlet for high-class single presentations. This volume
presents more than just excellent individual research results: it also offers
an important scholarly perspective. It marks a major contribution.

Stanislav J. Kirschbaum
York University, Toronto

Preface and Acknowledgements

The present volume is part of a larger multi-authored examination of ongoing developments in the foreign policy of the Russian Federation, with special focus on relations with Russia's near neighbours, the other former republics of the Soviet Union and the West, including both the members of the European Union and the United States.[1] The editors originally conceived of the project as a way to bring together analysts from across the world, many of them younger scholars, who are working on various aspects of Russian foreign and security policy. The first stage of the collaborative effort was the organisation of several panels on Russian foreign and security policy at the Eighth World Congress of the International Council for Central and East European Studies (ICCEES) held in Stockholm, Sweden, in July 2010. The editors were fortunate to entice a group of scholars to participate and present drafts of papers on these panels. The panels discussions contributed to the analysts editing and refining their arguments.

Immediately after the Congress the editors invited a number of other scholars who had presented papers at the ICCEES Congress that complemented the first group of analyses to join up with them in the publication project. This second group of papers added both depth and breadth to the analysis of Russian policy, as did several other papers not presented at the Congress, but directly relevant to the development of a comprehensive assessment of Russian relations either with its immediate post-Soviet neighbours or with the countries of the West.

The editors wish to express their deep appreciation to all of the participating authors for their important contributions to the ICCEES Congress, for their positive responses to editorial suggestions, for meeting deadlines, and for providing excellent and clear analyses of various aspects of Russian foreign and security policy. They wish to thank, as well, the many others without whose contribution this volume would not have appeared – the editors at Palgrave Macmillan, the anonymous readers who commented on various stages of the projects, the production staff, and others who have helped to ensure the clarity and readability of the final published text. Very special thanks go to Julia Vorobiova, a doctoral student at the University of Miami, for her invaluable assistance in ensuring accuracy in the references and editorial and formatting consistency across the chapters.

Maria Raquel Freire
University of Coimbra

Roger E. Kanet
University of Miami

Note

1. A second volume, edited by Roger E. Kanet and Maria Raquel Freire and titled *Russia and European Security*, will be published in 2012 by Republic of Letters Publishing, Dordrecht, The Netherlands.

Introduction: Russia and its Near Neighbours

Maria Raquel Freire and Roger E. Kanet

Relations between the Russian Federation and the West, including especially the European Union (EU) and the United States, have fluctuated significantly over the two decades since the collapse of the Soviet Union in 1991.[1] After a very brief period of seemingly close collaboration, relations began to fray, as the leadership in Moscow concluded that Western states were not taking its interests seriously. But, not until the emergence of Vladimir Putin as a vigorous new leader at the turn of the millennium and the revival of the Russian economy largely as a result of exponential increases in energy demands on the global markets was Russia in the position to push its own policy agenda and to challenge Western policy objectives, including those of the US. As others have noted (Sakwa, 2009), one can detect three rather clear periods in Russian policy towards and relations with the West from 1991 through to the end of the first decade of the twenty-first century. The first of these covers the years 1992 to 1995 – in fact, Sakwa divides this into two separate sub-periods – when Russia first followed Western initiatives, but soon began to reassert its own interests; a second period covering 1996 to 1999 that Sakwa terms the period of 'competitive pragmatism'; and, finally, the Putin and Medvedev years between 2000 and 2010, when Moscow clearly reasserted its autonomous policy objectives.[2] Russian policy towards the rest of the world underwent significant changes during these two decades, nowhere more noticeably so than in relations with both the West, which at the outset was at the centre of Russia's foreign policy approach, and to the countries of the 'Near Abroad'.

During the summer of 1999, when President Yeltsin selected Vladimir Putin as his last prime minister and then, a few months later, as his successor as president, Russia's position as a participant in global political and economic affairs had only recently reached its nadir. The

1

Russian economy and financial system had virtually collapsed in the summer of 1998. The Chechen secessionist movement had once again become a major issue in Russian domestic politics, as had the inability of Moscow to exert effective political control over much of the vast territory of the Russian Federation. Finally, the West, and NATO in particular, had ignored strongly voiced Russian opposition to expansion into what had been part of Soviet-dominated space in Central Europe and even stronger opposition to military intervention in Serbia to protect the Kosovar population.

Almost immediately after assuming the presidency, Vladimir Putin laid out his strategy for ensuring the reemergence of Russia as a major regional and global actor.[3] Central to this strategy was the reestablishment of effective central control by the government in Moscow over all of the territory of Russia. Putin accomplished this quite deftly during his first term as president by centralising the selection of regional political elites in the office of the president (for instance, by the abolition of elections for provincial governors), the gradual purging of the political opposition (often by the use of extralegal mechanisms), the silencing of the critical media, and the suppression of the remnants of secession in Chechnya. Putin was fortunate as well because the dramatic increase in the global demand for energy, of which Russia remains a major exporter, contributed to a visible rejuvenation of the Russian economy that continued until the worldwide financial collapse of 2008–09 (World Bank, 2008).[4] By the end of his first term in office, President Putin had overseen substantial political and economic gains that provided the foundations for a more assertive and less reactive foreign policy.

In the foreign policy realm, Russia under Putin continued to seek allies who shared a commitment to preventing the global dominance of the United States that represents, in the words of the official Foreign Policy Concept of the Russian Federation, a threat to international security and to Russia's goal of serving as a major centre of influence in a multipolar world. Throughout the 1990s, because of its weakened state as a major power, Russia had been forced to accept virtually any policy initiated by the United States and NATO. For President Putin, and for those who supported him, this situation had to change, and he was about to make clear that Russia would no longer accept what it viewed as the policy dictates of the West on issues such as NATO and EU expansion eastwards, support for what Moscow viewed as anti-Russian political forces in neighbouring post-Soviet states (the colour revolutions), and direct military intervention against Russian allies, as against the Serbs in Kosovo. Putin voiced this reorientation of Russian policy quite clearly in his statement to the Russian parliament and people in the spring of 2005 that 'the collapse of the Soviet Union was the greatest geopolitical catastrophe of the century' (Putin, 2005). Early in 2007, he repeated even more forcefully the message of Russia's refusal simply to accept Western encroachment and imposition, as it had previously been forced to do, when he attacked virtually all aspects of US foreign and security policy in a speech delivered at an international security conference in Munich (Putin, 2007).

When Putin turned the presidency over to his handpicked successor Dmitri Medvedev in May 2008, Russia had reemerged as a major player in European political and economic affairs and as the dominant actor across former Soviet space. However, Russia was also a much more authoritarian state internally, with significantly reduced political space for dissent, where brute force was used in dealing with those who dared question the government.[5]

This new assertive foreign policy reached its climax in 2008, with the Russian military incursion into Georgia and Moscow's recognition of the breakaway regions of Georgia as independent states. Probably the clearest message that Moscow meant for all others to take away from this military confrontation was that it would no longer accept continued Western expansion into former Soviet territory that it viewed as central to its own legitimate interests. Establishing its dominant role, at least along its periphery, is a core objective of Russian policy, and the fact was that Moscow would no longer deal with the rest of the world on any other terms except for those that it sets (Medvedev, 2008b). The foundation of this new role has been Russia's semi-monopoly over the extraction and distribution of natural gas and oil across much of Eurasia, and the growing direct influence that this semi-monopoly provides over the economies of neighbouring states.[6] The gas war between Russia and Ukraine in January 2009 and its implications for European consumers of Russian gas make clear the importance of both oil and gas exports to Moscow in its pursuit of its foreign policy objectives.[7]

Before continuing this discussion of recent Russian foreign policy, we should note at least briefly the relationship between the growing assertiveness in Russian foreign policy and domestic political developments. As Russia's leaders abandoned the halting efforts at democratisation that characterised the first decade of the Russian Federation and increasingly reestablished institutions and policies of an authoritarian state, they have also seized upon economic growth and Russian nationalism as the foundations on which to build support from broad segments of the population. The economic boom of the first decade of the twenty-first century that resulted in more than doubling the gross domestic product (GDP) per capita of the Russian population was an important element in the popularity of former President Putin and in the support for his policies.

Public opinion polls, as well as anecdotal information, indicate widespread public support for the return of Russia to great power status; more specifically, Russians overwhelmingly supported the Kremlin's decision to invade Georgia in August 2008 ('Half of Russians yearn for super-power status', 2008). Related to this broad sense of nationalism, the Putin–Medvedev leadership has increasingly focused on the dangers to Russia presented by foreign enemies, in particular the United States. The most recent version of the Foreign Policy Concept (2008) issued by President Medvedev in late July 2008, immediately prior to the intervention in Georgia, represents a break with earlier versions of the Concept, even though it in effect merely codified changes that had already occurred over recent years. Unlike the Concept issued at the beginning of the Putin presidency, it focuses on external, rather than internal, challenges to Russian security – with US global dominance at the very top of the list. In line with the extensive discussion of 'sovereign democracy' in Russia, the Concept stipulates that global competition is acquiring a civilisational dimension, which suggests competition between different value systems and development models within the framework of universal democratic and market economy principles. The new Foreign Policy Concept maintains that the reaction to the prospect of loss by the historic West of its monopoly in global processes finds its expression, in particular, in the continued political and psychological policy of 'containing Russia'.[8]

In the aftermath of the Georgian War, President Medvedev (2008a) presented the five principles guiding Russian foreign policy, which while putting forward new ideas, reinforced the understanding that had emerged in the Kremlin about a different international order, in which the US-centred international system is being replaced (Makarychev, 2010, p. 438). These principles, in line with the Foreign Policy Concept, include the primacy of international law, a multipolar international order, a non-confrontational and non-isolationist policy, the protection of diasporas and recognition of areas of influence. The combination of these five principles points to the goal of reestablishing a dominant position from which Russia will be able to operate, in line with the points that we have already discussed. President Medvedev has also added a new vector of research, innovation and technological development to Russian foreign policy, internally rooted but with clear expression in foreign relations, as for example in the most recent agreements with the

EU (Tolstaya, 2010). This is embedded in the discourse of modernisation and is conceived of widely to encompass military aspects as well as elements related to health and human resources. All of the major recent pronouncements concerning Russian foreign policy emphasise Russia's independence and sovereignty as the foundation on which to build all of Moscow's relations with the outside world.

By the autumn of 2008, immediately following the Russo-Georgian War, Russia's relations with both the United States and the European Union were strained to a point not seen since Soviet days. US plans for the construction of a Missile Defence System in Poland and the Czech Republic and the freezing of EU negotiations with Russia resulting from ongoing conflicts between Russia and several former Soviet dependencies and, more recently, the military intervention in Georgia were central to the deteriorated state of the relationship. In the following two years, however, important efforts were made to revive – 'reset', as US Vice President Biden put it (Whitlock, 2009) – relations between the two countries.[9]

In fact, the election of a new president in the United States in the latter part of 2008 contributed almost immediately to an improvement in the tone of relations between Washington and Moscow. Of a more concrete nature, the agreement on a new Strategic Arms Reduction Treaty (START), the US decision to restructure dramatically its plans for an anti-ballistic missile system, as well as agreements on transit across Russian territory to Afghanistan and on controlling nuclear development in Iran have all contributed to an improvement in Russian relations with the United States (Nation, 2010).

At the same time, Russia's relations with the European Union and with most of the major states of Europe have improved. Negotiations on a new foundation agreement between Russia and the European Union have resumed, although as of the end of 2010 they had still not resulted in an agreement. Russian relations with its Polish neighbour, the most important of the new post-communist members of NATO, have also improved significantly, thereby facilitating improved relations with the EU.

However, despite the improvements in relations, the generally hostile reasoning found in the 2008 version of the National Security Concept is repeated in the Russian Military Doctrine of 2010 (Office of the Russian President, 2010), a document that clearly underlines this understanding in Russia about Western containment policies. The blunt manner in which NATO's enlargement is identified as the primary external threat to Russia is indicative of this understanding. It was in the context of this tension with NATO's enlargement, as well as the irritating US proposal envisaging the development of a defence missile shield, that President Medvedev advanced with a proposal for a new European Security Treaty in Berlin in June 2008. The proposal went through various versions, from being an interstate organisation to including international organisations as members, but the fundamental idea underlining it rested with the Russian goal of limiting US influence while seeking to raise Russian influence, particularly in post-Soviet space. Through this new arrangement, Russia would ensure that no security decisions would be made without taking into account all members' interests, therefore assuring its right of oversight on European security. This proposal has lost momentum, but its relevance in the context of East–West tensions in which it emerged is fundamental to understanding the dynamics shaping Russian foreign policy towards the US, in particular, and regarding European security, more broadly.

The examination of Russian policy that follows is part of a larger examination that focuses on relations with both Russia's immediate neighbours in the present volume, *Russia and its Near Neighbours*, and on relations with Europe and the United States in a second volume entitled *Russia and European Security*.[10] The editors and authors recognise that they have not touched upon Russian policy in other areas of importance, beginning with Russian policy towards China, Japan and the two Koreas. Moreover re-emerging relations with former clients and allies in the Middle East, as well as important new economic relations with Latin America are not discussed in either volume.

In the chapters that follow in this volume, the focus will be on relations between Russia and the countries of Russia's immediate neighbourhood. The volume identifies as its main lines of analysis Russia's relations with its near neighbours, namely post-Soviet republics, and seeks to understand relations between these countries and Russia, which reveal the multidimensional character that has increasingly characterised the heterogeneous post-Soviet area. It analyses Russian foreign policy at a time when Russia has reemerged as the dominant political, economic and military actor in this area. As both Prime Minister Putin and President Medvedev have made most clear, a resurgent Russia is no longer willing to brook the expansion of Western – that is to say, both NATO and EU – involvement in what Moscow considers its areas of 'privileged interest'. The Russian military intervention in Georgia in August 2008 gave ample evidence of this fact. Political contexts, economic options and security alignments are therefore the focus of this analysis, which embeds Russia's relations with its neighbours in the broader dynamic framework in which these take place, with regard to other key actors as well as to fundamental issues, such as energy diplomacy. We hope collectively to make a contribution that adds to the study of Russian relations with its neighbours in post-Soviet space after its reemergence as a major regional and international actor.

With this objective in mind we have divided the book into three parts. The first part looks at determinants of Russian foreign policy following theoretically on the co-constitutive nature of the domestic and external settings in shaping and making policy. Looking at Russian understandings of its national identity and the definition of the national interest, the foreign policy choices of Russia – aimed at its projection as a great power – become clearer. In a chapter entitled 'Russia's vital and exclusive national interests in the Near Abroad', Ria Laenen employs an explicitly constructivist approach, in order to argue that national interests function in today's Russia in a much more encompassing manner than the narrow instrumentalist way in which they are often understood in analyses of Russian policy that are based on a realist or neorealist theoretical perspective. Here, national interests are regarded as a most interesting analytical category to explore the ideational genesis of Russia's foreign policy objectives in the Near Abroad. They emerge out of the interplay of both domestic and international factors, both of which contribute to the sense of national identity that lies as the base of conceptions of national interest. This approach to the analysis of Russian ideas of national interests contributes significantly to our understanding of Russian policy towards its near neighbours.

The chapter by Hanna Smith, entitled 'Domestic influences on Russian foreign policy: status, interests and *ressentiment*', deals with two main factors in the formation of foreign policy – national identity and national interests. Together they determine Russia's policy objectives and help explain contradictory elements in Russian politics. Internal weaknesses often play against the high international status that Russia seeks to achieve. Therefore in dealing with contradictions and in order to overcome what Smith terms a 'vicious circle' in Russian politics, it is fundamental that Russian authorities address structural issues allowing solid articulation between society and political power, in order to overcome internal constraints to the achievement of the goals of Russian foreign policy.

Luke March, in 'Nationalist grievance and Russian foreign policy: the case of Georgia', follows this same line of argument, focusing his analysis on the role of Russian nationalism in the definition of policies. The author argues that, contrary to prevalent views, Russian nationalism traditionally does not affect foreign policy, either directly or in an aggressive manner, constituting essentially a domestic tool for mobilising support. However, after 2008, this traditional linkage to internal discourse seems to assume different dimensions and elicit demands that might spill over into foreign policy. According to March, the August 2008 conflict in Georgia indicates a confluence of domestic and foreign policy discourses towards a nationalist approach. The chapter deals in detail with this interconnection, focusing on the war in Georgia as a case study and aiming to clarify the tension arising from the role of ideas and values in Russian politics, in particular with regard to a pragmatic, interest-based policy that has been characteristic of the presidencies of both Putin and Medvedev.

Also looking at the war in Georgia, in a chapter entitled 'The August 2008 Russo-Georgian War: which side went first?' John B. Dunlop analyses the developments leading to the outbreak of war, questioning the Russian arguments regarding the Georgian responsibility for initiating the August armed hostilities. The author digs into fundamental documents and public statements, as well as international fact-finding assessments seeking clarification on the decision to go to war. Dunlop draws at great length in his work on the findings of Andrei Illarionov, Pavel Felgenhauer and Yuliya Latynina, three well-known Russian analysts, who deconstruct language and discourse regarding information that was made public and that distorted many readings about who initiated this war. In this way, the chapter highlights the role of misinformation and manipulation with regard to decision-making and, more precisely, the taking of responsibility for foreign policy decisions with very concrete implications.

After discussing the determinants of foreign policy in Russia, the volume proceeds to its second part, which focuses on Russia and the Commonwealth of Independent States (CIS). The goal of this part's chapters is to clarify Russian relations within the CIS, and to show how foreign policy dynamics are a demonstration of the level of independence of these states with regard to Russia. Thus it is assumed that, despite asymmetries in relations between Russia and these states, these are bidirectional relations, meaning that different countries define and demand different relations with and towards Russia. These chapters focus on Russia's 'near neighbours', including the South Caucasus, Central Asia and the countries closer to EU borders, namely Ukraine.

In 'Whose 'Near Abroad'? Dilemmas in Russia's declared sphere of privileged interests', John Russell analyses the changing context of Russian relations with its neighbours in the framing of new relations with the US, particularly after the Obama administration took office.

The chapter looks at Russian opposition to the projection of Western interests, in particular US interests, in an area defined as a 'traditional sphere of interest' for Russia – NATO expansion and Russia's energy cuts in response during Putin's presidency, are illustrative. It then moves on to the warming up of relations between Russia and the US, which does not however hide persistent dilemmas related to transition and democratic governance, as well as development choices in Russia, particularly between a Western or a Eurasian model. This leads to what Russell describes as a 'Chill Peace' regarding 'what promises to be the dawn of a pragmatic new relationship between Russia and the West', and what this might deliver regarding Russia's relations in its neighbourhood, and the accommodation of external actors' interests in this new setting.

In 'Russia's European Security Treaty and the Kyrgyz Crisis', Graeme P. Herd guides the discussion towards the effects of the Russian proposal for a new European Security Treaty and how this could shape the security agenda in terms that are more favourable to Russia. The author goes through the details of the proposal and tests the advanced format regarding the case of Kyrgyz unrest and how this new institutional framework could have responded to it. The relevance of this proposal regarding the debate that it initiated is thoroughly discussed, and the case study developed helps the reader to understand Russian views regarding the management of security in its neighbourhood.

Also focusing on Central Asia, but pursuing a broader approach, Licínia Simão in 'Central Asia in Russian and US foreign policy: between continuity and "reset"' looks at the political dynamics in this area from the perspective of the 'reset policy' between the US and Russia, arguing, nevertheless, that the elements for cooperation were already in place before this new mood. The author looks at the policies of engagement of these two main players, and discusses how these affect Russian policies towards Central Asia. She argues that both actors prioritise short- to medium-term interests, while remaining suspicious of the other, particularly Russia about an enlarged US presence. In addition, the absence of cooperative frameworks where institutional relations could be solidified and provide the framework for sustained cooperation further hampers cooperation efforts. In order that Russia might pursue its interests in the area, it should engage in long-term strategic processes and aim simultaneously at the development of policies directed at the stabilisation of its southern borders.

In 'Russia's foreign policy in Central Asia: from Yeltsin to Medvedev', Diana Digol discusses the evolution of Russian policies towards Central Asia looking at the presidencies of Yeltsin, Putin and Medvedev, adding a different twist to the previous contribution. The author seeks to unpack the drivers of Russian foreign policy through these three presidencies, underlining the quest for great power status with Putin and Medvedev, and adding the more recent modernisation course that has been present in Russian discourse. She also looks at how these trends are reflected in Russia's strategic involvement in Central Asia. In her analysis, Digol acknowledges the role of external actors in shaping Russian policy, particularly that of the US, and that Russia has increasingly been attentive to Central Asia as a result of a more pragmatic, predictable and assertive foreign policy. The author argues that Russia is in the process of reasserting itself in Central Asia and that the context and setting offer positive prospects for such a reassertion.

The final part of the volume explores in detail the issue of energy policies and how the coincidence or not of policies and practices in this fundamental domain play in Russian foreign policy. In 'Strategy, security and Russian resource diplomacy', Matthew Sussex analyses Russia's coercive use of its energy resources, asking whether this constitutes a sensible policy for advancing Russian interests. The author argues that this coercive approach responds to Russia's strategic goals, mainly projecting its status as a great power and firmly framing the CIS states inside its area of influence. However, if, on the one hand this approach points to the primacy of Russia in an area described as of special influence, on the other hand it reveals severe limitations to Russian dealings with more powerful actors.

Bertil Nygren, in a chapter entitled 'Russian resource policies towards the CIS countries', focuses his analysis on President Medvedev's approach to energy and how he has been dealing with the inheritance of energy as a foreign policy tool, particularly regarding natural gas. The author does this exercise in how to manage energy as a foreign policy tool throughout the CIS space, identifying differences in approach and leverage and demonstrating that in essence, and despite concessions that have been made, Russian resource policy remains pretty much unchanged under President Medvedev from that which had been developed during the tenure of President Putin.

In 'Russia's energy policies in Eurasia: empowerment or entrapment?' Maria Raquel Freire also looks at energy diplomacy and its potential role as a Russian foreign policy tool. However, she examines this policy through a different prism, where she seeks to unpack the dynamics of empowerment and entrapment of Russia resulting from the complex network of relations of interdependency regarding production, transit and consumption, and including factors such as reliability, price bargaining and unforeseen fluctuations and control of production and transit routes. In this way, she argues, as much as Russia is empowered by energy diplomacy, it is also entrapped by the complex network of interdependence that the energy grid has created. The chapter provides evidence of this tension regarding Russian policies towards Eurasia and Western countries.

Focusing on the South Caucasus in 'Russian energy policy in the South Caucasus', Lilia A. Arakelyan and Roger E. Kanet highlight the key role of energy in Russia's policies in the South Caucasus, as well as Western attempts to reduce Russian influence in the region, in particular in the area of energy. They show that the three states of the South Caucasus are struggling to become truly independent players within their own territory, but that their intentions conflict with the geopolitical interests of other states. Russia's position in the South Caucasus is generally a strong one, they conclude. However, the fact that Russia largely ignored the region in the 1990s and that other actors – from regional states such as Turkey and Iran to others such as the United States and China – established themselves in various ways in the area has resulted in a much more competitive position for Russia as it attempts to dominate the region.

The various chapters in this volume highlight Russia's relations with its immediate neighbours in a context where the resurgence of Russia has been visible in policies and actions. The central argument is that this change in Russia's positioning towards its neighbourhood, with Russia assuming an objective policy of engagement and influence, is evident in its most recent dealings in political, economic and security terms. The authors agree that this has been most visible after the events in Georgia in the summer of 2008. Nevertheless, this does not mean that Russia has unlimited influence in the region, a fact that is detailed throughout the chapters. The contributors show this trend in Russian politics regarding different areas of activity, such as energy diplomacy or political–military relations, as well as through different theoretical lenses, including a discourse analysis approach, which constitutes an add-on to the understanding of the dynamics that underline the complexity of these relations. The chapters that follow therefore aim to bring to light Russia's resurgence, its meaning and how it has been rendered effective, despite limitations, by Russia in its relations with its heterogeneous immediate neighbourhood.

Notes

1. Portions of this Introduction are also included in the introduction to a companion volume, Roger E. Kanet and Maria Raquel Freire (eds), *Russia and European Security* (Dordrecht: Republic of Letters Publishing, 2012, in press).

2. Trenin (2010) provides a similar, but slightly different periodisation, including a fourth period that begins with the Medvedev presidency. Among the many recent examinations of Russian foreign policy since the collapse of the USSR, the most interesting include those by Shevtsova (2010), Trenin (2007) and Tsygankov (2006).
3. The goal of rebuilding Russia and the domestic and foreign strategies needed to achieve that goal are presented in the Foreign Policy Concept of the Russian Federation (2000).
4. The work of Lilia Shevtsova (2007) provides some of the clearest analyses on the erosion of democratic institutions in Putin's Russia.
5. The most heralded case concerns the treatment of Mikhail Khodorkovskii, one-time billionaire critic of Putin (Meier, 2009). Relevant as well is the significant number of journalists who have challenged the state's interpretation of developments only to be killed in unexplained circumstances (Hahn, 2010).
6. For a comprehensive examination of the role of energy in Russia's relations with neighbouring states, see Nygren (2008).
7. In the Ukrainian–Russian confrontation over gas supplies, as in the Georgian–Russian military conflict in the summer of 2008 over South Ossetia, Russia alone was not at fault. The leaders of both Ukraine and Georgia contributed significantly to the confrontations. On European reactions to the policies of these countries, see Taylor (2009). The victory of pro-Russian political leaders in Ukrainian elections in 2010 has seemingly resolved the outstanding differences between Russia and Ukraine.
8. It is important to recognise that the US decision to pursue a policy of a de facto containment of Russia beginning already by the mid 1990s, reinforced Moscow's concerns about security and its future role in areas adjacent to Russian territory and viewed as crucial to Russia's long-term interests.
9. For an excellent and brief examination of Russian–US relations in the twenty-first century, including a discussion of the role of domestic political interests, see Tsygankov (2010). For an examination of recent Russian policy towards Europe, see the editors' companion volume, Kanet and Freire (2012, in press).
10. Ibid.

References

Foreign Policy Concept of the Russian Federation (2000) Approved by the President of the Russian Federation, V. Putin, 28 June, available at: http://www.mid.ru/mid/eng/econcept.htm; also in *Johnson's Russia List*, JRL 2000, no. 4403, 14 July, available at: http://www.cdi.org/Russia/johnson (accessed 20 February 2011).

Foreign Policy Concept of the Russian Federation (2008) 'The Foreign Policy Concept of the Russian Federation: 31.07.2008', *MaximsNews*, News Network for the United Nations and the International Community, available at: http://www.maximsnews.com/news20080731russiaforeignpolicyconcept10807311601.htm (accessed 20 February 2011).

Hahn, Gordon (2010) 'Putting the murders of Russian journalists in perspective', *Russia: Other Points*, 21 November, available at: http://www.russiaotherpointsof

view.com/2010/11/putting-the-murders-of-russian-journalists-in-perspective. html (accessed 29 January 2011).

'Half of Russians yearn for super-power status' (2008) *Angus Reid Global Monitor*, 2 April, available at: http://www.angus-reid.com/polls/30420/half_of_russians_ yearn_for_super_power_status/ (accessed 29 January 2011).

Kanet, Roger E. and Maria Raquel Freire (eds) (2012, in press) *Russia and European Security* (Dordrecht: Republic of Letters Publishing).

Makarychev, Andrei (2010) 'La presidencia de Medvédev: el perfil cambiante de la Federación Rusa', *Anuario Internacional CIDOB 2010, Perfil de País: Federación Rusa*, pp. 435–42, available at: http://www.cidob.org/es/publicaciones/anuarios/ anuario_internacional_cidob/_internacional_cidob_2010_federacion_rusa_ perfil_de_pais (accessed 15 November 2011).

Medvedev, Dmitri (2008a) Interview given by Dmitry Medvedev to Television Channels Channel One, Rossiya, NTV, President of Russia, Moscow, 31 August, available at: http://archive.kremlin.ru/eng/speeches/2008/08/31/1850_ type82912type82916_206003.shtml (accessed 18 January 2011).

Medvedev, Dmitri (2008b) 'Russian President Medvedev's First Annual Address to Parliament', Rossiya TV, 5 November; translated in *Johnson's Russia List*, JRL 2008, no. 292, 6 November, available at: http://65.120.76.252/russia/johnson/ jrl-ras-archive.cfm (accessed 15 November 2011).

Meier, Andrew (2009) 'Who fears a free Mikhail Khodorkovsky?', *New York Times Magazine*, 18 November, available at: http://www.nytimes.com/2009/11/22/ magazine/22khodorkovsky-t.htm (accessed 29 January 2011).

Nation, R. Craig (2010) *Results of the 'Reset' in US–Russian Relations, Russie.Nei. Visions*, No. 53 (Paris: IFRI), available at: http://www.ifri.org/?page=contribution-detail&id=6156&id_provenance= (accessed 4 February 2011).

Nygren, Bertil (2008) *The Rebuilding of Greater Russia: Putin's Foreign Policy toward the CIS Countries* (Abingdon: Routledge).

Office of the Russian President (2010) *The 2010 Russian Military Doctrine*, 5 February, available at: http://www.worldpoliticsreview.com/documents/ show/133 (accessed 4 February 2011).

Putin, Vladimir (2005) President's Speech to the Federal Assembly, 24 April, BBC Monitoring, 'Putin focuses on domestic policy in State-of-Nation Address to Russian Parliament', source: RTR Russia TV, Moscow (in Russian), 08:00 GMT, 25 April, translated in *Johnson's Russia List*, JRL 2005, no. 9130, 25 April, available at: http://65.120.76.252/russia/johnson/jrl-ras-archive.cfm (accessed 15 November 2011).

Putin, Vladimir (2007) 'Putin slams US for making world more dangerous', *DW–World. DE Deutsche Welle*, 10 February, available at: http://www.dw-world. de/dw/article/0,2144,2343749,00.html (accessed 18 January 2011).

Sakwa, Richard (2009) *Power and Policy in Putin's Russia* (Abingdon: Routledge).

Shevtsova, Lilia (2007) *Russia: Lost in Transition* (Washington, DC: Carnegie Endowment for International Peace).

Shevtsova, Lilia (2010) *Lonely Power: Why Russia has Failed to Become the West and the West is Weary of Russia* (Washington, DC: Carnegie Endowment for International Peace).

Taylor, Paul (2009) 'Europeans souring on Ukraine, Georgia', Reuters, 14 January, reprinted in *Johnson's Russia List*, JRL 2009, no. 11, 16 January, available at: http://65.120.76.252/russia/johnson/jrl-ras-archive.cfm (accessed 15 November 2011).

Tolstaya, Yekaterina (2010) 'Medvedev's new vector in foreign policy', *Washington Post*, 25 August, available at: http://russianow.washingtonpost.com/2010/08/medvedevs-new-vector-in-foreign-policy.php (accessed 18 January 2011).

Trenin, Dimitri (2007) *Getting Russia Right* (Washington, DC: Carnegie Endowment for International Peace).

Trenin, Dimitri (2010) 'Rossiyskaya vneshnyaya politika: perspektiva 2020', *Russia 2020: Scenarios for the Future* (Moscow: Carnegie Moscow Center), available at: http://russia-2020.org/2010/10/06/russian-foreign-policy-perspective-2020/ (accessed 18 January 2011).

Tsygankov, Andrei P. (2006) *Russia's Foreign Policy: Change and Continuity in National Identity* (Lanham, MD: Roman and Littlefield).

Tsygankov, Andrei P. (2010) 'Rossiysko-amerikanskoe partnerstvo? "Russkaya ugroza" pod perom kritikov perezagruzki v SShA', *Vestnik Moskovskogo Universiteta: Politologiia*, no. 6, pp. 1–13.

Vogel, Heinrich (2011) 'Europe and Russia – the irritable neighborhood', unpublished paper presented at the Conference on Issues in Foreign Policy and National Security and the Challenges for Europe, organised by the Duitsland Institute, Amsterdam, 17–18 March.

Whitlock, Craig (2009) '"Reset" sought with Russia: Biden says', *Washington Post*, 8 February.

World Bank (2008) *The World Bank in Russia: Russian Economic Report*, No. 16, available at: http://siteresources.worldbank.org/INTRUSSIANFEDERATION/Resources/rer16_eng.pdf (accessed 15 November 2011).

Part I
Determinants of Russian Foreign Policy

1
Russia's 'Vital and Exclusive' National Interests in the Near Abroad

Ria Laenen

Introduction

Russia's national interests and its claim to great power status are often mentioned in the same breath by Russian foreign policy officials and in Russian policy documents.[1] One example is a quotation from an interview with Sergei Ryabkov, Russian Deputy Minister of Foreign Affairs, in which from the opening words 'national interests' are given centre stage, when Ryabkov attributes the deterioration of US–Russia relations to the different understandings of national interests by great powers. He states that:

> Every action taken by the government of any state is largely determined by its understanding of the country's national interests. Quite naturally, those understandings may differ, as sometimes occurs in relations between such great world powers as the United States and Russia. (Ryabkov, 2010, p. 207)

But what exactly is the nature of this linkage between national interests and great power status that are both key concepts in Russia's foreign policy discourse? In order to answer this question, I first propose a re-conceptualisation of national interests outside their classical realist understanding that is theoretically framed on the constructivist international relations (IR) paradigm. I remain convinced that constructivism as a theoretical framework can help us provide valuable insights into the link between Russia's identity and foreign policy. Various scholars have already delivered excellent work on Russian identity and foreign policy (for example, Prizel, 1998; and Neumann, 1996). However, a continued effort is needed to further the fine-tuning of the constructivist paradigm and to enhance the insights gained by it into Russia's enduring search for a post-Soviet identity. This chapter hopes to make a contribution to that effort.[2] I will explore Russia's definition of its national interests with regard to that one particular region of the world where it is most visibly promulgating its great power and national interests discourse – namely, the 'Near Abroad' understood here as the post-Soviet space, excluding the Baltic states.

I will first depict the main contours of the debate on national interests, as it took shape in post-Soviet Russia in the second half of the 1990s. I will then pay closer attention to the most recent developments in Russia's national interests discourse towards the Near Abroad in an attempt to determine whether substantial changes in the definition of national interests have taken place. More specifically, I am guided by the question of whether an analysis of Russia's definition of national interests can provide us with clues to explain the more assertive and aggressive turn in Russia's strategic choices towards the Near Abroad, with the Russian–Georgian War of August 2008 and the ensuing recognition of South Ossetian and Abkhazian independence by Moscow as the most eye-catching indications of this growing assertiveness (RIA Novosti, 2008).

To situate the material presented here within the broader context of foreign policy analysis, the reader should keep in mind the fact that this chapter's primary preoccupation is not with providing an assessment of Russia's foreign policy output, but rather with unravelling the process that comes ontologically before the actual foreign policy decision-making, being the formulation of the country's identity and interests.

A constructivist understanding of national identity

A constructivist definition of the concept of national interests is proposed here in order to gauge better the importance of national interests as the crucial link between Russia's identity and policy. Why constructivism? Are Putin and Medvedev not conducting a realist foreign policy then? Yes, they still largely consider the international system in zero-sum terms. Yes, they behave like rational actors making calculated policy choices. But there is more. Realism does not help us understand to the fullest degree the processes at work behind the definition of national interests. A constructivist approach allows us to study the complex processes at work in defining national interests and in formulating foreign policy – especially appealing are the domestic/external interactions and the treatment of both of these levels as equal (not considering one as being of secondary importance to the other). Constructivism provides a helpful approach to making sense of Russia's stance on national interests. As aptly put by William C. Wohlforth, constructivism deals with 'the basic dilemma of much of international relations theory: the difficulty of assigning relative weight to internal versus international factors when they continually influence one another' (Wohlforth, 1994, p. 107).

In terms of the analysis here, the main selling point of constructivism is its attention to ideational factors that allows us to take into account what is culturally specific to Russia, such as the historic link between Russia's identity and the concept of empire, while at the same time firmly embedding the case of Russia in a broader theoretical framework. In other words, the added value of constructivism for Russian studies lies in the fact that 'it systematizes the issues that traditional interpretive study of history and the study of Soviet or Russian foreign policy thinking have widely dealt with' (Pursiainen, 2000, p. 147).

Russian scholars have always stressed the need to contextualise Russian politics within the broader context of Russia's history and culture. In accordance with this tradition, it comes as no surprise that in Russia's foreign policy debate, 'most Russian foreign policy analysts examine military and economic capabilities in a broader cultural context and include in their discussions such topics as Russian geopolitical priorities, its imperial tradition, and its national character' (Tsygankov, 1997, p. 248). Constructivism falls into the category of reflective theoretical approaches with strong sociological components. Simultaneously, it can make Russian area specialists more aware of the fact that not only Russia, but 'any country is a composite of both unique and general factors' (Rosenau, 1987, p. 59), and that in that sense the Russian case can be treated as a case among many others without disregarding its area-specific features. A state's identity and, consequently, its interests and policy are constituted by interaction with other states in the international system, as well as by interaction with society at the internal level. While the state-centric approach has been challenged in IR in general, there has been a counteracting trend to reaffirm the pivotal role that the state still plays in the international system, as articulated by Valerie Bunce in this warning that:

> We must remember that states tend to be sticky – despite all the talk for many years of their impending decline, if not growing irrelevance in a globalised world featuring competing identities, competing sovereignties, and the expanding influence of transstate actors [...].

> The institution or bundle of practices that we know as the state [still is] the pre-eminent site for the construction of national interests. (Bunce, 2002, p. 6)

National identity has become so central to the discussion of post-Cold War politics and at the same time has been so vaguely defined and been used with such a great variation in meaning attached to it, that a further investigation of what is understood by 'national identity' cannot be regarded as a luxury but should be considered a bare necessity. National identity is conceived here as a particular conglomerate of ideas, constituted by a complex process of social interaction between state and society (internal dimension), as well as between the state and the international environment (external dimension).

As aptly formulated in one of the first major works on identity in IR, a constructivist approach to identity sees identity as follows:

> The term [identity] itself refers to mutually constructed and evolving images of 'self' and 'other', since it refers to images of individuality and distinctiveness ('selfhood') held and projected by an actor and formed and modified over time through relations with significant 'others'. (Jepperson et al., 1996, p. 59)

For Russia the West is mainly cited as its most significant other, but in the post-Soviet context the Near Abroad countries definitely also constitute a region with significant 'others' for Russia, while Russia still tends to see them as part of the 'self' to some degree. This lack of a clear boundary between 'self' and 'other' is precisely what makes Russia's stance towards the Near Abroad so interesting from the point of view of identity.

The most important function of national identity is that it provides a source of meaning for the purposes of a social actor's actions. National identity is one of the most important forms of collective identity that helps a social actor in rearranging material (from history, geography, collective memory and so on) within a space/time framework (Castells, 1997). As summarised by Stephen Krasner, 'The question is not how can I maximise self-interest but rather, given who or what I am, how should I act in this particular circumstance?' (Krasner, 1999, p. 5). National identity is viewed here as a nexus of ideas that is created by different processes that are continuously and simultaneously carrying on. National identity can be conceived of as being discursively constructed as the result of the interaction between the state and society internally, and the interaction between the state and the outside world externally. This means that this current research is based on the premise that national identity building is never completed. Suny's depiction of identities as 'provisional stabilities' offers a perfect illustration of this constant fluidity. According to Suny, identity can be thought of as stabilisation of a sense of self or group that is formed in actual historical time and space, in evolving economies, polities and cultures, as a continuous search for some solidity in a constantly shifting world – but without closure, without forever naturalising or essentialising the provisional identities arrived at (Suny, 1999).

Nonetheless, it has to be noted that national identity is not infinitely malleable, because there are certain cultural and geographical determinants of a state's national identity (for example, Russia's geographical location between East and West). A nation as a political community is based on a shared history and that national identity is rooted in the past. In the case of Russia, the close intertwining between the state's identity and the concept of empire that developed throughout history should definitely be singled out as a deeply rooted entanglement that is undeniably still having an impact on Russia's view of the Near Abroad.

National interests as the link between identity and interests

National interests are conceived of here as a medium that allows us to link national identity and policy, based on the idea that a state's national identity implies a particular set of interests and its consequent policy. Given the fact that national interest(s) as a concept is very elastic in use, in this section the conceptualisation of national interests as it is employed in this chapter is explained.

It is assumed here that a state's identity implies its interests. National interests are derived from the national identity or, as Suny put it, 'interests are tied to identities – that is, what we think we need is connected to who we think we are' (Suny, 1999, p. 144). National interests are about what a state wants to achieve, they describe 'the desired outcomes' (Frankel, 1970, p. 21). National interests usually deal with long-term and general policy objectives, not with concrete policy stipulations. The national interests are considered to define what is best for the nation, how the national resources and capabilities are to be used to achieve the long-term objectives to the ends of achieving what is best for the national society in terms of welfare and security. This implies that national interests do not belong exclusively to the domain of a nation's external policies; it might be used in the context of domestic politics as well. Nevertheless, there exists a 'tendency to confine the intended meaning to what is best for a nation in foreign affairs' (Rosenau, 1971, p. 239). They help specify, among other things, the goals that are to be protected and what constitutes a threat to the self (*in casu*, the Russian state). This study operates on the assumption that national interests are not exogenously given, but do emerge out of a process of social construction. 'Interests are not just "out there" waiting to be discovered' (Finnemore, 1996, p. 2). Constructivists see national interests as the product that emerges out of a process in which the culture, ideology, values and other sociological aspects play a constitutive role, as paraphrased by Wendt who says that 'the state is not a *tabula rasa* on which any interest can be written' (1999, p. 234).

Broadly speaking, the concept of national interests has two different functions in the foreign policy domain. These two functions were labelled by Alexander George and Robert Keohane as 'criterion' and 'justification' (1980). In the field of post-Soviet studies, national interests are most commonly studied in their justification function. This justification function concerns the instrumental way in which national interests are used to explain and legitimise policy decisions and actions. The emphasis on this function of national interests as a political tool follows from the realist approach summarised in the words of Rosenau 'as an instrument of political action, it [national interest] serves as a means of justifying, denouncing or proposing policies' (Rosenau, 1971, p. 239). So in realist thinking national interests are primarily seen as a rhetorical tool used by politicians to justify their actions and to mobilise support for them.

Transcending a pure instrumentalist understanding of national interests, I here adopt a different approach to the role of national interests, seeing them as an analytical tool that can help me explain why certain policy choices have been made. In doing this I focus more on the aforementioned criterion function of national interests. The criterion function refers to the fact that national interests play a role in policy decision-making in the sense that they provide the roadmap that outlines what is best for the state. In this function national interests stipulate the general directions to be followed by the state. Thus in this context and completely in line with constructivist thinking, interests are conceptually placed as coming before policy. As I explain later such an approach allows me to distance myself from ascribing Russia's increasing assertiveness towards the Near Abroad solely to one man, Vladimir Putin, as is often done in analyses of Russian policies.

Constructivism adheres to an idealist understanding of national interests. However it is important to underline the fact that in the constructivist approach followed here it is not denied that there exist 'realist' constraints to national interests. It is recognised that certain material factors to a certain extent determine the national interests of a state, such as its geographic location, economic (for instance, Russia's spectacular economic growth in the period 2000–08) and military capabilities. Wendt acknowledges the existence of 'rump' materialism that constrains the state's action, citing military strength, geography and natural resources as material capabilities that affect the possibility and likelihood of certain outcomes in international politics (Wendt, 1999). I concur with him when he says that 'idealist social theory is not about denying the existence of the real world. The point is that the real world consists of a lot more than material forces as such' (Wendt, 1999, p. 136). In national interests, in addition to material factors, values are incorporated and translated into goals. Thus instead of interpreting national interests in an instrumentalist rational choice model, constructivism understands national interests in a more ideational sense to be an aggregate complex of the state's aspirations reflecting its national identity. Russia's aspiration of being a great power is one of the leading motives in its search for a post-Soviet national identity.[3]

A constructivist re-conceptualisation of national interests does not deny that external stimuli originating from the international system are playing a role in the definition and redefinition of a state's national interests, but rather emphasises that these external stimuli are just one element in a larger group of constitutive factors in the process of the formation of an identity and interests. The external stimuli still leave every state with a broad range of policy possibilities. By conceptualising national identity as the conduit through which both external and domestic stimuli, of a material as well as an ideational nature, are incorporated into national interests, it is possible to explain variation in policy preferences among states.

The crystallisation of post-Soviet Russia's consensus on identity and interests

When examining the post-Soviet Russia's national interests debate, one can observe a pattern of evolution towards a consensus on Russia's identity and consequently on its interests. National interests are by no means a silent factor in post-Soviet Russian politics. In the 1990s, there emerged a heated societal debate over what exactly Russia's national identity and national interests should entail.[4] It soon became clear that the national interests in the post-Soviet context were being conceptualised as directly related to the distinctive needs and culture of the Russian state. This focus on the particular interests of the country contrasted with the universal meaning that was attached to national interests in Mikhail Gorbachev's new thinking and during the short honeymoon period with the West in the immediate aftermath of the breakup of the Soviet Union.

The position of national interests has become so central in the post-Soviet vocabulary of Russia's foreign policy that one can argue that the concept of national interests now functions as the theoretical or even ideological basis for Russia's foreign policy, comparable to the role fulfilled in Soviet times by Marxist–Leninist ideology. In sharp contrast to the ad hoc nature of Russia's foreign policy in the early post-Soviet years, a more consistent official discourse emerged in which Russia's national interests take central stage. National interests came to function truly as the intermediary between national identity and a more proactive policy or, as described in Russia's 2000 National Security Concept, 'They [national interests] have a long-term character and define the basic goals, the strategic and current tasks of the domestic and external state policy' (National Security Concept of the Russian Federation, 2000). By the end of the millennium the contours of Russia's national interests in the Near Abroad had taken shape and the main question did indeed become what strategies should be followed to ensure the protection of the national interests.

Capitalising on the energy-driven economic boost in the last decade, Russia's overall foreign policy output gained assertiveness. But the basic principles of that foreign policy, the core national interests, had already been formulated for a long time previously. With regard to Russia's interests in the Near Abroad, generally speaking, since the second half of the 1990s a consensus had emerged that Russia had well-defined national interests in the post-Soviet space.

That national interests involve more than just rational, calculated means–ends objectives is illustrated by the importance attached to patriotism in Russia's national interests discourse. A rise in Russian patriotism was, for instance, already an objective formulated in the 1996 State National Policy Concept, calling for the 'cultivation of a feeling of Russian patriotism'. In the text of that document not only language but broader concepts such as culture, traditions and also spiritual values are repeatedly defined as specific national features that need to be preserved and promoted (Concept of the State National Policy of the Russian

Federation, 1996). The tone set by the State National Policy Concept was continued in other major Russian policy documents, such as the 1997 and 2000 National Security Concepts and the Presidential State of the Nation speeches where again considerable emphasis was put on the preservation and strengthening of Russian national and spiritual values, as in this fragment:

> I am convinced that the development of society is inconceivable without accord on the common goals. And these are not only material goals. Spiritual and moral values are no less important. The unity of Russia is ensured by traditional patriotism, cultural traditions, and our common historical memory. There is a growing interest for national history, our roots, everything that is near and dear to all of us in the arts, theatre and cinema. (Putin, 2000)

Thus Russia refers not only to its natural resources, its size, its research technology potential (heavily stressed in President Medvedev's modernisation campaign) and its status as a nuclear power as elements of its great power status, but also to non-material elements such as its long history, rich cultural traditions and spiritual potential.

In contemporary Russia, indeed, Vladimir Putin can be singled out as a leading actor contributing significantly to the shaping and reshaping of Russia's identity and interests (Evans, 2008). Nevertheless the approach taken here underlines the fact that national interests are not a notion that can be given just any content by decision-makers. They are not a black box into which any notion or idea can be dropped and then promulgated by the state's officials. The national identity incorporates at least some level of convergence between the official state view and public opinion through the interaction between state and society. National identity is something that grows organically and discursively the interaction between state and society and cannot simply be forced upon a nation top-down. Nevertheless one must note that not only Putin, but also his predecessor Boris Yeltsin, actively sought what is referred to as a 'national idea' for Russia in a top-down manner.[5]

What can be said about the period since 2000, is that I have noticed in Russia an increasingly growing society-wide consensus on Russia's identity and its national interests in the Near Abroad. Indeed, as argued by one scholar, Putin understood the crucial importance of *soglasie*, of 'societal consensus' (Evans, 2008). The notion that Russia is a great power that has the right to behave accordingly in the Near Abroad seems to enjoy broad popular support in Russian society. Opinion polls organised by VTsIOM indicate that since 2007 an increasing number of respondents think that Russia has already achieved the status of great power (VTsIOM, 2010a and 2010b).

The Near Abroad as Russia's sphere of influence

The tension between great power ambitions, on the one hand, and regional power ambitions, on the other, present in Russian foreign policy in the 1990s, has disappeared. The Near Abroad has become the primary area where Russia is acting as a regional and global power all at once, using the post-Soviet space as the playing field for simultaneously confirming Russia's role as the sole dominant power in the region as well as its claim to be recognised as one of the 'happy few' great powers in the world. Arguably the label best suited to describe Russia's position in the Near Abroad is 'regional great power' or 'regional hegemon' (Laenen, 2008). It is more appropriate to speak about Russia's role in the Near Abroad as the role of 'hegemon', rather than as a neo-imperialist (Suny, 1999). In the case of (neo)imperialism, the root cause could be determined as a resurgent cultural-historical factor. The primary policy objective would be to establish full control over both the external and internal policies of the Near Abroad countries, thus expanding Russia's effective control beyond its own territorial sovereignty. By giving preference to the term 'great power hegemony', I aim to underline that Russia's policy toward the Near Abroad is in the first place a way to seek recognition by the West as still – or better again – belonging to the club of influential powers in international politics. In this sense I see the Russian–Georgian War of August 2008 and the ensuing recognition of the independence of South Ossetia and Abkhazia by Moscow not as primarily being directed at expanding Russia's territorial control in the region, but as sending out a message to the West in the first instance about drawing a line in the sand with regard to what Russia sees as its own sphere of influence as a great power. The tone was set in 2000 as follows:

> Russia is one of the world's strongest countries with a centuries old history and rich cultural traditions. Despite the complicated international situation and internal problems, it continues to play an important role in world processes based on its considerable economic, scientific-technical and military potential and its unique strategic location on the Eurasian continent. (National Security Concept of the Russian Federation, 2000)

In that period, before Russia's impressive economic growth, few international specialists regarded Russia as a great power. However, Condoleezza Rice wrote:

> It [Russia] still has many of the attributes of a great power: a large population, vast territory, and military potential. But its economic weakness and problems of national identity threaten to overwhelm it. [...] The United States needs to recognise that Russia is a great power. (Rice, 2000, p. 57)

In the Russian Foreign Policy Concept of 2008, it sounds very self-assured that the new concept was needed:

> with due account for the increased role of the country in international affairs, its greater responsibility for global developments and related possibilities to participate in the implementation of the international agenda, as well as in its development. (Foreign Policy Concept of the Russian Federation, 2008)

This regional great power sees the Near Abroad as an area where vital and exclusive Russian national interests are to be protected. Space and territory are crucial elements in any state's national identity, even more so in the national identity construction process of a former empire in search of a new identity. From Russia's identity concept as regional hegemonial power automatically follows the need for spatial control over a sphere of interest. A hegemonic identity type carries in itself the seeds for a high level of potential confrontation with the other actors in the international system, most specifically with other states that refuse to be part of the hegemon's sphere of interest, like Georgia, and with other hegemonial actors who claim interests in the same geopolitical space (like the US and to a certain extent also the EU). This statement by foreign policy official Ryabkov provides a good illustration of Russia's claim to the region as its exclusive sphere of interests:

> Quite naturally, we are fulfilling tasks traditional to any state, namely, creating a friendly environment. [...] Our partners outside the surrounding region should treat it with understanding. That space has no room for geopolitical games, which lead only to destabilization, as the experience in Georgia and Ukraine shows. (Ryabkov, 2010, p. 207)

In Russia's official discourse frequent references to 'vital national interests' occur, underlining a certain type of national interest regarded by the state as being of key importance to guarantee its survival. On this type of interests the state is assumed to be unwilling to make concessions. What makes Russia's definition of these vital interests so intriguing is the fact that they stretch beyond the protection of its own territorial integrity and welfare of its own state and into the neighbouring area of the Near Abroad. Framing national interests in this way immediately opens up the prospects of links with Russia's historical legacy of imperialism.

One of the key vital national interests as defined in the Near Abroad can be traced directly back to this legacy of imperialism: the national interest of defending and protecting the rights of the Russian 'compatriots' in the Near Abroad. This category of 'compatriots' is defined by Russia in a manner that is broader than ethnic Russians (Laenen, 2008). Russia's policy on passports is an interesting element in this policy towards its compatriots, providing Moscow with the legal tools for legitimising the claims to protection of these citizens, such as the majority of the citizens of South Ossetia and Abkhazia who hold Russian passports.

Recent developments: security interests prior to economic interests again?

While in the years 2000 to 2007, the official state view clearly prioritised economic development as the key national interest over all others, one can argue that since then security interests have once again been emphasised in a series of official security-related documents. In this section I attempt to discern changes in the prioritisation of Russia's national interests. Nevertheless I am fully aware that the national interests of economic growth, enhanced security and international great power status are mutually reinforcing and closely intertwined. The 2000 National Security Concept stated that:

> The implementation of Russia's national interests is possible only on the basis of stable economic development. This is why the national interests of Russia in this sphere are key to all other interests. (National Security Concept, 2000)

In Section II of the 2000 National Security Concept entitled 'The National Interests of Russia', a wide range of categories is mentioned as being part of the national interests: interests of the individual, of society and of the state; domestic and international national interests in the social sphere, in the spiritual life, in the domain of information, in the military sphere, in the sphere of ecology; and there is even a separate mention of national interests in the border sphere. Further on in Section IV of the document, it is stated that: 'Guaranteeing the national security and protecting Russia's national interests in the economic sphere are the priority direction of state policy' (National Security Concept, 2000).

The impact of the global economic crisis has left its footprints on the official documents that have been released. In the 2009 National Security Concept the dependence of the Russian economy on the export of raw materials is officially identified as a security threat (while at the same time linking Russia's international strength to its energy reserves). The strategy document compares the potential consequences of the global economic crisis to the devastation left by the activities of a large-scale military force (National Security Concept of the Russian Federation until 2020, 2009). By their very nature, national interests carry a strong security component since the physical survival of the state as a political entity is the most basic national interest of every state. Moreover as has been aptly formulated in a comprehensive study on Russia's security:

> A basic factor making the security challenge facing Russia more complex and disorienting than for others arises from the dense, inauspicious overlap between internal and external security. [...] In Russia's case, internal and external threats mingle at many points. (Legvold et al., 1999, p. 6)

This vague boundary between internal and external security threats is of crucial importance as a starting point for understanding Russia's definition of its national interests in the Near Abroad.

A sense of encroachment is one of the concerns of the Russians that is historically deeply rooted and translates into making security concerns a major constitutive part of Russia's national interests. Studying what a state sees as the most direct security threats offers a good indication of how the international environment is perceived. The basic security interests of Russia in the Near Abroad are directly derived from the threat perception that Russia sees in that region. That threat perception has undergone some changes since 2000 and has resulted in slight alterations in Russia's definition of its national interests in the region which can be clarified, when one takes the main sources of external threats to Russia enlisted in the 2000 National Security policy document (under Section III) as the reference point. Three of the seven threats formulated there emerge from the Near Abroad: 1) the possible appearance in the near future of foreign military bases and large military contingents in direct proximity to the Russian borders; 2) the weakening of the integration processes in the Commonwealth of Independent States (CIS); and 3) the outbreak and escalation of conflicts close to the state borders of the Russian Federation and to the external borders of CIS member states (National Security Concept, 2000).

With the first point, reference was made to NATO's eastwards enlargement. NATO is still seen as a major threat, or more precisely 'danger', to Russia's national interests (Military Doctrine, 2010). In the post-9/11 context the threat formulation became even more topical with the stationing of US troops in Central Asia in the context of the war on terror (for example, US military bases in Kyrgyzstan). Here it can be noted that from a Russian point of view the passive attitude of the CIS members towards the fight against terrorism in Afghanistan – compared to the active involvement of the US and its allies – was seen as a failure of the security cooperation arrangements in the post-Soviet space (Chufrin, 2009). Multipolarity was already introduced as a key feature of Russian foreign policy by Yevgeny Primakov and has since remained a primary objective of Russia's international strategy. Foreign Minister Sergei Lavrov began his overview of 2010 with the observation that the formation of a new multipolar world was continuing (Lavrov, 2010).

On the second point, the objective of CIS integration has been replaced by a more pragmatic choice for integration with core partners in the region, such as the customs union set up between Russia, Kazakhstan and Belarus.[6] The logic behind this strategic choice was expressed by former Russian Foreign Minister Igor S. Ivanov as follows:

> Should we continue to hold integration as an absolute value, for which we would pay any price and make any concessions to our partners? Or should we take a more pragmatic track, making sure that our fundamental national interests of security and economic development were met even at the price of deepening CIS integration? (Ivanov, 2002, p. 87)

The latest Foreign Policy Concept gives priority to moving forwards towards closer integration with the core CIS partners over CIS-wide integration, diplomatically wording this preference as follows:

> Russia forges friendly relations with all the CIS Member States on the basis of equality, mutual benefit, respect and regard for the interests of each other. Strategic partnerships and alliances are developed with

States that demonstrate their readiness to engage in them. (Foreign Policy Concept, 2008)

This seems to be typical great power behaviour in a globalised world. Just as Russia opts for bilateral relations to move on with interested key partners in the CIS; the US also consolidates its hegemonic position in Latin America by bilateral relations with core partner states, such as Colombia (Hakim, 2006). Indeed Russia's focus on bilateral relations with CIS countries, increasing their economic dependence on Russia, is an integral part of Russia's strategy of regaining great power status (Freire and Kanet, 2010, p. 89).

Conflicts in the Near Abroad are still perceived as having a potential of spilling over Russia's own borders. However, the main issues that threaten to destabilise the Near Abroad and have a spillover potential into Russia's own territory are no longer only ethnic conflicts, but are now more global threats such as international terrorism, extremism, drug trafficking and illegal migration (Foreign Policy Concept, 2008). Russia is by far the most powerful state in the region. Comparing Russia with the other former Soviet states dwarfs them in all possible aspects: population, territory, military capability, international status, natural resources, international economic ties and so on. This powerful position in the region serves Russia as an important source of identity confirmation as a great power. One of the domains in which Russia's regional great power ambitions became most clearly visible from very early on was its claim to the role of more peacekeeper in the region (Jonson, 1999). Increasingly the international environment has once again come to be viewed by Russia as a place from which are emanating threats to its national interests. The whole series of more recently released Russian security-related policy documents and speeches can be viewed in the wider context of Russia's identity and the reformulation of its interests.[7]

The very nature of the current international system viewed by Russia as a unipolar system unilaterally dominated by the US is seen as a threat to Russia's 'self', as the Russians have been advocating the development of a multipolar international system, trying to carve out for itself a place as one of the influential poles. Here I concur with Buzan when he sees that 'calls for multipolarity by Russia, China and others are not so much about making themselves into superpowers, as about the US giving up its superpower pretensions' (Buzan, 2005, p. 187).

Russia has been pointing not only to conflicts near its own state borders as a source of potential threat (for example, the link between instability in the South Caucasus and in the North Caucasus), but also to security threats along the external CIS borders (for example, soft security treats like drug trafficking via the porous border between Tajikistan and Pakistan). Russia claims to have national interests that stretch beyond the national borders into the whole of the CIS region. Russia has consistently raised concerns about the possible spillover effect of conflicts in the weak southern CIS underbelly into its own territory. Political and religious extremism, as well as ethnic nationalism, have been identified as potentially highly destabilising factors posing a threat to regional security and internal Russian security because they lead to ethnic and religious conflicts and terrorism. In this regard, again, domestic and external national security concerns are closely linked, as also became obvious in Russia's ambiguous stance on border policy. Already the law of 6 November 1996 on Russia's border policy explicitly states that its main objectives do not stop at the border of the Russian Federation, but also extend to the outer CIS borders. This stance was later reaffirmed in other official policy documents, the latest one being the most recent version of the Russian Military Doctrine approved by presidential decree on 5 February 2010.

Russia's continued focus on classic scenarios for military interstate action to guarantee security can be put in a wider historical context. The struggle to stabilise Russia's frontiers has been the most powerful objective in Russian foreign policy throughout history. 'In most cases in Russian history, stability was achievable only by engaging powerful neighbours through military action. In this way, Russia's own insecurity often resulted in the insecurity of others' (Gayoso, 2009, p. 243). It cannot be denied that there are some objective factors, such as the sheer size of the territory and the low density of population in some border areas that made border security a permanent preoccupation of the Russian state for centuries. This worry certainly gained prominence in the post-Soviet context with regard to Russia's borders with the southern, newly independent states. Given the inexperience of these new states with independence and their proximity to some of the world's hot spots (for instance, Turkmenistan's, Uzbekistan's and Tajikistan's border with Afghanistan), Russia's claims to security interests in that part of the post-Soviet space are not that far-fetched. Perhaps the single most innovative trend discernable in Russia's definition of its national interests is its government's full awareness that the domestic/external boundary is vague. This is acknowledged, for instance, in the 2008 Foreign Policy Concept, where it is stated that 'differences between domestic and external means of ensuring national interests and security are gradually disappearing' (Foreign Policy Concept, 2008).

Conclusion

Engaging with Russia remains one of the major challenges that the West will continue to face, as was confirmed in the recent NATO 'wisemen's report' (NATO, 2010). In this chapter it is suggested that a more attentive study of the process by which Russia's definition of its national interests evolves can offer valuable indications of the way in which Russia perceives itself in the international system and can thus help explain Russia's foreign policy behaviour. This is an explorative undertaking, having the modest ambition of suggesting a plausible interpretation of Russia's foreign policy towards the Near Abroad by focusing on the process of the definition of national interests that sets the broader framework in which actual foreign policy decisions are later taken. A constructivist account means first and foremost that national interests are seen here as the product of a complex process of social interaction and their content as reflecting the state's identity, making national interests dependent on the actor's identity and the social context.

It is argued here that – contrary to often heard opinions – no fundamental changes in Russia's national interests in the Near Abroad accompanied the transition from the Yeltsin to the Putin era, but that a confirmation and an intensification of the articulation of the growing consensus on Russia's great power identity and its ensuing interests instead took place. More subtle variations over time can be discovered when one examines the prioritisation of Russia's national interests. Indications are visible of the recent replacement of economic interests by security interests. In spite of the buzz about innovation and modernisation by President Medvedev, little on that topic can be found in Russia's definition of national interests in the Near Abroad. While during the early 2000s the maximisation of social and economic welfare was placed in the most prominent position, the pendulum has swung back to giving priority to security interests.

Perhaps this evolution can be seen as Russia's implicit recognition of its economic limitations and is an expression of the renewed sense of 'danger' threatening Russia's stability (both internally and externally). In that case, the continued insistence on traditional national security interests and great power thinking seem to me outdated and unsuitable to remedy Russia's more immediate security threats that emanate in the first place from within Russia (for instance, the demographic situation[8]). Indeed, as noted by one scholar, 'Russia sought to guarantee security in the region as a way of stabilizing the situation in Russia itself' (Kazantsev, 2008, p. 1083). But it is highly debatable whether this approach will serve Russia's national interests in the long term.

Notes

1. The term 'great power' (velikaya derzhava) was already used, for instance, in Russia's National Security Concept and Foreign Policy Concept, both of 2000.
2. Constructivism came to the fore in IR thinking in the second half of the 1990s as providing an alternative approach to dominant neorealist thinking; see, for instance, Katzenstein (1996); Adler (1997); and Checkel (1998). However more recently it has disappeared somewhat from the spotlight and was criticised by some for not having added substantive knowledge regarding or significant hypotheses on the behaviour of states. As explained in more detail further on the author relies mainly on the basic tenets of constructivist IR thinking as set out by Alexander Wendt in his 1999 volume entitled *Social Theory of International Relations*.
3. For an excellent analysis of how Russia has been trying to put into practice this aspiration of becoming a great power, see, for instance, Kanet (2007).
4. For one of the earliest academic articles that comprise part of this debate on Russia's national interests, see Bogaturov et al. (1992). The link between national identity, national interests and foreign policy was clearly discernable in that debate. See, for instance, Migranian (1997); Razuvaev (1993); and Sestanovich (1994).
5. In mid 1996, for instance, the official government newspaper launched a competition to find Russia's national idea. There was an essay contest and prominent public figures were provided with the opportunity to publish their views on the topic in the newspaper throughout the second half of 1996 (see 'Kto my?', 1996).
6. On the question of whether Belarus is still regarded as a core partner, given the increasing tensions between Minsk and Moscow and Belarus's overtures to the West, see, for instance, Stone (2011) who argues that Belarus since the signing of the December 2010 oil agreement has again become firmly placed within Russia's exclusive sphere of influence.
7. For instance, the 2008 Munich Speech by President Putin, the 2009 Berlin Speech by President Medvedev, the new 2009 version of the National Security Policy and the November 2009 European Security Draft Treaty.
8. See, for instance, the daunting statistics on Russia provided in the WHO's *Global Status Report on Alcohol and Health* (2011).

References

Adler, Emanuel (1997) 'Seizing the middle ground: constructivism in world politics', *European Journal of International Relations*, vol. 3, no. 3, pp. 319–63.

Black, Cyril (1962) 'Patterns of objectives', in Ivo J. Lederer (ed.), *Russian Foreign Policy: Essays in Historical Perspective* (New Haven, CT: Yale University Press), pp. 3–38.

Bogaturov, A., M. Kozhokin and K. Pleshakov (1992) 'Natsional'niy interes v rossiyskoy politike' (National interest in Russian policy), *Svobodnaya Mysl'*, no. 5, pp. 34–44.

Bunce, Valerie (2002) *Subversive Institutions* (Cambridge: Cambridge University Press).

Buzan, Barry (2005) 'The security dynamics of a 1 + 4 world', in Ersel Aydinli and James N. Rosenau (eds), *Globalization, Security, and the Nation State: Paradigms in Transition* (Albany, NY: State University of New York Press), pp. 177–97.

Castells, Manuel (1997) *The Power of Identity* (Oxford: Blackwell Publishers).

Checkel, Jeffrey T. (1998) 'The constructivist turn in International Relations theory', *World Politics*, vol. 50, no. 2, pp. 324–48.

Chufrin, G. (2009) 'ODKB v novykh geopoliticheskikh realiyakh' (SCTO [Collective Security Treaty Organisation] in the new geopolitical reality), *Rossiya i novye gosudarstva evrazii*, no. 2, pp. 5–13.

Concept of the State National Policy of the Russian Federation (Kontseptsiya gosudarstvennoy natsional'noy politiki Rossiyskoy Federatsii) (1996) Official website of Ministerstvo Inostrannykh Del (MID; Ministry of Foreign Affairs), available at: http://wwwmid.ru/nsosndoc.nsf/0e9272befa34209743256c630042d1aa/c6 d37e91be20bfc8c325707b004a2574?OpenDocument (accessed 15 December 2010).

European Security Treaty Draft (2009) 29 November, available at: http://archive. kremlin.ru/eng/text/docs/2009/11/223072.shtml (accessed 21 February 2011).

Evans, Jr, Alfred (2008) 'Putin's legacy and Russia's identity', *Europe–Asia Studies*, vol. 60, no. 6, pp. 899–912.

Finnemore, Martha (1996) *National Interests in International Society* (Ithaca, NY: Cornell University Press).

Foreign Policy Concept of the Russian Federation (2000) 28 June, available at: http://www.fas.org/nuke/guide/russia/doctrine/econcept.htm (accessed 21 February 2011).

Foreign Policy Concept of the Russian Federation (2008) 12 July, available at: http://archive.kremlin.ru/eng/text/docs/2008/07/204750.shtml (accessed 15 December 2010).

Frankel, Joseph (1970) *National Interest* (London: Pall Mall Press).

Freire, Maria Raquel and Roger E. Kanet (eds) (2010) *Key Players and Regional Dynamics in Eurasia: The Return of the 'Great Game'* (Houndmills: Palgrave Macmillan).

Gayoso, Carmen A. (2009) 'Russian hegemonies: historical snapshots, regional security and changing forms of Russia's role in the post-Soviet region', *Communist and Post-Communist Studies*, vol. 42, pp. 233–52.

George, Alexander and Robert Keohane (1980) 'The concept of national interests: use and limitations', in Alexander George (ed.), *Presidential Decisionmaking in Foreign Policy* (Boulder, CO: Westview Press), pp. 217–37.

Group of Advisers of the Presidential Administration of the Russian Federation (1997) *Rossiya v poiskakh idei: analis pressy* (Russia in Search of Ideas: A Press Analysis), G. Satarov (ed.) (Moscow: Presidential Administration).

Hakim, Peter (2006) 'Is Washington losing Latin America?', *Foreign Affairs*, vol. 85, no. 1, pp. 39–53.

Ivanov, Igor S. (2002) *The New Russian Diplomacy* (Washington, DC: Brookings Institution Press).

Jepperson, Ronald J., Alexander Wendt and Peter J. Katzenstein (1996) 'Norms, identity, and culture in national security', in Peter J. Katzenstein (ed.), *The Culture of National Security* (New York: Columbia University Press), pp. 33–78.

Jonson, Lena (1999) *Keeping the Peace in the CIS: The Evolution of Russian Policy*, Discussion Paper 81 (London: Royal Institute of International Affairs).

Kahl, Colin (1998) 'Constructing a separate peace: constructivism, collective liberal identity, and democratic peace', *Security Studies*, vol. 8, nos 2/3, pp. 94–144.

Kanet, Roger E. (ed.) (2007) *Russia: Re-emerging Great Power* (Houndmills: Palgrave Macmillan).

Katzenstein, Peter J. (ed.) (1996) *The Culture of National Security* (New York: Columbia University Press).

Kazantsev, Andrei (2008) 'Russian policy in Central Asia and the Caspian Sea region', *Europe–Asia Studies*, vol. 60, no. 3, pp. 1073–88.

Kortunov, Sergei (1998) 'Russia's national identity in a new era', paper series, Harvard University Strengthening Democratic Institutions Project, September.

Krasner, Stephen (1999) *Sovereignty: Organized Hypocrisy* (Princeton, NJ: Princeton University Press).

'Kto my?' (1996) 'Kto my? Kuda my idem? Konkurs "Ideia dlya Rossii"' (Who are we? Where are we going? Contest 'Idea for Russia'), *Rossiyskaya Gazeta*, 30 July.

Laenen, Ria (2008) 'Russia's Near Abroad policy and its compatriots during the first post-Soviet decade, 1991–2001: an empire in search of a new identity' (PhD thesis, Catholic University of Leuven).

Lavrov, Sergei (2010) 'Osnovnye vneshnepoliticheskie sobytiya 2010 goda' (Major foreign policy events of 2010), Ministerstvo Inostrannykh Del Rossiiskoi Federatsii (MID RF; Ministry of Foreign Affairs of the Russian Federation) Information and Press Department, available at: http://www.mid.ru/brp_ 4.nsf/0/ECFDB8F78179DDB8C3257806003A9CDB (accessed 2 January 2011).

Legvold, Robert, Karl Kaiser and Alexei G. Arbatov (eds), (1999) *Russia and the West: The 21st Century Security Environment* (London and Armonk, NY: M. E. Sharpe).

Medvedev, Dmitry (2008a) 'Medvedev sets out five foreign policy principles in TV interview', *Johnson's Russia List*, JRL 2008–163, 2 September, available at: http://www.cdi.org/russia/johnson/default.cfm (accessed 3 February 2012).

Medvedev, Dmitry (2008b) 'Poslanie Federal'nomy Sobraniyu Rossiyskoy Federatsii' (Address to the Federal Assembly of the Russian Federation), 5 November, available at: http://kremlin.ru/transcripts/1968 (accessed 18 January 2011).

Medvedev, Dmitry (2008c) 'Speech at a meeting with representatives of German political, parliamentary and social circles', Berlin, 5 June, in Russian, available at: http://archive.kremlin.ru/text/appears/2008/06/202133.shtml (accessed 16 February 2011).

Migranian, Andranik (1997) *Rossiya v poiskakh identichnosti* (Russia in Search of Identity) (Moscow: International Relations).

Military Doctrine of the Russian Federation (2010) 5 February, available at: http://news.kremlin.ru/ref-notes/462 (accessed 21 February 2011).

National Security Concept of the Russian Federation (Kontseptsiya natsional'noy bezopasnosti RF) (2000) *Diplomaticheskii vestnik*, no. 2, pp. 3–13.

National Security Concept of the Russian Federation until 2020 (Strategiya natsionalnoy bezopasnosti Rossiyskoy Federatsii do 2020 goda) (2009) 12 May, available at: http://www.scrf.gov.ru/documents/99.html (accessed 15 December 2010).

Neumann, Iver (1996) *Russia and the Idea of Europe: A Study in Identity and International Relations* (London: Routledge).

North Atlantic Treaty Organization (NATO) (2010) *NATO 2020: Assured Security; Dynamic Engagement: Analysis and Recommendations of the Group of Experts on a New Strategic Concept for NATO*, 17 May, available at: http://www.nato.int/nato_static/assets/pdf/pdf_2010_05/20100517_100517_expertsreport.pdf (accessed 15 December 2010).

Nygren, Bertil (2010) *The Rebuilding of Greater Russia: Putin's Foreign Policy towards the CIS Countries* (London: Routledge).

Prizel, Ilya (1998) *National Identity and Foreign Policy: Nationalism and Leadership in Poland, Russia and Ukraine* (Cambridge: Cambridge University Press).

Pursiainen, Christer (2000) *Russian Foreign Policy and International Relations Theory*, Finnish Institute of International Affairs (Burlington, VT: Ashgate).

Putin, Vladimir (2000) 'State of the Nation Address to the Federal Assembly: The state of Russia, a way to an effective state' (Moscow: Ministerstvo Inostrannykh Del Rossiiskoi Federatsii (MID RF; Ministry of Foreign Affairs of the Russian Federation, Information and Press Department).

Putin, Vladimir (2007) 'Speech of the President of the Russian Federation Vladimir V. Putin at the Munich Conference on Security Policy', 10 February, available at: http://www.securityconference.de/archive/konferenzen/rede.php?menu_2007=&menu_konferenzen=&sprache=en&id=179& (accessed 21 February 2011).

Razuvaev, Vladimir V. (1993) 'Natsional'naya identichnost'' i vneshnyaya politika Rossii' (National identity and Russia's foreign policy), *Kentavr*, no. 5, pp. 3–15.

RIA Novosti (2008) 'Russia recognizes Georgia's breakaway republics', 26 August, available at: http://en.rian.ru/russia/20080826/116291407.html (accessed 12 December 2010).

Rice, Condoleezza (2000) 'Campaign 2000: promoting the national interest', *Foreign Affairs*, vol. 79, no. 1, pp. 45–62.

Rosenau, James (1971) *The Scientific Study of Foreign Policy* (New York: Free Press).

Rosenau, James (1987) 'Toward single-country theories of foreign policy: the case of the USSR', in Charles F. Hermann, Charles W. Kegley, Jr. and James N. Rosenau (eds), *New Directions in the Study of Foreign Policy* (Boston, MA: Allen and Unwin), pp. 53–74.

Ryabkov, Sergey (2010) 'The view from Moscow: Q&A with the Deputy Minister of Foreign Affairs of the Russian Federation', *Journal of International Affairs*, vol. 63, no. 2, pp. 207–16.

Sestanovich, Stephen (ed.) (1994) *Rethinking Russia's National Interests*, Significant Issues Series, 16, 1 (Washington, DC: Center for Strategic and International Studies).

Stone, Matt (2011) 'Russia shores up Near Abroad with Belarus oil deal', *World Politics Review*, Briefing, 12 January, available at: http://www.worldpoliticsreview.com/articles/7538/russia-shores-up-near-abroad-with-belarus-oil-deal (accessed 21 February 2011).

Suny, Ronald Grigor (1999) 'Provisional stabilities: the politics of identities in post-Soviet Eurasia', *International Security*, vol. 24, no. 3, pp. 139–78.

Tsygankov, Andrei P. (1997) 'From international institutionalism to revolutionary expansionism: the foreign policy discourse of contemporary Russia', *Mershon International Studies Review*, vol. 41, no. 2, pp. 247–68.

Vserossiiskii tsentr izucheniya obshchestvennogo mneniya (VTsIOM) (All-Russian Center for the Study of Public Opinion) (2010a) 'Tseli Rossi v mire: razvitie ili sverchderzhavnost'?' (Goals of Russia in the world: development or superpower?), Press Release No. 1576, 7 September, available at: http://wciom.ru/index.php?id=459&uid=13799 (accessed 14 August 2011).

Vserossiiskii tsentr izucheniya obshchestvennogo mneniya (VTsIOM) (All-Russian Center for the Study of Public Opinion) (2010b) 'Kak nam postroit' velikoyu Rossiyu?' (How to build a great Russia?), Press Release No. 1601, 12 October, available at: http://wciom.ru/index.php?id=459&uid=13894 (accessed 14 August 2011).

Wendt, Alexander (1999) *Social Theory of International Relations* (Cambridge: Cambridge University Press).

Wohlforth, William C. (1994) 'Realism and the end of the Cold War,' *International Security*, vol. 19, no. 3, pp. 91–129.

World Health Organization (WHO) (2011) *Global Status Report on Alcohol and Health: Russia Country Profile*, available at: http://www.who.int/substance_abuse/publications/global_alcohol_report/profiles/rus.pdf (accessed 21 February 2011).

2
Domestic Influences on Russian Foreign Policy: Status, Interests and *Ressentiment*

Hanna Smith

Introduction

The formation of foreign policy rests in the first place on two factors. The first is national identity: it lurks in the background of questions that relate to beliefs, values, important national symbols, unity and feelings of belonging that have formed over the course of history. The second is the sum of national interests that define a country's needs, wishes and visions regarding the international community. Anne L. Clunan has argued that, in their turn, national identity and interest rest on two pillars: political purpose and international status (Clunan, 2009, p. 31). Political purpose encompasses beliefs about the appropriate system of political and economic governance and includes ideas about what values, principles, traits and symbols characterise the country, what values and principles should govern relations between countries and what the country's national mission is. International status includes questions of the positioning of one's country in an imagined international hierarchy of political, military, social and economic power. It involves ideas about the proper position, respect, deference, rights and obligations that one's country should be accorded, based on the group that one believes it belongs to (Clunan, 2009, pp. 31–2).

A great power mentality is at the core of Russian national identity and therefore the exact nature of Russia's identity has itself been difficult to detect and remains unresolved, since there are many different ways of being a great power: cooperative and respected, disruptive but recognised, small but morally powerful, large and yet lacking respect, capable but uncooperative, isolationist and developing, integrated but sovereign and so on. For Russia, foreign policy has been one of the most important factors in the creation of national unity and identity. When domestic policies and realities have been close to intolerable and have offered no signs of hope, national and personal pride have remained at the centre of Russia's foreign policy stance. It has mattered little whether Russia has been standing for or against someone, what has mattered most is that Russia is a great country that is most of the time misunderstood by others but has also achieved some recognition internationally. Foreign policy has obscured many weaknesses that Russia has had in other areas.

This chapter will begin by examining Russian 'greatpowerness', especially in the context of the new tone of its foreign policy set after President Putin's speech at the Munich Security Forum in 2007. Then the chapter will look into two aspects that are central to Russian foreign policy-making and also to its claim to being a great power. The domestic political arena is where the greatest challenges for Russian greatpowerness are present, in part because of history and in part because of Russia's own actions and the paths it chose to follow after the fall of the Soviet Union in 1991. The international political arena is where Russia seeks to achieve a high international status, and at present only a fully recognised great power status will suffice Russia's own self-image. Finally the chapter touches upon the issue of how these two often contradictory elements come together in the current arrangement of Russia's state leadership.

Russian greatpowerness

It is not a simple task to define the concept of power and it is therefore also hard to define what makes a country a great power. As Joseph S. Nye put it, 'power, like love, is easier to experience than to define or measure' (Nye, 1990, p. 177). This comparison is especially apt when it comes to analysing the place of Russia's great power status – *derzhavnost'* – in Russian domestic and foreign politics. For Russians *derzhavnost'* is more like an emotion, it is a craving for a status that most Russians strongly believe is theirs by right, by virtue of the enormous size of the country, its resources, its history. In the past this feeling has been expressed ideologically in terms of Russia as the defender of Christendom or as the guardian of international communism. However its roots are deeper than these obsolete ideologies. Russia's leading role in the Concert of Europe in the nineteenth century and its place as one of the two great superpowers for much of the twentieth century have left the impression that Russia is, and should be treated as, at least on a level with the world's other great powers. Russia's greatpowerness is based on its large size, military might and cultural impact, and yet it still does not translate into the economic power that has been the aim of Russian foreign and domestic policy for centuries without success. Furthermore Russia has been too weak to survive on its own and too large to have natural allies. The importance of *derzhavnost'* as a key element in Russian identity with an important impact on foreign policy-making has been recognised by scholars for some time. In a recent statement of this relationship, Margot Light has argued that:

> Russia was clearly not a superpower; indeed, it was questionable whether it was a great power. Yet to ordinary people, as well as to politicians, it was unthinkable that Russia could be anything less than this. The insistence that Russia should be regarded as a great power became an important theme in foreign policy statements and discussions and it remains an important driver of foreign policy. (Light, 2010, p. 229)

Light goes on to argue that 'Russia's identity could be established by defining its foreign policy principles' (ibid.).

'The Cold War has not returned, but Russia is now officially asserting itself as a great power, and behaving accordingly,' stated George Friedman (2007) after President Putin's speech at the Munich Security Forum in February 2007. While the war with Georgia in August 2008 was the most extreme manifestation of a new, more assertive direction in Russian foreign policy, most observers had noticed this new direction long before, with the Munich speech clearly marking a watershed regarding how Russia portrayed itself in the world arena. As Dmitri Trenin put it at the beginning of 2008, the Munich speech was a signal of 'Russia's return to the traditional status of an independent player on the international stage, unencumbered by any relationship of "complex subordination" to the West' (cited in Lyne, 2008). This was not mere rhetoric. As another observer noted in a review of Russian foreign policy for the year 2007, it was:

> the year Vladimir Putin implicitly compared the United States to the Third Reich. It was the year Moscow threatened to target its missiles at Europe and was accused of carrying out a cyber-attack on a NATO member. It was the year Russia pulled out of a key arms-control treaty and resumed strategic-bomber patrols. And it was the year that [...] the last remnants of the vaunted strategic partnership between Russia and the West appeared headed for the dustbin of history. (Whitmore, 2007)

The shift led some commentators to talk of a new Cold War, and while this never fully materialised the differences were clear.[1] Beforehand Russia's leading politicians concentrated on the need and aspiration to become a great power again, but with his Munich speech President Putin defined Russia as a great power. For example, in his 2000 State of the Nation speech Putin argued that:

> The only real choice for Russia is the choice of a strong country. A country that is strong and confident of itself. Strong not in defiance of the international community, not against other strong nations, but together with them. (Putin, 2000a)

And again in 2003:

> Now we must take the next step and focus all our decisions and all our action on ensuring that in a not too far off future, Russia will take its recognized place among the ranks of the truly strong, economically advanced and influential nations. (Putin, 2003)

The underlying message here is that Russia has been a great power, it has had its weak moments but it is a great country due to its potential and the future will show those that cast doubt over this claim that Russia will again be recognised as a great power. On other occasions Putin did not admit any doubts about Russia's great power status. In an interview with the newspaper *Welt am Sonntag* in June 2000, it was suggested to Putin that 'there is some concern in the West about renewed Russian claims to the status of a great power', to which he replied: 'Russia is not claiming a great power status. It is a great power by virtue of its huge potential, its history and culture' (Putin, 2000b). President Dmitri Medvedev has since the start of his presidency used the phrase 'Russia as a Great Power' on every possible occasion, from speeches in the domestic political arena to talks with the presidents of China, France and other nations. Russian greatpowerness can also be viewed as Sergei Kortunov from the Committee on International Affairs of the Duma's upper house described it,

> Russia is a great power in terms of its political importance, intellectual might and influence on global affairs, including as a permanent member of the UN Security Council and corresponding responsibilities. Apart from this, as well as the geopolitical situation and the existence of nuclear weapons (Russia is a military superpower without a doubt),

other proof of Russia's great power status are its current and future opportunities of a resource provider, its hard-working and intellectual population, and the high scientific and technological potential. These factors (territory, technological and human potential, and the existence of nearly all types of raw materials and resources) objectively make Russia a major world power. (Kortunov, 2006)

This description underlines a major feature of Russian claims to great-powerness – which was also present in many of Putin's earlier statements – its potential.

The undoubted source of Russian greatpowerness has been the Russian military and nuclear arsenal, as well as characteristics of imperialism. The characteristics of imperialism, weak or not, functioning or not, bring with them a notion of greatness too. As Richard Pipes put it:

Russia is torn by contradictory pulls, one oriented inward, hence isolationist, the other imperialist. The population at large, preoccupied with physical survival, displays little interest in foreign policy, taking in stride the loss of empire and the world influence that went with it. People pine for normality, which they associate with life in the West as depicted in foreign films and television programs. Depoliticized, they are unresponsive to ideological appeals, although not averse to blaming all their troubles on foreigners. But for the ruling elite and much of the intelligentsia, accustomed to being regarded as citizens of a great power, the county's decline to Third World status has been traumatic. They are less concerned with low living standards than the loss of power and influence, perhaps because inwardly they doubt whether Russia can ever equal the West in anything else. Power and influence for them take the form of imperial splendor and military might second to none. (Pipes, 1997, p. 68)

In this conception the empire has more to do with the size and influence of the country than with being a classic imperium with colonies. Russia's imperial character still lies in its image of a military power and a status that it has automatically through the size of the country.

According to Pipes's argument, for the ordinary people the status of a great power is not as important as it is for the elite and intelligentsia. However, opinion polls have recently shown a slightly different picture. In a poll taken by Fond obshchestvennoe mnenie (FOM) in August 2008, it was found that 60 per cent of those who answered the poll questions saw Russia as a great power. The most popular view of respondents regarding the source of Russia's greatpowerness concerned the size of the country (large territory), its strength (strong state), natural resources, 'Russia has always been a great power', Russia is feared, its voice is heard and it has a say in important international matters, Russia has authority in international matters and its army is powerful (FOM, 2008).[2] Also noteworthy is the fact that 72 per cent of all respondents place Russia among the ten most important countries in the world. Out of those, 44 per cent see Russia as belonging to the five leading countries and 7 per cent place Russia as a world leader (FOM, 2008). This opinion poll is only one example of how Russian people view their own country's position in the world order. One of the main themes of Putin's official speeches throughout his presidencies was Russia's belonging to the group of strong (Russian *velikaya*) nations. Towards the end of his second term in office, he dropped the conditionality and claimed Russia to be a great power. The opinion poll shows that this message has been delivered well. President Medvedev continues this tradition.

The fact that Russian greatpowerness has been a part of its identity, and has often been a uniting factor for the nation in hard times, also has a downside. The thirst for greatpowerness has had its costs. For the political elite it has been important to maintain the picture of Russia as a great power but the drive to play a part in global politics and also be influential in the world has made some domestic developments suffer as well:

> One legacy passed on to us from our Soviet foreign policy was a 'superpower mentality' and a subsequent striving to participate in any and all more or less significant international developments, which often bore a greater domestic cost than the country could afford. (Ivanov, 2002)

The problems that Russia has had during its history regarding reforms and modernisation efforts have often had their roots in the drive for great power status, either to maintain or to gain it. Russia has often embarked on the road to reforms when it has detected some weaknesses in its own system and the understanding has been that without reforms Russia's great power status might be questioned. However the limits of the reforms have also been defined by the framework of a great power status. Wars, the inflexibility of political structures and the fear of losing Great Power status have then worked in the opposite direction. One of the best examples is Mikhail Gorbachev's Russia. The reforms started precisely from the view that if the Soviet Union will not reform/modernise, it will lose its superpower status. The reforms then turned out to be half-hearted due to the fact that they led to the Soviet Union's great power status being questioned. This is well illustrated, especially regarding the thinking among the ranks of military leaders and the security service elite, by Mark L. Haas in his book *The Ideological Origins of Great Power Politics, 1789–1989* (2005, pp. 176–210). Soviet reactions to the events in Riga and Vilnius in early 1991 provide good examples – as do the wars in Chechnya and the five-day war between Russia and Georgia in 2008 – of the consequences of a state reacting on the basis of the view of itself as a Great Power.

The fundamental problem of Russia's great power status has always been its style of governance and its economic structure as compared to that of the Western economies. Celeste A. Wallander and Eugene B. Rumer have argued:

> What defines a great power if not a colossal geographic expanse, rapid economic growth, a vast nuclear arsenal, a permanent seat on the United Nations Security Council, and the unique ability to obliterate the United States at the flick of a switch? With all of these traits, plus vast quantities of energy resources and vital raw materials, wide-reaching political influence, and a dynamic leader, Russia appears to have what it takes to be a great power. The reality, however, is that these very elements that scholars and observers readily identify as key attributes are actually sources of weakness for Russia and thus significantly limit the country's ability to act as a desirable partner for managing the global challenges of terrorism, proliferation, underdevelopment, and instability. (Wallander and Rumer, 2003, p. 57)

As Wallander and Rumer show, Russian great power status is contradictory: on the one hand, it has it, and on the other hand, a shadow has been cast over it. The great power status is often an asset in Russian domestic politics and at the same time a stumbling block in domestic reforms. In the following section Russian greatpowerness and some aspects of Russian domestic politics are examined more closely.

Greatpowerness and domestic politics

The Russian view of itself has always contained a strong element of greatpowerness in it. This has impeded developments in governance and to some extent in economics. The question of the role of foreign policy in domestic politics has been widely debated and analysed. For a long time a view expressed by Bernard C. Cohen was extremely influential in locating the place of foreign policy among other policy areas: 'Foreign policy is more important than other policy areas because it concerns national interests, rather than special interests and more fundamental values' (Cohen, 1968, p. 580; Carlsnaes, 2002, p. 332). This view also suggested that foreign policy was treated by political elites differently from all other areas of public policy and was kept beyond democratic control and public scrutiny.

In Russia international politics seem to be very closely linked with different foreign policy variables – internal, external and historical experiences. Indeed international politics is one of the main factors in the formation of Russian identity. Since from a Western perspective Russian foreign policy still appears to be formed in ways conforming to Cohen's characterisation of foreign policy as a secretive and elitist policy, it is not an easy task to combine all of the aspects into one comprehensive picture that also reflects reality. Much of the most insightful analysis of Russian foreign policy sees both continuity and change as best describing Russian foreign policy and actions in international politics (Lo, 2002; Donaldson and Nogee, 2009; Trenin, 2007). Russians themselves have strongly expressed the link between domestic developments and foreign policy with regard to Russia's international status. Alexander II's foreign minister after the Crimean War of 1853–56, Alexander Gorchakov, saw two preconditions after Russia's defeat in the war for it to be able to rebuild its great power status in Europe:

> To avoid any external controversies that are likely to divert some domestic resources, so halting internal developments of Russia, as well as to forestall any territorial changes or shifts in the balance of power in Europe. (Ivanov, 2000)

This statement reflects Russian foreign policy-making at times when peace for domestic development and territorial integrity form a central part of its foreign policy strategy. In modern times and in the case of the new Russian Federation the war in 1994 in Chechnya went against both of these factors. The period under Alexander II after the Crimean War is often compared to the time after Gorbachev came to power in the Soviet Union in 1985 (Bunce, 1993). Both leaders had the same task – to maintain and lift up Russia as a great power at a 'time of weakness'. Many other historical comparisons have been made, and in some cases have been cultivated by the leaders themselves, for example Nicholas I and Leonid Brezhnev, Peter the Great and Vladimir Putin, Ivan the

Terrible and Joseph Stalin. Taken together these parallels give a strong indication that Russian domestic developments have followed similar paths and that the challenges and problems have remained extensive, as well as the need for reforms at regular intervals.

This observation also puts domestic developments and events at the core of foreign policy-making. Furthermore all of the leaders have worked with the assumption that Russia is either a great power or needs to be displayed as a great power again before the eyes of the outside world. The domestic situation in Russia has dictated both the challenges and the possibilities of Russian foreign policy-making. This leaves very little space for foreign policy-planning and long-term thinking, it has also given a distinct flavour to situations where external factors have prompted some type of action by the Russians. This is one of the defining factors explaining why Russian foreign policy appears unpredictable and prone to extreme reactions to apparently innocuous external developments. However deeper structural analyses show that, disregarding who the leader is or what type of governance Russia has had, there are foreign policy traditions that are always in the background of Russian foreign policy-making and also define the country's goals. As Bobo Lo has written: 'One of the most noteworthy aspects of Russian foreign policy in the post-Soviet era has been the extent to which it has been shaped by domestic factors' (Lo, 2002, p. 26). The strong connection between domestic politics and foreign policy has much to do with the great power identity that Russia has.

One aspect of great power behaviour is an assertive nature. This element has its roots in domestic politics and usually has a negative effect on foreign relations. It can also be used in alliance building and as the basis for a form of cooperation, but since its nature is to be 'against something' it also presents an opposite pole – 'the other'. Historical memory and the fact that Russia has suffered from invasions and physical aggression from all directions, north, south, east and west, throughout its history have created very deep-rooted suspicions and a sense of insecurity vis-à-vis the outside world and increased the divisions between 'us' and 'them' (Lo, 2002, p. 72). As Jack Snyder has argued, 'a state's foreign policy is shaped by the myths it holds about how to achieve security' (Snyder, 1991, pp. 109–10). Even if there have been noteworthy attempts by the Russian political elite to conduct foreign affairs in the manner of the twenty-first century, historical experiences do still play a major role in all Russian international relations. The blame can be put on the supremacy of great power thinking in Russian policy-making.

The influence of great power thinking on domestic policies and the reciprocal negative effect on Russia's external relations as well as its own internal development can be illustrated by examining Russian politics during the Chechen Wars, in the war on terrorism, the five-day war with Georgia and in the broader Russian politics of *ressentiment* (an image of enemy).

Russia's wars

The Chechen Wars

It can be argued that it was the First Chechen War (1994–96) that started the vicious circle that Russia has found difficult to break out of – democracy and war seldom go hand in hand with ease. The First Chechen War was also the first challenge to the great power status of the new Russian Federation. It has often been regarded as aimed at preventing the Russian Federation from breaking up. It started in an environment of regime breakdown and at the beginning of a process of democratisation. It presented Russia with the following dilemma: war may affect subsequent democratic change and democratic change may affect the subsequent outbreak of war (Crescenzi and Enterline, 1999, p. 76). However the reasons for the First Chechen War can also be viewed differently. The regime of Dzhokar Dudayev did not initially ask for independence from Russia but for a favourable deal between Chechnya and the centre. But the traditional assertive aspect of greatpowerness does not allow for opponents to adopt a negotiating position. Dudayev's challenge to Russia as a great power came on two fronts: first, it attempted to put the weakened centre in a negotiating situation; and second, with the demand for independence it questioned the sovereignty of the state, the Russian Federation that had been born of the ashes of the Soviet Union.

The First Chechen War was not portrayed by the Russian state as a war against terrorism, but some of the methods of the Chechen fighters like hostage-taking in Budyanovsk in 1996 allowed the Russian authorities to use the word 'bandit' and the word 'terrorism' was also flashed. Already in 1994 an amendment regarding terrorism was introduced into Russian criminal law (Jonson, 2004, p. 123). The first federation law on the fight against terrorism came into force in July 1998. The First Chechen War was a humiliation for the Russian army, and led to a massive decline in Yeltsin's popularity and dealt a heavy blow to Russia's status as a great power. However it is interesting to note that, despite the humiliating failures of the Russian military, during 1993–2000 the Russian army was the public institution that enjoyed more trust than any other public institution in Russia.[3] The First Chechen War was planned to be a blitzkrieg that would show that the central authority in Russia had the country under its control, would boost the army and demonstrate to the world that Russia was still a mighty force. Somehow it seems that the lessons from history were forgotten by Yeltsin, and also perhaps by Putin. War is seldom quick and often results in unexpected and unwanted outcomes (the example of Iraq also highlights this). Russian Tsar Nicholas II was persuaded by his interior minister Vyacheslav Plehve that 'a quick and victorious war' (Pipes, 1990, p. 2) against Japan in 1904 would boost his popularity as tsar. As history knows the opposite happened, the tsar lost his authority, the army revealed significant weaknesses and Russia began looking like an ageing titan in European politics and indeed underwent a full regime change after some years. One could argue that the war against Japan was the beginning of the end of Russia as a tsarist empire.

The results were perhaps not as dramatic for Yeltsin, but many of the same elements were involved. In the international arena and in foreign relations the war in Chechnya resulted in increasing tensions, and many problems that especially the European Union (EU) experiences today with Russia have their origins in the First Chechen War. After a promising start Russia's already troubled relationship with the Organization for Security and Co-operation in Europe (OSCE) soured quite soon after the August 1996 Khasavyurt peace accord was signed and never fully recovered. Even if in Russian minds the idea at the beginning of the war was to boost the role of the OSCE at the expense of the North Atlantic Treaty Organization (NATO), as it turned out Russia's actions in Chechnya had the opposite effect, ensuring that the first NATO enlargement went ahead while the role of the OSCE remained more or less the same. Russia's status as a great power has suffered as a result. The First Chechen War had shown to the world that Russia was not a military threat to it and that action by Western countries even against Russian wishes was possible.

On the domestic scene the power elite of Russia led by Yeltsin weakened significantly because of the war. The internal power struggles after the First Chechen War paved the way for what was to come in Russian politics – the Putin era with a strong hand. The legacy of Yeltsin's presidency for the Russians was twofold. First, Russians themselves considered Russia's weak democracy as chaos, a disgrace and a time of uncertainty. Yeltsin had fallen into the same trap as Gorbachev – he had made a great country much smaller in the eyes of others, and Russian greatpowerness was questioned. Second, for the Russians Western behaviour towards their country was very contradictory and represented double standards. Because of the fear of a return of communism, Western governments and institutions turned a blind eye to the shortcomings of Russian democracy, an action that was interpreted in Russia as being given a 'carte blanche' for domestic affairs while 'business as usual' would continue in international politics. This misperception by the Russians and the weakness displayed by its Western partners was very much down to the results of the First Chechen War and have ever since characterised Russia's relations with the West.

The Second Chechen War and the war on terror

Even if the First Chechen War was doubtless a mistake and represented a failure on the part of the Yeltsin administration and the army, it continued to attract the attention of power elites in Moscow. The Russian military needed a mission in order to survive, the leadership a reason to boost nationalism, and revenge would enhance Russia's great power image. Chechnya once again presented them with such an opportunity. Furthermore the Russians' experience in the First Chechen War had given them the impression that strong-handed action – even if the First Chechen War was a humiliation – was still the best way to demonstrate state power. An interesting feature of the decision to renew hostilities was that it came not from the Defence Ministry but from the Interior Ministry. The kidnapping of an interior ministry official led to Minister of the Interior Sergei Stepashin calling for a new mission in Chechnya. Plans regarding Chechnya were already being laid out in early 1999 (Evangelista, 2002, p. 79). The scenario that a 'war strategy' was already in place also fits in with Putin's claim during his first meeting with President Clinton in the summer of 1999 that al-Qaeda had troops in Chechnya and was planning action against Russia (CoFR, 2004). The fight against terrorism was also raised at the June 1999 Commonwealth of Independent States (CIS) summit in Minsk, where the CIS countries signed a document for cooperation in this matter (Treaty on Cooperation, 1999). A new victorious war would restore stability in the Russian Federation and the West would see that Russia was indeed a force to be reckoned with.

In contrast to the First Chechen War, when official discourse focused on the internal threat posed by Chechnya, in the Second Chechen War discourses also presented an external threat in the form of international terrorism. A fight against an external enemy is well suited to a great power image. The Russian presidential administration began arguing in the international arena about the threat of international terrorism with the start of the Second Chechen War in 1999. Foreign Minister Igor Ivanov spoke in favour of international cooperation against terrorism at the fifty-fourth General Assembly of the United Nations in September 1999. In October the UN Security Council passed two resolutions, one regarding the action against the Taliban government in Afghanistan and one about international cooperation against terrorism (UN Security Council Resolution 1267, 1999; UN Security Council Resolution 1269, 1999). Once elected President of Russia, Putin continued talking about the threat of international terrorism. When he met with leaders of the European Union and the United States, he continually brought up the issue of the growth of terrorism in Afghanistan and warned about links between the terrorist camps in Afghanistan and groups of Islamic fundamentalists in Europe (Hill, 2002). The fight against terrorism had become one of the major priorities of the Russian state well before 9/11. All of the major foreign and security policy documents stressed the danger of terrorism; the Russian national security concept portrayed international terrorism attempting to weaken and split Russia, in the military doctrine terrorism was named as the most dangerous factor threatening Russia's internal unity, and the Russian foreign policy doctrine stressed the importance of international cooperation in the fight against international terrorism. All three major foreign and security policy documents were published in 2000 (Russian Foreign Policy Concept, 2000; Russian Military Doctrine, 2000; Russian National Security Concept, 2000).

The Second Chechen War and the war against terrorism united all of Russia's political factions: liberals, communists, nationalists, the army and security institutions as well as public opinion that was moved to support the Russian president and his government. S. J. Main wrote:

> In fighting in the south, Russia not only hopes to restore consti-
> tutional order and, of course, reassert its territorial integrity in the
> region, but also to send a warning shot across the bows of anyone
> who might have thought that Russia would quietly slip away from
> the region, like a thief in the night. As Russia has been a key player
> in the area, for better or worse, for over 300 years, it is not going to
> quietly slip away. (Main, 2000, p. 35)

The Russian public very much shared this view. Opinion polls showed that the Russian population overwhelmingly supported the war (73 per cent were in favour) as late as March 2000 (Sperling, 2001). The

Second Chechen War began in August 1999. Only a very few newspaper articles questioned the operation. Evgeni Krutikov wrote in the newspaper *Izvestia*, 'Why do we Russians do all this and what exactly do our leaders want to gain by using all this force?' (Krutikov, 1999). A specialist in security issues and a member of the Duma, Alexei Arbatov warned against the war in an article in *Obshaya Gazeta* titled 'Never step into the same war twice' (Arbatov, 1999). It already looked then that the war might be long and drawn out. Defence Minister Igor Sergeyev stated at the end of October that the Russian troops would never leave Chechnya (Busza, 1999).

One of the clear explanations of why Putin's new war in the old place – the Second Chechen War – and the concept of terrorism gained so much support was that after the very stormy years of Yeltsin's administration the feeling of insecurity had grown so great that both the political elite and the public were ready to unite against a common enemy. At the same time Russia was acting like a great power in the international arena and the Russian military was again taken more seriously. In the war against terrorism Russia was and is a valuable partner to the US and to European countries.

The five-day war with Georgia

The First Chechen War was clearly a result of the institutional weakness of Russia, of pressure from the military and security elites and of the use of nationalist rhetoric about Chechnya. The Second Chechen War was needed to create a picture of a state that honours order and stability. The war on terrorism worked as a scapegoat for all of the internal troubles and faults that Russia had and Russia's status in the international arena once again became more noticeable. These wars had all had their internal purposes more or less successfully fulfilled when it came to restoring the image of a strong state. However the wars did not cross international boundaries. The war that did so was that between Russia and Georgia in August 2008. Russians argue that it was not a war between Russia and Georgia but a war between Georgia and South Ossetia and Georgia and Abkhazia where Russia only helped the weaker part, just as the Western coalition helped Kuwait when Iraq invaded it or when NATO decided to go into action in defence of Kosovo Albanians. But the fact remains that according to all international documentation prior to the war, South Ossetia and Abkhazia were part of Georgia. The Russian argument for launching the war was its right to protect Russian citizens outside Russian borders. This argument has been on the rise in the Russian domestic political arena and has had a significant impact on Russian foreign relations. A noteworthy fact is that Russian politicians adopted this in official rhetoric and then in the national security strategy of 2009 after the United States had already done so in 2002.

Ressentiment

After empires break up the former imperial power faces the problem of finding a new identity to replace the imperial one. This is much more problematic in the case of states that lack developed institutions and are in flux following a period where Marxism–Leninism was the prevailing ideology. In the late nineteenth century the elites of the Russian Empire resorted to state-sponsored xenophobia and exclusivity as the foundation of political order. Sometimes the politics of *ressentiment* go down better with the populace than does openly isolationist or imperialistic rhetoric (Prizel, 1998, p. 412).

The politics of *ressentiment* rest on accusing outside forces of causing every problem that arises on the domestic front. It is not at all a new phenomenon in Russian history. It was also frequently used during the Soviet era. One good example can be seen in Nina Andreeva's famous letter 'I cannot give up my principles' in *Sovetskaya Rossiya* on 13 March 1987. Published as an article, it claimed that the attacks on the dictatorship of the proletariat and the former political leaders in the heat of *glasnost* must owe their origin to professional anti-communists in the West, who have long advocated 'the so-called democratic slogan of anti-Stalinism' (Sakwa, 1999, pp. 441–6). Another more recent example of the same type of argument can be found in Putin's speech of 4 September 2004:

> We winked at our own weakness, and it is the weak who are always beaten up. Some want to tear away a large part of our wealth, while others help these aspirants in so doing. They still believe that Russia poses a threat to them as a nuclear power. Terrorism is just another instrument implementing their designs. (Putin, 2004)

In statements of this kind today it remains unspecified just who is Russia's 'foe'. During the Soviet era it was clear that it was the West and the capitalist system. Andrei Illarionov also warns about the influence from outside: 'It is critical for Russia to breed immunity against destructive ideas, which are occasionally imported from countries generally viewed as advanced and developed' (Illarionov, 2005). Illarionov calls for a selective approach to ideas that come from the West – some are good and some are bad for Russia. He points out that not only have freedom of the individual, the market economy and democracy entered Russia from the West, but also Marxism and socialism (Illarionov, 2005).

The concept of *ressentiment* is often used to describe a situation where the ruling elite accuses foreign powers of trying to weaken it. It is often also based on a suspicion that stems from insecurity about one's own identity and a feeling of being looked down upon by others. Building up a strong sense of identity is seen as important and national unity is regarded as a crucial element in this. The Russian commentator, Sergei Markov, has stated that 'the Russian mentality is by nature defensive, and has been thus for hundreds of years. The myth that Russia is surrounded by enemies is widespread, and politicians use this to their advantage' (Smith, 2006). *Ressentiment* is a typical characteristic of a state governed by an elite in which institutions have not developed. *Ressentiment*-type behaviour in Russia includes government accusations of Russian oligarchs living abroad trying to weaken the Russian government and create a detrimental image of it in the West, and claims that citizens' organisations, particularly those getting funding from abroad, are hotbeds of anti-government political activity. Georgians have been made the scapegoats of the growing hatred towards foreigners, and international terrorism is regarded as a threat to Russia's unity. Some major Western firms have also been accused of trying to hijack Russia's important raw material resources for themselves.

The concept of *ressentiment* is of use to the understanding of Russian foreign policy since it highlights Russian suspicions towards anything that comes from outside of its own society. This feeling has deep roots in the Russian past where, in order to survive, it needed to defend itself against many acts of aggression. This factor is often neglected in analyses of Russian foreign policy. In the Western discourse Russia is the aggressive one with traditional imperialist ambitions and a great power mentality. The concept of *ressentiment* is very helpful in explaining Russian foreign policy where great power ambitions exist at the same time as the mentality of an occupied country. Aleksandr Muzykantsky further explains this suspicion, using sociologist Igor Yakovenko's definitions about Russian mentality, according to which part of Russian mentality is characterised by Manicheanism. Manicheanism sees the world as an arena of the eternal struggle between two forces – light and dark, good and evil. In this struggle there are 'us' and 'them'. A Manichean mentality needs an enemy, real or imaginary. In interstate relations, stereotypical enemies of the Manichean type are: 'a hostile environment, imperialist circles, backstage intrigues or simply "forces of darkness" that are out to destroy, dismember or take control of everything' (Muzykantsky, 2005). This type of a worldview sounds like something directly out of nineteenth-century Russian literature, but the evidence of even the official statements speaks to the fact that Russian ruling elites divert into the politics of *ressentiment* when it is too difficult to say 'we don't know what to do'. A great power always knows what to do. As long as *ressentiment* politics prevails in Russian political discourse, the Russian state remains a weak great power and any effort at reform will only be halfhearted. The main controversy of this tactic is that it is often successful. Only by admitting its own internal weaknesses in a transparent way can Russia shake off the politics of *ressentiment* and start building a modern great power.

Greatpowerness and international status

The great power mentality in Russia is deeply embedded in foreign policy behaviour in the multilateral context as well. The Russian aspiration to be one of the great powers of the world provides a constraint to domestic politics and a more cooperative line in its foreign policy. In the Russian view of multipolarity the principle of equality has a strong presence but only works in the context of great power relations.

Russian foreign policy-makers seem to accept the maxims described by Robert O. Keohane concerning the importance of international institutions even if they are not always successful in world politics:

> Superpowers need general rules because they seek to influence events around the world. Even an unchallenged superpower such as the United States would be unable to achieve its goals through the bilateral exercise of influence: the costs of such massive 'arm-twisting' would be too great. (Keohane, 2002, p. 27)

But at the same time Russians find it very difficult to cooperate in multilateral agreements and protocols where Russia would be one among others, small and big countries alike, and furthermore the multilateral format of international organisations and forums makes it possible for Russian diplomacy to create actively a broad base of supporters for its conceptual approaches to the issues (Ivanov, 2002, p. 47). The Russian understanding of great power status does not include equality among all states or any possibility of interfering in the state affairs of a great power. As much as it looks as though Russia understands the use and meaning of international organisations and international relations in the multilateral context, the influence of the past centuries of Russia's international status still lurks in the background of its actions and views about how international relations should be conducted and foreign policy statements follow this line accordingly.

Russia still seeks to belong and to be one of the 'big players' in international organisations. The example of the Council of Europe illustrates this well. Russia has been playing by the Council's rules during the first decade of its membership, however all the while it has sought to find ways to change agendas and unwritten rules.[4] Russia has wanted to take its place among the 'big' countries within the Council, thus formalising the superiority of the great powers. Despite this attitude it can also be argued that Russia does very much understand and is acquainted with today's multilateral structures and mechanisms and how multilateralism works in theory.[5] The multilateral system provides an opportunity for Russia to create for itself a leading role, especially in regard to those organisations where Russia has a dominant position such as the one that it has in the CIS and UN or the Shanghai Cooperation Organisation (SCO). The case of the OSCE is an interesting one since there Russia has demonstrated both a willingness to work with the multilateral framework and to use it in conflict situations, while simultaneously opposing the involvement of the organisation (for example, in the case of Chechnya). The troubles that the OSCE has had with Russia and vice versa are also due to the two contradictory trends: the principle of equality and the superiority of the great powers. The tension between these two creates a deadlock in Russia's behaviour in the OSCE. This also translates into the general framework of Russian foreign policy creating a clear tension between great power thinking based on the realist view and the equality principle that has a base in institutionalism and also in elements of democratic peace theory. According to Bobo Lo, Russia views multipolarity as a plutocratic multilateralism and so does not have any commitment to multilateralism, if that means the democratisation of international relations where big and small are making decisions on an equal basis.[6]

Russia has long been interested in Western international organisations and has shown a great interest in dealing with NATO countries in the multilateral context. The concept of cooperation with NATO seems to work, despite a number of problems and disagreements, and one of the reasons for its success is that Russia is seen as an equal without membership and veto rights. However in Russian eyes there is one international organisation that stands above all others – the United Nations. The role of the UN in Russian foreign policy argumentation has steadily grown. Russia has always stressed the importance of the UN but in Putin's multivector and multidirectional foreign policy programme, the UN has gained an even bigger role:

> In the course of Russia's realization of its foreign policy programme, the United Nations has begun to play an extremely important role.

In the Russian view, the UN represents the central collective mechanism for shaping the multipolar world order and regulating world politics. It is the backbone of the emergent international system based on international law, the UN Charter and multilateral approaches to global and regional problems. (Kassianova, 2002)

The UN is an organisation that Russia does not need to seek membership of as it is already a member, and it also suits its views as to how great powers should be able to manoeuvre inside of an international organisation. With the veto right given to all of the permanent members of the UN Security Council, Russia among them, UN decisions can rarely be unsatisfactory for permanent Security Council members. Russia – as the main heir to the Soviet Union – has been with the UN since its foundation and therefore the rules and practises that exist have been created with Russia as a member. This is a very important aspect in today's Russian multilateralism. Furthermore the UN is also a place where Russia seeks greater legitimacy (Kassianova, 2002).

At the multilateral level the 'clubs' that Russia is keenest on are both the G8 and the G20. Membership in the G8 was the ultimate goal of the Russian Federation after the fall of the Soviet Union and was seen as proof of Russian greatpowerness. In fact that was not a new trend. Soviet President Mikhail Gorbachev made the first overtures to the organisation in the late 1980s (Dalziel, 2002). Russia was looking to enhance the prestige of its international image from the club: 'Moscow's original desire to join was clearly based on considerations of prestige. After the fall of the Soviet Union, Moscow was in dire need of confirmation of its status as a major power' (Lukyanov, 2007). As far as the Russians are concerned, Russia became a member of the G8 at the 1998 Birmingham summit. When in 2002 Russia was granted the status of host for the G8 summit of 2006, it was interpreted as a signal that Russia was now a full-fledged member with as great a role and as much prestige as the others. As Pavel K. Baev has written: 'The privilege of chairing the G8 was hailed by the Russian leadership as a unique opportunity to demonstrate their country's rising power and re-assert its coveted great-power status' (Baev, 2008, p. 58).

At the time Russia was not even ranked among the world's top ten economies. G8 membership indicated both that Russian great power status has been and will be determined by something other than economic might, and that the other great powers, especially the great economic powers, cannot keep Russia out:

In international relations Russia still behaves like a major power, a legitimate member of the G8, as opposed to any other 'normal country' of the middle rank. In other words, Russia is boxing above its weight – a country with a GDP similar to that of the Netherlands or Turkey can hardly be seen as a leading industrial power in the world. Yet it is evident that the Russian leadership aspires to a more exalted role in the world. (Barnes and Owen, 2006, p. 17)

It is clear that Russia pays special attention to achieving recognition of its international status as a great power through different international organisations. In most of its encounters with international organisations Russia's motives are connected to the status of a great power. Russian rhetoric also circulates around this status.

Conclusion: the two-headed eagle – greatpowerness as domestic political purpose and international status

Soviet foreign policy was, according to a study by Marshall D. Shulman in 1965, more rational than was thought in the West, less focused on personalities than was supposed and similar to two different great power types of behaviour – one militant and direct and the other long-term and cooperational. According to Shulman, this had already been the case in imperial Russia (Shulman, 1965). In both Russian domestic and foreign policies these two traditional lines are also present. To some extent they are personalised by the 'two-headed eagle' leadership, also known as the 'tandem' leadership. President Medvedev represents the more long-term and cooperational line and Prime Minister Putin represents the militant and direct line.

Parallels to a dual leadership in Russian history are hard to find and one needs to stretch both one's knowledge and imagination to find one: Peter the Great and his weak brother Ivan? Perhaps a more relevant parallel is in the relationship between tsar and prime minister after 1905. Tsar Nicholas II withdrew from hands-on everyday governmental work and the prime minister was left to take care of the state. However the decisions still ultimately had to be taken by the tsar. The prime minister's hands were tied since the tsar still retained full power over the state. For example, he had the right to appoint ministers and conduct wars. Many historians argue that nonetheless the system worked well for a certain period. But it would seem that the model was only really effective as long as an exceptional prime minister – Stolypin – was in office, and at the same time the tsar chose largely to absent himself from the power to which he was entitled.

Translated into today's Russia this would indicate that the strong man is Putin but that the system works as long as the president himself does not want to exercise his powers fully. As Fraser Cameron puts it, 'it suits both to play the "good cop, bad cop" role from time to time, but in reality there are no fundamental differences between the two' (Cameron, 2010). The 'bad cop' or rather the 'strong man' image goes down well on the domestic front while the 'good cop' image is needed internationally. However the tough stance presented by Putin at home includes statements on international policy, and this creates a weakness internationally where the aggressive tone cannot be moderated. Analysis of different statements by Russia's leaders reveals that Russia's self-image as expressed by the political leadership is contradictory. On the one hand can be seen harsh self-criticism and a realistic picture of the problems, and on the other hand there is praise for the Russian past and its achievements as well as rhetoric in favour of hard measures to maintain stability. Alongside the list of faults is as long a list of successes and idealised views of the possibilities for the future of Russia.

Domestically Russia cannot show any weaknesses in international politics, but as a consequence it ends up alone and in a defensive position in the global arena. That in turn brings more assertiveness and bitter words into domestic politics. Russia has created for itself politics of a 'vicious circle' where it will continue to exhaust itself unless it is ready to admit to some weaknesses, make some real structural changes and heal the gap between society and political power. But anything short of greatpowerness is unacceptable domestically, and as long as Russian leaders obey the constraints of domestic politics, such changes in international politics are unlikely to be achieved.

Notes

1. For a balanced discussion of the significance of the Munich speech, see Monaghan, 2008, pp. 719–22.
2. The opinion poll was conducted on 23–24 August 2008. The war in Georgia was in early August. This poll also shows that in the eyes of the Russian people, the war only reinforced Russia's great power status, and not the other way around.
3. Public Opinion survey conducted by VTsIOM in Sperling (2001).
4. Interview with Council of Europe official, Strasbourg, 20 June 2006.
5. Interview with Irina Kobrinskaya, analyst, Moscow, 21 June 2004.
6. Interview with Bobo Lo, researcher, Moscow, 22 June 2004.

References

Arbatov, Alexei (1999) 'Never step into the same war twice', *Obshaya Gazeta*, no. 39, 30 September–6 October.

Baev, Pavel K. (2008) 'Leading in the concerts of great powers – lessons from the Russian G8 chairmanship', in Elana Wilson Rowe and Stina Torjesen (eds), *The Multilateral Dimension in Russian Foreign Policy* (London: Routledge), pp. 58–68.

Barnes, Hugh and James Owen (2006) *Russia in the Spotlight: G8 Scorecard*, January (London: Foreign Policy Centre).

Bunce, Valerie (1993) 'Domestic reform and international change: the Gorbachev reforms in historical perspective', *International Organizations*, vol. 47, no. 1, pp. 107–38.

Busza, Eva (1999) 'Chechnya: the military's golden opportunity to emerge as an important political player in Russia', (Program on New Approaches to Research and Security in Eurasia), PONARS Eurasia, *Policy Memo.*, No. 98, December (Washington, DC: George Washington University).

Cameron, Fraser (2010) *New York Times*, 11 February.

Carlsnaes, Walter (2002) 'Foreign policy', in Walter Carlsnaes, Thomas Risse and Beth A. Simmons (eds), *Handbook of International Relations* (London: Sage), pp. 331–49.

Clunan, Anne L. (2009) *The Social Construction of Russia's Resurgence – Aspirations, Identity and Security Interests* (Baltimore, MD: Johns Hopkins University Press).

Cohen, Bernard C. (1968) 'Foreign policy', in David L. Sills (ed.), *International Encyclopedia of the Social Sciences* (New York: Macmillian and Free Press).

Council of Foreign Relations (CoFR) (2004) 'Terrorism, Q & A – Russia', London, available at: http://cfrterrorism.org/coalition/russia.html (accessed 23 August 2005).

Crescenzi, Mark J. C. and Andrew J. Enterline (1999) 'Ripples from the waves? A systemic, time-series analysis of democracy, democratisation and interstate war', *Journal of Peace Research*, vol. 36, no. 1, pp. 75–94.

Dalziel, Stephen (2002) 'Analysis: Russia's place in G8', BBC website, 27 June, available at: http://news.bbc.co.uk/2/hi/business/2069587.stm (accessed 11 November 2011).

Donaldson, Robert H. and Joseph L. Nogee (2009) *The Foreign Policy of Russia: Changing Systems, Enduring Interests* (Armonk, NY: M. E. Sharpe).

Evangelista, Matthew (2002) *The Chechen Wars: Will Russia Go the Way of the Soviet Union* (Washington, DC: Brookings Institution Press).

Fond obshchestvennoe mnenie (FOM) (2008) 'Opros naseleniya, Mezhdunarodnoe polozhenie Rossii i zadachi rossiyskoy vneshney politiki', Moscow, 28 August, available at: http://bd.fom.ru/report/cat/inter_pol/mesto_v_mire/ (accessed 13 November 2011).

Friedman, George (2007) 'Russia's great-power strategy' (Austin, TX: STRATFOR Global Intelligence), 13 February.

Haas, Mark L. (2005) *The Ideological Origins of Great Power Politics, 1789–1989* (Ithaca, NY: Cornell University Press).

Hill, Fiona (2002) 'Extremists and bandits: how Russia views the war against terrorism', (Program on New Approaches to Research and Security in Eurasia), PONARS Eurasia, *Policy Memo.*, No. 246, April (Washington, DC: George Washington University).

Illarionov, Andrei (2005) 'A long-term project for Russia', *Russia in Global Affairs*, no. 3, July–September, available at: http://eng.globalaffairs.ru/number/n_5342 (accessed 13 November 2011).

Ivanov, Igor S. (2000) *Vneshnyaya politika Rossii i mir (Russian Foreign Policy and the World)* (Moscow: ROSSPEN).

Ivanov, Igor (2002) *The New Russian Diplomacy* (Washington, DC: Brookings Institute Press).

Jonson, Lena (2004) *Vladimir Putin and Central Asia: The Shaping of Russian Foreign Policy* (London: I. B. Tauris).

Kassianova, Alla (2002) 'Russian diplomacy in the 21st century multilateralism put to work', (Program on New Approaches to Research and Security in Eurasia), PONARS Eurasia, *Policy Memo.*, No. 262, October (Washington, DC: George Washington University), available at: http://csis.org/files/media/csis/pubs/pm_0262.pdf (accessed 13 November 2011).

Keohane, Robert O. (2002) 'International institutions: can interdependence work?', in Robert O. Keohane (ed.), *Power and Governance in a Partially Globalized World* (London: Routledge), pp. 27–38.

Kortunov, Sergei (2006) *Should Russia Claim Great Power Status* (Moscow: RIA Novosti, 25 September).

Krutikov, Yevgeni (1999) 'Chechen rakes', *Izvestia*, 28 September.

Light, Margot (2010) 'Russian foreign policy', in Stephen White, Richard Sakwa and Henry E. Hale (eds), *Developments in Russian Politics* (Basingstoke: Palgrave), pp. 225–44.

Lo, Bobo (2002) *Russian Foreign Policy in the Post-Soviet Era: Reality, Illusion and Mythmaking* (Basingstoke: Macmillan).

Lo, Bobo (2003) *Vladimir Putin and the Evolution of Russian Foreign Policy* (London: Royal Institute of International Affairs and Blackwell Publishing).

Lukyanov, Fyodor (2007) 'G8 membership as an exercise in legitimacy', *Russia in Global Affairs*, no. 2, April–June, available at: http://eng.globalaffairs.ru/redcol/n_8712 (accessed 13 November 2011).

Lyne, Roderic (2008) 'Reading Russia, rewiring the West', *Open Democracy*, 12 October, available at: http://www.opendemocracy.net/article/terrorism-theme/reading-russia-rewiring-the-west (accessed 12 November 2011).

Main, S. J. (2000) 'Counter-terrorist operations in Chechnya: on the legality of the current conflict', in A. C. Aldis (ed.), *The Second Chechen War* (Camberley: Conflict Studies Research Centre), pp. 19–37.

Monaghan, Andrew (2008) '"An enemy at the gates" or "From victory to victory"? Russian foreign policy', *International Affairs*, vol. 8, no. 4, pp. 717–33.

Muzykantsky, Alexsander (2005) 'A yardstick for Russia', *Russia in Global Affairs*, no. 3, July–September, available at: http://eng.globalaffairs.ru/number/n_5340 (accessed 3 November 2011).

Nye, Joseph S. (1990) 'The changing nature of world power', *Political Science Quarterly*, vol. 105, no. 2, pp. 177–92.

Pipes, Richard (1990) *The Russian Revolution 1899–1919* (London: Collins Harvill).

Pipes, Richard (1997) 'Is Russia still an enemy', *Foreign Affairs*, vol. 76, no. 5, pp. 65–78.

Prizel, Ilya (1998) *National Identity and Foreign Policy: Nationalism and Leadership in Poland, Russia and Ukraine* (Cambridge: Cambridge University Press).

Putin, Vladimir (2000a) 'Annual Address to the Federal Assembly of the Russian Federation', 8 July (Moscow: The Kremlin), available at: http://archive.kremlin.

ru/eng/speeches/2000/07/08/0000_type70029type82912_70658.shtml (accessed 13 November 2011).

Putin, Vladimir (2000b) 'Interview with the newspaper *Welt am Sonntag* (Germany)', 11 June, available at: http://archive.kremlin.ru/eng/text/speeches/2000/06/11/0000_type82916_129866.shtml (accessed 13 November 2011).

Putin, Vladimir (2003) 'Annual Address to the Federal Assembly of the Russian Federation', 16 May (Moscow: The Kremlin), available at: http://archive.kremlin.ru/eng/speeches/2003/05/16/0000_type70029type82912_44692.shtml (accessed 13 November 2011).

Putin, Vladimir (2004) Address, 4 September, Kremlin Archive, available at: http://archive.kremlin.ru/eng/speeches/2004/09/04/1958_type82912_76332.shtml (accessed 13 November 2011).

Russian Foreign Policy Concept (2000) Available at: http://www.fas.org/nuke/guide/russia/doctrine/econcept.htm (accessed 13 November 2011).

Russian Military Concept (2000) Available at: http://www.armscontrol.org/act/2000_05/dc3ma00 (accessed 13 November 2011).

Russian National Security Concept (2000) Available at: http://www.mid.ru/bdomp/ns-osndoc.nsf/e2f289bea62097f9c325787a0034c255/a54f9caa5e68075e432569fb004872a6!OpenDocument (accessed 13 November 2011).

Sakwa, Richard (1999) *The Rise and Fall of the Soviet Union, 1917–1991* (London: Routledge).

Shulman, Marshall D. (1965) *Stalin's Foreign Policy Reappraised* (New York: Atheneum with Harvard University Press).

Smith, Sebastian (2006) 'Enemies at the gate: Russia's siege mentality in polls run-up', Agence France-Presse, Moscow, 17 October.

Snyder, Jack (1991) *Myth of Empire: Domestic Politics and International Ambition* (Ithaca, NY: Cornell University Press).

Sperling, Valerie (2001) 'Opposition to the war in Chechnya: antimilitarist organizing in Russia', (Program on New Approaches to Research and Security in Eurasia), PONARS Eurasia, *Policy Memo.*, No. 224, December (Washington, DC: George Washington University).

Treaty on Cooperation among States Members of the Commonwealth of Independent States in Combating Terrorism (1999) Minsk, 4 June.

Trenin, Dmitri (2007) *Getting Russia Right* (Washington, DC: Carnegie Endowment for International Peace).

United Nations Security Council Resolution 1267 (1999) On measures against the Taliban, 15 October.

United Nations Security Council Resolution 1269 (1999) On international cooperation in the fight against terrorism, 19 October.

Wallander, Celeste A. and Eugene B. Rumer (2003) 'Russia: power in weakness', *Washington Quarterly*, vol. 27, no. 1, pp. 57–73.

Whitmore, Brian (2007) 'Russia: Cold War lite', RFE/RL, 26 December, available at: http://www.rferl.org/content/article/1079299.html (accessed 13 November 2011).

3
Nationalist Grievance and Russian Foreign Policy: The Case of Georgia

Luke March

Introduction

'The Russians are coming.' Western discussion in the last half-decade has focused on an increasingly 'assertive' and even 'aggressive' Russian foreign policy underpinning growing confidence about Russia's global position. From a Russia that could only say 'yes' to the West in the 1990s, the West was apparently now confronting a Russia that could, and would, say 'no' (Connor, 2007, pp. 383–91).

For many analysts this assertive stance was associated with distinct ideational underpinnings that sought to challenge Western liberalism. Although 'sovereign democracy' was the most obvious example, many also argued that anti-Western nationalism moved from the margins to the mainstream of Russian discourse in the Putin era (Joo, 2008, pp. 217–42; Umland, 2009, pp. 5–38; Breslauer, 2009, pp. 370–6). Moreover this nationalism had apparently begun ineluctably to influence Russian foreign policy and to deepen the rhetorical and cognitive dissonance between Russia and the West. Indeed, as Edward Lucas argued, 'the ideological conflict of the New Cold War is between lawless Russian nationalism and law-governed Western multilateralism' (Lucas, 2009, p. 14).

The Russia–Georgia conflict of August 2008 seemed initially only to authenticate this narrative. Russia's recognition of Abkhazia and South Ossetia in defiance of Euro-Atlantic positions appeared to be the tipping point when a highly nationalistic Russia began to substantiate its rhetoric and to export its internal values in an attempt to revise the post-Cold War order, or as one of the most influential authors on the conflict wrote:

> by the summer of 2008 [...] an increasingly nationalistic and revisionist Russia was [...] rebelling against a system that it felt no

longer met its interests and had been imposed on it during a moment of temporary weakness. (Asmus, 2010, p. 7)

Hindsight has clearly confounded this view somewhat. While the exact catalysts for the conflict will long remain hotly debated, Georgian President Mikheil Saakashvili's reputation has suffered significantly as the view that he provoked Russian intervention rather than vice versa has gained currency (particularly in Europe). More widely, the United States–Russia 'reset' has involved a marked change of climate and de-escalation of rhetoric. Russia itself has focused increasingly on internal modernisation and immediate fears that it was to pursue overt annexation of other contested regions like Crimea and Transnistria have receded. Finally, Russian President Dmitri Medvedev's modernisation rhetoric is associated with increased efforts to control domestic nationalist excesses via greater law enforcement (Kozhevnikova, 2010).

So what did the 'five-day war' between Russia and Georgia in August 2008 reveal about the influence of nationalism on Russian foreign policy? Was it the driving force in Russian conduct during the conflict, as some Western analysts initially assumed, and if so, why has it apparently diminished in official foreign policy discourse since 2008? Does nationalism present a significant obstacle to the 'modernisation' and 'resetting' of Russian policy?

In this chapter I will trace the foreign policy influence of Russian nationalism from the Putin to the Medvedev eras, focusing specifically on Russian nationalist arguments for and reactions to the August 2008 conflict. Although this is not the primary focus here, it should of course be noted that 'nationalism' is not the sole preserve of the Russian authorities (Western and particularly Georgian approaches also regularly articulate policies that non-natives could regard as 'nationalist'). Moreover contrary to a prevalent view that has regarded Russian nationalism as inevitably expansionist and militarist, I do not consider it as negative by itself (Pipes, 1984). Indeed, I will argue that traditionally, Russian nationalism has rarely affected foreign policy directly or in an aggressive way; rather, the causative arrows need to be reversed. The Russian state has generally tried to insulate itself from the constrictive effects of ideational factors and – particularly in the Putin era – sought to exploit nationalism as a tool largely for domestic mobilisation purposes. However, this mobilisation of domestic nationalism – whereby nationalism is now the 'politically correct' domestic discourse – which was largely unchecked until 2008, has risked becoming self-fulfilling, creating demands that are increasingly hard to control and which spill over into foreign policy. The August 2008 conflict does indeed show Russian domestic and foreign policy discourses becoming congruent around a nationalist stance to an arguably unprecedented degree. However the Russian elite seems aware of this and has since 2009 deliberately sought to return to non-ideational, non-nationalist rhetoric. Nevertheless without more fundamental domestic change, this is likely to remain a superficial 'reset' that does not circumvent the likelihood of nationalism increasingly affecting Russian foreign policy.

Nationalism and foreign policy: from 'managed' to unmanageable?

Observers disagree about the role of nationalism in Russian foreign policy. This is unsurprising. As John Breuilly argues, there is a fundamental conceptual problem with analysing governmental – as opposed to opposition – nationalism unless there is an obvious, direct link to a nationalist movement: 'nationalist' governments whose policies defend 'national interests' and that other states might regard as 'assertive' or 'aggressive' are so universal that 'governmental nationalism' becomes a meaningless category (Breuilly, 1993, pp. 10–11). In Russia there is no such obvious, direct, link.

Three broad approaches can be identified. Liberal views tend to assume that domestic ideas and constituencies are determining in general and nationalism has become more relevant – and dangerous – in particular. For example, analysts have traced the influence of anti-Western neo-Eurasianists like Aleksandr Dugin and Mikhail Leont'ev over the political establishment – in particular the number of leading Russian executive and legislative figures in Dugin's International Eurasian Movement – including presidential aide Aslanbek Aslakhanov and South Ossetian President Eduard Kokoity (Liverant, 2009). For some, indeed, Putin has himself been heavily influenced by neo-Eurasianist ideas (Liverant, 2009). For many, increasing domestic authoritarianism ineluctably tends towards anti-Western nationalism in foreign policy (Sherr, 2009, pp. 196–224; Hassner, 2008, pp. 5–15; Shevtsova, 2009, pp. 61–5). For them Russian foreign policy has become increasingly driven by its domestic imperatives. Most notably the Kremlin doctrine of 'sovereign democracy' was motivated primarily by the need to defend against regional 'colour revolutions' and allegedly marked a fundamental existential challenge to the West (Krastev, 2007).

By contrast many – primarily, but not exclusively, realists – argue that even under Putin Russia remains a predominantly pragmatic, non-ideological state motivated largely by traditional high-level security concerns, material interests and economic opportunism – this is the Russia Inc. outlined by Dmitri Trenin (Trenin, 2007; Donaldson and Nogee, 2009; Mankoff, 2009). The highly consolidated elite can conduct foreign policy independently of domestic interest when necessary (as in Putin's notorious pro-Western shift after 9/11). Of course, the Russian foreign policy elite themselves largely share this realist view, seeing their policy as one of pragmatic and rational national interests based around *raison d'état*.

Certainly no account will completely dismiss either internal or external factors, but arguably more persuasive are broadly constructivist accounts that do not assume that external or internal factors are dominant, but place the interaction of internal and external factors at the centre of analysis and focus on their subjective mediation via the policy process (Hopf, 2002; Tsygankov, 2010). For instance, externally projected 'national interests' are themselves always subjectively defined through the prism of domestic nationalism – a state can only agree such interests if national identity itself is defined.

Focusing on the domestic–foreign policy nexus reveals a complex and often changing picture. However certain longer-term trends can be identified. For example, Astrid Tuminez argues that the Russian Imperial and Soviet foreign policy traditions shared a desire to prioritise interests of state over nation and to insulate foreign policy-making from nationalism (Tuminez, 2000). Such nationalism was regarded as useful for domestic consolidation but seen as both constricting and even dangerous when exported into the foreign policy realm. When nationalism did affect foreign policy more directly, this was usually in conditions of international and national crisis and profound elite divisions; it was more usually used simply to reinforce traditional views of Russia as a 'great power' (Tuminez, 2000). Such a tradition continued into the post-Soviet era. For instance, the 1990s ushered in unprecedented competition between three broad – and in their own way 'nationalist' – conceptions of foreign policy (see Table 3.1), in which the hard-line nationalists were the most publicly vocal. However the elite gave the hard-liners only rhetorical concessions – for instance, by forming the Russian–Belarusian Union – but generally regarded their policies as geopolitically confrontational and economically counterproductive, at least when relations with the West were good (Tsygankov, 2009a, pp. 189–202).

During the Putin era, a strict demarcation between foreign policy and domestic nationalism has been increasingly hard to draw. First, the foreign policy consensus has been dominated by the statists, who have

Table 3.1   Foreign policy images of Russian elites

	Westernisers	Statists	Hard-line nationalists
Foreign policy objectives	Integration with the West	Sovereignty; great power status	Empire; cultural independence
Foreign policy methods	Alliances with the West	Flexible alliances	Alliances against the West

Source: Tsygankov, 2009a, p. 190.

an ambiguous relationship to nationalism. On the one hand, although some analysts regard them as 'pragmatic' nationalists (Jackson, 2003; Allison et al., 2006), this is not true at an ideological level – their central concepts are statehood (gosudarstvennost') and great power status (derzhavnost'), and even domestically when they talk about 'nation' (rarely), this is generally defined in civic, multiethnic terms – Putin has talked about *Rossiiskaya natsiya* not *Russkaya natsiya* (nation of Russian citizens rather than ethnic Russian nation). In addition, statist politicians like Vladislav Surkov – the author of 'sovereign democracy' – have spoken harshly about the national-patriots. It is hardly accurate to describe as 'nationalists' politicians who rarely use the term and more convincing to regard the statists as conservatives, for whom stability, pragmatism and national tradition are more important than 'nation' as an independent entity and ideological construct (Bladel, 2008).

On the other hand, the statists are attitudinally proto-nationalistic because of their Soviet heritage. For instance, following Stalin, they are unable to regard their own nationalist inclinations self-critically: 'nationalism' is a negative concept reserved for 'extremist' anti-state actors while state policies are invariably 'patriotic' (Laruelle, 2009a). Moreover owing to continuities in Tsarist and Marxist–Leninist security traditions, much of the foreign policy elite thinking has – particularly that of the powerful Kremlin *silovik* ('securocrat') faction – 'still displayed features of [...] renounced ideology' (de Haas, 2010, p. 7). For many, they have less a coherent ideology than an engrained foreign policy mindset or instinct derived from a traditionalist *realpolitik* mentality (Trenin and Lo, 2005; Bladel, 2008). This mindset emphasises foreign – especially Western – threats, a zero-sum emphasis on geopolitics and 'spheres of influence' – overall an illiberalism and naked realism (Lo, 2003). This mindset arguably gives statists a more elective affinity to the hard-line nationalists than Westernisers, and so they are not as equidistant between the two groups as Table 3.1 might indicate. Even when the rhetoric of statist foreign policy is not fully nationalistic, its substance is; its pursuit of 'great power status' is almost a national mission; it sees the state itself in quasi-nationalistic emotional and even spiritual terms. Moreover the often articulated tone of defiance exhibits *ressentiment*, the sense of envy that reinforces particularistic pride and xenophobia as parts of national identity, which in Russia has been historically directed at the West (Breslauer, 2009; Greenfeld, 1993). As James Sherr has argued, 'a feeling of *obida* (injury) at perceived humiliation by the West [...] became foundations of policy [...] at least as potent as Soviet ideology had been' (Sherr, 2009, p. 205). Overall then, the dominance of statist ideas has allowed the more pragmatic nationalist ideas to act as 'conceptual "road maps"' helping to steer foreign policy (Jackson, 2003, p. 173).

Second, the foreign policy-making process has become more centralised since the Yeltsin era. This has ambiguous effects: on the one hand, the Kremlin – in both domestic and foreign policy – is theoretically able to dictate a more unified foreign policy line and ignore hard-line nationalists even to a greater degree than in the 1990s. On the other hand, the 'black box' of the Kremlin is very difficult to observe. Foreign policy-making is apparently restricted to a very narrow circle of trusted advisers and the presidential administration (Sergunin, 2008, pp. 59–96; Trenin and Lo, 2005; Kryshtanovskaya and White, 2005, pp. 1065–75). Naturally this places an emphasis on personal connections, behind-the-scenes lobbying and other indirect forms of influence from which hard-line nationalists might unduly benefit. For instance, it is argued that Aleksandr Dugin's influence is 'immense' among the Russian political establishment, while Putin's favoured journalist is Mikhail Leont'ev and his confessor is the nationalist Priest Archimandrite Tikhon Shevkunov (Liverant, 2009). None of this is verifiable (and indeed it is hard to identify consistently neo-Eurasianist ideas in Putin's public pronouncements) but it does indicate how the closed policy process might actually benefit nationalists with high levels of access to central decision-makers.

Third, despite this centralisation, public discourse is far from irrelevant in policy-making. Certainly the Kremlin is known to be an assiduous analyst of public opinion. Indeed, Putin's public image has been regarded as deliberately co-opting liberal, communist and nationalist ideas to serve his 'father of the nation' status (Sakwa, 2009). In this way publicly articulated nationalist ideas can inform Kremlin policy. Indeed, it can be argued that the Kremlin's nationalism is mainly an attempt to co-opt ideas that have a popular resonance in the service of regime goals (Laruelle, 2009a). It is not unimportant then that the State Duma, which although it has minimal direct policy influence still plays a large role in affecting political debate, has since 2003 been dominated by parties of a statist or hard-line nationalist inclination. The Duma parties' 'opposition' has been much constrained, and indeed these parties rarely dissent from Kremlin foreign policy except in a more nationalist direction, particularly in periods of perceived national existential crisis when they basically act as cheerleaders for the regime.

Fourth, under Putin, foreign and domestic policies have become more cohesive and interlinked overall and with regard to nationalism in particular. Just as the political system has been dubbed 'managed pluralism' whereby the elite demarcates the broad boundaries of 'healthy' democracy and periodically intervenes to maintain these boundaries, so can the Kremlin's approach to nationalism be dubbed 'managed nationalism' (March, 2012). As I have explored in greater depth elsewhere, this managed nationalism consists of three interlocking spheres (March, 2012):

1. *Official nationality* is so named because it is functionally equivalent to Tsarist Official Nationality in terms being only quasi-nationalist (state interests are prior to the nation's) and in its broader aim of co-opting patriotic sentiment in the interests of internal and external regime stability. It is contained in official Kremlin statements; presidential addresses; and foreign policy doctrines that articulate the *gosudarstvennik* position: this is a relatively moderate, pro-European, secular and pragmatic conservatism most cogently articulated in the doctrine of 'sovereign democracy' – modernisation and democratisation *à la Russe*.
2. *Cultural nationalism* is principally the mainstream intellectual and media discourse and symbols that aim to reinforce the historical, moral and social aspects of a distinct Russian 'national' way of life and thereby build a sense of national solidarity.
3. *Political nationalism* is simply domestic electoral and social mobilisation around nationalist motifs.

What is clear is that the state actively shapes the relationship among these three spheres: official nationality sets down the parameters for the cultural and political sphere that are allowed some autonomy within – and even, occasionally, beyond – these limits as long as they do not fundamentally challenge it.

Finally, and of most relevance to the Georgia case, is that the cultural and political spheres periodically escape the regime's control and risk creating a self-sustaining momentum to which the Kremlin has to respond. For instance, the dominant feature of cultural and political nationalism has become a 'civilisational nationalism' that emphasises the uniqueness of Russian 'civilisation' and contrasts it against the 'other' (increasingly the West or pro-Western governments in Georgia, Ukraine and Moldova) (Laruelle, 2007). Civilisation nationalism portrays Russia as a 'besieged fortress', the Russian authorities are the only force preventing national destruction and the population needs to 'rally round the flag' against external enemies who are motivated by 'Russophobia' (Feklyunina, 2010). Given state control of the electronic media, which largely marginalises non-loyal and liberal voices, a vicious circle of 'civilisational nationalism' is created: the state helps create a media dominated by nationalism, which then re-informs Kremlin policy. This civilisational nationalism often directly contradicts the pro-European, modernist and pragmatic elements of official nationality, but has proved highly useful for domestic mobilisation purposes, since such mechanisms 'combine [...] openness to the West with effective discrediting of all Western voices by means of creating a virtual conflict with the West over a third area' (Filippov, 2009, p. 1825). Indeed, the elite has occasionally deliberately stoked conflict to these ends.

Moreover a large number of interconnected think tanks have emerged that promulgate different forms of conservative nationalism across the political spectrum. There is a huge cross-fertilisation of personnel and ideas – for instance, many of the 'nationalist' think tanks overlap with official structures around the dominant pro-presidential party United Russia – meaning that elite and nationalist views are in many cases one and the same and often marginal nationalist views can come to more public prominence (Laruelle, 2009b). Although relatively liberal think tanks, such as the Institute of Contemporary Development (INSOR), Carnegie or the Center for Political Technologies, still maintain a high profile – especially outside Russia – the proliferation of well-funded nationalist think tanks and the dominance of nationalist discourse on state-run media means that these have tended to go against public opinion: pro-Kremlin think tanks flood the market with nationalist ideas.

In addition, 'civilisational' arguments, which were traditionally exclusively associated with the hard-line nationalists, have been increasingly visible even in official domestic and foreign policy. For example, despite the civic and multiethnic elements noted above, the key features of Russianness in Kremlin discourse – noted in particular in its strictures against the 'falsification of history' – have become the 'commitment to [...] Russian culture: language, history, values of statehood and patriotism, the idea of the strong and great Russia, uniqueness of the Russian civilization' (Panov, 2010, p. 93). Similar arguments, which put Russia's cultural status at the centre of analysis, have been noted in foreign policy. One reason for this is an increasing Russian emphasis on 'soft' power and attempts to promote Russian history and culture as a pole of attraction to compete with a West perceived to be declining (Tsygankov, 2009b, pp. 347–69). Accordingly a proliferation of mechanisms have sought to project Russian values abroad, from the *Russia Today* English-language TV channel, to the Paris- and New York-based Institute for Democracy and Cooperation and the Russkii Mir foundation headed by Kremlin-connected Vyacheslav Nikonov, which specialises in the promulgation of the Russian language and culture beyond Russia's own borders.

Nevertheless the Kremlin demonstrates a profound reluctance to allow sustained social mobilisation around nationalist ideas (for instance, by demoting the most articulate nationalist politicians like Dmitri Rogozin). Indeed, Boris Kagarlitskii argues that the Kremlin is scared of 'dangerous' nationalists like Dugin (Weir, 2008). However despite the official preference for enlightened patriotism, the Kremlin actually has few genuine safeguards against unenlightened nationalism: the authorities' frequent repudiation of liberal democracy and the extinction of domestic liberalism gives an inbuilt bias towards illiberal versions of nationalism. Moreover if theorists of nationalism are right, illiberal nationalism is inherent to authoritarian or semi-authoritarian systems, which lack the representative institutions and cultures of compromise that might digest nationalism into milder forms. As Michael Mann argues, 'Mild nationalism [...] is democracy achieved, aggressive nationalism is democracy perverted' (Mann, 1995, p. 62).

The ensuing sections of this chapter will show exactly this. While Russian nationalism is but one of several factors provoking Russian intervention in Georgia in 2008, the infusion of formerly marginal nationalist sentiments into mainstream Russian thinking in the 2000s led to a self-fulfilling prophecy whereby Georgia was repeatedly denigrated as being itself an aggressive, nationalistic, weak, untrustworthy and profoundly hostile state that was a pawn of nefarious Western geopolitical interests. This predisposed the Russian elite to see the worst in Georgian intentions and to prepare accordingly. Ultimately, 'liberal' Medvedev took the 'aggressive' response of 'coercing Georgia to peace' in part in order to demonstrate his 'patriotism' to an expectant public, and took a position virtually indistinguishable from that of hard-line nationalists. Since 2008, the perception of Russian rebirth has resulted in a new emphasis on civilisational nationalism in foreign policy. Although Russia's economic difficulties and the 'reset' have marked a partial return to pragmatism and the dissipation of foreign policy nationalism, there is little to prevent this nationalism from increasing once more in the longer term.

The domestic hard-line nationalists

Russia's hard-line nationalists have maintained a consistent and inflexible position regarding Georgia. Indeed, most of their contemporary sentiments were already evident in the early 1990s, when high-level politicians such as Supreme Soviet Chairman Ruslan Khasbulatov and Deputy Sergei Baburin expressed open sympathy for the secession of Abkhazia, South Ossetia and Adzhara from Georgia on the basis of their nostalgia for the USSR and cultural ties with Russia, which had – in their view – acted as the historical guarantor of their statehood (Niedermaier, 2008). Georgian policy under its first post-Soviet president, 'nationalist demagogue' Zviad Gamsakhurdia, was widely regarded as aggressively nationalist even by neutral observers (Jackson, 2003, p. 114). Nevertheless the Russian nationalists went further, arguing that Georgia had committed 'genocide' against the Abkhaz and South Ossetians in 1992–93, and was itself an inherently nationalist and aggressive state. Yet they maintained an unswerving hostility towards Georgia's second president, Eduard Shevardnadze, for his alleged complicity in the collapse of the USSR. Politicians like Baburin developed close ties with the Abkhaz leadership in particular, often visited the region and allegedly assisted them with supplies (including arms) (Jackson, 2003, p. 114). The nationalists and communists dominated the Duma until 1999 and mainly affected Russia's relations with Georgia by using blocking tactics. Above all, the Duma blocked the ratification of the 1994 Georgian–Russian Friendship Treaty and an additional treaty in 1995 (Filippov, 2009).

The nationalists have consistently seen Georgia as a troublemaker and zone of instability. They were utterly unimpressed by its 'so-called democracy' – Aleksandr Dugin saw Georgia as a failed state, while Vladimir Zhirinovskii regarded it as a complete US client that falsified its elections (Dugin, 2008b; Zhirinovskii, 2008). As might be expected, the nationalists regarded the Rose Revolution as profoundly negatively from the outset, seeing it as destabilising for the whole North Caucasus, and a foothold for US influence in the region. They were also hostile to Saakashvili straight away, seeing him as a US puppet, whose real masters resided in Washington. They took the lead in denigrating him as a 'mad and bad' Hitler or Pinochet-style dictator (Zhirinovskii, 2007). Nor did they conceal their revanchist aims, basically supporting a policy of divide and rule against Georgia and its forcible incorporation into the Russian sphere of influence. As nationalist politicians like Zhirinovskii and Dugin argued, this could be achieved simply by the recognition of the unrecognised states and military action against Saakashvili.

Official discourses concerning Georgia

Until the Putin period, such nationalist views were officially marginalised in Russia's ineffectual State Duma. The Yeltsin administration – although not the military high command, which detested him – maintained largely benign relations with Shevardnadze and usually simply ignored parliamentary outrage. It gave official support to Georgian territorial integrity and supported multilateral mechanisms for achieving autonomy for the unrecognised entities within the Georgian state. However official rhetoric masked an essentially pro-Abkhaz approach at the 'implementation level', whereby unofficial support for the separatists was used to keep Georgia firmly in the Russian sphere of influence and hinder resolution of the 'frozen conflicts' (Nygren, 2005, pp. 156–81).

It is easy to forget that Moscow's view of Tbilisi had already started to deteriorate markedly before the Rose Revolution and that this revolution was not as pivotal as some accounts suggest (Lapidus, 2007, pp. 138–55). Georgia's orientation towards NATO membership from 2002 onwards was critical in this evolution, as were disputes about alleged Georgian support for Chechen separatists residing in the Pankisi Gorge in Northern Georgia (Nygren, 2005). Nevertheless Moscow was, initially at least, not nearly as critically disposed towards Saakashvili in the aftermath of the Rose Revolution as the nationalists were and hoped for an improvement in relations (Novikov and Sysoev, 2004). Indeed, Moscow was sufficiently pragmatic in 2003–04 to intercede on Saakashvili's behalf to facilitate first Shevardnadze's peaceful resignation and later that of Aslan Abashidze, whom Saakashvili unseated as President of Adzhara.

By 2005–06, the decline in mutual relations was evident: the initial flashpoint was a dispute about smuggling, but geopolitical rivalry after the Orange Revolution and Saakashvili's marked tilt westwards and poor personal relations with Putin were more lasting catalysts (Simonyan, 2005). Clearly the August conflict cannot be understood without the prospect of Georgia's entry into NATO and the Western recognition of Kosovo in 2007–08, which Moscow continually portrayed as an unacceptable Western geopolitical démarche that would encourage separatism in the Commonwealth of Independent States (CIS).

Alongside this mutual antipathy, official Moscow increasingly began to share the nationalist view of both the Georgian state and Saakashvili personally as being unstable and aggressive. Putin's personal distaste for Saakashvili became evident.[1] As with Ukraine, Moscow often denigrated any 'democratic' achievements of the colour revolutions. In the doctrine of 'sovereign democracy' promulgated above all in 2005–07, Georgia and Ukraine were the archetypes of non-sovereign states, with formal democratic procedures but de facto governed from abroad – by the US.

However even until early 2008, Moscow's official rhetoric upheld the virtues of international law and Georgian territorial integrity. Yet, as later became evident, the de facto rhetorical and material support for the unrecognised entities only increased: most notably by the 'passportisation' of the Abkhaz and Ossetians, which later allowed Georgian residents to be regarded as not just compatriots, but Russian citizens; similarly visa restrictions against Georgians – which however excluded residents of separatist areas – de facto undermined Georgian territorial integrity. More and more, Russia recognised the separatist entities' rights to 'self-determination' and separatist leaders were increasingly described as full-fledged presidents and granted state visits to Moscow (Solov'ev and Novikov, 2006).

The cross-fertilisation of discourses

At a rhetorical and even implementation level then the Russian authorities were increasingly coming to share some of the suspicions and proclivities of the hard-line nationalists. The de facto cross-fertilisation of discourses became most graphical in the anti-Georgian campaign of October–November 2006, which was 'the first incident of officially endorsed ethnic discrimination in contemporary Russia' (Kozhevnikova, 2007b).

The campaign was initially prompted by a diplomatic spat over the Georgian arrest of Russian 'spies' and their provocative display on Georgian TV on 27 September 2006. A Soviet-type campaign ensued with some Aesopian signals from the top. In early October, Putin declared the need for regional authorities to 'protect the interests of Russian manufacturers and Russia's native population' in the country's outdoor markets (Lenta.ru, 2006b). This was taken as code for the harassment of (particularly Georgian) immigrants by local officials and extreme nationalist groups alike, since a central theme of the campaign was that of Georgian criminality. In particular, the Georgian diaspora was portrayed as providing the financial support for Georgian aggression against

Russia. Official measures were taken centrally with coordinated activity against 'illegal' immigrants. The Federal Migration Service had to deny reports that it was setting up a special department for Georgians (Lenta. ru, 2006a). The police in several regions demanded lists of pupils with 'Georgian surnames' in schools. Mass deportations followed, alongside several deaths in custody. Notable too was the targeting not just of Georgian citizens, but of Russian citizens of Georgian origin such as the author Boris Akunin (Grigorii Chkhartishvili). The campaign was even supported by (relatively) moderate pro-state media like *Izvestiya*. More remarkable was that extreme nationalist groups interpreted the campaign as official endorsement for their actions (for example, the Movement Against Illegal Immigration declared that it was ready to help the regime 'rid the country of Georgians') (NEWSru.com, 2006).

In time-honoured fashion, this campaign ran out of the control of its initiators as those lower down the administrative chain over-fulfilled the plan and it had to be reined back. This tendency was not helped by the lack of attention towards the effects of the campaign on its Georgian victims in the state-run media. However even the nationalist commentator Mikhail Leont'ev soon declared on his Channel 1 programme *Odnako* that the idea of closing Georgian restaurants and a mass expulsion of Georgians was 'stupid' and that the campaign was not directed against Georgians as a people (although he did admit that it helped Georgians get rid of 'parasites' like Saakashvili themselves) (Leont'ev, 2006). The Russian Public Chamber condemned the campaign on 12 October and it had run out of steam by November, after Putin on 26 October announced that 'ethnically motivated' law enforcement actions were 'inadmissible' (Putin, 2006). Once more the authorities' exploitation of ethnic sentiment from the top had led to an autonomous 'demand from the bottom' that the Kremlin had to deflate lest it lost control of the nationalist agenda. However this campaign directly inspired the anti-Estonian campaign of March 2007, which marked a new degree of coordination and sophistication.

Of course one should not over-emphasise the role of domestic nationalism in the buildup to August 2008. This conflict clearly fulfilled some of Russia's long-articulated military and security aims: namely, its determined opposition to Georgian NATO membership, its insistence on primacy in its sphere of influence and fundamental opposition to pro-Western centrifugal tendencies in the CIS. Above all, it aimed to show that Russia was back as a regional and global player, and that the West could not act against it with impunity (Monaghan, 2008; de Haas, 2010).

Nevertheless the hard-line nationalists played a significant role in escalating internal and external tension. Nationalist forces outside and inside parliament (especially the Liberal-Democratic Party of Russia (LDPR) and the Communists) called repeatedly for recognition of the unrecognised entities throughout 2008, and were only partly assuaged when Moscow upgraded relations with Abkhazia and South Ossetia in April 2008 (this action in itself ratcheted up expectations that would be difficult to de-escalate later on). One of the most prominent troublemakers, Aleksandr Dugin, visited South Ossetia several times in 2008, when his Eurasian Youth Movement helped train the Ossetian militias and participated in sporadic fighting (*Spiegel Online*, 2008). Dugin repeatedly expressed his preference for the military invasion of Georgia, occupation of Tbilisi and partition of the Georgian state, and in the aftermath of the conflict continued to inflate the number of South Ossetian deaths and called for imperial renaissance and incorporation of Georgia within the Russian sphere of influence: 'Georgia must orientate itself toward Russia, not in order to get back its irredeemably lost territories, but in order not to lose its remaining ones' (Babitskii, 2010). Similarly Mikhail Leont'ev used his *Odnako* programme to disparage American values and the idea of a 'world community' and attack Saakashvili as a 'reptile' and 'war criminal' (Leont'ev, 2008).

The well-articulated Western and Georgian narrative that Russia pushed Georgia into a long-prepared snare by provoking it into overreacting has been best summed up by Svante E. Cornell and S. Frederick Starr: 'Did Saakashvili fall into a trap? [...] [E]ven if he had not, a pretext would have been found to proceed with the campaign as it had been planned' (Cornell and Starr, 2009b, p. 9).[2] Although compelling, this argument is one-sided, ignoring Georgia's own nationalism and the cycle of provocations on both sides that led to conflict, let alone any US culpability (Cheterian, 2009b, p. 155). Moreover Russian arguments that Dmitri Medvedev had little choice but to pursue military intervention and recognition of the separatist entities are self-serving but cannot simply be dismissed. Arguably, as a new president widely derided as a liberal fig leaf with little domestic or foreign legitimacy, Medvedev's own political position would have been critically weakened had he not taken a hard line to defend Russian 'citizens' (Monaghan, 2008). Moreover much of Russian policy appeared improvised and the decision to recognise Abkhazia and South Ossetia took most residents by complete surprise (Garb, 2009, p. 235). Also suggestive of a lack of forward planning 'was the fact that during the two weeks between the war and the recognition, pundits in Russia were in consensus and busy explaining to the public what a huge geopolitical mistake it would be to give the separatists official recognition' (Filippov, 2009, p. 1842).

However in other ways Russia was responding to long-articulated strategies. Moscow certainly carries culpability in stoking the domestic sentiments to which it had to respond. As Sakwa notes, domestic anti-Western sentiment has ebbed and flowed, but the tide tends to be higher after each ebb (Sakwa, 2008, pp. 241–67). Not coincidentally, George W. Bush and Mikheil Saakashvili were regarded in Russian public opinion as Russia's chief enemies long before August 2008. More generally, Russian discourse over Georgia conformed to long-rehearsed patterns of rallying round the flag against foreign enemies: in the aftermath of the conflict, both Medvedev and Putin emphasised the geopolitical roots of the war and the prime role of US interests in Georgia. Not coincidentally, Medvedev got some of his strongest support from hard-line nationalists who had previously regarded him as 'toothless'. For example, *Zavtra* regarded Medvedev as coming of age as an independent and authoritative politician (Lentsev, 2008). Arguably, August 2008 marks the peak of symbiosis between the authorities, nationalists and the wider population with the Kremlin prioritising domestic opinion. As Sakwa argues, 'the Russian focus was on the domestic audience and the state-directed electronic media went into overdrive to present the Kremlin's case to its people' (Sakwa, 2010, p. 13). Overall, in September 2008, both Putin and Medvedev reached historically high levels of popular approval – 88 per cent and 83 per cent, respectively, according to surveys by Russia's Levada Center.

Most notably, in the aftermath of August 2008, elite and nationalist discourses towards Georgia became virtually indistinguishable in their analysis of the origins and outcomes of the war (if not quite the longer-term strategic lessons). Both quickly consolidated around a discourse of Georgian 'aggression' against a defensive and unoccupied South Ossetian population. Both Medvedev and Putin described the alleged death of 2000 South Ossetians during the Russo-Georgian War as 'genocide'. Georgians in general and Saakashvili in particular were war criminals firing on peacekeepers and unarmed inhabitants in the dead of night.

Even though the Russian prosecutor general quickly revised the number of South Ossetian civilian deaths markedly downwards to 162 this information was not widely publicised, and the shared official/nationalist discourse has continued to be dominant, with only marginal changes and nuances ever since (Akhvlediani, 2010, pp. 113–40). This is not to deny that a number of Russian analysts have been extremely critical of Russian military conduct during the war, even including prominent Russian nationalist Aleksandr Prokhanov who argued that in military strategy at least Russia actually lost the war (Prokhanov, 2009). However these analysts largely ignore political questions. While Western discourse can be accused of anti-Russian bias, there are arguably far greater nuances and even disagreements among Western positions (see Table 3.2).[3]

The shared Russian discourse continues to ignore the historical roots of the conflict in general, and any Russian culpability in particular. Such historical narrative refers only to previous Georgian atrocities in the 1990s and Georgian 'aggression' in the 2000s. A number of Russian publications and films (for example, *War of 08.08.08. The Art of Betrayal*) reinforce an emotional message focusing on Russian solidarity with the beleaguered town of 'Tskhinval' – as the Russians now named Tskhinvali, by symbolically adopting its spelling in South Ossetian – and convey incredulity at the (alleged) criminal and inhuman barbarity of the Georgian forces (trained and funded by the US) (Akhvlediani, 2010). Images of Saakashvili chewing his tie or cowering in terror at the approach of a Russian jet are repeatedly shown to indicate the cowardliness and rashness of the Georgian side.

Russian commentators continue to insist that not just intervention in Georgia but even Russian recognition of secessionist entities was absolutely inevitable and forced upon Russia by Georgian aggression. Intervention is regarded as a moral, humanitarian issue in order to defend Russian citizens (following NATO's rationale for intervention in Kosovo). For example, Vyacheslav Nikonov regards the event (with a much over-used phrase) as 'Russia's 9/11' – that is to say, as an existential challenge to which any viable state would have to respond (Nikonov, 2008). Even neo-Eurasianist Aleksandr Dugin regards intervention as more of a moral than geopolitical issue, although geopolitics are not absent since he regards Georgia as a Eurasian and not a European civilisation whose national interests lie with Russia (Dugin, 2008a). Most mainstream Russian commentators regard recognition of Abkhazia and South Ossetia as an incontrovertible fact that can under no circumstances be reversed – the non-recognition of these states by most of the international community is either simply ignored or regarded as temporary. The salient fact is that Russia, by showing that it can stand up for its interests irrespective of global opinion, has been transformed from a post-Soviet to a global power as part of a newly multipolar system, and that Washington suffered a strategic defeat (Pavlovskii, 2009, pp. 6–9).

Even the publication in September 2009 of the EU's Tagliavini report did not change the dominant narrative (the report was of the

Table 3.2 Divergent Russian/Western foreign policy images, Russian–Georgian relations

Points of controversy over the Russo-Georgian War	Hard-line Westernisers	Moderate Westernisers	Statists	Hard-line nationalists
Image-promoting constituency	Georgia: US pro-Georgia lobby; Russian liberals	EU; Obama administration	Russian establishment	Pro-establishment media
Nature of Georgian state	Beacon of democracy	Flawed democracy	Unstable, non-sovereign state	Failed state
Russia's aims in Georgia	Imperialist aggression	Aggressive pursuit of sphere of influence	Pragmatic cooperation; sphere of influence	Russian dependency; sphere of influence
Causes of five-day war	Russian aggression and 'trap'	Russian provocation/ invasion: Georgian overreaction	Georgian aggression/ genocide; Russian humanitarian intervention/self-defence	Georgian genocide; Russian humanitarian intervention/ self-defence
Consequences of five-day war	Existential challenge to Euro-Atlantic institutions	Regional destabilisation; problematic Russia–West relations	Regional stability; need to rethink European security	Regional stability; weakening of Euro-Atlantic alliance
Attitude to Saakashvili	Exemplary democrat	Flawed democrat	(War) criminal	War criminal/fascist
Future dynamics of Russo-Georgian relationship	Need for principled Western/NATO containment of Russian expansionism	Need for confidence-building and protection of Georgian sovereignty; NATO membership postponed	Georgian sovereignty respected within post-conflict borders; Russia–Georgia relations to resume post-Saakashvili	Post-conflict borders the first stage in Russian imperial renaissance

Source: Author's conceptualisation.

Independent International Fact-Finding Mission on the Conflict in Georgia, headed by Ambassador Heidi Tagliavini and mandated by the Council of the EU to investigate the origins and the course of the conflict in Georgia) (IIFFMCG – CEIIG, 2009). Although balanced coverage was present (Gabuev, 2009), official Russian discussion focused largely on Georgia's culpability for the outbreak of hostilities and said virtually nothing about the report's disputation of any evidence of genocide in South Ossetia, its allegations of ethnic cleansing of Georgians there or its conclusion that Russian intervention was not legally justified in the first place and was disproportionate in its result. In this regard, an October 2009 edition of the *Sudite Sami* programme on Channel 1 hosted by Maxim Shevchenko was instructive: only the Carnegie Foundation analyst Aleksei Malashenko differed – and then only marginally – from the general consensus that Georgia was entirely culpable for the conflict, even planning it in advance, that recognition of the separatist entities was inevitable and that, in MP Sergei Markov's view, the Tagliavini report 'inflicts a colossal blow on the Saakashvili regime' (Pervyi Kanal, 2009).

Overall, as evident in Table 3.2, whereas nationalist and statist approaches still differ in their broader conceptions of foreign policy, they are fused almost into one when it comes to the specific issue of Georgia.

In essence, they share a common understanding of the overall Georgia–Russia relationship, the August 2008 conflict's causes and immediate outcomes. The differences are largely in degree and are most evident in their proposed solutions: extreme nationalists such as Dugin call for an imperialist, expansionist policy towards Georgia, Ukraine and other CIS states, whereas official views focus on preservation of the post-conflict status quo of a weakened non-NATO Georgia alongside proposals to revise European security institutions. However even these distinctions are sometimes hard to draw, when prominent establishment politicians like Andrei Kokoshin, deputy leader of the pro-Putin United Russia Party's Duma faction have argued that the only 'disproportionality' of the Russian response in August 2008 was that it was 'too soft' and did not make a Yugoslav-style strike against Georgian infrastructure (Pervyi Kanal, 2009).

Clearly, then, the main influence of Russian nationalism on foreign policy towards Georgia is both Russia's deliberate stoking of domestic nationalist sentiment to support its foreign policy aims and the more subtle co-mingling of official and nationalist foreign policy proclivities that results. Whether this is a long-term result remains to be seen, because the signals are ambiguous. Certainly in mid 2008, Medvedev's demands that the Georgian government respect the Russian government, its people and values indicated the increasing projection of a 'sense of grievance into its foreign policy' (Caryl, 2009). In particular, Medvedev's 2008 foreign policy concept mentioned, for the first time, global politics taking on a 'civilisational dimension', arguably giving the nationalist foreign policy stance a doctrinal legitimacy it had previously lacked (*Rossiiskaya gazeta*, 2008).

However since the peak of the conflict, Moscow's official rhetoric has become more restrained and less incendiary. The word 'genocide' has been dropped from high-level discourse and the emphasis has been on rationality and common interests. As Foreign Minister Sergei Lavrov said in the immediate aftermath of the Russia–Georgia conflict, the only ideology determining foreign policy is 'common sense and the supremacy of international law' (Lavrov, 2008). Even during the conflict, Medvedev was at pains not to repeat the pogrom-like campaign of 2006 by insisting on the political – not ethnic – basis of the conflict, and has repeatedly warned against domestic nationalist extremism. Moscow's policy towards Georgia has now changed tone and is more of a charm offensive among the Georgian population, with Medvedev stressing Russia's centuries-old friendship with ordinary Georgians.

Nevertheless in other respects Moscow's policies have changed little. The Kremlin has expanded its attempts to delegitimise the Georgian 'regime', which it continues to regard as criminal and now largely ignores except when it can embarrass it – for example, by rebuilding in Moscow in December 2010 a memorial to World War II veterans that was demolished in the Georgian city of Kutaisi just twelve months previously. Medvedev openly stated that he regarded Saakashvili as a 'political corpse' (Civil.ge, 2010). Moscow also uses methods tried and tested in other West-leaning CIS states, namely courting potential pro-Russian 'fifth columnists' – such as former Georgian parliamentary speaker Nino Burdzhanadze and former Georgian Prime Minister Zurab Nogaideli – and hosting congresses of Georgian citizens in Moscow. This approach might offer a resumption of relations after Saakashvili demits office; however it offers no long-term solution if a new Georgian president also seeks to leave Russia's self-delineated sphere of influence.

Georgia has not remained a sticking point in wider relations with the West, particularly because as part of the 'reset', the US and Russia have agreed to disagree over Georgia. Indicatively, the draft new foreign policy document leaked to *Newsweek* in May 2010 prioritises business and businesslike links with the West and sidelines the Georgian issue entirely – indeed, it does not even mention Georgia directly, although it does argue for the need to 'actively oppose the attempts of extra-regional forces to interfere in Russia's relations with CIS countries' (Gaaze and Zygar, 2010). Therefore, perhaps the truest difference between statist and hard-line nationalist foreign policy views is that for the statists in the Russian authorities, nationalism is far less consistently interesting than money.

Conclusion

Russian nationalism has been an often misunderstood catalyst in Russian foreign policy towards Georgia. It was neither an all-dominant motivating force, nor an irrelevant element. Its most obvious effect has been as a volatile component in domestic views of foreign relations, which have strongly pushed the domestic consensus in a more nationalist direction. The Russian authorities, as keen observers of public opinion, have felt compelled to respond to this public consensus domestically and abroad, but have as often directly provoked it with the aim of domestic regime consolidation, actively stoking nationalist sentiments to cement their internal legitimacy.

Nationalist *ressentiment* has long been part of the rhetorical arsenal of the statist Russian foreign policy-makers. However in the middle to late 2000s, the domestic oversupply of conservative nationalism and the undersupply of more liberal variants have increasingly begun to influence and directly contaminate Russian foreign policy on both a rhetorical and even conceptual level. Russian foreign policy towards Georgia is one area where the nationalist tiger has threatened to escape the cage, with state and nationalist discourses becoming increasingly intertwined, indistinguishable and self-reinforcing.

Whether this fundamentally changes the role of nationalism in Russian foreign policy in the long term is still unclear. There are reasons to be sceptical. In particular, the Putin–Medvedev administrations have never consistently and completely based either their domestic or foreign legitimacy on ethnic Russian nationalism; rather, they have a thoroughly instrumental approach – more often trying to control and co-opt it. Furthermore as Medvedev's attempts to limit domestic anti-Georgian sentiment show, the Kremlin remains very reluctant fully to endorse social mobilisation on the basis of nationalism. Since 2008, Russia has once again tried to move its foreign policy towards a more pragmatic, interest-based policy that indicates its continued fundamental hesitancy about prioritising the role of ideas and values in international relations – even when these values are Russia's own. This fits in with the time-honoured pattern identified by authors such as Tuminez: the Kremlin seeks to remain independent in foreign policy-making and to avoid policies that commit it to risk. In August 2008, this golden rule was briefly dropped but was soon reinforced.

Nevertheless the Kremlin is arguably playing a dangerous game by using nationalism as a resource that can be tapped into at will administratively to suit regime goals, given the risks of continually stoking domestic nationalism and then depriving it of an outlet. Certainly, there is little in Russian domestic discourse since 2008 to indicate that the nationalist tiger has been securely caged, still less tamed. Whereas the Weimar Russia scenario – extreme nationalist takeover – remains very much an unlikely worst case (Kailitz and Umland, 2010), more probable is a continued incompatibility between the Russian authorities' foreign policy goals – interest-based, pragmatic, multilateral – and domestic aims – values-based, subjective, unilateral – which will cause contradictions to arise and severe tensions for both, particularly given Russian declared interests in resetting international relations and modernising domestically. August 2008 shows that resolving these tensions with a more consistently civilisational nationalist policy is highly tempting for the authorities. Although the longer-term gains of such a policy are likely counterproductive, the policy is a direct product of the structure of the domestic political system, in particular its lack of developed democracy. A more democratic Russia would still most likely have national interests and national specifics distinct from Europe and the US (for example, a strong emphasis on state sovereignty and domestic political centralisation). However if Mann is right, the only long-term solution to a zero-sum, assertive and 'aggressive' nationalism 'is to achieve democracy – especially federal, inter-regional democracy'. He adds however: 'Unfortunately, this is easier said than done' (Mann, 1995, pp. 62–3).

Notes

The author wishes to acknowledge the support of the British Academy (Overseas Conference Grant) in this research.

1. Albeit Putin reserved his most choice expressions such as wishing to 'hang him [Saakashvili] by the balls' for private conversation with world leaders (Pravda.ru, 2008).
2. See also the chapter by John B. Dunlop in this volume.
3. For instance, John B. Dunlop's chapter in this volume highlights the profound disagreements some Russian liberals and US analysts have with the EU's Tagliavini report of 2009.

References

Akhvlediani, Margarita (2010) 'The fatal flaw: the media and the Russian invasion of Georgia', in Paul B. Rich (ed.), *Crisis in the Caucasus: Russia, Georgia and the West* (Abingdon: Routledge), pp. 113–40.

Allison, Roy, Margot Light and Stephen White (2006) *Putin's Russia and the Enlarged Europe* (Malden, MA: Wiley-Blackwell).

Asmus, Ronald D. (2010) *A Little War that Shook the World: Georgia, Russia, and the Future of the West* (New York: Palgrave Macmillan).

Babitskii, Andrei (2010) 'Dugin: Gruziya dolzhna orientirovat'sya na Rossiyu dlya togo, chtoby ne poteryat' ostaln'nye territorii', *Ekho Kavkaza*, 15 May, available at: http://www.ekhokavkaza.com/articleprintview/2042713.html (accessed 3 November 2010).

Bladel, Joris van (2008) 'The dual structure and mentality of Vladimir Putin's power coalition: a legacy for Medvedev', *Report*, FOI-R-2519-SE (Stockholm: FOI, Swedish Defence Research Agency), available at: http://www2.foi.se/rapp/foir2519.pdf (accessed 8 November 2011).

Breslauer, George W. (2009) 'Observations on Russia's foreign relations under Putin', *Post-Soviet Affairs*, vol. 25, no. 4, pp. 370–6.

Breuilly, John (1993) *Nationalism and the State* (Manchester: Manchester University Press).

Caryl, Christian (2009) 'The Russians are coming?', *New York Review of Books*, 12 February, available at: http://www.nybooks.com/articles/archives/2009/feb/12/the-russians-are-coming-2/ (accessed 3 November 2010).

Cheterian, Vicken (2009) 'The August 2008 war in Georgia: from ethnic conflict to border wars', *Central Asian Survey*, vol. 28, no. 2, pp. 155–70.

Civil.ge (2010) 'Medvedev: Saakashvili is a "political corpse"', n.d., available at: http://www.civil.ge/eng/article.php?id=19379 (accessed 3 November 2010).

Connor, Walter D. (2007) 'A Russia that can say "no"?', *Communist and Post-Communist Studies*, vol. 40, no. 3, pp. 383–91.

Cornell, Svante E. and S. Frederick Starr (2009a) 'Introduction', in Svante E. Cornell and S. Frederick Starr (eds), *The Guns of August 2008: Russia's War in Georgia* (Armonk, NY: M. E. Sharpe), pp. 1–9.

Cornell, Svante E. and S. Frederick Starr (eds) (2009b) *The Guns of August 2008: Russia's War in Georgia* (Armonk, NY: M. E. Sharpe).

de Haas, Marcel (2010) *Russia's Foreign Security Policy in the 21st Century: Putin, Medvedev and Beyond* (London: Routledge).

Donaldson, Robert H. and Joseph L. Nogee (2009) *The Foreign Policy of Russia: Changing Systems, Enduring Interests*, 4th edn (Armonk, NY: M. E. Sharpe).

Dugin, Aleksandr (2008a) 'A. Dugin: "Gruziya mozhet raspast'sya"', KM.ru, 26 September, available at: http://uncensored.km.ru/uncensored/index.asp?data=26.09.2008+8:00:00&archive=on (accessed 3 November 2010).

Dugin, Aleksandr (2008b) 'Mengrely sleduyushie', Russia.Ru, 19 August.

Feklyunina, Valentina (2010) 'Russia as a "besieged fortress"', unpublished paper, Prospects for Wider Cooperation, International Council for Central and East European Studies (ICCEES) 8th World Congress, Stockholm, 26–31 July.

Filippov, Mikhail (2009) 'Diversionary role of the Georgia–Russia conflict: international constraints and domestic appeal', *Europe–Asia Studies*, vol. 61, no. 10, pp. 1825–47.

Gaaze, Konstantin and Mikhail Zygar (2010) 'Let there be sun again', *Russkiy Newsweek*, 9 May, available at: http://www.runewsweek.ru/country/34166/ (accessed 3 November 2010).

Gabuev, Aleksandr (2009) 'Rossii i Gruzii pridetsya bit'sya ob doklad', *Kommersant'*, no. 182, 1 October, available at: http://www.kommersant.ru/doc.aspx?DocsID=1246965 (accessed 3 November 2010).

Garb, Paula (2009) 'The view from Abkhazia of South Ossetia ablaze', *Central Asian Survey*, vol. 28, no. 2, pp. 235–46.

Greenfeld, Liah (1993) *Nationalism: Five Roads to Modernity*, new edn (Cambridge, MA: Harvard University Press).

Hassner, Pierre (2008) 'Russia's transition to autocracy', *Journal of Democracy*, vol. 19, no. 2, pp. 5–15.

Hopf, Ted (2002) *Social Construction of International Politics: Identities and Foreign Policies, Moscow, 1955 and 1999* (Ithaca, NY: Cornell University Press).

Independent International Fact-Finding Mission on the Conflict in Georgia: Report (IIFFMCG – CEIIG) (2009) Available at: http://www.ceiig.ch/Report.html (accessed 8 November 2011).

Jackson, Nicole J. (2003) *Russian Foreign Policy and the CIS: Theories, Debates and Actions*, annotated edn. (New York: Routledge).

Joo, Hyung-min (2008) 'The Soviet origin of Russian chauvinism: voices from below', *Communist and Post-Communist Studies*, vol. 41, no. 2, pp. 217–42.

Kailitz, Steffen and Andreas Umland (2010) 'Why the fascists won't take over the Kremlin (for now): a comparison of democracy's breakdown and fascism's rise in Weimar Germany and post-Soviet Russia', preprint (Moscow: Publishing House of the State University, Higher School of Economics), available at: http://kueichstaett.academia.edu/AndreasUmland/Papers/235639/Why_the_Fascists_Wont_Take_Over_the_Kremlin_for_Now_A_Comparison_of_Democracys_Breakdown_and_Fascisms_Rise_in_Weimar_Germany_and_Post-Soviet_Russia (accessed 8 November 2011).

Kozhevnikova, Galina (2007a) 'Antigruzinskaya kampaniya: Gosudarstvennaya propaganda i obshchestvennoe soprotivlenie', *SOVA Center*, 4 May, available at: http://www.sova-center.ru/hate-speech/publications/2007/05/d10770 (accessed 3 November 2010).

Kozhevnikova, Galina (2007b) 'Radical nationalism in Russia and efforts to counteract it in 2006', *SOVA Center*, 22 May, available at: http://www.sova-center.ru/en/xenophobia/reports-analyses/2007/05/d10896/ (accessed 3 November 2010).

Kozhevnikova, Galina (2010) 'Manifestations of radical nationalism and efforts to counteract it in Russia during the first half of 2010', *SOVA Center*, 30 July, available at: http://www.sova-center.ru/en/xenophobia/reports-analyses/2010/07/d19436/ (accessed 3 November 2010).

Krastev, Ivan (2007) 'Russia as the "Other Europe"', *Russia in Global Affairs*, 17 November, reprinted in *Russia in Global Affairs*, no. 4, October–December 2007, available at: http://eng.globalaffairs.ru/number/n_9779 (accessed 3 November 2010).

Kryshtanovskaya, Ol'ga and Stephen White (2005) 'Inside the Putin Court: a research note', *Europe–Asia Studies*, vol. 57, no. 7, pp. 1065–75.

Lapidus, Gail (2007) 'Between assertiveness and insecurity: Russian elite attitudes and the Russia–Georgia crisis', *Post-Soviet Affairs*, vol. 23, no. 2, pp. 138–55.

Laruelle, Marlène (ed.) (2007) *Sovremennye interpretatsii russkogo natsionalizma* (Stuttgart: ibidem-Verlag).

Laruelle, Marlène (2009a) *In the Name of the Nation: Nationalism and Politics in Contemporary Russia* (Basingstoke: Palgrave Macmillan).

Laruelle, Marlène (2009b) 'Inside and around the Kremlin's black box: the new nationalist think tanks in Russia', *Stockholm Paper*, October, Institute for Security and Development Policy, available at: http://www.isdp.eu/images/stories/isdp-main-pdf/2009_laruelle_inside-and-around-the-kremlins-black-box.pdf (accessed 8 November 2011).

Lavrov, Sergei (2008) 'Litsom k litsu s Amerikoi: Mezhdu nekonfrontatsiei i konvergentsiei', *Profil'*, 13 October, available at: http://www.profile.ru/items/?item=27218 (accessed 3 November 2010).

Lenta.ru (2006a) 'Migratsionnaya sluzhba Rossii ne nashla u sebya "gruzinskogo" otdela', 5 October, available at: http://lenta.ru/news/2006/10/05/fms1/ (accessed 3 November 2010).

Lenta.ru (2006b) 'Prezident RF prikazal razobrat'sya na rynkakh s inostrantsami', 5 October, available at: http://lenta.ru/news/2006/10/05/putin/ (accessed 3 November 2010).

Lentsev, Ivan (2008) 'Triumf duumvirata', *Zavtra*, 13 August, available at: http://zavtra.ru/cgi//veil//data/zavtra/08/769/24.html (accessed 3 November 2010).

Leont'ev, Mikhail (2006) 'Analyticheskaya programma "Odnako" s Mikhailom Leont'evym', *Pervyi Kanal*, 5 October, available at: http://www.1tv.ru/news/print/99387 (accessed 3 November 2010).

Leont'ev, Mikhail (2008) 'Analiticheskaya programma "Odnako" s Mikhailom Leont'evym', *Pervyi Kanal*, 10 August, available at: http://www.1tv.ru/news/print/29950 (accessed 3 November 2010).

Liverant, Yigal (2009) 'The prophet of the new Russian empire', *Azure*, no. 35, available at: http://www.azure.org.il/include/print.php?id=483 (accessed 3 November 2010).

Lo, Bobo (2003) *Vladimir Putin and the Evolution of Russian Foreign Policy* (Malden, MA: Wiley-Blackwell).

Lucas, Edward (2009) *The New Cold War: How the Kremlin Menaces both Russia and the West* (London: Bloomsbury Publishing).

Mankoff, Jeffrey (2009) *Russian Foreign Policy: The Return of Great Power Politics* (Lanham, MD: Rowman & Littlefield).

Mann, Michael (1995) 'A political theory of nationalism and its excesses', in Sukumar Periwal (ed.), *Notions of Nationalism* (Budapest: Central European University Press), pp. 44–63.

March, Luke (2012, forthcoming) 'Nationalism for export? The domestic and foreign-policy implications of the new "Russian idea"', *Europe–Asia Studies*.

Monaghan, Andrew (2008) 'The Russo-Georgian conflict: immediate report', NATO Defense College Research Division, August, available at: http://www.ndc.nato.int/research/series.php?icode=3 (accessed 8 November 2011).

NEWSru.com (2006) 'Natsionalitsy podderzhali Putina: DPNI reshilo pomoch' prezidentu ochistit' stranu ot gruzin', October 6, available at: http://www.newsru.com/russia/06oct2006/dpni_print.html (accessed 3 November 2010).

Niedermaier, Ana K. (2008) *Countdown to War in Georgia, Russia's Foreign Policy and Media Coverage of the Conflict in South Ossetia and Abkhazia* (Minneapolis, MN: East View Press).

Nikonov, Vyacheslav (2008) 'Moment istiny', *POLITY foundation*, 3 September, available at: http://www.polity.ru/articles/moment_i2.htm (accessed 3 November 2010).

Novikov, Vladimir and Gennadii Sysoev (2004) 'Mikhail Saakashvili poluchil vid na vizy', *Kommersant'*, 13 February, available at: http://www.kommersant.ru/doc.aspx?DocsID=449512 (accessed 3 November 2010).

Nygren, Bertil (2005) 'Russia's relations with Georgia: the impact of 11 September', in Jakob Hedenskog et al. (eds), *Russia as a Great Power: Dimensions of Security under Putin* (Abingdon: Routledge), pp. 156–81.

Panov, Petr (2010) 'Nation-building in post-Soviet Russia: what kind of nationalism is produced by the Kremlin?', *Journal of Eurasian Studies*, vol. 1, no. 2, pp. 85–94.

Pavlovskii, Gleb (2009) 'Predislovie', in Kirill Tanaev and Pavel Danilin (eds), *Voina i mir Dmitriya Medvedeva* (Moscow: Evropa), pp. 6–9.

Pervyi Kanal (2009) 'Tragediya Tskhinvala: vinovnyi nazvan', 1 October, available at: http://www.1tv.ru/prj/sudsami/vypusk/print_version/2144 (accessed 3 November 2010).

Pipes, Richard (1984) *Survival is not Enough: Soviet Realities and America's Future* (New York: Simon & Schuster).

Pravda.ru (2008) 'Georgia's Saakashvili nervously giggles to Putin's intention to hang him by the balls', 14 November, available at: http://english.pravda.ru/world/ussr/14-11-2008/106700-saakashvili_putin_balls-0/ (accessed 18 November 2010).

Prokhanov, Aleksandr (2009) 'Esli zavtra voina', *Zavtra*, 4 March, available at: http://www.zavtra.ru/cgi/veil/data/zavtra/09/798/11.html (accessed 3 November 2010).

Pukhov, Ruslan (ed.) (2009) *The Tanks of August* (Moscow: Centre for Analysis of Strategies and Technologies).

Putin, Vladimir (2006) 'Prezident skazal pro … ', *Vremya novostei*, 26 October, available at: http://www.vremya.ru/2006/197/52/164083.html (accessed 3 November 2010).

Rossiiskaya gazeta (2008) 'Kontseptsiya vneshnei politiki Rossiiskoi Federatsii', 12 July, available at: http://www.rg.ru/2008/05/26/koncepciya-dok (accessed 3 November 2010).

Sakwa, Richard (2008) '"New Cold War" or twenty years' crisis? Russia and international politics', *International Affairs*, vol. 84, no. 2, pp. 241–67.

Sakwa, Richard (2009) *Putin: Russia's Choice*, 2nd edn (Abingdon: T & F Books).

Sakwa, Richard (2010) 'The five-day war of 2008 through the prism of conspiracy theories', paper, Prospects for Wider Cooperation, International Council for Central and East European Studies (ICCEES) 8th World Congress, Stockholm, 26–31 July.

Sergunin, Alexander (2008) 'Russia's foreign-policy decision making on Europe', in Ted Hopf (ed.), *Russia's European Choice* (Basingstoke: Palgrave), pp. 59–96.

Sherr, James (2009) 'The implication of the Russia–Georgia War for European security', in Svante E. Cornell and S. Frederick Starr (eds), *The Guns of August 2008: Russia's War in Georgia* (New York: M. E. Sharpe), pp. 196–224.

Shevtsova, Lilia (2009) 'The return of personalized power', *Journal of Democracy*, vol. 20, no. 2, pp. 61–5.

Simonyan, Yurii (2005) 'Krainimi sdelali mirotvortsev', *Nezavisimaya gazeta*, 22 September, available at: http://www.ng.ru/cis/2005-09-22/5_morotvorcy. html (accessed 3 November 2010).

Solov'ev, Vladimir and Vladimir Novikov (2006) 'Otbiranie zemel'. Rossiya otkazyvaet Gruzii i Moldavii v territorial'noi tselostnosti', *Kommersant'*, 2 June, available at: http://www.kommersant.ru/doc.aspx?DocsID=678700 (accessed 3 November 2010).

Spiegel Online (2008) 'Road to war in Georgia: the chronicle of a Caucasian tragedy', August 25, available at: http://www.spiegel.de/international/ world/0,1518,574812,00.html (accessed 3 November 2010).

Trenin, Dmitri (2007) *Getting Russia Right* (Washington, DC: Carnegie Endowment for International Peace).

Trenin, Dmitri and Bobo Lo (2005) *The Landscape of Russian Foreign Policy Decision-Making* (Washington, DC: Carnegie Endowment for International Peace).

Tsygankov, Andrei (2009a) 'From Belgrade to Kiev: hard-line nationalism and Russia's foreign policy', in Marlene Laruelle (ed.), *Russian Nationalism and the National Reassertion of Russia* (Abingdon: Routledge), pp. 189–202.

Tsygankov, Andrei (2009b) 'Russia in the post-Western world: the end of the normalization paradigm?', *Post-Soviet Affairs*, vol. 25, no. 4, pp. 347–69.

Tsygankov, Andrei P. (2010) *Russia's Foreign Policy: Change and Continuity in National Identity*, revd edn (Lanham, MD: Rowman & Littlefield).

Tuminez, Astrid S. (2000) *Russian Nationalism since 1856: Ideology and the Making of Foreign Policy* (Lanham, MD: Rowman & Littlefield).

Umland, Andreas (2009) 'Rastsvet russkogo ul'tranatsionalizma i stanovlenie soobshchestva ego issledovatelei', *Forum noveishei vostochnoevropeiskoi istorii i kul'tury*, vol. 6, no. 1, pp. 5–38.

Weir, Fred (2008) 'Moscow's moves in Georgia track a script by right-wing prophet', *EVRAZIA*, 23 September, available at: http://evrazia.org/modules. php?name=News&file=article&sid=4089 (accessed 4 November 2010).

Zhirinovskii, Vladimir (2007) 'Zhirinovskii nazval Saakashvili "gruzinskim Pinochetom", sposobnym "krov'yu Gruziyu zatopit"', NEWSru.com, 8 November, available at: http://newsru.com/arch/russia/08nov2007/pinochet.html (accessed 4 November 2010).

Zhirinovskii, Vladimir (2008) 'V Gruzii bystree rozhdayutsya novye staliny, chem novye demokratii', Regnum.ru, 11 January, available at: http://www.regnum. ru/news/941117.html (accessed 4 November 2010).

4
The August 2008 Russo-Georgian War: Which Side Went First?

John B. Dunlop

Introduction

This chapter examines the findings of three well-known Russian commentators who take exception to the Medvedev–Putin regime's official view on the question of which side initiated hostilities at the time of the five-day Russo-Georgian War of August 2008. The three commentators are: Andrei Illarionov, who served as President Putin's senior economic adviser in the Russian presidential administration during the period 2000–05; Pavel Felgenhauer, a leading military affairs journalist who writes for the thrice-weekly pro-democracy newspaper *Novaya gazeta*; and Yuliya Latynina, another influential journalist who regularly publishes in *Novaya gazeta*, on the websites ej.ru and Gazeta.ru, and who also hosts a popular weekly radio programme on Ekho Moskvy Radio.[1]

On 24 June 2010, President Dmitri Medvedev, during a joint press conference with President Obama held in the East Room of the White House, stipulated that the 2008 war was a 'conflict that was initiated by Georgia's leadership' (Calmes, 2010). As we shall see, Illarionov, Felgenhauer and Latynina contest this assertion by the Russian president. In addition to examining the views of the above-mentioned three commentators, this chapter also seeks to compare what they write concerning the outbreak of hostilities with the findings of the Independent International Fact-Finding Mission on the Conflict in Georgia (IIFFFMCG) of the Council of the European Union. That body, whose head of mission was Ambassador Heidi Tagliavini of Switzerland, made its lengthy report concerning the conflict public on 30 September 2009 (Council of the European Union, 2009).[2]

Illarionov's findings

By far the most significant contribution to an understanding of the root causes of the August war (on the Russian side) has been the prodigious research effort put in by Andrei Illarionov. In the future no one will be able to write in an informed fashion about the war without first assimilating the huge amount of material that Illarionov has posted on the Internet. Of particular value are the highly detailed chronology and collection of documentary and analytical materials that Illarionov posted in 2009 on the site of the publication *Russkii zhurnal* (Illarionov, 2009f). Illarionov has also attempted to boil down and synthesise the information posted on the site of *Russkii zhurnal* in a lengthy four-part article appearing in *Novaya gazeta* in late June and at the beginning of July 2009 (Illarionov, 2009e). An English-language version of this essay, together with a detailed chronology of events, appeared in Illarionov's contribution to the 2009 collection *The Guns of August 2008: Russia's War in Georgia*, edited by Svante E. Cornell and S. Frederick Starr (Illarionov, 2009h). In addition to these publications, Illarionov on 20 February 2009 posted a useful chronology of actions taken by both the Russian and Georgian sides in the period leading up to the conflict on the site livejournal.com (Illarionov, 2009c). To take one example, he reported that Russia first placed tanks on the territory of South Ossetia on 3 February 2003, while Georgia first did so on 7 August 2008. In addition, Illarionov gave several lengthy interviews to Ekho Moskvy Radio, in which he further documented his version of events (Illarionov, 2009a, 2009d and 2009f). He also granted an interview to Radio Liberty on the same topic (Illarionov, 2009b). It is worth noting that the long Tagliavini report fails to acknowledge in any way Illarionov's ground-breaking research. While the report does footnote two other articles appearing in the compendium edited by Cornell and Starr, it passes in silence over Illarionov's seminal contribution to the volume.

This chapter will first summarise Illarionov's chronology and his documentation of the build-up on the Russian side in preparation for the August war. Then it will examine his description of the immediate run-up to the war, beginning in late July of 2008. In Illarionov's view, the antecedents to the August war stretch back as far as 1999, when Vladimir Putin became prime minister of Russia. From 1999 onwards, Illarionov asserted, there developed a pattern of constant, unrelenting aggression on the part of Russia against its southern neighbour. First, he noted, Russia chose to supply the separatist leadership of South Ossetia with massive armaments:

> By supplying South Ossetia with heavy military equipment in February 2003, the Russian government deliberately chose a military solution to the conflict with Georgia. By providing the South Ossetian regime with seventy-five additional T-72 tanks and huge stocks of weaponry and ammunition in May and June 2004, the Russian government further paved the way for future, even larger-scale, military action. (Illarionov, 2009h, p. 50)

By the time of the August war in 2008, South Ossetia boasted the most tanks per capita of any state or sub-state entity on the globe: 1758 tanks and light tanks per 1000 of population, higher than such militarised countries as Israel (531) and North Korea (177) (Illarionov, 2009g, pt 2, p. 13). During the period 2004–08, Russia also constructed military bases near Java in South Ossetia that were not subject to international monitoring (Illarionov, 2009g, pt 1, *passim*).

Russia also, Illarionov wrote, repeatedly turned a sympathetic ear to the requests of President Eduard Kokoity and the parliament he controlled to recognise South Ossetia's independence from Georgia. Thus, for example, 'the South Ossetian parliament, in March 2002, adopted a resolution requesting the Russian authorities to recognize the independence of the republic and to admit it into the Russian Federation' (Illarionov, 2009h, p. 52). On March 13, 2008,

> the Russian State Duma, in a closed session, discussed a report prepared by the Russian secret services and the Ministry of Foreign Affairs on a strategy for achieving the independence of Abkhazia and South Ossetia. On March 21, 2008, it adopted a special resolution endorsing both requests for recognition. (Illarionov, 2009h, pp. 67–8)

By the end of 2002, Illarionov observed, Eduard Kokoity, the former wrestler and shadowy businessman who had emerged as Russia's choice to head up the South Ossetian regime 'began filling positions in the governmental bureaucracy with representatives of the Russian power ministries (e.g., defence, security and intelligence, etc.)' (Illarionov, 2009h, p. 53). At the time of the August war, Illarionov noted, South Ossetia's Defence Minister was Lieutenant General Vasilii Lunev, a graduate of the Moscow High Military College, who had previously been first deputy commander-in-chief of the Siberian Military District. The Secretary of the Security Council – and former republican Minister of Defence – was Lieutenant General Anatolii Barankevich, a native of the Russian Far East, who had previously served in the Siberian Military District and the Volga and North Caucasus Military Districts. The Minister at the Ministry of Internal Affairs (Ministerstvo Vnutrennikh Del; MVD), Lieutenant General Mikhail Mindzaev, had previously served in the Federal Security Service of the Russian Federation (Federal'naya sluzhba bezopasnosti Rossiyskoi Federatsii; FSB special forces) and as deputy chief of staff at the Ministry of Interior of the Republic of North Ossetia-Alania. The head of the republican KGB (the Soviet name was retained), Lieutenant General Boris Attoev, had formerly served in the FSB central directorate in Moscow and as chief of the FSB branch of Kabardino-Balkariya (Illarionov, 2009h, pp. 81–2).

It is inconceivable, Illarionov concluded, that these high-ranking Russian generals would have supported a course contrary to the wishes of Vladimir Putin and the Russian *siloviki* (power ministers). Another point repeatedly stressed by Illarionov was the importance of the passportisation process. During the spring and summer of 2002, the Russian government began preparations for the distribution of Russian passports to residents of South Ossetia (as well as of Abkhazia and Adjara). 'In June 2002, the Russian parliament adopted the necessary amendments to the Russian law on Citizenship, which evoked a strong protest from [then] Georgian president Eduard Shevardnadze' (Illarionov, 2009h, p. 53). Once the Rose Revolution in Georgia had taken place in late 2003 and Mikheil Saakashvili had been elected president, this passportisation process was accelerated. By early April 2003, while Shevardnadze was still president, 56 per cent of the population of South Ossetia had received Russian passports (Illarionov, 2009g, pt 1, p. 4). By mid August of 2006, that figure had swollen to 98 per cent (Illarionov, 2009g, pt 1, p. 15).

The Tagliavini EU report, it should be pointed out, insisted that this Russian passportisation process was in fact contrary to international law. For the process to have been legal, Ambassador Tagliavini underlined the point that:

> An explicit consent of the home country is required. Georgian law, however, does not recognize dual citizenship [...]. The vast majority of purportedly naturalized persons from South Ossetia and Abkhazia are not Russian nationals in terms of international law [...]. They were still citizens of Georgia at the time of the armed conflict of

August 2008, and in legal terms they remain so to this day [...].
(Council of the European Union, 2009, vol. 1, p. 18)

In his discussion of the run-up to the conflict, Illarioniov noted that, in
June of 2008, the South Ossetian authorities set up an Internet website
entitled 'Ossetian genocide' (Illarionov, 2009h, p. 70). This site was
apparently preparing the ground for charges of genocide against Georgia
once hostilities broke out. On 20 July, a cyber-attack against Georgian
government sites was launched; such attacks were to mushroom during the conflict (Illarionov, 2009g, pt 1, p. 33). On 6 July, the North
Caucasus Military District began its 'Caucasus–2008' military manoeuvres, 'with the participation of 8,000 servicemen from the army, interior
forces, and the FSB including 700 armoured units, and with support
from the Air Force and Black Sea Fleet' (Illarionov, 2009h, p. 71). On 2
August, just five days before the outbreak of hostilities, these manoeuvres officially ended, 'but troops participating in the manoeuvres did
not leave their positions' (Illarionov, 2009h, p. 73). In the days leading
up to the conflict, Illarionov observed, Russia took a number of steps
suggesting that it had decided to provoke a conflict. On 2 August,
Russian state television, radio and print journalists 'ready and eager to
report on a war that had not yet begun' started arriving in Tskhinvali;
by 7 August, their number had reached 50 (Illarionov, 2009h, pp. 72–3).
Only one non-Russian journalist, a Ukrainian, was included. This process has become known to students of the war as 'the prepositioning of
journalists'.

During the first week of August, Illarionov noted, the South Ossetian
authorities evacuated more than 20,000 civilians to North Ossetia.
'This number constituted more than 90 per cent of the population of
the future area of battle and about 40 per cent of the total population
of South Ossetia' (Illarionov, 2009h, p. 73). At the same time, an officially controlled mobilisation of 'volunteers' and Cossacks began in
the North Caucasus, with the first 300 crossing the Russian–Georgian
border on 4 August. Most of these volunteers were assigned to the
19th Infantry Division of the North Caucasus Military District or to
the North Ossetian Peacekeeping Battalion; others signed contracts
with the South Ossetian Ministry of Defence (Illarionov, 2009h, p. 74).
Illarionov also noted the semi-clandestine filtering of Russian military
units into South Ossetia. This filtering process followed a key meeting
held in Tskhinvali on 2 August attended by a Russian deputy minister
of defence, General of the Army Nikolai Pankov, the Deputy Chief
of Russian Military Intelligence and Commander-in-Chief of the

58th Army, Anatolii Khrulev, plus the two generals in charge of the 530-soldier Russian and South Ossetian peacekeeping forces, as well as high-ranking South Ossetian *siloviki* and President Kokoity (Illarionov, 2009g, pt 1, p. 37).

On 3 August, an intelligence-collecting battalion of the 42nd Motor-Rifle Division arrived in South Ossetia (Illarionov, 2009g, pt 1, p. 37). The following day, 4 August, medical and communications units of the Russian 58th Army arrived in the republic, and the next day several armoured units as well as 40 artillery systems and an intelligence battalion of the 33rd Special Airborne Storm-Trooper Brigade with full armaments moved through the Roki Tunnel into South Ossetia (Illarionov, 2009h, p. 74). On the evening of 6 August, the leadership of the North Caucasus Military District was deployed to Java in South Ossetia (Illarionov, 2009h, p. 75). Finally, on 7 August, between 3:41 and 3:52 a.m., a column of Russian armour was moved through the Roki Tunnel to the territory of South Ossetia (Illarionov, 2009g, pt 1, p. 47). In September 2008, Illarionov pointed out, the Russian authorities were to admit to the existence of this armoured column but asserted, misleadingly, that it had merely represented a rotation of Russian peacekeepers.[3] Illarionov cast a wide net in seeking to locate information demonstrating that major elements of the Russian military had been clandestinely inserted into South Ossetia in advance of the hostilities. In the documentation section of the *Russkii zhurnal* materials, Illarionov cited South Ossetian official and unofficial websites and blogs, as well as numerous Russian newspapers, websites and blogs, including official (for instance, the army newspaper *Krasnaya zvezda*), central (for instance, *Nezavisimaya gazeta*) and provincial (for instance, *Permskie novosti*, *Vechernii Saransk* and *Gazeta Yuga* [Kabardino-Balkariya]) to show the unlawful presence of regular Russian military units, that is to say units not attached to the Russian peacekeeping contingent, in South Ossetia before the outbreak of the conflict late on the seventh and early on the eighth of August.

We now move on to perhaps the central theme of Illarionov's research: namely, the question of which side began the war? On 28 July, he reported, the South Ossetian forces,

> for the first time fired at the joint peacekeeping forces and OSCE [Organization for Security and Co-operation in Europe] observers. The next day [29 July], also for the first time, South Ossetian forces shelled villages with ethnically mixed populations that were under Georgian control. (Illarionov, 2009h, p. 72)

On 5 August, the South Ossetian minister of internal affairs, Lieutenant General Mindzaev, gave 'an order for the destruction of the [ethnic Georgian] village of Nuli' (Illarionov, 2009g, pt 1, p. 43). On 6 and 7 August, South Ossetian forces shelled and subjected to mortar-round attack a number of ethnic Georgian villages, including Nuli. On the sixth, two Georgian peacekeepers were wounded. On the seventh in the morning, the bombardments increased in strength; three Georgian soldiers were wounded. Then, later that same day, 'A post of Georgian peacekeepers from Avnevi is bombarded [...]. Two Georgian peacekeepers are killed. This is the first fact of the death of [Georgian] peacekeepers in the zone of conflict' (Illarionov, 2009g, pt 1, p. 49). Informed that large units of Russian armour were moving through the Roki Tunnel and that even larger units were poised to do so, and that the bombardment of Georgian villages was continuing and becoming heavier, President Saakashvili, as is well known, gave an order at approximately 11:30 p.m. on the seventh to begin a military operation. Illarionov saw this decision by the Georgian president as having been fully justified.

Felgenhauer's findings

The well-known Russian military journalist Pavel Felgenhauer has expressed agreement with Illarionov's point of view. The Georgians, as Felgenhauer saw it, fell victim to a rather brilliantly executed *maskirovka* (camouflage; the term is mine, not his), which was followed by an unexpected blitzkrieg offense. 'The Russians and their separatist allies in Abkhazia and South Ossetia', he wrote,

> prepared and executed in August 2008 a war which the Georgians did not predict or expect. The Georgians, until they were plunged headlong into the fighting, appear to have prepared only for a replay of previous confrontations in the Abkhazia and South Ossetia regions in the early 1990s [...]. But this time, the Russian military staged an all-out invasion, planning to totally decimate and destroy the Georgian military – in effect, a full demilitarization of Georgia, as well as to overthrow the hated pro-Western regime of President Mikheil Saakashvili. For this purpose, the Russian staffs mobilized and prepared for action tens of thousands of servicemen from the Navy, Air Force and Army [...]. Russia, led by former KGB agent Vladimir Putin, managed to hide its preparations and intentions not only from the Georgians but from Western governments and intelligence services. (Felgenhauer, 2009, pp. 162 and 165)

Felgenhauer made reference to a number of the same sources that had also been highlighted by Illarionov to demonstrate that it was Russia, and not Georgia, that went first: 'After the war', Felgenhauer summed up,

> multiple reports and interviews given by Russian soldiers were published in different Russian newspapers, including the official Defence Ministry daily *Krasnaya zvezda*. These provided first-hand evidence that Russian troops indeed began the invasion of Georgia and actually crossed the border through the Roki Tunnel before the Georgian troops attacked the Ossetian positions in the Tskhinvali region.[4] (Felgenhauer, 2009, p. 168)

Moscow, Felgenhauer contended,

> wanted its military action in Georgia in August 2008 to be seen merely as a reaction to 'Georgian aggression' against Tskhinvali [...] and against Russian peacekeepers in the region. However, this official Russian position ignores the simple fact that an invasion of such magnitude would require long-term preparations involving the entire Russian military, including, the Army, Air Force and Navy.[5] (Felgenhauer, 2009, p. 165)

In a response to an American critic, Felgenhauer wrote on 1 September 2008:

> The good professor [...] does not, apparently, understand the difference between the deployment into battle of a combined army task force, supported by air and navy, and a limo or pizza delivery service that can be expected to turn up in an hour after receiving an order [...]. If the Russian response would have been indeed only a reaction to a sudden Georgian attack, it would have taken at least a week to send a vanguard force into South Ossetia and a month to organize a full-scale invasion. (Felgenhauer, 2008b)

The Tagliavini report

In contrast to the views expressed by Illarionov and Felgenhauer, the Tagliavini EU report faulted Georgia, rather than Russia, for initiating the conflict. As Ambassador Tagliavini wrote in her introduction to the report:

> On the night of 7 to 8 August 2008, a sustained Georgian artillery attack struck the town of Tskhinvali. Other movements of the Georgian

armed forces targeting Tskhinvali and the surrounding areas were under way, and soon the fighting involved Russian, South Ossetian and Abkhaz military units and armed elements. (Council of the European Union, 2009, pt 1, p. 10)

The report continued:

There is the question of whether the use of force by Georgia in South Ossetia beginning with the shelling of Tskhinvali on the night of August 7th, was justifiable under international law [...]. It was not [...]. Even if it were assumed that Georgia was repelling an attack, e.g., in response to South Ossetian attacks against Georgian populated villages in the region, according to international law, its armed response would have to be both necessary and proportional. (Council of the European Union, 2009, pt 1, pp. 22–3)

'An additional legal question', the report continued,

is whether the Georgian use of force against Russian peacekeeping forces on Georgian territory, i.e., in South Ossetia, might have been justified. Again it is in the negative. There was no ongoing armed attack by Russia before the start of the Georgian operation. Georgian claims of a large-scale presence of Russian armed forces in South Ossetia prior to the Georgian offensive on August 7th could not be substantiated by the Mission.[6] (Council of the European Union, 2009, pt 1, p. 23)

It seems clear that the report's authors would likely have come to different conclusions if they had taken into consideration Illarionov's research. The EU report, it should be emphasised, does not uniformly support the Russian position on the conflict. 'The Russian side', Ambassador Tagliavini observed,

justified their military intervention by their intention to stop an allegedly ongoing genocide of the Ossetian population by the Georgian forces, and also to protect Russian citizens residing in South Ossetia and the Russian contingent of the Joint Peacekeeping Forces deployed in South Ossetia in accordance with the Sochi agreement of 1992. (Council of the European Union, 2009, pt 1, p. 21)

In point of fact, the report concluded, there was no genocide of South Ossetians, a total of 162 Ossetian civilians, it reported, lost their lives.

As we have seen, the report also emphasised that the South Ossetians remained Georgian and not Russian citizens under international law (Council of the European Union, 2009, pt 1, p. 21). Therefore only the Russian claim that there was a need to protect Russian peacekeepers in South Ossetia retained a degree of validity in the eyes of the authors of the report.

Latynina's findings

Yuliya Latynina has taken vigorous exception to the claim of the Tagliavini report that it was Georgia that initiated the conflict. Latynina's most complete response to the Tagliavini report was posted on the website ej.ru on 3 May 2010 (Latynina, 2010a).[7] She noted that:

> The war, in the opinion of Tagliavini, begins at precisely that moment when Georgia delivers a blow to Tskhinvali. True, here the respected commission stipulates that this was preceded by various complicated events [...]. A question for Ms. Tagliavini: in June of 1941, Finland declared war against the USSR. This was preceded by such a minor detail as the bombing by the Red Army of scores of Finnish population points, but without a declaration of war. Is Ms. Tagliavini certain that the [...] Soviet–Finnish war should be dated from the moment of its declaration by Finland? (Latynina, 2010a)

'Ms. Tagliavini', Latynina continued,

> carries out a coup in world politics, introducing a new definition of war. A war, it turns out, is begun by he [*sic*] who responds to the actions of an aggressor [...]. So when Ossetian 'volunteers' burn Georgian villages – that is not a war. But if they [the Georgians] respond to this, then here you, accursed ones, have started a war. Following the logic of the Tagliavini commission, the Georgians ought not to have responded. Even if Russian tanks had reached Tbilisi, and the Georgians had responded, they, the swine, would have started a war. The logic is irreproachable: if the Georgians had not responded, there would have been no war. (Ibid.)

'The [Tagliavini] commission' Latynina concluded,

> should have established under what conditions the shelling [of Tskhinvali] was conducted. For example, it should have established

why several days before the perfidious attack on Tskhinvali almost the entire civilian population [of the city] was evacuated, and why [Russian] journalists were brought in large numbers to illuminate the perfidious Georgian aggression. (Ibid.)

She stressed that the commission ought to have established why 'the Georgian village of Nuli' was set on fire by the South Ossetians on 7 August and burned to the ground. According to the Tagliavini Commission, 'Georgia had no right to send a single shell into the city [of Tskhinvali]. But the opposite side had a right to burn down Nuli, and that was not an infringement of human rights' (ibid.).

This stance of the Tagliavini Commission, Latynina, summed up in her rejoinder,

is cowardice. Cowardice not even in the face of an international dictator but before an international hooligan [that is to say, Vladimir Putin]. There would be nothing bad in this cowardice if the people who exhibited it did not pretend to the rule of arbiters. (Ibid.)

The Tagliavani report, she concluded witheringly, 'is a new Munich' (ibid.).

Like Andrei Illarionov, whose work she cited at times, Latynina referenced South Ossetian websites and blogs to demonstrate that Russia and its allies did indeed go first. At approximately 8:30 p.m. on the evening of the seventh, after the Georgian village of Nuli had been completely destroyed,

the Ossetian militia were celebrating a victory over the Georgians [...]. On the evening of the 7th in Tskhinvali they celebrate the taking of Nuli. Nuli is destroyed, struck by artillery, not by mortar fire, but by artillery. And several hours later we are informed that the vile Georgian fascists have entered the peaceful village of Khetagurovo [...]. This is a principle of double-think: who attacked whom? (Latynina, 2008c)[8]

In September 2009, Latynina observed during one of her weekly radio programmes:

If you look, for example, at what the South Ossetian blogs were saying on the morning of the seventh [of August], I quote here from messages posted on the site http://osradio.ru/index.html: 'Ossetians, your task is to fill to overflowing one of the largest morgues in Europe, the one in the city of Gori.' 'The Georgian fascists must receive their own Stalingrad.' 'We haven't yet bombed peaceful Tbilisi, but we soon will.' 'The 58th [Army] is already in the city [Tskhinvali], we have to remove the [Georgian] enclaves at any price [...].' (Latynina, 2009a)

And Latynina went on to comment:

'The war has begun' and 'The 58th [Army] is already in the city' were written on the afternoon of the seventh and on the evening of the seventh 'the accursed fascist Saakashvili' delivered a blow to the peacefully sleeping Tskhinvali. (Ibid.)[9]

Illarionov endorses Latynina's findings

In an interview given to Ekho Moskvy Radio, Illarionov, like Latynina, focused on the shelling of Georgian villages in South Ossetia:

The bombardment of the population points of Avnevi and Nuli took place two days before the bombardment of Tskhinvali. And the population points of Avnevi and Nuli were de facto wiped off the face of the earth. During the course of this bombardment on the 6th and 7th of August [...] several Georgians were killed, including Georgian peace-keepers. Two Georgian peacekeepers were killed at about 2:00 p.m. on 7 August, almost a day before there arrived the first information about the deaths of Russian peacekeepers. (Illarionov, 2009d)

The destroyed Georgian village of Nuli, Illarinov noted elsewhere, contained a population of approximately 2000 (Vol'tskaya, 2009). Another point emphasised by Illarionov was that the damage inflicted on Tskhinvali by the Georgians had been intentionally exaggerated by Russian and South Ossetian propaganda outlets. In an October 2008 interview with Ekho Moskvy Radio, Illarionov recalled that:

I visited South Ossetia and Tskhinvali [shortly after the war] [...]. In Tskhinvali, judging from the streets I succeeded in visiting, from 5%–10% of the buildings were destroyed [...]. My personal impression rather seriously correlates with the [satellite] photos taken by UNOSAT [the UNITAR (United Nations Institute for Training and Research) Operational Satellite Applications Programme], which show that about 5% of the buildings on the territory of Tskhinvali were destroyed. (Illarionov, 2008; Unosat.org, 2008; Goble, 2008)

In contrast to the Tagliavini report, Illarionov insisted that Russian peacekeepers based in South Ossetia had attacked the Georgian peacekeepers first, and not the other way around. He remarked in an interview that:

We have information that the Georgian side made a declaration to the Russian side that it did not intend to attack the Russian peacekeepers [...]. Such a statement exists, and it was confirmed by the Russian side, it was confirmed by [General] Kulakhmetov [head of the Russian peacekeepers] and so on. And we know this: those Russian peacekeepers which were present at their posts, not one of those posts was attacked, no-one suffered, no-one was killed and no-one was wounded [...]. The Georgian peacekeepers did not open fire on the Russian forces because they had such an order. (Illarionov, 2009d)

What did occur, he explained, was that at approximately 5:50 a.m. on 8 August, Russian peacekeepers opened fire on the Georgian forces. At 6:20 a.m. the Georgian forces returned fire.

In his useful book, *A Little War that Shook the World*, Ronald D. Asmus (2010) of the German Marshall Fund, a former US State Department official under President Bill Clinton, has acknowledged the value of Illarionov's research in helping him grasp the root causes of the 2008 war. Asmus observed that:

Andrei Illarionov in an exhaustive study of Russia's war preparations, has argued that some 1,200 Russian soldiers along with medical and communication units were already in South Ossetia illegally by August 7, with another 12,000 troops poised [to cross the border] [...]. Subsequent sources and press reports [...] suggest that elements of the 135th and 693rd Regiments of the Fifty-eighth Army and Twenty-second Special Forces Brigade, as well as several tank units had already moved into South Ossetia between August 2 and the evening of August 7 – and some of those units started fighting the Georgians early on August 8 when they entered Tskhinvali. (Asmus, 2010, p. 22)

The fact is, Andrei Illarionov has summed up his findings,

that that version of events which has received broad dissemination thanks to the propaganda efforts of the Russian official authorities cannot withstand a confrontation with reality. There are revealed a colossal number of errors, falsifications and open lies. (Illarionov, 2009a)

'Much available evidence', he has remarked elsewhere, 'refutes the often-heard claim that the Georgian government under Mikheil Saakashvili played a crucial role in provoking the war' (Illarionov, 2009h). Pavel Felgenhauer has arrived at a similar conclusion:

> This war was not an improvised reaction to a sudden Georgian military offensive in South Ossetia, since masses of troops cannot be held for long in 24-hour readiness. The invasion was inevitable, no matter what the Georgians did. (Felgenhauer, 2008d).

Conclusion

To conclude this analysis, an independent scholar, Andrei Illarionov, and two leading journalists, Pavel Felegenhauer and Yuliya Latynina, have raised probing questions concerning the official Russian state version of which side initiated the August 2008 conflict. In my view, the version advanced by Illarionov, Felgenhauer and Latynina constitutes an accurate account of what transpired. Their version accords with my own independent research into the origins of the conflict as well as with the findings of a well-informed former United States diplomat, Ronald D. Asmus (Dunlop, 2009; Asmus, 2010). Future unbiased students of the war will want to commend Illarionov, Felgenhauer and Latynina for their courage and honesty and for the originality of their investigative research.

Notes

1. I selected these three commentators because they represented the most influential and, in my view, the most trenchant critics of the Medvedev–Putin regime's conduct of the conflict. Felgenhauer's articles predate Illarionov's publications. Latynina cites Illarionov's work but also does her own independent digging; furthermore she ventures into numerous areas not covered by Illarionov. As for myself, I put in a rather massive research effort that included all of the material cited by the three authors as well as a number of items not referenced by them. Due to space constraints, this chapter will focus exclusively on developments in South Ossetia. Events taking place in Abkhazia will not be covered.
2. On the EU report, see Barry and Kanter (2009). I have singled out the EU report for special attention because of the great weight accorded to it by spokespersons for the Medvedev–Putin leadership and by Russian public opinion. Part three of the EU report, it should be noted, devotes 250 pages to citing official Russian documents and official responses to questions posed by the EU in seeking to provide Russia's authorised view of the inception of the conflict. As will be seen, my approach to the vexed question of the inception of the conflict is largely chronological.

3. Illarionov noted: 'In accord with the [agreed upon] rules, the rotation of
   peacekeepers is carried out once every half year, in a mutual accord of the
   sides, during the daytime, with an advanced notification of one month'
   (Illarionov, 2009f, pt 1, p. 47). None of these conditions were observed.
   Moreover, 'the last rotation of Russian peacekeepers in the zone of conflict
   was achieved on 31 May 2008' (ibid.).
4. Of particular significance here is Zhirnova, 2008. The author related these
   words of a hospitalised captain from the 135th Motor-Rifle Regiment: '"My
   byli na ucheniyakh," nachinaet rasskaz kapitan Sidristyi. "Eto otnositel'no
   nedaleko ot stolitsy Yuzhnoi Osetii. Nizhnii Zaramakh—prirodnyi zapoved-
   nik Severnoi Osetii. Vot tam posle planovykh uchenii i stoyali lagerem, no 7
   avgusta noch'yu prishla komanda na vydvizhenie k Tskhinvalu. Podnyali
   nas po trevoge—i na marsh. Pribyli, razmestilis', a uzhe 8 avgusta utrom
   tam popykhnulo s takoi siloi, chto mnogie dazhe rasteryalis.'" ('We were on
   maneuvers,' Captain Sidristyi began his account. 'It was a place located not
   far from the capital of South Ossetia. Nizhnii Zaramakh was a nature preserve
   in North Ossetia. There, after finishing the planned maneuvers, we stood in
   a camp, but on 7 August, at night, there came a command for us to move to
   Tskhinvali. We were placed on alert and then ordered to march. We arrived
   and settled in, but already on the eighth, in the morning, things flared up
   with such force that many even became bewildered.') This article was subsequently taken down from the *Krasnaya zvezda* website.
5. For similar assertions, see Felgenhauer, 2008a, 2008c and 2008d.
6. In the section of the Tagliavini report entitled 'Military events of 2008' (vol.
   2, ch. 5), the author seems less categorical than does the author of the report's
   introduction: 'At the time of the writing of the report, the Mission was not in a
   position to consider the Georgian claim concerning a large-scale Russian military
   incursion into South Ossetia before 8 August 2008 as substantiated. However,
   there are a number of reports and publications, including of Russian origin,
   indicating the provision by the Russian side of training and military equipment
   to South Ossetian [...] forces prior to the August 2008 conflict. They also indicated an influx of irregular forces from the territory of the Russian Federation
   in early August as well as the presence of some Russian forces in South Ossetia
   apart from the Russian PKF [peacekeeping] battalion, prior to 14.30 hours on 8
   August 2008' (Council of the European Union, 2009, p. 221).
7. See, too, Latynina, 2009b.
8. For similar comments by the journalist, see Latynina, 2008a and 2008b.
9. During her 7 August 2010 weekly radio programme, Latynina observed that
   'the General Procuracy has [now] admitted that Russia began the war in
   August 2008'. For her detailed discussion of the Procuracy's admission, see
   Latynina, 2010b. For the Procuracy's statement, see General'naya Prokuratura
   Rossiiskoi Federatsii, 2010. See also Itar-Tass, 2010.

References

Asmus, Ronald D. (2010) *A Little War that Shook the World: Georgia, Russia, and the Future of the West* (New York: Palgrave Macmillan).

Barry, Ellen and James Kanter (2009) 'European report on Georgia War faults both sides', *New York Times*, nytimes.com, 1 October, available at: http: nytimes.com/2009/10/01/world/europe/01russia.html?scp=1&sq=European% 20report%20on%20Georgia%20war%20faults%both%sides&st=cse (accessed 24 July 2010).

Calmes, Jackie (2010) 'Obama and Medvedev talk economics', *New York Times*, nytimes.com, 25 June, available at: http://www.nytimes.com/2010/06/25/ world/europe/25prexy.html (accessed 24 July 2010).

Cornell, Svante E. and S. Frederick Starr (eds) (2009) *The Guns of August 2008: Russia's War in Georgia* (Armonk, NY: M. E. Sharpe).

Council of the European Union (2009) Independent International Fact-Finding Mission on the Conflict in Georgia (IIFFMCG – CEIIG) (Tagliavini report), Geneva, September, available at: http://www.ceiig.ch/pdf (accessed 24 July 2010).

Dunlop, John B. (2009) 'Georgia didn't pick that fight,' *Hoover Digest*, No. 1, 22 January, available at: http://www.hoover.org/publications/hoover-digest/ article/5545 (accessed 10 January 2011).

Felgenhauer, Pavel (2008a) 'Eto byla ne spontannaya, a splanirovannaya voina', *Novaya gazeta*, 14 August, available at: http://www.novayagazeta.ru/ dta/2008/59/04.html (accessed 24 July 2010).

Felgenhauer, Pavel (2008b) 'Pavel Felgenhauer response to Professor Herspring Posting on *JRL*', *Johnson's Russia List*, no. 161, 28 August, available at: http:// www.cdi.org/russia/johnson/2008-161-10.cfm (accessed 24 July 2010).

Felgenhauer, Pavel (2008c) 'S chem Gruziya podoshla k voine', *Novaya gazeta*, no. 11 August, available at: http://www.novayagazeta.ru/data/2008/58/09. html (accessed 24 July 2010).

Felgenhauer, Pavel (2008d) 'The Russian–Georgian War was preplanned in Moscow', *Eurasia Daily Monitor*, 14 August, available at: http://www.jamestown. org/single/?_cache=1&tx_ttnews (accessed 24 July 2010).

Felgenhauer, Pavel (2009) 'After August 7: the escalation of the Russia–Georgia War', in Svante E. Cornell and S. Frederick Starr (eds), *The Guns of August 2008: Russia's War in Georgia* (Armonk, NY: M. E. Sharpe), pp. 162–80.

General'naya Prokuratura Rossiiskoi Federatsii (The Prosecutor General's Office of the Russian Federation) (2010) 'Novosti', genproc.gov.ru, 27 July, available at: http://genproc.gov.ru/news-12594/ (accessed 26 August 2010).

Goble, Paul (2008) 'Window on Eurasia: UN satellite photos undercut Russian claims about South Ossetia', Vienna, VA, 10 September, available at: http:// windowoneurasia.blogspot.com/2008/09/window-on-eurasia-un-satellite-photos.html (accessed 24 July 2010).

Illarionov, Andrei (2008) 'Situatsiia v Yuzhnoi Osetii i Gruzii', echo.msk.ru, round-table discussion, 24 October, available at: http://www.echo.msk.ru/ programs/razvorot/548457-echo/ (accessed 24 July 2010).

Illarionov, Andrei (2009a) 'Andrei Illarionov: Lukavye tsifry rossiisko-gruzinskoi voiny', echo.msk.ru, 24 June, available at: http://echo.msk.ru/programs/ figure/600923-echo.phtml (accessed 24 July 2010).

Illarionov, Andrei (2009b) 'Godovshchina bitvy za Yuzhnuyu Osetiyu', svobodanews.ru, RFE/RL, 6 August, available at: http://www.svobodanews.ru/ articleprintview/1794407.html (accessed 24 July 2010).

Illarionov, Andrei (2009c) 'Kto byl pervym?' livejournal.ru, 20 February, available at: http://aillarionov.livejournal.com/70169.html (accessed 24 July 2010).

Illarionov, Andrei (2009d) '"Narod protiv" Andreya Illarionova', echo.msk.ru, 8 September, available at: http://echo.msk.ru/blog/video/618624-echo.phtml (accessed 24 July 2010).

Illarionov, Andrei (2009e) 'Kak gotovilas' voina', *Novaya gazeta*, no. 66–9, 24 June, 26 June, 29 June and 1 July, available at: http://www.novayagazeta.ru/politics/44604.html (accessed 24 July 2010).

Illarionov, Andrei (2009f) 'Rossiisko-gruzinskaya voina byla sprovotsirovana rossiiskimi vlastyami?' echo.msk.ru, 8 September, available at: http://www.echo.msk.ru/programs/opponent/618330-echo-phtml (accessed 24 July 2010).

Illarionov, Andrei (2009g) 'Rossiisko-gruzinskaya voina: Dokumenty i materialy', *Russkii zhurnal: rabochie tetrady, Zhurnalnyi zal, Kontinent* (Moscow: Russkii Zhurnal), pts 1 and 2, p. 263, available at: http://magazines.russ/ru/continent/140/ill16html and http://magazines.russ.ru/continent/2009/140/illar.html (accessed 24 July 2010).

Illarionov, Andrei (2009h) 'The Russian leadership's preparation for war, 1999–2008', in Svante E. Cornell and S. Frederick Starr (eds), *The Guns of August 2008: Russia's War in Georgia* (Armonk, NY: M. E. Sharpe), pp. 49–84.

Itar-Tass (2010) 'South Ossetia military official put on trial as spy for Georgia', Itar-Tass, 27 July, available at: http://dlib.eastview.com/browse/doc/22234310 (accessed 25 October 2010).

Latynina, Yuliya (2008a) 'Dvesti km tankov. O rossiisko-gruzinskoi voine', ej.ru, 29 November, available at: http://ej.ru?a=note&id=8611 (accessed 24 July 2010).

Latynina, Yuliya (2008b) 'Kod dostupa', echo.msk.ru, 9 August, available at: http://www.echo.msk.ru/programs/code/532628-echo.phtml (accessed 24 July 2010).

Latynina, Yuliya (2008c) 'Kod dostupa', echo.msk.ru, 25 October, available at: http://www.echo.msk.ru/programs/code/548878-echo-phtml (accessed 24 July 2010).

Latynina, Yuliya (2009a) 'Kod dostupa', echo.msk.ru, 26 September, available at: http://www.echo.msk.ru/programs/code/622622-echo.phtml (accessed 24 July 2010).

Latynina, Yuliya (2009b) 'Utka ot Shpigelya', Gazeta.ru, 27 March, available at: http://www.gazeta.ru/column/latynina/296578.shtml (accessed 24 July 2010).

Latynina, Yuliya (2010a) 'Doklad Ta[g]liavini i padenie evro', ej.ru, 3 May, available at: http://www.ej.ru/a=note&id=10074 (accessed 24 July 2010).

Latynina, Yuliya (2010b) 'Kod dostupa', echo.msk.ru, 7 August, available at: http://echo.msk.ru/programs/code/701229-echo.phtml (accessed 9 August 2010).

Unosat.org (2008) 'Satellite damage assessment for Tskhinvali, South Ossetia, Georgia', (Unosat is the UNITAR (United Nations Institute for Training and Research) Operational Satellite Applications Programme), 22 August, available at: http://unosat-maps.web.cern.ch/unosat-maps/GE/Russia_ConflictAug08/UNOSAT_GEO_Tskhinvali_Damage_Overview_19aug08_Highres.pdf (accessed 24 July 2010).

Vol'tskaya, Tat'yana (2009) 'Chto zhe vy ne pogibli?', svobodanews.ru, 13 September, available at: http://www.svobodanews.ru/article/1821512.html (accessed 24 July 2010).

Zhirnova, Irina (2008) 'Zhizn' prodolzhaetsya', *Krasnaya zvezda*, 3 September.

Part II
Russia and the CIS

5
Whose 'Near Abroad'? Dilemmas in Russia's Declared Sphere of Privileged Interests

John Russell

Introduction

In the immediate aftermath of the Russo-Georgian War of 2008, when the idea for an article on this topic was first conceptualised, experts on East–West relations were still coming to terms with the consequences of the definitive breakdown of the coalition formed after 9/11 to prosecute the 'global war on terror'. As a consequence relations between Russia and the West reached what was probably a post-Cold War low. Just over two years later, we are witnessing a very recent but potentially very significant upturn in this relationship, as this analysis will seek to demonstrate.

In retrospect, by 2005, the signs of the breakdown of the post-9/11 coalition were already apparent, although by no means obvious to all. For, despite setbacks in Afghanistan and Iraq, George W. Bush, fresh from winning a second term as president, still led a self-confident United States administration that on behalf of the world's only super-power was forcefully putting into practice ideas of the new American century, which had been generated ever since it became clear that the USSR was disintegrating (most notably Krauthammer, 1990–91).

Russia, buoyed by escalating oil revenues and a popular, assertive leader, was emerging under the presidency of Vladimir Putin – a representative of the powerful *siloviki* faction (drawn from the armed forces, law enforcement bodies and intelligence agencies) within Russian politics (Bremmer and Charap, 2006–07) – from what he characterised, in the wake of the Beslan school massacre of September 2004, as a period of national humiliation and weakness:

> We showed weakness, and the weak are trampled upon. Some want to cut off a juicy morsel from us while others are helping them. They

are helping because they believe that, as one of the world's major nuclear powers, Russia is still posing a threat to someone, and therefore this threat must be removed. (Putin, 2004)

Energetic Russian opposition to the projection of US power outside of the North Atlantic Treaty Organization's (NATO) traditional sphere of interest[1] and, at least in the Putin administration's perception, into Russia's own back yard through its policies of deploying a missile defence shield in Eastern Europe (Slocombe, 2008) and NATO expansion into the former Soviet Union, combined with Russia's exercise of its 'energy' card on its neighbours in Eastern and Central Europe during freezing winters between 2006 to 2009, led to speculation towards the end of the first decade of the twenty-first century of the emergence of a new Cold War. Indeed, the full title of Edward Lucas's bestseller on this topic, published in 2008, was *The New Cold War: How the Kremlin Menaces both Russia and the West* (Lucas, 2008).

Even the spy scandal in the summer of 2010 between Washington and Moscow seemed to hearken back nostalgically to the Cold War era. Yet despite Lucas's 'I-told-you-so' protestations (Lucas, 2010), the fact is that both in Russia (Bayer, 2010) and the West (Hearst, 2010) this scandal tended to give rise to more comedy (and captivation with Anna Chapman's charms) than complaint and, more importantly, signally failed to derail a perceptible warming in US–Russian relations, underlining just how misplaced had been much of the hyperbole over the new Cold War.

Russia's resurgence, combined with the manifest failure of the strategy of 'shock and awe' (itself a concept created in 1996 as a strategy for the US armed forces to achieve 'Rapid Dominance' by destroying an adversary's will to resist) (see Ullman and Wade, 1996) to achieve results that the US desired in both Afghanistan and Iraq, and the continuing rapid rise to superpower status of China, meant that even before the August war of 2008 there was no longer such a pressing requirement to continue to exaggerate Islamic fundamentalist-inspired terrorism as the biggest threat to the West's security. The notion of such a 'Green Peril', in the absence of any obvious alternative, conveniently replacing the threat to the West emanating from the USSR, had been articulated almost as soon as the Soviet menace had disappeared.[2]

With a form of postwar stability returning to Russia's rebellious North Caucasus republic, Chechnya, and growing public concern in the West over the open-ended powers granted to governments through counter-terrorist legislation, much of the utility of prosecuting the 'global war on terror' had clearly evaporated for both Russia and the West. Moreover as a recent article by a US military academic makes clear, the strategy of 'shock and awe' has proved unsuitable against 'authoritarian governments and ideological or faith-based non-state actors' (Bartholomees, Jr, 2010), in other words against regimes like Putin's or al-Qaeda.

The subsequent world economic crisis ensured that neither the US nor its Western allies could afford to impose foreign policy outcomes on Russia, as the Russo-Georgian conflict clearly demonstrated. The heightened distrust of Russia's future intentions in its 'Near Abroad' reminded this scholar, who is old enough to remember well the original Cold War, of a similar panic after the Soviet Union's invasion of Czechoslovakia forty years earlier in 1968, which resulted not only in an unprecedented period of East–West détente, but also in the United Kingdom's belated entry into the European Economic Community in an attempt to present a unified West European front against any further Soviet aggression.

As the Russo-Georgian War was the first major foreign policy crisis in Dmitri Medvedev's presidency, its successful (from the Russian viewpoint) outcome in checking NATO expansion and revealing the weakness of the US commitment to defending its policies in the contested neighbourhood, offered him the opportunity to signal that, as in 1968, having secured its most pressing aim, it was not the Kremlin's intention to go further. The chance to manifest this change of policy came with the election of Barack Obama, the subsequent pressing of the 'reset' button and the respective visits of the Russian and US presidents to each other's country. Judging from Medvedev's announcement of a new foreign policy concept in Moscow on 12 July 2010, the US and the European Union were identified as Russia's key partners in the drive to modernise, technologically and politically, the country's structures.

However, although the warming relations between the two presidents have altered quite dramatically relations between Russia and the West, important dilemmas emanating from the 'Near Abroad' remain to be resolved. Thus whereas my fellow panellist at the ICCEES VIII World Congress in Stockholm in July 2010, Richard Sakwa, employed the concept of a 'cold peace'[3] to represent the current state of Western–Russian relations, I prefer to use the term 'Chill Peace' to describe what promises to be the dawn of a pragmatic new relationship between Russia and the West.

I will argue that this relationship, which following Yeltsin's initial failed attempt at transition to democracy and Russia's assertive resurgence under Putin, might be recognised as the third relationship since the collapse of communism in the USSR, is based more upon recognition of potential dangers arising from a series of dilemmas in Russia's 'Near Abroad' than from real and immediate threats that either side is perceived currently to pose to the other.

For the purposes of this analysis, I have identified two closely related dilemmas: a security dilemma (emanating from strong states) in Central and Eastern Europe; and an insecurity dilemma (arising in weak states) in the former states of the Soviet Union (excluding the Baltic countries) over the question of democratic governance (what the European Union's Commissioner for External Relations and European Neighbourhood Policy, Benita Ferrero-Waldner, in her speech at the United Nations in 2007 termed the EU's combination of 'soft and smart power') (Ferrero-Waldner, 2007). A third and arguably related dilemma – Russia's choice of its future path of development – Western (European) or Eurasian, will not form part of this analysis.

Although strictly speaking the Near Abroad relates only to those non-Russian former Soviet states that are currently members of the Commonwealth of Independent States (CIS), this analysis will cover the Baltic states as well as countries of the former Soviet bloc in Eastern and Central Europe, insofar as they customarily see themselves as being on the precarious border between the 'democratic' West and 'authoritarian' Eurasia and thus seek to allay their security concerns by advocating a more assertive US-led NATO policy vis-à-vis Russia.

Russia's proclamation of a sphere of 'privileged interest' was one of President Medvedev's five principles of Russia's foreign policy laid down after the Russo-Georgian conflict in August 2008 and concerned regions 'that are home to countries with which we share special historical relations and are bound together as friends and good neighbours' (Russia Profile Weekly Experts Panel, 2008).

Although both the US and the UK refuse to recognise the Commonwealth of Independent States as a sphere of Russian 'privileged interest', their measured reaction to the change of government in Ukraine in February 2010 and their lack of action over civil unrest in Kyrgyzstan in June of that year indicate that, in practice, this at least is no longer perceived as a cause for major confrontation. Indeed, such was the lack of interest on the part of NATO in getting involved in Kyrgyzstan, that Fyodor Lukyanov, editor of *Russia in Global Affairs*, was moved to complain recently that Russia had effectively been left alone to deal with the Near Abroad as a 'zone of responsibility' (Lukyanov, 2010a).

Yet for all of the political, economic and social ills besetting the US and her partners in NATO at present, there remains a firm and widespread belief amongst its citizens and voters that its own and the world's interests are best served by promoting the spread of good governance, human rights and economic freedoms. Insofar as there resides a desire in Russia itself, let alone in the Near Abroad, to modernise, albeit only partly according to the Western template, the West's continued engagement with the former Soviet republics is much more than simply the moral issue, which Georg Sørenson has termed the 'value dilemma' (Sørenson, 2007). While it might be considered as axiomatic that it would be in neither Russia's nor the West's interests, let alone those of the peoples caught up in the dilemma of the Near Abroad to allow Europe's huge Eurasian neighbour to modernise and engage more closely with the US and member states of the European Union, while the countries in Eastern Europe, the Caucasus and Central Asia were held back from such a course, the resurgence of Russia, against the background of the rapid rise of China, has called into question whether democracy is the best, let alone the only, path towards economic development (McFaul, 2010).

Eastern Europe's security dilemma

In his September 2007 article in *Security Dialogue*, Sørenson explicitly rejects the 'realist' view of international relations that a security dilemma is inescapable while stating that 'the liberal view that the security dilemma can be transcended among liberal (postmodern) states is correct' (Sørenson, 2007, p. 362). Using the European Union as an example of integration between and cooperation among strong postmodern states, he postulates that the classical Cold War security dilemma in Europe is over.

However herein is a problem. For by his own definition Russia remains recognisably a modern, not a postmodern, state governed by 'a centralised system of democratic rule, based on a set of administrative, policing and military organisations, sanctioned by a legal order, claiming a monopoly of the legitimate use of force, all within a defined territory' and with 'a segregated national economy, self-sustained in the sense that it comprises the main sectors needed for its reproduction' (Sørenson, 2007, p. 361). Derek Averre usefully further identifies 'postmodern' states as representing 'normative', and 'modern' states 'structural', power (Averre, 2009, p. 1690).

The stringent accession terms of the European Union's *acquis communautaire* were designed to ensure the postmodern status of all of its new members from the former Soviet bloc, so there should be no question of a security dilemma in Central and Eastern Europe, especially as all are also members of NATO. Clearly a security dilemma no longer exists between West European countries and Russia. However insofar as NATO expansion into the former Soviet bloc (indeed, into the former Soviet Union) is regarded as a threat to Russian security by the Kremlin, there is a recognisable security dilemma between NATO on the one hand, and Russia on the other. This was admitted in February 2010 in Russia's latest strategic doctrine, which identifies NATO for the first time as posing its greatest external *danger* (Military Doctrine, 2010). It is worth emphasising in the context of this chapter that the word *threat* was used in this document only to cover the following five contingencies:

1. A drastic deterioration in the military–political situation (interstate relations) and the creation of the conditions for the utilisation of military force.
2. The impediment of the operation of systems of state and military command and control of the Russian Federation, the disruption of the functioning of its strategic nuclear forces, missile early warning systems, systems for monitoring outer space, nuclear munitions storage facilities, nuclear energy facilities, atomic and chemical industry facilities, and other potentially dangerous facilities.
3. The creation and training of illegal armed formations and their activity on the territory of the Russian Federation or on the territories of its allies.
4. A show of military force with provocative objectives in the course of exercises on the territories of states contiguous with the Russian Federation or its allies.
5. A stepping up of the activity of the Armed Forces of individual states (groups of states) involving partial or complete mobilisation and the transitioning of these states' organs of state and military command and control to wartime operating conditions.

During the elaboration of this doctrine, the single biggest irritant to Russia was the Pentagon's declared intention to construct a missile defence shield in the Czech Republic and Poland, ostensibly to intercept incoming Iranian missiles, but unambiguously perceived by the Kremlin as directed against Russia. In retaliation, in a move that exemplifies graphically how the security dilemma operates, much to the consternation of the Czechs and Poles, the Russians indicated that they would site short-range missiles in Kaliningrad.

Obama's subsequent announcement in September 2009 that the US was abandoning the shield disappointed 'hawks' in both the US and

Russia, as well as the leaders of Central and East European countries who feared that their security was being sacrificed for the greater goal of US–Russian rapprochement (Harding and Traynor, 2009), but it was generally well received in Western Europe and laid the foundations for the signing of a new Strategic Arms Reduction Treaty (symbolically termed New START and signed in Prague) between Russia and the US in April 2010 (US Department of State, 2010).

Russian public opinion was quick to register its approval of the warming of relations. The percentage of Russians polled who recognised an improvement in US–Russian relations rose from February to June 2010 from 31 to 46 per cent, with those noticing a deterioration falling over the same period from 9 to 5 per cent, respectively ('Opros', 2010). Even Obama's fallback plan to locate the missile shield in Bulgaria and Romania to target more emphatically Iran rather than threaten Russia's intercontinental ballistic missile (ICBM) capacity (Weitz, 2010), left open the door for Russian participation (Iliev, 2010), thus potentially avoiding a further spiral in the security dilemma – although the fervour with which the two Balkan states reacted to the prospect of US missiles being located in their countries did not go unnoticed in Moscow, prompting the leader of the pro-Russian breakaway Transdniester Republic in Moldova to invite the Kremlin to base Russian missiles on its territory (BBC News, 2010a). A Russian military analyst recently dismissed the US anti-ballistic missile (ABM) strategy as a means to keep Europe militarily dependent on its transatlantic partner and thus keep the US military-industrial complex happy with the prospect of new contracts and orders (Khramchikhin, 2010), yet another example of the 'mirror image' view of Western societies projected by 'official' opinion-forming Russians.

An example of military issues still to be resolved between NATO and Russia is the question of the ratification of a new Conventional Armed Forces in Europe Treaty that would address serious Russian concerns over the imbalances brought about by the 'defection' of so many former Warsaw Pact troops to NATO. Since August 2008, this has been complicated by the stationing of Russian troops in Abkhazia and South Ossetia, regions that the West still considers to be an integral part of Georgian territory (Arbatov and Oznobishchev, 2010).

That a security dilemma does not operate between Western Europe and Russia can be explained by the fact that the Russian authorities do not feel threatened by NATO in the North Atlantic area – North America and Northern and Western Europe – but do, as is hinted at in the new Military Doctrine (2010), by its presence in Central and Eastern Europe. By the same token, the former socialist states feel secure from Russia mainly due to the umbrella provided by NATO, which they wish would follow a more assertive policy towards Russia.

Understandably, NATO's inability and/or unwillingness to stand up to Russia over South Ossetia has led to considerable insecurity in the capitals of Russia's NATO neighbours, especially in the Baltic states of Estonia and Latvia, which are home to large minorities of ethnic Russians.[4] The Russian authorities have repeatedly referred cases of alleged human rights violations by the Estonian and Latvian governments to the European Court of Human Rights (Fawn, 2009). In addition, like Georgia, Estonia claims that it has been the target of cyber-attacks emanating from Russia (Traynor, 2007; Michael, 2010) (the 2008 NATO Report on the attacks on Georgia was compiled by the Cooperative Cyber Defence Centre of Excellence based in Tallinn, Estonia; see Tikk et al., 2008).

A recent example of the disagreement between 'old' and 'new' EU and NATO members is provided by Baltic reactions to the confirmation in March 2010 that France was to sell four Mistral amphibious assault vessels to Russia, with France claiming that Russia should be treated as a partner, not an enemy, and Estonia, Latvia and Lithuania reminding its Western ally that Russia held seaborne military exercises in the Baltic in 2009 (The Tocqueville Connection, 2010). France might wish to emulate Germany in its bid to become a major trading partner with Russia, particularly after the agreement over the Nord Stream pipeline, which is planned to deliver gas directly to Germany, much to the annoyance on financial and energy security grounds of Poland, Lithuania and Estonia (as well as on environmental grounds of Finland and Sweden) (Socor, 2008).

By their bilateral agreements with Russia, Germany and France can be seen to be following the US's example of putting its own national interests (that is to say, a non-confrontational relationship with Russia) above the perceived security interests of allies in Central and Eastern Europe. In Germany's case, disenchantment with its responsibilities for bailing out profligate EU members in the Mediterranean exhibiting less than full transparency in governance, might well have prompted the European Union's biggest economy to promote energetically a more rewarding relationship with Russia. Given the track record of the EU's influence on Russia's development, there are grounds for concluding that the more pragmatic (less value-laden) countries of Europe, such as Germany and France, might consider that bilateral relations with the energy giant to the east might give them more influence and success (Haukkala, 2009).

Any further German disenchantment with the process of EU enlargement might not facilitate the spread of the European idea to those countries of former Yugoslavia such as Serbia and Montenegro, which have strong historical ties with Russia but seek membership of the European Union and NATO (despite having been the targets of NATO attacks during the Balkan wars). If other West European countries were to follow Germany's lead, one might anticipate that manifestations of excessive Russophobia on the part of the EU's 'new' members in Central and Eastern Europe, might be regarded by their Western allies as an undesirable obstacle to normalising the kind of relations with Russia that are envisaged in the new 'Partnership for Modernisation' launched in Rostov-on-Don in June 2010 (Europa – Press Releases, 2010).

However the narrow victory in the Polish presidential elections achieved by Bronislaw Komarowski in July 2010 was generally welcomed by the Russian leadership, as well as by leaders of EU and NATO countries. Insofar as better relations with Russia objectively make good economic as well as political sense, the poignant circumstances of his predecessor's demise near Smolensk in April, the exaggerated role of traditional anti-Russian sentiment that has figured so prominently in Polish politics may well have reached an historic turning point. Poland's reluctance to comply with Russia's extradition request for Chechen rebel envoy Akhmed Zakayev in September 2010, and Moscow's apparent understanding of this position, may well have served as a litmus test for the depth of this transformation (*Eurasia Daily Monitor*, 2010; Jones, 2010).

By the same token, as the perceived threat from NATO enlargement recedes, it is unlikely that Medvedev's administration will risk the benefits accruing from the new-found warmth in bilateral relations with the US by pushing too hard for his much heralded (in Russia if not in the West) new European security architecture that circumscribes the power of both NATO and the Organization for Security and Co-operation in Europe (OSCE). As Bobo Lo has demonstrated, a comparison of his speech on this topic in London in April 2009 with those made earlier in Berlin and Evian in 2008 reveals a much more conciliatory tone towards NATO (Lo, 2009).

In present circumstances therefore the security dilemma in Eastern Europe remains a potential source of danger rather than a genuine threat to the security of either Russia or the West. Moreover in his assessment of ten factors that had shaped current Russian foreign policy, Fyodor Lukyanov listed Medvedev's modernisation campaign, Obama's decision to 'reset' relations, the New START treaty, Russia's turn towards prioritising Asia, the crisis in the EU and the breakthrough in relations with Poland – all six of them containing the potential to reduce the security dilemma that has emerged in Central and Eastern Europe (Lukyanov, 2010b).

The insecurity dilemma in the Near Abroad

The West's overriding priority currently in the Near Abroad is stability, followed by a containment of any attempt to reconstitute the threat posed to the West by the Soviet Union. The strategy to achieve both has been a mixture of 'soft' power (that is to say, spread of the Copenhagen Criteria that are perceived to have reaped such rich rewards in terms of security, development and economic integration in those states in Central and Eastern Europe that have joined the European Union and/or NATO) (Gänzle, 2009, p. 1716) and 'hard' power (attempts to exploit Russia's weakness by seeking to replace it as the dominant power in the Near Abroad). Whereas under the George W. Bush administration, the latter was given priority, Obama's use of 'smart' power (the appropriate mix of 'soft' and 'hard' and power for any given situation) has switched Western emphasis to the former.

Of course significant gains in the US Congress by the Republican Party (particularly its Tea Party tendency) in the November 2010 midterm elections might well have put the brakes on or even reversed Obama's attempts at productive engagement with Russia, as indeed might the decision that Putin rather than Medvedev will run for the Russian presidency in 2012.

That Russia considers security as its overriding vital interest in the Near Abroad is apparent from the text of the new Russian Military Doctrine, adopted on 5 February 2010, which identifies as threats, foreign support for 'illegal armed formations' on the territory of the Russian Federation or on that of its allies and military exercises of 'a provocative nature' on the territory of its neighbours (Military Doctrine, 2010). Whereas the latter relates to those states already in or aspiring to join either the European Union or NATO or both, the former appears to refer only to interference in the domestic affairs of Russia (for example, Chechnya) and its allies (for example, Tajikistan).

The major difference between the states of the former Soviet bloc now within the European Union and/or NATO and those that remain in the CIS but aspire to eventual membership of either or both organisations, is that the former might be categorised as relatively strong postmodern states and the latter as relatively weak modernising states, particularly when measured against the standards set by the European Union's *acquis communautaire*. Russia stands apart in that while it clearly fails to pass the governance and several other tests of EU membership, it could hardly be described as either a weak or an unstable state. It does however contain relatively weak, or at least potentially unstable, regions most notably in the North Caucasus, including Chechnya, to which Sørenson's dilemma of liberal values might apply.

A further part of Russia's Near Abroad that is not discussed here, but that could play an important role in NATO–Russian relations, is the Arctic, which is 'weak' only insofar as international and national jurisdictions over the region are the subject of a potentially dangerous dispute over access to and ownership of natural resources (Howard, 2010).

Drawing on the work of Jeremy Weinstein, John Porter and Stuart Eizenstat (2004, pp. 12–13), Sørenson identifies three 'grave problems' or gaps in 'weak' states. Of these, neither the 'security' gap (inability/unwillingness to maintain basic order within the state's territory) nor the 'legitimacy' gap (the state offers little or nothing, and gets no support in return) seems to be particularly acute in the Near Abroad, so that only the 'capacity' gap (the inability/unwillingness to provide other basic social values, such as welfare, liberty and the rule of law) appears at all endemic (Sørenson, 2007, pp. 365–6). This implies that the insecurity dilemma in the Near Abroad is not particularly pressing at present, but certainly has the potential to become more acute if the interests of all concerned parties are not taken into account.

Although Sørenson's analysis concerns more directly former colonial states, particularly in Africa, the degree to which the former states of the USSR – or indeed republics within present-day Russia – were part of a Soviet empire also remains disputed. Sergei Markedonov, for example, insists that the polyethnic nature of the Soviet state and its leadership – Stalin after all came from one of the so-called Russian 'colonies' – the contiguous nature of the Russian landmass and the lack of a single national-based ideology, mark out the USSR from classical European empires (Markedonov, 2010, p. 10).

The colonial typology nonetheless is strongest in the Caucasus – North and South – and in the five Central Asian states – Kazakhstan, Kyrgyzstan, Tajikistan, Turkmenistan and Uzbekistan – which are potentially – or, currently in the case of Kyrgyzstan, actually – unstable insofar as their stability is shored up, first and foremost, by regimes whose authoritarian nature falls well short of European Union standards of governance. As the examples of Chechnya, South Ossetia and Kyrgyzstan illustrate, ethnic violence, border disputes and repression of separatist, religious or dissident movements are a widespread feature of the region.

Armenia, Azerbaijan, Georgia, Moldova and Ukraine are all – as well as, potentially, Belarus – on a clearer trajectory towards what might be recognised as 'Europeanisation' (Sedelmeier, 2006) than either Russia or the Central Asian states of the former Soviet Union, but all have had, are still experiencing or have the potential for a degree of instability. For example, all four of the 'frozen' conflicts concerning unrecognised states (Abkhazia, Nagorno-Karabakh, South Ossetia and the Transdniester republic) are located in this group and Russia has intervened (in the case of Georgia and the Ukraine) or (in the other four cases) might be predicted to obstruct any further movement towards integration into European institutions. Although the objection clearly is greater vis-à-vis NATO membership, Russia's rejection of the EU's European Neighbourhood Policy, launched in May 2004 (Dangerfield, 2009), exposes a genuine dilemma in the South Caucasus as well as in Belarus, Moldova and Ukraine.

Of course, to all intents and purposes the threat to Russia inherent in this insecurity dilemma passed with the rolling back since August 2008 of the 'colour revolutions' of 2003–05 in Georgia, Ukraine and Kyrgyzstan, all perceived by the Russian authorities to have been facilitated, if not provoked, by the West (Trenin, 2006). In Georgia this was achieved in the August war, the subject of John B. Dunlop's preceding chapter in this volume. In Ukraine it was the signing of the bilateral agreement in April by Medvedev and newly elected Ukrainian President Viktor Yanukovych that extended the Russian lease on its Crimean naval base for twenty-five years, in exchange for a 30 per cent discount on the amount that Ukraine pays for Russian natural gas (Feifer, 2010) and, in Kyrgyzstan, with then President Kurmanbek Bakiyev's threat to close the US airbase at Manas in 2009 (BBC News, 2009). These events, together with the operationalising of a customs' union between Russia, Belarus and Kazakhstan in July 2010 (RIA Novosti, 2010), have all helped to ease Russia's sense of insecurity.

However Russian reaction to the recent Kyrgyz crisis, which had resulted in more than 2000 dead, bore little resemblance to their so-called 'humanitarian' intervention in South Ossetia, causing some Russian observers to question whether China, rather than the West, was the main danger to Russia's 'sphere of privileged interests' in Central Asia.

Russian military analyst Aleksandr Golts, for example, commented in the *Moscow Times* on 22 June 2010 that:

> The conflict in Kyrgyzstan has demonstrated that Russia is incapable of being even a regional leader. Although the Kremlin is obsessed with US interference in the region, their real concern should be

that China will fill the vacuum and become the region's leader. The Chinese are in a much better position to pick up the ball that the Kremlin has dropped in Central Asia. (Golts, 2010)

Journalist Yulia Latynina's (2010) assessment of Moscow's hold on the whole region was characteristically blunt and even more damning:

> The problem is that Kyrgyzstan is only the tip of the iceberg. Ever since the Russians abandoned Kyrgyzstan, all of Central Asia is deteriorating into something akin to what equatorial Africa turned into after the British left.
>
> Kyrgyzstan is the first to go down the drain because it was created as a phantom state by Stalin. It was a land of valleys and mountains and was divided into clans and families along geographical barriers. The Ferghana Valley in the south – the best piece of real estate in the country – was divided between Uzbeks, Tajiks and the Kyrgyz in a way that made the current conflict inevitable.
>
> Kyrgyzstan is already a failed state, but other Central Asian nations are catching up. There is Turkmenistan, which was home to Saparmurat Niyazov – or Turkmenbashi ('the leader of all Turkmen') – the first post-Soviet president who built himself a gold statue that used to revolve 360 degrees every 24 hours so that it always faced the sun. It seems that Niyazov's personal physician, Gurbanguly Berdymukhammedov, and the country's chief of security conspired to unseat Turkmenbashi, but Niyazov conveniently died. The physician proceeded to become the new leader and sent the chief of security to prison.
>
> In addition, there is Uzbekistan, a mix of stiff Communist has-beens and holdovers from Central Asian feudalism. The Turkmen scenario can easily be repeated in Uzbekistan – and Uzbekistan is soaked in Islamic fundamentalism like a rag in gasoline. (Latynina, 2010)

Clearly the current situation in Central Asia, especially in Kyrgyzstan, provides sufficient evidence of unresolved questions generating potential dangers that might lead to a clash of Western, Russian, and possibly Chinese, interests. Fyodor Lukyanov identified Kyrgyzstan as 'the first post-Soviet state to be almost officially described as a "failed state"', whilst recognising that Western inaction had played a generally positive role in US–Russian relations (Lukyanov, 2010b).

If one applies, as Sørenson does, Isaiah Berlin's concepts of 'negative liberty' as 'autonomy, self-determination, freedom of choice, ability to act unobstructed by others' and 'positive liberty' as 'being your own master […] not held down by disease, poverty, ignorance or tyranny' (Sørenson, 2007, p. 369), one might recognise that the states of Russia's Near Abroad generally speaking enjoy 'negative liberty' but deny many of their subjects 'positive liberty'. Insofar as the Western liberal model purports to optimise the chances of 'positive liberty' for all, then its spread to Russia's Near Abroad might be seen to be a natural progression and a good thing not only for the inhabitants of this region but also for the international community as a whole.

That this might not be regarded as so either by the Russian leadership or by political and business elites in those states that benefit from 'negative liberty' is equally clear. This is the substance of the dilemma, which is particularly acute for those states in the Near Abroad that have set their course of development on a 'European' trajectory.

Sørenson might recognise this as a 'value dilemma' for the West, in that as liberals we are faced with the choice of intervening in states to impose 'positive freedom' – as in Kosovo in 1999 – (NATO, 1999), what he calls the 'Liberalism of Imposition' or prioritise the concept of territorial integrity and leave states to determine their own 'negative liberty' – as with the Russians in Chechnya in 1994–96 and 1999–2006 – (Russell, 2007), termed the 'Liberalism of Restraint' (Sørenson, 2007, p. 367).

The paradox is that the Russian leadership, which rejects the 'values' basis of Western foreign policy, clearly used the precedent of NATO intervention in Kosovo to justify their own incursion into South Ossetia (Schaeffer, 2009). Given the inconsistency of NATO in applying the 'Liberalism of Imposition', revealed anew in the 'Arab Spring' of 2011, there is a temptation to suggest that it is only recognised when, as in the case of Kosovo, it was considered to be in the interests of the alliance, or its driving force, the US, so to do. This however misses the important role of the rule of law, which continues to be observed in the main in Western states,[5] which is by no means always the case in countries such as Russia, where there remains a large element of non-constitutional 'prerogative' power exercised by political elites. The projection of 'soft' and 'smart' power that forms an intrinsic part of Western democracy promotion does carry a certain appeal within Russia, let alone within the Near Abroad.

Sørenson quotes the 'fundamental' principles embodied in the Millennium Declaration endorsed by more than 150 states at the UN General Assembly in 2000, including Freedom, Equality, Solidarity, Tolerance, Respect for Nature and Shared Responsibility, admitting that 'there is a good deal of rhetoric behind this apparent consensus' (Sørenson, 2007, pp. 366–7).[6]

The two factors that in my opinion determine the level of acceptability of the spread of good governance are: (a) if Russia, or any of its neighbours in the Near Abroad, feels that its vital interests are being sacrificed on the altar of liberal democracy, then any attempt to spread Western values will be met with resistance; and (b) the more that Western countries live up to their international obligations and undertakings, the less cynicism there will be in Russia and the Near Abroad that the West is guilty of employing double standards.

Conclusion

The signs are that a perceptible warming has occurred in Russia's relations with the West since the Obama–Medvedev 'reset' strategy began to bear its first fruits in the course of 2010. With the US admission, finally, that it is in its own interests to 'read Russia right' (Trenin, 2005) and take into account Russia's vital interests, a much more sensitive foreign policy has reduced the deep-seated if exaggerated fears of the Russian leadership over US intentions in what had hitherto been portrayed as a unipolar world.

By the same token, the realisation that the US cannot afford, financially or politically, to be the world's policeman, has led to a downgrading of the values-led rhetoric of the Bush era and a promotion of the pragmatic interests of the US and her allies. This has suited such European partners as France, Germany and Italy, who have long found accommodation with Russia easier than has been the case with the Anglo-Saxon approach favoured by the United States and the United Kingdom.

Both of these factors have reduced perceptibly the pressure produced by mutually perceived 'threats' emanating from the NATO–Russia confrontation both in Eastern Europe and the 'Near Abroad'. However, although the threats have been reduced, the dangers (potential threats) of policy clashes between the West and Russia in both areas remain to be addressed. The heightened anxiety at present of the Baltic states, in particular, over any diminution in the US's commitment to upholding their liberty is understandable, although a greater degree of diplomatic sensitivity – after all, the cyber-attack was preceded by widespread anger in Russia over the perceived lack of respect for a monument to the Soviet 'liberators' of Estonia in Tallinn – might serve to emphasise that political solidarity based on shared interests and values can be as effective for such issues as military support.

In the Near Abroad, the outcomes in Georgia and Ukraine have gone a long way towards dampening Russian fears of further NATO encroachment. It no longer seems credible that the West might resort to force in order to compete for control over this region. The danger here depends to some extent on a Russian recognition that it can have no veto on the aspirations of its neighbours and that good governance on its borders increases rather than decreases its security. The fly in this ointment at present is the deep misgiving over the speed and scope of EU enlargement and the negative impact that this has had on the concept of European integration.

The rise of the BRICS (Brazil, Russia, India, China and, since 2011, South Africa), the economic success of bureaucratic corporate capitalism in South East Asian countries and even the increasingly independent path being adopted by Turkey appear to offer alternative templates for development to the Euro-Atlantic model. Although the South Caucasian states, Belarus, Moldova and Ukraine, might well still see their futures in 'Europeanisation', there is no certainty that those in Central Asia would not prefer to follow the Shanghai Cooperation Organisation (SCO) route. In Russia the rise in popularity in the first decade of the twentieth-first century of Aleksandr Dugin's neo-Eurasianism is seen as a direct challenge to the global dominance of Western liberal democracy (Dugin, 2004).

Even before the world economic crisis it had become apparent that the liberal undertakings proclaimed in the UN's Millennium Declaration could barely be upheld by most liberal democracies, let alone by developing and modernising countries unless it was clearly in their interests so to do. Such undertakings will only become universal therefore when it is perceived to be in the interests of all, or at least the overwhelming majority of signatories, to respect them. The pragmatism of the 'liberalism of restraint' presently appears to outweigh the value-laden 'liberalism of imposition', even if this means that illiberal regimes, in practice, can treat their own people with little regard to their international commitments confident in their impunity against sanctions by the international community, as the official Chinese reaction to the award of the 2010 Nobel Peace Prize to Liu Xiaobo exemplifies (BBC News, 2010b).

What is certain however is that a similar degree of recognition is required by the West that Russian security interests must at least be considered and understood in order to build the mutual trust necessary to transform this geopolitically vital contested area from a landscape of the hitherto dangerous 'zero-sum' confrontation into the 'win-win' scenario that would represent a far more rational outcome for all concerned parties. This should not deter those in the West who genuinely believe that liberal democracy promises a more efficient, effective and prosperous future for those in the Near Abroad from defending this viewpoint with both vigour and rigour.

Notes

The author acknowledges the financial assistance of the British Academy for providing a bursary enabling him to attend the 2009 International Studies Association (ISA) Conference in New York where this project took shape.

1. Forcefully articulated by President Putin in his address to the 43rd Munich Conference on Security Policy in February 2007 (Putin, 2007).
2. See, for example, an article dating from 1992 by Leon T. Hadar.
3. See his chapter, 'The cold peace: making sense of Russia's relationship with the West', in Roger E. Kanet and Maria Raquel Freire (eds), *Russia and European Security* (Dordrecht: Republic of Letters Publishing, 2012, in press).
4. The justification for Russia's invasion of Georgia was to protect Russian citizens in South Ossetia, its own 'peacekeepers' and those inhabitants of the region who had taken up the Russian offer of citizenship prior to the conflict.
5. Of course, there are those who claim that since 9/11, democracy in the West has become more formal than real, see Golub (2006).
6. For the Millennium Declaration, see UNGA, 2000.

References

Arbatov, Aleksei and Sergei Oznobishchev (2010) 'Pushki – pod kontrolem, kompromiss dostignut' (Field guns – under control, compromise reached), *Nezavisimoe voennoe obozrenie*, 9 July.

Averre, Derek (2009) 'Competing rationalities: Russia, the EU and the "shared neighbourhood"', *Europe–Asia Studies*, vol. 61, no. 10, pp. 1689–713.

Bartholomees, Jr, J. Boone (2010) 'The issue of attrition', *Parameters*, vol. 40, no. 1, pp. 5–19.

Bayer, Alexei (2010) 'Spying is a laughing matter', *Moscow Times*, 12 July.

BBC News (2009) 'Kyrgyzstan moves to shut US base', 4 February, available at: http://news.bbc.co.uk/1/hi/world/asia-pacific/7868586.stm (accessed 16 July 2010).

BBC News (2010a) 'Russia asks Bulgaria to explain US Missile Shield Plan', 18 February, available at: http://news.bbc.co.uk/1/hi/world/europe/8523124.stm (accessed 16 July 2010).

BBC News (2010b) 'International reaction to Liu Xiaobo Nobel Peace Prize', 8 October, available at: http://www.bbc.co.uk/news/world-europe-11499931 (accessed 20 October 2010).

Bremmer, Ian and Samuel Charap (2006–07) 'The *siloviki* in Putin's Russia: who they are and what they want', *Washington Quarterly*, vol. 30, no. 1, pp. 83–92.

Dangerfield, Martin (2009) 'The contribution of the Visegrad Group to the European Union's "Eastern" policy: rhetoric or realism?', *Europe–Asia Studies*, vol. 61, no. 10, pp. 1735–55.

Dugin, Aleksandr (2004) 'Eurasian idea', 3 August, available at: http://www. evrazia.info/modules.php?name=News&file=print&sids=1984 (accessed 16 July 2010).

Eurasia Daily Monitor (2010) 'Poland detains rebel Chechen envoy as violence continues in the North Caucasus', Jamestown Foundation's *Eurasia Daily Monitor*, vol. 7, no. 167, 17 September, available at: http://www.jamestown. org/programs/edm/single/?tx_ttnews%5Btt_news%5D=36875&tx_ttnews%5B backPid%5D=484&no_cache=1 (accessed 27 September 2010).

Europa – Press Releases (2010) 'EU and Russia launch new partnership for modernisation', 1 June, available at: http://europa.eu/rapid/pressReleases Action.do?reference=IP/10/649&format=HTML&aged=0&language=EN& guiLanguage=en (accessed 16 July 2010).

Fawn, Rick (2009) '"Bashing about rights"? Russia and the "new" EU states on human rights and democracy promotion', *Europe–Asia Studies*, vol. 61, no. 10, pp. 1777–803.

Feifer, Gregory (2010) 'For Yanukovych a fleet-footed dash to repair Russia divide', *RFE/RL Features*, 29 April, available at: http://www.rferl.org/content/ For_Yanukovych_A_Fleet_Footed_Dash_To_Repair_Russia_Divide/2028075. html (accessed 6 July 2010).

Ferrero-Waldner, Benita (2007) 'The European Union and the world: a hard look at soft power', speech at Columbia University, New York, 24 September, available at: http://www.eu-un.europa.eu/articles/en/article_7330_en.htm (accessed 6 July 2010).

Gänzle, Stefan (2009) 'EU governance and the European neighbourhood policy: a framework for analysis', *Europe–Asia Studies*, vol. 61, no. 10, pp. 1715–34.

Golts, Alexander (2010) 'Very little collective security', *Moscow Times*, 22 June 2010, available at: http://www.themoscowtimes.com/opinion/article/very-little-collective-security/408780.html (accessed 16 July 2010).

Golub, Philip S. (2006) 'The will to undemocratic power', *Le Monde Diplomatique* (English edn), no. 9, available at: http://www.eurozine.com/articles/2006-09-27-golub-en.html (accessed 16 July 2010).

Hadar, Leon T. (1992) 'The Green Peril: creating the Islamic fundamentalist threat', *Cato Policy Analysis*, no. 117, 27 August, available at: http://www.cato. org/pubs/pas/pa-177.html (accessed 6 July 2010).

Harding, Luke and Ian Traynor (2009) 'Obama abandons Missile Defence Shield in Europe', *Guardian*, 17 September.

Haukkala, Hiski (2009) 'Lost in translation? Why the EU has failed to influence Russia's development', *Europe–Asia Studies*, vol. 61, no. 10, pp. 1757–75.

Hauner, Milan (1992) *What is Asia to Us? Russia's Asian Heartland Yesterday and Today* (London: Routledge).

Hearst, David (2010) '"Russian spies" bungle was epic', *Guardian*, 29 June.

Howard, Roger (2010) 'Russia's new front line', *Survival*, vol. 52, no. 2, pp. 141–56.

Iliev, Nick (2010) 'Top Russian general bids to deploy anti-ICBM missiles in Bulgaria and Romania', *Sofia Echo*, 2 June.

Jones, Gareth (2010) 'Analysis: Polish–Russian thaw seen safe despite crash concerns', Reuters, 11 October, reproduced in *Johnson's Russia List*, JRL 2010, no. 191, 12 October, available at: http://www.reuters.com/article2010/10/11/ us-poland-russia-idUKTRE69A2IZ20101011 (accessed 12 October 2010).

Khramchikhin, Aleksandr (2010) 'Amerikanskaya PROpaganda' (author's note: PRO is the Cyrillic rendition of ABM (anti-ballistic missile)), *Izvestiya*, 8 July.

Krauthammer, Charles (1990–91) 'The unipolar moment', *Foreign Affairs*, vol. 70, no. 1, pp. 22–33.

Latynina, Yulia (2010) 'An imitation empire', *Moscow Times*, 30 June.

Lo, Bobo (2009) 'Medvedev and the new European security architecture', *Central European Reform Policy Brief*, July, available at, http://www.cer.org.uk/pdf/pbrief_medvedev_july09.pdf (accessed 6 July 2010).

Lucas, Edward (2008) *The New Cold War: How the Kremlin Menaces both Russia and the West* (London: Bloomsbury).

Lucas, Edward (2010) 'Russia's spooks: they've never gone away', *Daily Telegraph*, 3 July.

Lukyanov, Fyodor (2010a) 'Russia's zone of responsibility', *Russia in Global Affairs*, 10 July.

Lukyanov, Fyodor (2010b) 'Top 10 events shaping Russia's foreign policy', *Moscow Times*, 20 July.

Markedonov, Sergei (2010) *Turbulentnaya Evraziya* (Turbulent Eurasia) (Moscow: Academia).

McFaul, Michael (2010) 'Democracy and economic modernization: the causal relationship', *Yaroslavl Forum Working Paper*, 9–10 September, reproduced in *Johnson's Russia List*, JRL 2010, no. 182, 29 September, available at: http://www.cdi.org/Russia/johnson/default.cfm (accessed 30 September 2010).

Michael, Alex (2010) 'Cyber probing: the politicisation of virtual attack', Defence Academy of the United Kingdom, *Special Series*, 10/12, September, pp. 1–24.

Military Doctrine of the Russian Federation Approved by Edict of the President of the Russian Federation (2010) 5 February, available at: http://text.document.kremlin.ru/SESSION/PILOT/main.htm (accessed 16 July 2010).

North Atlantic Treaty Organization (NATO) (1999) 'NATO's role in relation to the conflict in Kosovo', *NATO and Kosovo: Historical Review*, 16 July, available at: http://www.nato.int/kosovo/history.htm (accessed 15 December 2010).

'Opros: Vse bol'she rossiyan zayavlyaet ob uluchshenii otnosheniy RF i SShA' (Poll: more Russians say relations between the Russian Federation and USA are improving) (2010) *Nezavisimaya gazeta*, 7 September, available at: http://www.ng.ru/politics/2010-07-09/2_opros.html (accessed 23 December 2010).

Putin, Vladimir (2004) 'Excerpts from Putin's Address', BBC News, 4 September, available at: http://news.bbc.co.uk/1/hi/world/europe/3627878.stm (accessed 6 July 2010).

Putin, Vladimir (2007) Address to the 43rd Munich Conference on Security Policy in February 2007, available at: http://www.securityconference.de/archive/konferenzen/rede.php?menu_2007=&menu_konferenzen=&sprache=en&id=179& (accessed 23 December 2010).

RIA Novosti (2010) 'Customs Union of Russia, Belarus, Kazakhstan to become fully operational', 6 July, available at: http://en.rian.ru/world/20100706/159703796.html (accessed 16 July 2010).

Russell, John (2007) *Chechnya – Russia's 'War on Terror'* (Abingdon: Routledge).

Russia Profile Weekly Experts Panel (2008) 'Is Russia turning unilateralist?', *Russia Profile*, 12 September, available at: http://www.russiaprofile.org/page.php?pageid=Experts%27+Panel&articleid=a1221237697 (accessed 16 July 2010).

Sakwa, Richard (2012, in press) 'The cold peace: making sense of Russia's relationship with the West', in Roger E. Kanet and Maria Raquel Freire (eds), *Russia and European Security* (Dordrecht: Republic of Letters Publishing).

Schaeffer, Sebastian (2009) 'The Kosovo precedent – directly applicable to Abkhazia and South Ossetia', *Caucasian Review of International Affairs*, vol. 3, no. 1, pp. 108–10, available at: http://cria-online.org/6_11.html (accessed 16 July 2010).

Sedelmeier, Ulrich (2006) 'Europeanisation in new member and candidate states', *Living Reviews in European Governance*, available at: http://www.livingreviews.org/lreg-2006-3 (accessed 16 July 2010).

Slocombe, Walter B. (2008) 'Europe, Russia and American missile defence', *Survival*, vol. 50, no. 2, pp. 19–24.

Socor, Vladimir (2008) 'Germany, Russia bypassing others with Nord Stream Project', Jamestown Foundation's *Eurasia Daily Monitor*, vol. 5, no. 109, 9 June, available at: http://www.jamestown.org/single/?no_cache=1&tx_ttnews%5Btt_news%5D=33702 (accessed 16 July 2010).

Sørenson, Georg (2007) 'After the security dilemma: the challenges of insecurity in weak states and the dilemma of liberal values', *Security Dialogue*, vol. 38, no. 3, pp. 357–78.

The Tocqueville Connection (2010) 'France's warship plan raises Baltic hackles', 2 March, available at: http://www.ttc.org/20100302161324_SSV29.htm (accessed 6 July 2010).

Tikk, Eneken et al. (2008) 'Georgian cyber attacks: legal lessons identified', *Analysis Document*, Cooperative Cyber Defence Centre of Excellence, Tallinn, Estonia, November, pp. 1–45, available at: http://www.carlisle.army.mil/DIME/documents/Georgia%201%200.htm (accessed 6 July 2010).

Traynor, Ian (2007) 'Russia accused of unleashing cyber war to disable Estonia', *Guardian*, 27 May.

Trenin, Dmitri (2005) 'Reading Russia right', *Carnegie Endowment Policy Brief*, October, available at: http://carnegieendowment.org/files/pb42.trenin.FINAL.pdf (accessed 16 July 2010).

Trenin, Dmitri (2006) 'Russia leaves the West', *Foreign Affairs*, vol. 85, no. 4, pp. 87–96.

Ullman, Harlan K. and James P. Wade (1996) *Shock and Awe: Achieving Rapid Dominance* (Washington, DC: National Defense University), available at: http://www.dodccrp.org/files/Ullman_Shock.pdf (accessed 6 July 2010).

United Nations General Assembly (UNGA) (2000) Resolutions, 55th Session, A/RES/55/2, 18 September, available at: http://unstats.un.org/unsd/mdg/Resources/Static/Products/GAResolutions/55_2/a_res55_2e.pdf (accessed 16 July 2010).

US Department of State (2010) 'New Strategic Arms Reduction Treaty (New START)', 8 April, available at: http://www.state.gov/t/vci/trty/126118.htm (accessed 16 July 2010).

Weinstein, Jeremy, John Porter and Stuart Eizenstat (2004) *On the Brink: Weak States and US National Security* (Washington, DC: Center for Global Development).

Weitz, Richard (2010) 'Realities: Russia, NATO and missile defence', *Survival*, vol. 52, no. 4, pp. 99–120.

6
Russia's European Security Treaty and the Kyrgyz Crisis

Graeme P. Herd

Introduction

Russia's European Security Treaty (EST) proposal has been characterised as 'Moscow's first attempt in 20 years to formulate a coherent foreign-policy vision' (Lukyanov, 2009, p. 94). It was advanced at the height of an official state narrative that portrayed Russia as a 'sovereign democracy', excluded and marginalised from strategic decision-making. The world was marked by a Unites States-dominated 'unipolar decision-making process' and a 'bloc', or more specifically a 'NATO-centric approach' within Europe predominated and created imbalances and tensions and has 'shown its weakness' (Medvedev, 2008). Through 2009 and 2010, Russia's narrative as elaborated by a very active Foreign Minister Sergei Lavrov has evolved to focus more on restoration and the necessity of 'conservative' or 'technological modernisation' of Russia to consolidate its reemergence as a centre of global power in a multipolar, polycentric and therefore stable world order.

In this period Russia has shepherded its EST through various conferences and meetings. While declaratory rhetoric and aspiration marked the first eighteen months of the EST's rollout, the bare-bones concept was given flesh in a draft text elaborated in November 2009 (Medvedev, 2009). For many analysts, this text appeared to be designed to downgrade or replace the Organization for Security and Co-operation in Europe (OSCE). However Russian Foreign Minister Sergei Lavrov characterised the hosting of the OSCE Summit (Astana, 1–3 December 2010) as follows:

> Recall that the OSCE came out of hibernation only after Russian President Dmitry Medvedev had put forward his initiative for

a European Security Treaty. It shook the OSCE, and set the task of creating a single and indivisible security space in which each state would feel secure, regardless of participation in military–political alliances. (RIA Novosti, 2010b)

In July 2010, President Medvedev offered an assessment of the EST and its reception and progress:

I am pleased to note that although this initiative received quite a chilly, not to say hostile, response at the outset, it has now become subject of lively discussions, and not only with our traditional partners such as Germany, France and Italy but with the majority of participants of the Euro-Atlantic security system. Therefore, we must take this issue further. (Medvedev, 2010)

Aleksandr Grushko, the Russian Deputy Foreign Minister, was even more upbeat in his assessment:

As for the European security treaty, a draft has been sent to all the heads of state of the Euro-Atlantic region. They include not only European states, but also Central Asian countries, the USA and Canada. We continue to receive replies. Approximately 20 countries have replied at the top level, their reaction is unequivocally positive. (Interfax News Agency, 2010a; RIA Novosti, 2010a)

Both the German and Russian Foreign Ministers issued a joint statement that reinforced this picture of progress:

We intend to build on the European continent, a space of stability and security without dividing lines and demarcations. A significant contribution to launching the dialogue on this topic has been made by the Russian initiative for a European Security Treaty. Our common position is that the security of one state cannot be achieved at another's expense. On the contrary, it is determined by the highest possible degree of security for your neighbour. Therefore, we intend to jointly conduct a broad dialogue on European security, to delve deeper into the different points of view on this matter and to overcome contradictions. This is especially true of confidence-building measures, disarmament and arms control initiatives and conflict resolution. (Lavrov and Westerwelle, 2010)

The EST should have been dead on arrival: its rollout in June 2008 was eclipsed by the August Russo-Georgian conflict. Rather than delegitimising the treaty proposal, Russia argued that this conflict merely reinforced its central logic and so its necessity. The fact that the conflict took place, Russia argued, demonstrated existing institutional structures and mechanisms – all of which had their genesis in the Cold War period – were ill-suited to address root causes of societal crises in the twenty-first century. During the conflict and in its immediate aftermath, talk of a 'New Cold War' underscored the notion that the Cold War remains unfinished business.[1] NATO's continued geopolitical expansion into the grey zone – the countries in between, Georgia, Ukraine, Moldova and Belarus – is stated by Russia and reiterated by some Collective Security Treaty Organisation (CSTO) states as further evidence, but this understanding is not shared throughout Europe or the US.

The perception of NATO within NATO, for example, is increasingly one of weakness – a central debate is on how to avoid the very real possibility that strategic withdrawal from Afghanistan underscores strategic failure is underway – rather than vibrant discussions focused on how NATO might better exercise balance of power politics in the Black Sea region or project power through Eurasian space. In June 2011, US Defence Secretary Robert Gates, for example, warned that NATO could face 'a dim if not dismal' future if military spending shortages and national caveats were not addressed, given that his generation's 'emotional and historical attachment to NATO' is 'aging out' (Burns and Butler, 2011) The Russian argument that existing institutional structures and mechanisms do not work – as evidenced by the NATO–Kosovo conflict of 1999 and Russia–Georgia conflict of 2008 – but would if only there were a legally binding basis to underpin cooperation is also contested.

Many EU and NATO states argue that these two conflicts point to the need to build on and make better use of the framework of existing tried and tested institutions, structures and mechanisms – including the OSCE, the NATO–Russia Council and the Euro-Atlantic Partnership Council – by working to modify, reform and strengthen them, rather than replace them with an all-encompassing legally binding treaty. As Robert Blake, US Assistant Secretary of State for South and Central Asian Affairs noted: 'We see no need for new treaties in Europe in addition to the existing security architecture. We feel that we already have a very good system and mechanisms' (Makedonov, 2010).

The attribution of multiple motives: 'Heads I win; tails you lose?'

Russia has argued that in terms of end goals and outcomes, it wants a legally binding treaty signed by all states. According to one proponent:

> The very idea of reviving the intergovernmental dialogue on security in Europe reflects the legal universalism of Russian politics that has been characteristic of this country throughout almost all of its history since Peter the Great and that is typical of Medvedev's political style. (Mezhuyev, 2009, p. 103)

A legally binding treaty removes ambiguity, builds trust and confidence and lessens threat perception and misperception; the argument being that a treaty would make explicit expectations and so increase predictability in international relations. This allows Russia, Europe and the US finally to leave behind Cold War mindsets and collectively address the real and shared threats to global stability.[2] This latter point, the focus on a cooperative US–EU–Russian 'condominium' or 'triangular construction' as the objective 'basis for political cooperation in the Euro-Atlantic region' serves a larger purposes – it could, in the words of Sergei Lavrov, 'become a major element of the new coordinate system on the world's geopolitical map and work to strengthen the position of the whole European civilisation in an increasingly competitive world' (Lavrov, 2010b).

However since 2008, a period marked by evolving narratives concerning Russia's role in the world and regime continuity (in the shape of the Medvedev–Putin tandem), virtually all analysis and assessments of the proposed EST highlight the issue of hidden agendas and purposes, declared and undeclared outcomes have been raised, if only by some to be dismissed as a non-issue (Fedorov, 2009; Lo, 2009; Karaganov, 2009; Monaghan, 2008). This contention could mask a number of factors, including: a residual distrust of Russia's resurgence, on occasion spilling over into outright Russophobia; a predilection for conspiracy theory-based explanations that is an enduring characteristic of post-Soviet security politics; a response to the gap between the rhetoric of June 2008 and the reality of August 2008; and an attempt to account for a draft treaty document published in November 2009 that lacks substance, is vague, inconsistent and contradictory (Kuhn, 2010). This latter point rests on the notion that collective self-regulation occurs when: 'a group of states attempts to reduce security threats by agreeing to collectively punish any member states that violate the systems rules' (Downs, 1994, p. 18).

It follows that for collective security systems to function effectively: all states, especially the powerful, sign a legally binding treaty – there must be a universality of membership; all states must agree which state in any given conflict is the aggressor, and all states must be both able and willing actively to oppose aggression and the aggressor, resorting to the threat of collective action against an aggressor as the last resort. There must be a high degree of commitment and automaticity within the system if there is to be a reliable promise of redress to potential victims of aggression. Does the draft treaty give confidence that these preconditions are in place?

'Heads I win'

If the treaty is signed, the hidden agenda argument runs, a legally binding treaty results in a freezing of the status quo – an outcome that is to Russia's advantage given the reality of current power differentials. If the EST were to come into force and each state rigorously monitored the behaviour of other states, looking to see whether current or future actions of others could affect their own security even in an unintended way, then what might be the outcome? Let us examine the draft treaty articles with this question in mind.

Article 1 of the draft treaty promotes the principle of 'indivisible, equal and undiminished security'. To that end, 'Any security measures taken by a Party to the Treaty individually or together with other Parties, including in the framework of any international organisation, military alliance or coalition, shall be implemented with due regard to security interests of all other Parties.' The 1975 Helsinki Accords, the 1990 Charter of Paris for a New Europe and the 1999 Charter for European Security all stipulate that states are free to choose which alliances they join – a stipulation that in the EST is 'ominously omitted' (Onyszkiewicz, 2010), though in its preamble it suggests that it is 'guided by the principles' embodied in these treaties. Dmitri Trenin notes that the EST 'if enacted, would de facto abolish other treaties, including the Washington one' (Trenin, 2009, p. 2). The assumptions of solidarity and shared responsibility can be questioned – might states rather act according to their own immediate interests and priorities, privileging this above the longer-term interests of the preservation of peace in the system? Adam Roberts remarked that collective action is most likely against 'especially glaring aggressive actions by military powers of the second rank' (Roberts, 1993, p. 289). Reality is rarely as accommodating.

Article 2 stipulates that the use of state territory 'with the purpose of preparing or carrying out an armed attack against any other Party or Parties to the Treaty or any other actions affecting significantly the security of any other Party or Parties to the Treaty' should not take place. To that end, Article 3 allows any signatory to request of another, 'information on any significant legislative, administrative or organisational measures taken by that other Party, which, in the opinion of the Requesting Party, might affect its security'. Who decides whether a certain activity significantly threatens or affects the security of other parties? The state(s) that plan(s) to carry out the activity or the state(s) that feel(s) under threat? If Ukraine, for example, had refused to renegotiate the status of Russia's Black Sea Fleet so that it can remain *in situ* after 2017, could Russia not have claimed that this would have significantly threatened its security? Definitional clarity is lacking: 'preparing for armed attack' is itself a contested notion, a matter of opinion, subjective and context-specific. Could not a state claim that it is mobilising for self-defence when it is in fact preparing for armed attack? Can cyber-attacks be counted as an armed attack? Is this dependent on the objects of the attack and the consequences of the impact (for example, disabling critical infrastructure, such as an air defence network)? Does Article 3 invalidate the possession of an offensive capability?

Article 4 stipulates that, in order 'to settle differences or disputes that might arise between the Parties in connection with its interpretation or application', consultations and conferences between the parties can take place (reiterated in Article 8). Article 5 (para 3) notes that: 'Any Party not invited to take part in the consultations shall be entitled to participate on its own initiative.' Article 6 (para 3) stipulates that: 'The Conference of the Parties shall be effective if it is attended by at least two-thirds of the Parties to the Treaty. Decisions of the Conference shall be taken by consensus and shall be binding.' Thus any single participating state on any issue would have veto rights over the decision of the others. Article 7 notes that every Party has the right of self-defence under UN Charter Article 51, but what are states, their coalitions or alliances allowed to do if the actors of the 'common security space' cannot agree on collective measures? Article 8 outlines the decision-making mechanism that would apply and adjudication procedures. For a conference to be held, two-thirds of the signatories to the treaty need to be present, four-fifths for an Extraordinary Conference, with binding decisions 'taken by unanimous vote'. In other words, a single veto determines whether enforcement takes place.

Liberal institutionalist theory argues that decision-making in intergovernmental fora, such as the one outlined in Article 4, allows for joint resolutions that raise the reputational costs of the failure to act and conference diplomacy facilitates bargaining and provides political cover – policy-makers feel more obliged to adopt policies that they could defend internationally. But is the decision-making mechanism in this case fit for the purpose? How exactly do parties to the treaty react, mobilise and coordinate ad hoc responses? Questions of burden sharing, authority, coordination of ad hoc responses remain unaddressed. The draft does not outline how defectors from the collective security system could be punished. If by sanctions, could these be applied without violating the norm of non-intervention in a state's domestic affairs? What are the tools in the toolbox – mediation, conciliation, economic sanctions, preventative or coercive use of force deployments, peacekeeping or peace enforcement? Can we gain timely consensus on when they are to be used, how they are to be sequenced/combined, when escalated then de-escalated?

Given these operational ambiguities, how would parties that sign such a treaty avoid collective inactivity? If states are determined to instrumentalise the treaty then it is clear how they would be prevented from doing so. Would not strategic paralysis in and between Moscow, Brussels and Washington prevail? If so might then the primary aim of the consensus principle be to freeze the political and territorial status quo in Europe, as changes that reinforce current trends only serve to diminish further Russia's power relative to the West? Evidence to support this contention is found in the implicit logic of the EST; namely, Russia will have the power of veto over all security-related decisions of NATO and the EU, just as it does in the OSCE (Aron, 2010, p. 2; Onyszkiewicz, 2010). Given that 'security' can be widened to include political, economic, environmental and societal as well as military matters, Russia acquires a carte blanche veto power over all strategic decision-making in Euro-Atlantic space. In this reading the EST proposal is primarily a tactical initiative whose main purpose is to demonstrate that a functioning collective security area is unattainable. As well as freezing political and territorial space, the EST has been interpreted as attempting to return Europe to the normative legal world of 1945. The legally binding nature aims to reestablish the primacy of a state-centric system of international law as enshrined by the principles of the 1945 UN Charter, Article 2, which protects sovereign states, and eliminates the advances of international law during the last sixty years by disregarding the principles enshrined in the Helsinki Final Act of 1975 (the rights of peoples to self-determination and individuals to human rights) and the UN General Assembly (UNGA) Resolution 2625 (Declaration on Principles) (Dunay and Herd, 2009), which qualify and balance sovereignty and accept that European state borders should not be absolute, fixed and inviolable under any and all circumstances.

'Tails you lose'

If the EST fails to garner support, Russia will gain the freedom and additional legitimacy to build its own 'sphere of privileged interest' even more overtly, consolidate and institutionalise its control over post-Soviet space. This contention is centred in a paradox: failure by key Western Euro-Atlantic states to ratify a legally binding treaty represents a successful outcome for Russia and its friends and allies. Russia is able to argue that in an open and transparent manner it advanced an alternative to the status quo in multiple international forums, repeatedly and at the highest levels. Its proposal was rejected, primarily by EU and NATO member states. These states rejected it as the status quo best upholds their state interests. To avoid a double standard, Russia will now look to see how best it can preserve and secure its own interests. In this sense, apparent failure to achieve the stated primary intended outcome cloaks strategic success – the achievement of the undeclared real purpose of the proposal – the consolidation and institutionalisation of Russian influence in post-Soviet space: 'All these models have had a common aim: The European order which Russia desires should, on the one hand, not be antagonistic or discriminatory and, on the other hand, potentially replace NATO or make it superfluous' (Mutzenich, 2010, p. 67).

This outcome would then result in a redivision of Europe and the long-term coexistence of two groups of states operating on the basis of partly different principles: in the politico-military sphere this can be understood as market-authoritarian or neutral non-NATO and market-democratic NATO. In the process, the solidarity of Western space – particularly of the NATO alliance – will have been undermined and the EST 'divide and conquer' process will have been proven effective.[3] This would especially be a concern if a minority of NATO states demonstrate a willingness to sign the treaty proposal, while a majority oppose it.

Kyrgyzstan: the challenge of fragile states and regional crises

Given that the Kyrgyz crisis of April and June 2010 is the latest catastrophic event to have disrupted Euro-Atlantic space, it is worth examining the crisis in light of the logic, principles and rationale of the EST. The Kyrgyz crisis shares and exemplifies many of the challenges, obstacles and dilemmas generated by complex emergencies. It embodies the nature of wars amongst peoples rather than between states, conflict generated by state failure rather than interstate rivalry, catastrophes of which their second and third order cascading transborder and international effects can be worse than the first order, and in which few strategic blueprints exist to provide post-conflict management roadmaps, let alone 'security solutions'. In short it captures one type of strategic threat identified by the EU Security Strategy of 2003, US National Security Strategy (NSS) of 2002, 2006 and 2010, and Russia's NSS of 2010 – regional crisis and fragile states – and so offers a profound contemporary prism through which to ask: if the EST had been in force, what would have been the result?

On 10 June in the southern Kyrgyz city of Osh violence erupted, spreading to Jalalabad two days later, with reports of armed gangs, interethnic violence, rape and stampedes at border crossings into Uzbekistan. The OSCE and Office of the United Nations High Commissioner for Refugees (UNHCR), as well as Rosa Otunbayeva, the acting interim government Prime Minister and President, stated that over 200 people had been killed, over 2000 wounded, with 400,000 (8 per cent of the Kyrgyz population) displaced – 300,000 internally, 100,000 as refugees into the neighbouring Uzbekistan province of Andizhan. China, India, Turkey, South Korea, Germany and Russia amongst others, airlifted their foreign nationals out of the area of conflict to Bishkek and beyond.

What were the causes of such violence and what are the likely implications? The UNHCR has stated that: 'We have strong indications that this event was not a spontaneous interethnic clash, we have some indications that it was to some degree orchestrated, targeted and well planned' (Agence France-Presse, 2010a). A report by the OSCE Minorities High Commissioner noted 'attempts at ethnic cleansing' (Deutsche Presse-Agentur, 2010). Latent interethnic animosity can be understood as the trigger for the civil conflict in the south and as the means by which violence was instrumentalised by Bakiyev clan leaders, behind-the-scenes power brokers, former advisers and security service loyalists and organised crime figures, to serve other ends. (Melvin, 2011; Human Rights Watch, 2011).

According to the Kyrgyzstan's 2009 Census Report, 'the Kyrgyz share in the total population has increased from 64,9% in 1999 to 70,9% in 2009. The share of Uzbeks living in the country, in the total population has made up 14,3%, Russians – 7,8%' (National Statistical Committee, 2009, p. 18). Although ethnic Uzbeks only constitute a fraction of the total population, they form a majority in some southern provinces. These communities had historically coexisted and cooperated, ethnic intermarriage was high, Osh and Jalalabad residents identified themselves more by city residence than ethnicity and many were bi- or trilingual – Kyrgyz, Uzbek and Russian-speaking. Nevertheless ethno-nationalist tendencies under the Bakiyev regime resulted in a gradual 'Kyrgyzisation' of local government functions (school directors, hospital administrators, local government officers). Uzbeks dominated economic structures. In addition to social stratification, the global financial crisis resulted in a reduction in remittance money and workers returning to the region from Russia, placing greater pressures on infrastructure and provisions.

Violence created a power vacuum and this served two ends. First, it provided the means by which the Bakiyev clan could reassert its control over the extremely lucrative drug trade flows in the south. Osh and Jalalabad are major drug transit hubs where heroin is repackaged before being exported by plane, train or land. The large and heterogeneous Bakiyev clan ('eight brothers and the eight brothers each with eight sons') was heavily implicated in drug trafficking. According to informed media sources: 'After Kurmanbek Bakiyev came to power, all drug lords were killed, and (his elder brother) Zhanybek Bakiyev consolidated most of the drug trafficking in his hands' (Leonard, 2010; Weir, 2010). President Bakiyev himself disbanded the relatively successful Drug Control Agency (part-funded by the UN and US) in October 2009, placing drugs policing under the Interior Ministry. The US State Department characterises this move as a 'significant blow to regional counternarcotics efforts' (Leonard, 2010).

Second, violence served a political objective – namely to demonstrate that the interim government was not in control of the situation, and would have to postpone or cancel the planned referendum of 27 June to adopt a new Constitution underpinning a parliamentary rather than presidential republic. In May 2010, an unedited and unauthenticated 40-minute audio recording played on national TV (KTR), capturing an alleged conversation between Maxim and Janysh Bakiyev, stating the need to recruit 500 men to organise and ferment chaos – 'We need to find 500 bastards' (AKIpress News Agency, 2010; Meo and Orange, 2010, p. 30). Pierre Morel, the EU Special Representative for the region, points his finger at a combination of Bakiyev clan members and loyalists who made a 'concerted effort' to provoke the clashes in a bid to regain power (Radio Free Europe, 2010a). The political analyst Mars Sariev unpicks the nature of this grouping in greater detail, noting that the violence boosted the emergence of a nascent political opposition to the interim government. This opposition consists of *siloviki* – former military and security generals who held high positions under Bakiyev. Omurbek

Suvanaliev, a former interior minister and current leader of the Ata-Jurt Party based in southern Kyrgyzstan and Miroslav Niyazov, a former military general and current head of the El Armany Party are cited as two prominent examples, and Sariev predicts that: 'As the state falls apart and destabilization continues, I think there could be a seizure of power' (Radio Free Europe, 2010b).

The political weakness of the interim government should not be overlooked, particularly its inability to exert authority over the Interior Ministry and army garrisons in the south, which human rights observers and Rosa Otunbayeva have accused of being complicit in attacks, robberies and violence: 'We have been left with a demoralized police force, stuffed with Bakiyev personnel [...]. We have security forces, many of whom joined one side in this conflict in the south' (Solovyov, 2010, p. 19A; 24.kg website, 2010). The interim government consists of an alliance of three former opposition parties and its authority is commensurate with its ability to take a united stance. Unfortunately the glue that holds this alliance together is opposition to the ousted Bakiyev regime, particularly the former president himself and immediate family members, rather than a clear vision of Kyrgyzstan's future political order.

It was in this context that the constitutional referendum planned for 27 June 2010 went ahead. Rosa Otunbayeva argued that: 'Holding this referendum has become necessary because we must create a legal framework If we allow any delays, this will threaten us with further instability' (Solovyov, 2010; Kyrgyz Television 1, 2010a). It must be held in order to address the Bakiyev legacy of 'corruption, lawlessness and judicial arbitrariness' and 'leave behind the Bakiyev constitution forever, which would again restore the former clannish and mafia-style pyramid of power' (Kyrgyz Television 1, 2010b). Finance Minister Temir Sariev stated that: 'Cancelling the referendum would mean success for those destructive forces. That's why the majority of the population demands the referendum proceed as planned, whatever the difficulties and moral issues involved. The fate of the state and the people is at stake' (Radio Free Europe, 2010b).

The referendum was monitored by a total of 189 international observers, representing more than 30 countries and 18 international organisations (for example, CSTO, the Commonwealth of Independent States (CIS), OSCE, the Shanghai Cooperation Organisation (SCO) and the Office for Democratic Institutions and Human Rights (ODIHR)), plus 30 accredited foreign media outlets. More than 90 per cent voted 'yes', and around 8 per cent voted against it. Some 2.7 million people were eligible to vote, and the turnout was nearly 70 per cent (Shuster, 2010). Despite this, Kamchybek Tashiyev, a prominent politician from southern Kyrgyzstan and a leader of the Ata Zhurt Party and former Emergency Situations minister, predicted that: 'Kyrgyzstan is not yet prepared for the transition to a parliamentary form of government and needs strong presidential power. We are not ready for that even geopolitically,' arguing that 'the leading political forces will not recognize the referendum results' (Interfax News Agency, 2010b). Other Bakiyev loyalists supported this contention. Zaynidin Kurmanov, ex-Speaker of the Jogorku Kenesh (parliament), stated that: 'The holding of an illegitimate referendum, and as a result, the adoption of the illegitimate constitution of a parliamentary republic could result in an escalation of protest demonstrations' (Panfilova, 2010; Lillis, 2010).

Rosa Otunbayeva reportedly invited the CSTO to intervene with peacekeepers on 12 June when the violence was at its height, but then retracted this invitation, so sparking serious debates as to the likelihood of an external intervention force – perhaps a UN-mandated peacekeeping mission and/or third party mediators that would form a political buffer zone. Kimmo Kiljunen, the Special Representative for Central Asia of the OSCE Parliamentary Assembly, raised the notion of an international police operation that would create an 'atmosphere of trust' and enhance stabilisation efforts (Radio Free Europe, 2010a). The crisis presents an opportunity to move beyond zero-sum logic into relationships based on multilateral cooperation, building trust and addressing shared threats collectively.

Such interventions would aim to prevent localised violence from spreading and facilitate humanitarian crisis relief operations. Pierre Morel noted the potential spillover effects: the situation is 'difficult, very difficult, because apart from the future of the country, it puts into question the security and stability of the entire Central Asian region' (Radio Free Europe, 2010a). The potential of such dislocation and dysfunctionality to spill over are high and the consequences could be strategic in nature, including: the disruption of freight rail between Afghanistan and Uzbekistan exacerbating social tensions in Northern Afghanistan; Kyrgyzstan as a Uighur insurgent base, threatening stability in China's neighbouring Xinjiang province; and the consolidation of an economic black hole in southern Kyrgyzstan that dramatically increases drug transit and so HIV/AIDs in Russia/China. The case for an intervention was not without foundation.

However arguments to counter intervention are powerful. Military–political debates centred on the realisation that getting an intervention force into Kyrgyzstan would be easier than getting it out. The complex emergency looked set to present a quagmire and credibility trap that would be expensive, prolonged and more than likely bloody. In a 'war among the peoples' (no borders or uniforms), intervention forces run the risk of being caught in the crossfire and disowned if the provisional government falls, and so perceived of as an occupying force, one that would be caught up in internal power struggles. For Russia a dilemma presented itself: Russian intervention under the cover of the CSTO risked failure; although the CSTO had never yet undertaken a collective security operation, failure to intervene brought into question the CSTO's purpose and capability (in terms of resources, equipment and political will to enact collective security responsibilities through peace-keeping missions). Was the CSTO a Potemkin-like structure, designed to support imperial illusions ('sphere of privileged interest') but unable to withstand realities ('sphere of reluctance')? As Dmitri Trenin notes: 'The most the CSTO proved capable of was a meeting of the Secretaries of the Security Councils of the organization's member states. That is a good thing, but it is clearly not enough' (Trenin, 2010, p. 2). The real dilemma facing Russian interests can be restated: too much violence had a potential to return Bakiyev to power or, worse, the potential for extra-regional spillover; too little unrest and interethnic clashes would fail to delegitimise the emergence of a democratic political movement in Central Asia, and in particular the Otunbayeva government and its determination to hold a referendum on a parliamentary system of government.

What light does the Kyrgyz case study and the issue of intervention shed on the EST? Had a legally binding EST been in place, would this complex emergency have been resolved sooner? If the CSTO was not to intervene, why did the CSTO, on Russia's initiative, initially oppose the intervention of the OSCE, which has just agreed to send a 52-person police mission? One logical path that assumes promotion of the EST as shaping Russian policy choices might run as follows: the CSTO, although legally binding, is a collective defence organisation and is therefore unable to intervene to ameliorate intra-state conflicts as this type of threat was not covered by its mandate; the OSCE, although a collective security organisation, was prevented from intervening because it could not gain consensus given that it was politically rather than legally binding, reinforcing the Russian contention after the Georgian crisis of August 2008 – the OSCE, due to its consensus-based decision-making foundational principle, was ineffective. Russia would like to suggest that only a legally binding consensus-based EST can effectively, efficiently and legitimately address sources of insecurity. In reality an OSCE politically binding consensus-based efficient and effective response de facto undercuts the argument that a legally binding EST is needed – hence the Russian reluctance to agree to its mission. This reluctance can also be explained by Russia's unwillingness to set precedents whereby pan-European collective security organisations can involve themselves in intra-state conflicts, particularly those within Russia's 'sphere of privileged interest' – the EST as currently drafted 'would enshrine the principle of avoiding external force to settle national disputes and so would mean no interference in the problems in the northern Caucasus, including Chechnya' (Onyszkiewicz, 2010). This necessity is implicitly acknowledged by President Medvedev's announcement that the charter documents of the CSTO will be amended in order to create a more effective and efficient organisation with broader powers and 'anti-crisis mechanisms' (Interfax News Agency, 2010c).

The Kyrgyz crisis highlights serious flaws in the EST. The draft treaty text calls for collective self-regulation only in the context of violations of state sovereignty and territorial integrity by other states in the state-centric international system. Non-state actors, whether they are terrorist groups, organised criminals or political extremists, as well as ethnic violence, or a combination thereof, involved in intra-state conflict with spillover potential to other states and societies within the potential collective security regime, are not addressed by the draft treaty text. This is all the more surprising as containment of the potential consequences of such intra-state conflict cannot be guaranteed even within the collective security regime – that is, from Vancouver to Vladivostok. The Kyrgyz example suggests that Afghanistan in South Asia and China in East Asia could have had their sovereignty and territorial integrity violated had this complex emergency spiralled out of control. In a sense the EST is touchingly nostalgic for a lost era of interstate warfare, absolute sovereignty and centralised elite decision-making structures. It unconsciously betrays an almost Brezhnevian sympathy for strategic stagnation and status quo in a contemporary context in which the structural and systemic root cause of instability tend to be increasingly non-state based and solutions lie in human security and development agendas that are targeted at individuals, societies and regions. In cases where groups have a distinct identity and region, are subject to systematic discrimination and the central regime rejects reasonable proposals for minority rights and no peaceful alternatives exist for the advancement of competing values that would render war unnecessary, new states emerge. Restoration of the status quo ante undermines the credibility of the collective security system among those with grievances.

It can be noted that the Treaty on Conventional Armed Forces in Europe (CFE Treaty) and Council of Europe provide two examples of legally binding arrangements in Europe and both have difficulties despite their legally binding character. Decision-making based on consensus gains democratic procedural legitimacy but at the potential price of its effectiveness or performance outcome. Every intergovernmental institution based on this consensus principle would inevitably face this classic trade-off, irrespective of whether a treaty is politically or legally binding. Replacing the OSCE by a consensus-driven EST only displaces rather than eliminates this challenge. A fundamental problem with collective security theory is that it 'proposes a legal response to issues that remain fundamentally political' (Miller, 1999, p. 323).

A second fundamental problem is that the only legal wrong that the EST draft treaty addresses is interstate aggression – an armed attack by one party to the treaty on another. Fragile states and the threat of proliferation, terrorism, cyber-attacks, finance, critical infrastructural, food-production or migration, are illustrative of strategic insecurity today. The insecurities of countries with a geographical proximity to fragile states may resonate and become amplified, a phenomenon underlined by the spillover effects of the events in Tunisia, Egypt and Libya during the Arab Spring of 2011. Shared network membership – whether it be critical infrastructure or food production and supply chains, migration flows, cyber or financial systems connectivity – make all states more vulnerable to crisis. In addition, the greater the interconnectivity of systems, the more likely it is that totally unprecedented Black Swan-type events have disastrous results, as exemplified by the Fukushima nuclear reactor catastrophe caused by the tsunami that hit Japan in 2011. The greater frequency and impact of such systemic shocks, with unintended consequences, spillovers and cascading second- and third-order effects, can be more devastating and the resultant disorder much harder to manage than the initial source of insecurity. Increasing synergy, interconnectivity and coupling of complex systems generate unpredictable non-linear behaviour and effects. They create a power vacuum, raising questions of authority and control – who 'owns' the crisis, who must manage it? The management of such threats suggests procedures and mechanisms in place that can constantly calibrate a negotiated equilibrium point between effectiveness (joint approach in terms of what is appropriate) efficiency (timeliness and cost in terms of what is affordable) and legitimacy (moral and political in terms of what is acceptable of responses).

Conclusion

Where does the EST go from here? In July 2010, Armenia declared itself supportive of the EST (ARMInfo News Agency, 2010), while Romania opposed it (Agence France-Presse, 2010b), and this fundamental divergence on the perceived utility of the EST in Euro-Atlantic space suggests an eventual stalemate in the discussion process. By mid 2010, perceptions, narratives and the mood music between Russia and Western interlocutors around the EST proposal had become all-important (Shupe, 2010, p. 4). How should the West relate to Russia in general and in post-Soviet space in particular, and how should Russia relate to the West? There is no agreement within the West as to how to relate to Russia and post-Soviet space, partly as a result of the West's ability to act strategically, partly because of intra-European and transatlantic splits – 'the West' is an increasingly incoherent concept. There is no agreement in Russia as to how to engage westwards, partly because of the complete estrangement of the political elite from the West over the last twenty years, and partly due to a lack of willingness to address the domestic 'elephant in the room' – the opposition of internal vested interests to modernise Russia's economy and society as this implies a different political order – that is, one that is democratic.

Russia has initiated a debate: are the European security architecture and its structures and norms fit for the purpose of security? If not, how can they be strengthened and made to work more efficiently, effectively and with greater legitimacy? How does the Russia–EU reset with its 'partnership for modernisation' agenda impact on this debate, or the joint Medvedev–Merkel proposal to create a council to coordinate Russian and EU foreign policy, or indeed Prime Minister Putin's proposal 'for the creation of a single European economic, energy, and human complex stretching from the Atlantic to the Pacific – a kind of "Union of Europe"' (Karaganov, 2011)? Charles Kupchan has even suggested that Russia integrates into NATO:

> There are, of course, many other options for pursuing a pan-European order, such as fashioning a treaty between NATO and the Russia-led Collective Security Treaty Organization; elevating the authority of the Organization for Security and Cooperation in Europe (OSCE), of which Russia is a member; or picking up on Russia's proposal for a new European security treaty. (Kupchan, 2010)

Rather than such a radical step, in the shorter term the process of discussions, exchanges of perspectives and consultations engendered by the EST initiative are more likely to help build mutual trust and confidence as this deficit is the underlying fundamental source of tension between Russia and many other states in Euro-Atlantic space. What can NATO do to address this deficit in Russia; what can Russia do to address this deficit in NATO?

Discussions through the EST to reassess European security structures and propose reforms to existing institutions and practice are valuable as in this sense they address the real agenda – lack of trust. Some rebalancing of the various dimensions of the OSCE, with an increased importance attributed to its politico-military dimension may be the outcome, as well as the launching of arms control negotiations and the provision of further Euro-Atlantic legitimacy to the CSTO. Two general conclusions can be drawn. First, that the process of discussions generated by the EST proposal has been more important in terms of rebuilding trust (or at least halting the deterioration of trust) than in forging a consensus that can be implemented. For Russia the EST has demonstrated that Moscow is a major European player when it comes to thinking strategically about European security. Process has trumped. Second, while the EST proved a useful focal point for engagement and the exchange of perspectives through 2008–10, by 2011 it is apparent that the utility of this particular vehicle in its present form is reaching an end. The OSCE Astana Summit declaration paid lip service to the concept and ideal of a collective security community, but did not advance practical discussions on its implementation. As Audronius Azubalis, OSCE Chairperson-in-Office and Lithuanian Foreign Minister, noted in a discussion of OSCE priorities for 2011, the OSCE's internal Corfu Process where EST discussions began under the Greek Chairmanship in 2009 will continue:

> At the same time we do not intend to get involved in 'reinventing the wheel': A sufficient mass of political commitments, instruments, and negotiating formats has been developed within the organization in order to achieve specific results in various areas. (Azubalis, 2011)

The EST was always hamstrung by the fact that the concept was insufficiently technically pertinent – to be diplomatic – as well as by the unwillingness of other major state actors to downgrade existing structures in return for the uncertainty of the new.

Hitherto for Russia the EST's utility has been to demonstrate that it is actively engaged in shaping the security agenda in Euro-Atlantic space.

Looking to the future as the EST proposal passes its regional sell-by date, it may prove to be a more versatile and transferable template. As Russian Deputy Minister of Foreign Affairs Aleksey Borodavkin noted at an Asia–Pacific forum:

> For a variety of reasons the region lacks a coherent system of collective security arrangements. While the question in the Euro-Atlantic area is one of improving the existing structures so as to create a common security space from Vancouver to Vladivostok – the focus of our initiative for a European Security Treaty in particular – we observe in the Asia–Pacific region, from Vladivostok to Vancouver, a clear shortage of such mechanisms, along with their insufficient effectiveness. (Borodavkin, 2010)

If so, the common denominator between Euro-Atlantic space and the Asia–Pacific region will be that Russian collective security proposals, though never realisable, provides Russia with a much needed voice in both regional security contexts. Ironically the greatest driver for reviving the EST proposal is the ongoing and accelerating power shift from the US and Europe to East and South Asia. China's rise and Russia's need to balance that rise in soft coalition with Europe and the US provides the impetus for more practical and substantive progress in rebuilding trust: the EST vehicle has still some road to travel.

Notes

1. 'European security has become wobbly in all its aspects over the previous twenty years. This includes the erosion of the arms control regime, atrophy of the OSCE, emergence of serious conflicts and the danger of their uncontrolled escalation, and the attempts to turn frozen conflicts into active ones. Statements like "everything is all right, let's do business as usual" fail to convince. In my view, key issues to analyse in the current situation are the theory and practice of the comprehensive approach to security, including the future of the OSCE and an integrated and pragmatic solution in the form of a treaty on European security advocated by Russia' (Lavrov, 2010a).
2. 'Only in this way is it possible to "turn over the page" and finally resolve the question of "hard security", which has been haunting Europe throughout its history' (Lavrov, 2010b, 2010c; Trenin, 2009).
3. 'The treaty obliges the signatories to support one another militarily in the event of armed attack and can therefore be interpreted as in direct competition with the promise of mutual assistance (Article 5) contained in the North Atlantic Treaty' (Mutzenich, 2010, p. 66); 'many western countries responded with the suspicion that the proposal served merely to "divide and conquer" [...].

In particular points 3 and 4 aim unmistakably at the weakening of NATO's role in Europe' (Shupe, 2010, p. 3).

References

24.kg website (2010) 'Kyrgyz police officers, soldiers accused of marauding in Kyrgyz southern city', 24.kg website, Bishkek, in Russian, 24 June, available at: http://www.24kg.org/osh/77390-v-gorode-oshe-kyrgyzstan-nekotorye-milicionery-i.html (accessed 18 October 2010).

Agence France-Presse (2010a) 'UN agencies fear escalation in Kyrgyz "Ethnic tinderbox"', Geneva, 15 June, available at: http://www.expatica.com/ch/news/swiss-news/un-agencies-fear-escalation-in-kyrgyz-ethnic-tinderbox-_76787.html (accessed 11 November 2011).

Agence France-Presse (2010b) 'Romania rejects Russia's EU security proposal', 2 June, available at: http://www.expatica.ru/news/russian-news/romania-rejects-russia-s-eu-security-proposal_73166.html (accessed 11 November 2011).

AKIpress News Agency (2010) 'Recordings of telephone conversations with voices of famous individuals posted on YouTube', Kyrgyzstan, 20 May, available at: http://www.highbeam.com.doc/1G1-227017390.html (accessed 3 February 2012).

ARMInfo News Agency (2010) 'Russia's European Security Treaty in harmony with Armenia's security efforts: Secretary of Armenian National Security Council', 25 June, available at: http://www.arminfo.info.home (accessed 3 February 2012).

Aron, Leon (2010) 'Dmitri Medvedev's Glasnost: the pudding and the proof', *Russian Outlook*, American Enterprise Institute for Public Policy Research, Winter, p. 2, available at: http://www.aei.org/article/foreign-and-defence-policy/regional/europe/dmitri-medvedevs-glasnost-the-pudding-and-the-proof/ (accessed 3 February 2012).

Azubalis, Audronius (2011) 'Golden millimetres of progress: Audronius Azubalis, head of the Organization for Security and Cooperation in Europe, talks about the tasks facing the OSCE, which this year is headed by Lithuania', Gazeta.ru website, Moscow, in Russian, 2 February, available at: http://www.accessmylibrary.com/article-1G1-248647184/lithuanian-foreign-minister-details.html (accessed 18 October 2010).

Ban Ki-Moon (2009) 'The ice is melting', *New York Times*, 17 September, available at: http://www.nytimes.com/2009/09/18/opinion/18iht-edban.html?ref=global (accessed 18 October 2010).

Borodavkin, Aleksey (2010) Text of 'Speech by Russian Deputy Minister of Foreign Affairs Aleksey Borodavkin at the Theoretical and Practical Conference organized by the Federation Council of the Federal Assembly of the Russian Federation on the theme of "The Asia–Pacific Region and Russian National Security"', Ministry of Foreign Affairs, Moscow, 19 March, available at: http://www.mid.ru/brp_4.nsf/e78a48070f128a7b43256999005bcbb3/e2d6cdc4691c2e5ac32576eb00488a39?OpenDocument (accessed 18 October 2010).

Burns, Robert and Desmond Butler (2011) 'Gates: NATO alliance future could be "dim, dismal"', *Associated Press*, 10 June, available at: http://news.yahoo.

com/s/ap/20110610/ap_on_re_eu/eu_gates_nato_doomed (accessed 12 June 2011).

Deutsche Presse-Agentur (2010) 'OSCE says attempted ethnic cleansing underway in Kyrgyzstan', Deutsche Presse-Agentur, Vienna, 15 June, LexusNexus (accessed 3 February 2012).

Downs, George W. (1994) *Collective Security: Beyond the Cold War* (Ann Arbor, MI: University of Michigan Press).

Dunay, Pál and Graeme P. Herd (2009) 'Redesigning Europe? The pitfalls and the promises of the European Security Treaty Initiative', in Institute for Peace Research and Security Policy at the University of Hamburg (ed.), *OSCE Yearbook 2009* (Baden-Baden: Nomos), pp. 77–98.

Ebinger, Charles E. and Evie Zammbetakis (2009) 'The geopolitics of Arctic melt', *International Affairs*, vol. 85, no. 6, pp. 1215–32.

Fedorov, Yuri (2009) *Medvedev's Initiative: A Trap for Europe*, Research Paper 2/2009 (Prague: Association for International Affairs), available at: http://www.amo.cz/publications/medvedevs-initiative-a-trap-for-europe-.html?lang=en (accessed 18 October 2010).

Human Rights Watch (2011) 'Distorted justice: Kyrgyzstan's flawed investigations and trials on the 2010 violence', 8 June, available at: http://www.hrw.org/node/99483 (accessed 21 June 2011).

Interfax News Agency (2010a) 'Russia's partners agree on need to revamp European security structure – official', Moscow, in Russian, 28 May (LexisNexis).

Interfax News Agency (2010b) 'Kyrgyz politician expects constitutional referendum to fail', Moscow, in Russian, 26 June (LexisNexis).

Interfax News Agency (2010c) 'CIS security bloc should learn from NATO, EU, bolster institutions – Medvedev', Moscow, in Russian, 20 August (LexisNexis).

Karaganov, Sergey (2009) 'The magic numbers of 2009', *Russia in Global Affairs*, no. 2, April–June, available at: http://eng.globalaffairs.ru/printver/1279.html (accessed 18 October 2010).

Karaganov, Sergey (2011) 'Standing still in front of a "window of opportunity"', *Rossiyskaya Gazeta* website, Moscow, in Russian, 18 May, available at: http://en.rian.ru/valdai_op/20110523/164176390.html (accessed 11 November 2011).

Kuhn, Ulrich (2010) 'Medvedev's proposals for a new European security order: a starting point or the end of the story?', *Connections: The Quarterly Journal*, vol. 9, no. 2, pp. 1–16.

Kupchan, Charles A. (2010) 'NATO's final frontier: why Russia should join the Atlantic Alliance', *Foreign Affairs*, vol. 89, no. 3, pp. 100–12, available at: http://www.foreignaffairs.com/articles/66217/charles-a-kupchan/natos-final-frontier (accessed 18 October 2010).

Kyrgyz Radio First (2010) 'Top Kyrgyz security officer warns of recurrence of ethnic violence', Bishkek, in Russian, 25 June.

Kygyz Television 1 (2010a) 'Interim leader notes importance of constitutional referendum for Kyrgyzstan', Bishkek, in Russian, 22 June.

Kyrgyz Television 1 (2010b) 'Kyrgyz interim leader urges nation to back new constitution in Sunday referendum', Bishkek, in Russian, 24 June.

Lavrov, Sergey (2010a) Text of unofficial translation of article by Russian Foreign Minister Sergey V. Lavrov, *Revue Defense Nationale*, May issue, 'Euro-Atlantic: equal security for all', Ministry of Foreign Affairs website, Moscow, 24

May, available at: http://www.ln.mid.ru/brp_4.nsf/e78a48070f128a7b432569 99005bcbb3/ef1f3c48ad0e5959c325772d0041fa53?OpenDocument (accessed 18 October 2010).

Lavrov, Sergey (2010b) 'Russian Foreign Minister Sergey Lavrov interview with the Weekly News Magazine *Itogi* published on November 26, 2007', Russian Ministry of Foreign Affairs website, Moscow, 18 May, available at: http://www.un.int/russia/new/MainRoot/docs/off_news/261107/newen1.htm (accessed 18 October 2010).

Lavrov, Sergey (2010c) 'Russian diplomacy in a changing world', *Federal Year Book*, vol. 23, Ministry of Foreign Affairs website, Moscow, 7 May, available at: http://www.mid.ru/brp_4.nsf/0/4E37152B4A140C1EC325771C004C7DBB (accessed 24 December 2010).

Lavrov, Sergey and Guido Westerwelle (2010) 'Repair', *Rossiskaya Gazeta*, Russian Foreign Minister Sergey Lavrov and German Vice Chancellor and Foreign Minister Guido Westerwelle, 31 May.

Leonard, Peter (2010) 'Heroin trade a backdrop to Kyrgyz violence', *Associated Press Worldstream*, Jalal-Abad, Kyrgyzstan, 24 June, available at: http://abcnews.go.com/International/wireStory?id=11000057&page=1 (accessed 11 November 2011).

Lillis, Joanna (2010) 'Kyrgyz leaders urged to halt "illegitimate" referendum', *The Independent*, London, from Bishkek, 25 June, available at: http://www.independent.co.uk/news/world/asia/kyrgyz-leaders-urged-to-halt-illegitimate-referendum-2009983.html (accessed 18 October 2010).

Lo, Bobo (2009) 'Medvedev and the New European Security Architecture', openDemocracy, 3 August, available at: http://www.opendemocracy.net/article/email/medvedev-and-the-new-european-security-architecture (accessed 18 October 2010).

Lukyanov, Fyodor (2009) 'Rethinking security in "Greater Europe"', *Russia in Global Affairs*, 5 September, available at: http://eng.globalaffairs.ru/number/n_13589 (accessed 18 October 2010).

Makedonov, Lev (2010) 'European security denunciation', Gazeta.ru website, Moscow, in Russian, 3 February, available at: http://www.gazeta.ru/politics/2010/02/03_a_3319348.shtml (accessed 11 November 2011).

Medvedev, Dmitry (2008) 'Text of Speech at World Policy Conference in Evian, France', President of Russia website, 8 October, available at: http://www.president.kremlin.ru/eng/speeches/2008/10/08/2159_type82912type82914_207457.shtml (accessed 18 October 2010).

Medvedev, Dmitry (2009) Draft of the European Security Treaty, Russian Presidential Executive Office, 29 November, available at: http://eng.kremlin.ru/news/275 (accessed 18 October 2010).

Medvedev, Dmitry (2010) Text of Speech at meeting with Russian ambassadors and permanent representatives to international organizations, President of Russia website, 14 July, available at: http://eng.kremlin.ru/transcripts/610 (accessed 24 December 2010).

Melvin, Neil (2011) 'Promoting a stable and multiethnic Kyrgyzstan: overcoming the causes and legacies of violence', Central Eurasia Project, *Occasional Papers Series No. 3*, Open Society Foundations, March, pp. 1–62, available at: http://www.soros.org/initiatives/cep/articles_publications/publications/occasional-paper-3-20110307 (accessed 21 June 2011).

Meo, Nick and Richard Orange (2010) 'Princeling and the revolution: a tape recording allegedly shows that the son of the deposed Kyrgyz leader planned the recent wave of ethnic violence in a bid to seize power', *Sunday Telegraph*, London, 20 June, p. 30.

Mezhuyev, Boris (2009) 'Towards legal universalism: the origins and development of the Medvedev initiative', *Russia in Global Affairs*, vol. 7, no. 3, pp. 103–9, available at: http://www.isn.ethz.ch/isn/Current-Affairs/Security-Watch/Detail/?fecvnodeid=106619&fecvid=33&ots591=0c54e3b3-1e9c-be1e-2c24-a6a8c706 0233&lng=en&v33=106619&id=105699 (accessed 18 October 2010).

Miller, Lynn H. (1999) 'The idea and reality of collective security', *Global Governance*, vol. 5, no. 3, pp. 303–32.

Monaghan, Andrew (2008) *Russia's 'Big Idea': 'Helsinki 2' and the Reform of Euro-Atlantic Security*, NATO Research Report, NATO Research Division (Rome: NATO Defence College), 3 December, available at: http://www.ndc.nato.int/research/series.php?icode=3 (accessed 18 October 2010).

Mutzenich, Rolf (2010) 'Security with or against Russia? On the Russian proposal for a "European Security Treaty"', *Internationale Politik und Gesellschaft Online: International Politics and Society*, no. 2; electronic edn (Berlin: IPG-Redaktion), available at: http://www.rolfmuetzenich.de/lectures_and_publications/index_2010.php?oid=1977 (accessed 18 October 2010).

National Statistical Committee of the Kyrgyz Republic (2009) 'Main social and demographic characteristics of population and number of housing units', E. F. Konovalov (ed.), *Population and Housing Census of the Kyrgyz Republic of 2009*, Book I (Bishkek: The Committee).

Onyszkiewicz, Janusz (2010) 'Europe should be wary of the Russian bear's embrace', *EuropesWorld*, Summer, 18 July, available at: http://www.europesworld.org/NewEnglish/Home_old/Article/tabid/191/ArticleType/articleview/ArticleID/21668/Default.aspx (accessed 18 October 2010).

Panfilova, Viktoriya (2010) 'Kyrgyzstan is continuing to arm: the referendum could result in an escalation of the conflict in the Republic', *Nezavisimaya Gazeta*, Moscow, in Russian, 25 June, available at: http://www.ng.ru/cis/2010-06-25/6_kirgizia.html (accessed 24 December 2010).

Radio Free Europe (2010a) 'EU envoy warns of regional risk from Kyrgyz instability', 23 June, available at: http://www.rferl.org/content/EU_Envoy_Warns_Of_Regional_Risk_From_Kyrgyz_Instability/2080537.html (accessed 3 February 2012).

Radio Free Europe (2010b) 'As Kyrgyzstan prepares for referendum, government faces predictions of collapse', 24 June, available at: http://www.rferl.org/content/As_Kyrgyzstan_Prepares_for_Referendum_Government_Faces_Predictions_Of_Collapse/2081294.html (accessed 3 February 2012).

RIA Novosti (2010a) 'Russia sees improved atmosphere in Euro-Atlantic diplomacy', 19 May, available at: http://en.rian.ru/russia/20100519/159079630.html (accessed 24 December 2010).

RIA Novosti (2010b) 'Russian foreign minister interviewed on OSCE summit', Ministry of Foreign Affairs website, Moscow, in English, 9 December, available at: http://www.accessmylibrary.com/article-1G1-243948393/russian-foreign-minister-interviewed.html (accessed 12 December 2011).

Roberts, Adam (1993) 'United Nations and international security', *Survival*, vol. 35, no. 2, pp. 3–30.

Russia and CIS Military Weekly (2010) 'Ukraine willing to discuss new European Security Treaty', Kyiv, 2 April.

Shupe, Cortnie (2010) 'Cooperation with the Kremlin', *Spotlight Europe*, Bertelsmann Stiftung, January, available at: http://aei.pitt.edu/12876/ (accessed 18 October 2010).

Shuster, Simon (2010) 'Kyrgyzstan endorses new constitution: new Constitution strips power from the President and gives more authority to Parliament', *Globe and Mail Online*, 28 June, available at: http://www.theglobeandmail.com/news/world/asia-pacific/kyrgyzstan-endorses-new-constitution/article1621116/ (accessed 18 October 2010).

Solovyov, Dmitry (2010) '4 die in raid by Kyrgyz Security Forces: rights groups say soldiers beat villagers', *The Gazette*, Montreal, from Osh, Kyrgyzstan, 22 June, p. 19A.

Trenin, Dmitri (2009) 'From a "Treaty to replace all treaties" to addressing Europe's core security issues', *Web Commentary*, Carnegie Endowment for International Peace, 30 November, available at: http://www.carnegieendowment.org/publications/index.cfm?fa=view&id=40470 (accessed 18 October 2010).

Trenin, Dmitri (2010) 'The Kyrgyz Bell', Carnegie Endowment for International Peace, Op-Eds/Articles, Moscow, 29 June, available at: http://www.carnegie.ru/publications/?fa=41126 (accessed 18 October 2010).

Weir, Fred (2010) 'Kyrgyzstan failure could boost Afghan drug trade, Islamist radicals', *Christian Science Monitor*, 25 June, available at: http://www.csmonitor.com/World/Asia-South-Central/2010/0625/Kyrgyzstan-failure-could-boost-Afghan-drug-trade-Islamist-radicals (accessed 25 December 2010).

7
Central Asia in Russian and US Foreign Policy: Between Continuity and 'Reset'

Licínia Simão

Introduction

Central Asian politics remain a backwater of world affairs. During Soviet rule this remote area, at the heart of the Eurasian landmass, was virtually isolated from the world. After independence from the Soviet Union a host of new actors engaged with the region, including the United States, which prioritised the promotion of liberal democracy and security cooperation, aimed at contributing to the region's peaceful development. This was a period of ambivalence in Russian policies towards Central Asia, reflecting the ongoing debates on Russia's post-Soviet foreign policy. The region was regarded by some as a burden at a time of economic strife, and by others as an important buffer zone from instability in South Asia, including Islamic militants from Afghanistan and Pakistan making their way to the South and North Caucasus.

Following the events of 9/11, the US presence in Central Asia changed considerably, both in size and nature. Security concerns became prominent, whereas competition with Moscow over energy resources in the Caspian was at its height. Moscow under President Putin's leadership continued a policy of the reassertion of power in the 'Near Abroad', as set out by Russian Foreign Minister Yevgeny Primakov during the late 1990s. In this regard, President Putin was careful to support US moves to establish military bases, in what the US National Security Strategy of September 2002 called an 'area of instability'. Although Moscow shared the concern with terrorist networks operating in Afghanistan and Pakistan, it sought to ensure that US military presence in Central Asia did not become permanent.

The arrival of President Obama at the White House was much awaited as an encouraging change in US–Russia dealings. The deterioration of relations under the Bush and Putin leaderships was unprecedented in the post-Cold War context, as was the lack of interest and priority attributed to relations with Moscow by the US foreign policy establishment (Ikome and Motsamai, 2009, p. 2). Therefore the agenda was overloaded with highly important issues, in great need of being addressed. In Central Asia the prospect of normalised and cooperative relations between Moscow and Washington meant the possibility of decreasing regional competition, despite the permanence of points of tension. These included the maintenance of the US transit centre in Kyrgyzstan; competition over access to energy resources in the Caspian; and prospects for increased military cooperation with Uzbekistan. The potential for improvement under Obama and Medvedev therefore remains high.

This chapter addresses the ongoing dynamics in Central Asia, from the perspective of the 'new' relations between the US and Russia. It argues that the elements pushing for a cooperative approach between the US and Russia in Central Asia existed prior to the arrival of the Obama and Medvedev administrations. The main factor in this regard is the shared security concern over Afghanistan. It also argues that both presidents have developed a policy of continuity towards Central Asia, which does not reflect the announced wish to redesign relations between Moscow and Washington. This is visible in the US pursuit of short-term goals in Central Asia and the instrumental use of improved relations with Russia to achieve these goals. Conversely, Russia continues to regard the US's lack of interest in Russian interests in Central Asia a major point of concern. For that matter the chapter uses the concept of multilevel hegemony (Deyermond, 2009) to assess the current state of affairs in US–Russia relations in Central Asia under the reset policy.

Hegemonic competition in Central Asia

As some authors suggest, Russia is bound to remain a 'key player' in Central Asia, although it is 'no longer its destiny' (Garnett et al., 2000, p. 71). This means that any process of hegemonic reaffirmation by Russia in this region will conflict with the global hegemon's presence, that is to say the United States, and its active dealings in the region. We can therefore speak of multilevel hegemony (Deyermond, 2009) taking place in Central Asia, including a global hegemon (the US), a regional hegemon in reaffirmation (Russia), an aspiring subregional hegemon, Uzbekistan (Deyermond, 2009, pp. 162–4; Buzan and Waever, 2003, p. 425), and external potential hegemons such as China and India (Laruelle et al., 2010). This complex scenario makes the calculations of all of the actors involved highly uncertain, potentially increasing strategic competition rather than cooperation towards addressing the region's security challenges, as discussed in more detail below.

The multilevel hegemony model is particularly well suited to addressing the complex power relations developing in Central Asia, by providing an analytical framework where the interests of the different actors in Central Asia can be assessed in relational terms, that is to say how each actor's interests are restricted or advanced by its relations with other hegemons in this regional context. When interests among hegemons coincide, Ruth Deyermond (2009, p. 151) calls this a 'matrioshka model of hegemony [where] the different level hegemons can accommodate one another peacefully and where their interests coincide they can form alliances'. The model is also relevant to assess the conflict potential in scenarios where regional hegemonic competition takes place, as seems to be the case in Central Asia. Multilevel hegemony conceives hegemony 'as a multi-layered concept, in which hegemony at one level poses challenges to, but does not necessarily erase, hegemony at another' (Deyermond, 2009, p. 157). Furthermore when contemplating the possibility of multilevel hegemonic competition, the potential for conflict between the different hegemons must be assessed based on complex relations, where competition and cooperation are possible at different levels. What then are the possibilities of accommodation and cooperation at the subregional Central Asian context? And how has the challenge posed by the global hegemon to the regional hegemon been managed at the regional level? Can there be payoffs from other areas of interaction between hegemons, which could impact relations in the Central Asian regional complex?

If we look at how the US and Russia have managed their own ambitions in the region, the argument can be made that US presence and assistance to Central Asia have both gradually increased since the end of the Cold War, and have displayed clear peaks of interest, justifying a more active engagement. This was the case during the 1990s with energy resources around the Caspian; after 9/11, there was the global war on terror; and now under Obama the concentration of war efforts in Afghanistan has again put Central Asia at the forefront of the US's immediate priorities. This has been perceived by the regional hegemon, Russia, as a challenge to its interests and its position in the Central Asian context, consolidating competition for power as a major factor in regional relations.

There are two levels of problems with this situation. First, the lack of a US comprehensive, long-term commitment to Central Asian stability and security and the practice of policy-making based on short-term interests will induce half-hearted commitments to democratic reforms and human rights issues in a region where authoritarianism is rewarded. These are issue areas that the global hegemon could use to its advantage when compared to other regional hegemons such as Russia or China, but which surprisingly have actually resulted in a weakening of US influence in the region. Second, these waves of US engagement and partial disengagement have overlapped with Russia's own efforts to reassert its influence in the region. In the 1990s, both were competing for access to energy resources, and still are; in 2001, Russia was in the process of reversing its declining influence; and since the events in Andijan in 2005, Russia has consistently increased its influence in Central Asia, again clashing with the Obama administration's war efforts in Afghanistan. This has meant that the US has either needed Russian support to reach its regional goals, or has had to compete with Russia, especially considering that cooperation with the aspiring subregional hegemon, Uzbekistan, has not resulted in positive outcomes for the US.

The reset policy is unlikely to change this state of affairs, despite the numerous opportunities for cooperation towards enhanced regional and global stability. The war in Afghanistan is, of course, a major opportunity for cooperation to develop. Russia has stated its commitment to assist Western war efforts and it shares a genuine interest in seeing radical Islamic terrorism curbed in its Near Abroad, as well as in limiting the pernicious impact that the increasing illicit drug trade has on its own society. However Russia also regards the war in Afghanistan as a trump card in its relations with the United States and NATO (Stepanova, 2009, p. 2), increasing Russia's strategic relevance for both actors. The potential exists that neither will the US successfully define a coherent strategy to fight narcotics and transnational terrorist activities in Central Asia backed by adequate resources, nor will Russia acknowledge the absolute necessity for stable institutions in Afghanistan, if these two related problems are to be eradicated.

The complex security context of Central Asia

Central Asia does not today face major classical security threats. The establishment and consolidation of sovereign nation states has been mainly a peaceful process. One of the areas that remains a source of tension and potential conflict is the arbitrary nature of borders and the problem of their delimitation. Borders in Central Asia were drawn up under Stalin with the purpose of assuring that the largest titular nations in the Soviet Union were entitled to a republic. Large ethnic minorities were left outside the republics' borders in order to avoid a consolidation of national ethnic identities that could challenge the central power in Moscow. While during the Soviet period borders were of little importance, after 1991 they became issues of contention. One of the most important steps taken to address border issues was China's decision to reach agreement with Kazakhstan, Kyrgyzstan and Tajikistan on defining and demilitarising their 3000-kilometres-long common border (Xing, 2001, p. 154), largely within the framework of the Shanghai Forum (which became the current Shanghai Cooperation Organisation (SCO)). An area where border delimitation has still not been possible is the Caspian Sea, hampering the development of energy resources (Pratt and Schofield, 1997).

The Fergana Valley presents by far the most complex issue regarding the delimitation of borders, with large portions of the Uzbek–Kyrgyz and Uzbek–Tajik borders still disputed. Adding further tension is the fact that the valley is the most fertile area in the whole of the Central Asian region, with natural resources such as land and water being highly disputed. Although most of these disputes have been managed at the local level among the different communities, the potential exists for them to gain national proportions (Swanstrom et al., 2005, p. 17). Uzbekistan's concerns with terrorism and its fight against the Islamic Movement of Uzbekistan (IMU) have made border management and cross-border security in the Fergana Valley, where the IMU is more active, a regional problem. Illustrating this, after two bomb explosions in Tashkent in 1999, Uzbekistan sealed off its borders in the valley and launched airstrikes on IMU positions in the south of Kyrgyzstan without Bishkek's consent, killing about twelve Kyrgyz (ICG, 2002a, p. 14). The presence of large Uzbek enclaves in Kyrgyzstan has also created tensions between the two countries, as well as with Tajikistan, which hosts a large Uzbek minority in the north. This has provided Tashkent with leverage over its smaller neighbours on other issues, including water disputes and the fight against radical Islamic threats, which Tashkent is willing to use as a means of consolidating a subregional hegemonic position.

Border disputes become far more complex when they overlap with non-traditional security threats of a transnational nature. Transnational organised crime has become entrenched in Central Asia, feeding off the highly profitable drug trade from Afghanistan and undermining state institutions. Most of the drug trafficking from Afghanistan now occurs along the Silk Road through Central Asia (Fenopetov, 2006), partly because of the lack of functional border controls. Much as with terrorist concerns, drug trafficking is contributing to the process of hardening intra-Commonwealth of Independent States (CIS) land borders (Allison, 2001, p. 258), hampering economic integration and social development. Drug trafficking has also affected the legitimacy of national institutions (Lubin, 2004, p. 364), leading to severe cases of state infiltration (Cornell, 2006), especially in Kyrgyzstan and Tajikistan. The political crisis of April 2010 in Kyrgyzstan, with the violent ousting of President Bakiev, shed light on the level of cooperation of the ruling elite with criminal networks operating in the south of Kyrgyzstan and illustrated the dangers of mixing ethnic, regional and social divisions with criminal interests (Marat, 2008, 2010).

The widespread drug trade throughout Central Asia has also contributed to increasing levels of pandemics and drug consumption, thereby affecting the fragile social fabric of the region. Poverty levels remain extremely high in Central Asia. From 1990 to 1996, the Central Asian economies declined by 20 to 60 per cent of gross domestic product (GDP), only managed by extensive borrowing that in turn led to high debt rates (Hill, 2002). Although the states of the region have experienced economic growth rates over recent years, the impact of the international financial crisis has been high in the region, halting Kazakhstan's impressive growth rates and radically limiting the remittances sent home by Kyrgyz and Tajik migrants working in Russia (Pomfret, 2009; Gullette, 2010).

The lack of sustainable and widespread economic development in Central Asia also reflects the uneven distribution of natural resources between the energy-rich states of Kazakhstan, Turkmenistan and Uzbekistan and their poorer neighbours, Tajikistan and Kyrgyzstan. The latter however control water resources, providing them with leverage, especially over Uzbekistan, whose economy largely relies on intensive cotton-growing (ICG, 2005, pp. 2–6). Moreover hydroelectric power production has become a major area of investment in both countries, creating a source of revenue and national affirmation, but disrupting water flows to neighbouring countries. The lack of comprehensive regulations on water use, as well as arrangements for swaps of energy for water, has made water management an urgent objective in order to avoid further security concerns in Central Asia (ICG, 2002b).

A final issue shaping Central Asian security is the concern with terrorism and the domestic and geopolitical implications it has in the region. Although radical Islamic terrorism poses a real threat for the peoples of Central Asia, there has been an instrumental use of Islam to reinforce authoritarian trends. This has been the case in Uzbekistan, but also in

Tajikistan and to a more limited extent in Kyrgyzstan (*The Economist*, 2010). September 11 and the US engagement in the region further reinforced this trend to regard any Islamic movement as a security threat, criminalising the resurgent religious movement in Central Asia. Russia has also regarded the Islamic movements operating in Central Asia, with links to Afghanistan, as a major threat to its security, especially in the North Caucasus. This has proven an important area of cooperation between Washington, Moscow and the regimes in Central Asia, potentially with important spillover for regional stability. However the outcome has been a reinforcement of authoritarian and repressive regimes, unable to address the security threats posed by transnational terrorist networks operating freely across Central Asian borders, while using radical Islam as a banner to restrict civil liberties and freedom of expression.

Spillover effects from the activities of Islamic militants operating in the Afghan–Tajik border zone have been particularly visible in Tajikistan, which is experiencing the biggest surge of violence since the end of the civil war in 1997 (Tutubalina, 2010). This is another area where US and Russian interests have coincided, both regarding the goal of consolidating secular regimes in Central Asia and curbing radical Islamic movements and as regards the methods to do so. The major difference is perhaps visible in the open support for local authoritarian regimes, which Moscow and Beijing have provided and which the US has tacitly maintained through its reluctance to support political freedoms and human rights when its interests rest mainly in saving US soldiers' lives in Afghanistan (Stern, 2009).

Central Asia in US and Russian politics

From independence to 9/11

In the immediate post-Cold War period, US and Russian policies towards Central Asia displayed movements in opposite directions. On the one hand, after the breakup of the Soviet Union, Russian elites in Moscow demonstrated a lack of vision regarding the future of relations with the former empire, with some elements even advocating 'shed[ding] the onerous burden of the Central Asian underbelly' (Solzhenitsyn, quoted in Rashid, 1994, p. 39; see also Jonson, 2001, pp. 96–7). Russia spearheaded the creation of the CIS, aimed at managing a 'civilised divorce' between the Soviet Republics and leading them to independence (Sakwa and Webber, 1999; Markedonov, 2010). The US, on the other hand, regarded cooperation with the region as a necessary step to ensure the sovereignty and independence of these fragile new states, and passed the Freedom Support Act in 1992, which aimed at the formation of a coherent framework for engagement with Eurasia (Wishnick, 2002, p. 3; Hill, 2001, p. 97).

Although in the immediate period following independence there were other priorities both on the US and Russian agendas, Central Asia increased in importance in the following years. With the arrival at the White House of President Bill Clinton, the US commitment to the promotion of political and economic liberal reforms in Central Asia, which was presented as a major priority of its early engagement, was balanced by a visible interest in the energy resources of the Caspian region (Hill, 2001). Furthermore security concerns that, in the absence of Russia's control, these states would fall prey to radical Islamic groups seeking to destabilise the region, created another issue bearing on a US principled approach to the region. This presented enormous risks for regional security, not least due to the presence of nuclear-related technology throughout the former Soviet space and the potential to destabilise US allies in the vicinity, namely Turkey. Finally, this would also potentially pose a threat to US investments in energy development and transportation (Nichol, 2003, p. 3). The US made security and military cooperation, including denuclearisation, a central feature in its foreign policy towards Russia and the CIS (Giragosian, 2004, pp. 45–6). Military cooperation was closely associated with a wider goal of democracy and liberal economy promotion, in the hopes that a virtuous cycle would be initiated and expanded to other areas of the globe.

US rhetoric about the region, especially during Clinton's second administration, firmly promoted the idea that the development of energy resources from the Caspian would act as a catalyst for prosperity and the consolidation of economic and political independence of the region (Blank, 2001, p. 131). However the outcome of the energy development promise was far more modest than suggested (Olcott, 1999), and people throughout Central Asia have been falling into a continuous cycle of impoverishment, authoritarian repression and instability. On the one hand, US engagement with the regimes of Central Asia was far less principled than expected (Anderson and Beck, 2000, p. 87), with the US regarding Uzbekistan as a key partner in curtailing Russian influence in Central Asia, despite the regime's atrocious record on human rights (Luong and Weinthal, 2002, pp. 63–5). On the other hand, the announcement by US Deputy Secretary of State Strobe Talbott (1997) that Washington regarded investing in conflict resolution and avoiding a new 'Great Game' around the Caspian region as a priority, did not materialise.

By the year 2000, the US had engaged in extensive military and security cooperation with Central Asia, assisting the region in its anti-terrorist efforts, and further integrating it into multilateral frameworks, such as NATO, through the Euro-Atlantic Partnership Council and the Partnership for Peace (PfP) and the Organization for Security and Co-operation in Europe (OSCE). Energy development was advancing, based on Azerbaijani and Kazakh commitments to the Baku–Tbilisi–Ceyhan pipeline. This project benefitted Turkey, while avoiding Russian and Iranian territories and consolidating US influence in the Caspian (Jafalian, 2004, pp. 152–4; Rashid, 2002, p. 184). Overall the US goals of intertwining democracy and liberalised economies with regional prosperity and security failed to address the complex nature of relations in Eurasia, but clearly established the US as a challenger to Russia's regional hegemony in Central Asia. Washington's interests led it to rhetorically refuse competition, while strategically pursuing it. This left the US ill prepared to address the root causes of radical and militant Islam in the region, which came to dominate the 2000s, as well as to deal with the permanence of Central Asian ruling elites, actively supported by Moscow in the name of regime stability.

Russia's relations with the newly independent states of Central Asia were both complicated and facilitated by the previous legacy. The prioritisation of the West in Russia's immediate post-Soviet foreign policy was the result of a combination of a nationalist mood and President Mikhail Gorbachev's policies of openness and approximation to the West (Jackson, 2003, p. 55). This meant that the former empire was initially neglected, both out of the necessity of concentrating energy and resources in managing the problems inside Russia, and due to the perception that any attempt to engage in national politics in Central Asia would be poorly received locally. In fact, the trend among Central Asian nations reflected uncertainty regarding the newly acquired independence and the challenges that immediately fell upon national leaders. Departing from the acknowledgement of this reality, by December 1991, Russia, Belarus and Ukraine established the CIS and, by 1993, the five Central Asian states joined the organisation, recognising a 'functional necessity of cooperation' to suppress their lack of military and economic self-sufficiency (Sakwa and Webber, 1999, p. 381). Thus collaboration with Russia was both necessary due to the limitations of de facto sovereignty in Central Asia, and unwanted in countries enjoying a period of nationalist affirmation.

In terms of security the civil war in Tajikistan represented a central challenge to Russia's relations with the region and to its ability to influence the reshaping of regional relations. Russian troops, which had been left behind from the Soviet period, intervened in the conflict and Russia pursued conflict resolution policies within the framework of the CIS (Akiner, 2001, pp. 45–6). Radical Islamic movements operating in the Fergana Valley were another central concern in Russian–Uzbek relations. Despite the strained relations and the disagreement on how to address the situation in Tajikistan, both Uzbekistan and Russia, along with Kazakhstan and Kyrgyzstan, agreed in Tashkent to establish the Collective Security Treaty (CST) by mid 1992, finally consolidating security and military cooperation within the framework of the CIS (Cutler, 2007, p. 112).[1]

Russian policies towards Central Asia changed considerably, favouring stronger engagement by the mid 1990s, with Prime Minister Primakov advocating 'Eurasianism' as the main tenet in Russia's dealings with the Near Abroad. This reflected a desire to recover great power status for Russia (Jonson, 2001, p. 97), including a regional hegemonic position in the CIS, and an opportunity to consolidate a doctrine of special Russian interests in the former USSR already initiated under Yeltsin and Foreign Minister Andrei Kozyrev. The Foreign Policy Concept of the Russian Federation and the Military Doctrine of 1993 confirmed Russia's attempt to be regarded as the political and security guarantor in the former USSR (a regional hegemon), as well as the right of Russia to intervene in the CIS to protect Russian citizens abroad (Foreign Policy Concept of the Russian Federation, 1993).

During Yeltsin's second term in office (1996–99), Russia sought to consolidate its presence in the CIS, balancing between recognition of the newfound independence of its neighbours and acknowledgement of its security needs. Russia regarded with concern and sought to counterbalance the increased Western encroachment in and around the Caspian and Central Asia that it perceived as being directed against Russian interests and posing a challenge to its efforts to reestablish itself as a regional hegemon. New pipelines were being designed to avoid its territory, NATO was pursuing eastwards expansion and seeking to deepen its relations with CIS countries through the PfP, and the US was pursuing bilateral military cooperation with Central Asia, leading to the establishment of the Central Asian Peace Keeping Battalion (Centrazbat) (Burghart, 2007, p. 8). This set the stage for a sharp increase in competition with the US in the years prior to and after 9/11, which culminated in the war in Georgia in 2008.

From 9/11 to the Obama–Medvedev era

A new security and foreign policy vision for Russia had been consolidated in the lead-up to the 2000 Russian presidential elections.

The Foreign Policy Concept of the Russian Federation and the Military Doctrine of 2000 clearly regarded the curtailment of Russian interests by other states as a major threat, whereas the promotion of a multipolar world order was underscored as a fundamental principle that should guide international relations (Jonson, 2001, p. 99). Both documents reflected recognition of the limits of the Western models of economic and political development for Russia. The 1998 financial meltdown and the socioeconomic crisis that followed exposed the limited assistance that the West was willing to extend to Russia and demanded a new model, more suited to the advantages that Russia had. This meant placing the exploitation of natural resources at the heart of the economy at a time when international markets were coming around and favouring oil and gas exporters. Politically Russia was also far from achieving the democratic standards that the West expected. The security challenges faced in the North Caucasus and Russia's management of the wars in Chechnya left it exposed to wide international criticism, consolidating the view that Russia needed its own model of political development (Kobrinskaya, 2005, p. 78).

These issues facilitated Moscow's rapprochement with Central Asian leaders. After a decade of difficulties in the consolidation of independence and of disillusionment with the promises of the West, Central Asian leaders also sought to reengage Russia in regional affairs. Under President Putin, Moscow began to play a carefully crafted game of reasserting its presence in Central Asia and the Caspian. This meant institutionalising cooperation efforts with each state in the Near Abroad, as well as making use of strategic assets such as energy relations and military basing rights to consolidate Russia's presence (Laruelle, 2007). President Putin displayed a clear understanding of Central Asia's regional dynamics, as well as a strong commitment to non-interference in domestic issues, largely welcomed by local regimes. Illustrating this, one of President Putin's first decisions was to make Kazakhstan a top priority in Central Asia, signing a new cooperation agreement with Astana shortly after his election (Cutler, 2007, p. 117). This provided Russia with two advantages: first, it brought a difficult partner closer to Moscow, while improving relations with an important ally of the West in the extraction of resources from the Caspian; second, it fed into the strategic competition for subregional dominance that Kazakhstan and Uzbekistan maintain in Central Asia. Another example is the political support provided by Moscow to the fragile and authoritarian regimes in Central Asia, following the wave of colour revolutions in Eurasia. This policy had its apex in the open support to the Uzbek President, after the Andijan events of 2005. Moreover President Putin's commitment to fighting international terrorism became a central feature of Russia's foreign policy after 9/11 (Wilhelmsen and Flikke, 2005, p. 391), resonating positively with Central Asian leaders.

Overall Moscow's policies focused on two main issues. First, Moscow was committed to reestablishing institutional cooperation in Central Asia, both bilaterally and multilaterally in two main areas: military and economic. Under Putin, Russia negotiated bilateral military agreements with Kyrgyzstan in 2003 (Eurasianet, 2002), with Tajikistan in 2004 (RFE/RL, 2004) and with Uzbekistan in 2005 (EurasiaNet, 2005), while there is a well-established military cooperation with Kazakhstan. At the multilateral level Russia led the transformation of the CST in 2002 into the Collective Security Treaty Organisation (CSTO). Moscow promoted the Eurasian Economic Community (EurAsEC) as a central tool in deepening Russia's economic ties with the region. Uzbekistan joining the CSTO and the EurAsEC in 2006, can be seen as a major victory for Moscow and a central step towards consolidating Russia's regional hegemonic dominance (Laruelle, 2007; Trenin, 2007, p. 99).

Second, Russia also sought to deepen economic ties with Central Asia, tapping into the region's energy and mineral reserves, including oil, gas, hydropower and mining (Trenin, 2007, pp. 106–10). Russia was willing to pay higher prices for more energy in order to ensure control over the production and export of oil and gas from Central Asia. This goal was further advanced by the close links between the state and the major energy companies in Russia, such as Lukoil and Gazprom, their actions of which can be seen as reinforcing the political objectives of the Kremlin (Baev, 2004, p. 272). Finally, Russia also invested in hydroelectric power in Tajikistan and Kyrgyzstan, which are the main sources of energy-related revenue in the two countries.

As Russia gradually sought to counter its declining role in Central Asia, the events of 9/11 and the US-led global war on terror presented Moscow with a challenge (Antonenko, 2001). With the US decision to intervene militarily in Afghanistan, Central Asia was put at the heart of US strategy. The immediate response by Central Asian leaders was to facilitate US operations and allow the establishment of two US military bases, Manas in Kyrgyzstan and Khanabad in southern Uzbekistan. This Central Asian cooperative mood can partly be explained by a shared concern with Islamic threats coming from Afghanistan, but also as a strategic assessment that closer cooperation with the US could further reinforce these countries' multivector foreign policies and keep Russia's hegemonic appetite under control. Washington was adamant in assuring both Moscow and local regimes that its presence in Central Asia would be short-lived and limited to the operational needs of the war in Afghanistan, portraying its interests in Central Asia as coinciding with those of the ascending regional hegemon and subregional one. However as Baev argues, by 2003, President Putin realised that 'the Bush Administration neither intended to withdraw from Central Asia nor had the ability to build up a military presence there to such a degree that it would become the dominant regional power' (Baev, 2004, pp. 274–5), providing opportunities for Russia in Central Asia.

Although increased US engagement in Central Asia following 9/11 created important new options for local regimes, by the end of the Bush administration's term Russian and Chinese presence in the region had been further consolidated. These two actors represent an incredible challenge to US policies in the region in terms of their economic and security interests, as illustrated by the development of the Shanghai Cooperation Organisation. This context of increased competition demanded from the US a more carefully crafted policy, balancing its security and energy interests with support for political and economic reforms (Fried, 2005, p. 6; Boucher, 2006, pp. 1–2); a policy defined as aimed at 'help[ing] Central Asian nations to have options'.

The balancing of interests and principles has also been complicated by the active US military basing policy in the region. As Alexander Cooley has argued (2008, p. 89), 'In both countries [Kyrgyzstan and Uzbekistan], the relatively small the U.S. presence […] went from being relatively depoliticized to a highly visible and contested political issue domestically.' This raised questions as to the impact of the US military presence in providing implicit support to the regimes in power. Nevertheless after the Andijan events of 2005, the US was extremely critical of the Uzbek regime, demanding an independent international investigation and cutting back many of its assistance programmes. This deprived the global hegemon of the strategic cooperation with the subregional hegemon, leaving Russian–Uzbek and Russian–Chinese cooperation free from constraints. Overall by the end of President Bush's mandate, the US was pursuing a policy of narrow interests in Central Asia, constrained by a growing Russian and Chinese presence and the consolidated authoritarian nature of local regimes.

Russia–US relations resetting

The election of President Medvedev in 2008 presented Russia with an option for the continuity of the policies pursued under Putin (Freire and Simão, 2008). This coincided with Russia's growing assertive realism in the international arena and its desire to rebuild the foundations of the Russian state (Kanet, 2008, p. 8; Freire, 2009, p. 129), which had been developing for a number of years. During this process relations with the West and especially with the US severely deteriorated, leaving a highly charged agenda unaddressed until the Obama administration arrived at the White House in November 2008. The issues pressing on Russia–US relations included the announced deployment of a US Missile Defence System in Poland and the Czech Republic, the war in Afghanistan, the Iranian nuclear programme, postwar Georgia and the need to reach a new Strategic Arms Reduction Treaty (START) agreement and relaunch the nuclear non-proliferation regime.

The potential for cooperation was therefore high should the political will exist, although the two presidents had yet to identify clearly their foreign policy priorities in the aftermath of the Putin and Bush years. Medvedev, for his part, had presented a liberal agenda of modernisation for Russia that many hoped could reinforce relations with the West, in a potential '1990s revisited' (Averre, 2010). This set the tone for a new era of relations with the US, should the new administration be willing to engage and address Russia's grievances. Therefore the message coming from Russia was one of cautious optimism, sceptical as to what this new era might bring as far as the redefinition of a post-Cold War order is concerned. Illustrating this, the new National Security Strategy of the Russian Federation until 2020 of May 2009 was innovative in having a clear link between Russia's ability to defend its national security and the country's economic potential (de Haas, 2009, p. 3; National Security Strategy, 2009), according to Medvedev's modernisation agenda. Nevertheless although this was a clear departure from Cold War language and perspectives, from the external dimension both NATO and the US remained central references to Russia's security both as important partners and as potential threats (Jolkver, 2009).

On the US side, one of the first decisions of the Obama administration was to reengage Russia by changing the rhetoric towards Moscow and by looking to build on the substantial bilateral agenda that they shared. US Vice President Joe Biden's speech at the Munich Security Conference in 2009 was the launch pad for the reset policy. In his words, 'It's time to press the reset button and to revisit the many areas where we can and should be working together with Russia' (Biden, 2009). Overall during 2009, both countries moved towards more positive terms and took important steps towards cooperation, culminating with the signing in Prague of a new START agreement. Russia also agreed to UN sanctions on Iran, following US guarantees that the Missile Defence

System in Eastern Europe was being reconsidered (Winchester, 2009, p. 46; Cooper, 2009).

Another potential area of cooperation between Moscow and Washington is the war in Afghanistan. In this regard the decision of the Kyrgyz Parliament in February 2009 to terminate the US leasing of the Manas airbase, which is fundamental to US military operations in Afghanistan, caught the new US administration by surprise (EurasiaNet, 2009). Moscow's reaction was to offer Russian airspace to replace the Kyrgyz facilities, in a clear attempt to force the US to acknowledge that the road to Afghanistan runs through Moscow (Mankoff, 2009). Finally, during his visit to the Kremlin in July 2009, Obama signed an agreement with Russia allowing US military goods to transit through Russian territory. The volume of supplies transited through the Northern Distribution Network has expanded, effectively making Russia a central partner in Afghanistan (White House, 2010).

The reset policy has been highly controversial, with its critics saying that the US is playing into Russia's games, putting forward concessions with little to show for (FPI, 2010; Cohen, 2010). Its supporters underline the need to redefine and rebuild relations, based on a more comprehensive and institutionalised foreign policy (Ikome and Motsamai, 2009, p. 3). A central step in this regard has been the establishment of a new overarching bilateral presidential commission, chaired by the two Presidents and with Secretary of State Hilary Clinton and Foreign Minister Sergei Lavrov coordinating its work. The commission has thirteen working groups and covers a wide spectrum of issues, from nuclear security to business, civil society and education, among others (Plater-Zyberk, 2009, p. 6; see also the website of the US–Russia Bilateral Presidential Commission). Although this work has been fundamental to allowing a relaxation in relations, moving forward important issues, in Eurasia there is less reason for optimism.

In fact the dynamics that were under way when President Medvedev arrived at the Kremlin and the lack of US capability to redesign a new strategic approach to Central Asia has left regional dynamics mainly unchanged since the reset button was hit. Russia has pursued a policy of increased economic and military presence in Central Asia, distributing financial assistance and investing in highly profitable and strategic sectors in regional economies (Barry, 2009). However despite these efforts to reinforce a 'sphere of privileged interests', Russia has found that 'dealing with Central Asian neighbours is no easier than it has been over the course of the past two decades' (Kanet, 2010, p. 93). For the US the hardest lessons to be learned are related to the political crisis in April 2010 in Kyrgyzstan.

The presence of the Manas transit centre and the management of relations with the Bakiev regime were fraught with contradictions and the potential coalescence of corrupt practices were exposed by the political crisis (Maher, 2010). We can therefore say that competition between the US and Russia is still on in Central Asia, and that so far no major changes have been visible in the management of regional issues.

For the Central Asian multivector foreign policies, competition for influence among several hegemons serves the purpose of protecting the regional elites from one-sided pressure. Competition has favoured the status quo and has provided limited responses to regional challenges. As argued above the reset policy is unlikely to change the current state of affairs, as there is little evidence that long-term US and Russian foreign policy goals have changed towards a cooperative effort in stabilising Central Asia. For Russia, safeguarding its regional hegemonic position, especially against the US military presence, has been a major priority. As Deyermond (2009, p. 171) argues, even if peaceful hegemonic coexistence has been possible in Central Asia, Russia has made preservation of its hegemonic role in Central Asia in the security sphere a crucial aspect of its policies. As the US prepares to disengage from Afghanistan, the challenge to Russia's hegemonic position in the security field might diminish, and this might mean less risk of hegemonic conflict, but it will also test Russia's ability to provide for regional security. Moreover hegemonic competition on trade, financial assistance and soft power will be maintained in a broad spectrum of aspiring regional hegemons, including China and India. Both scenarios indicate a reinforcement of the status quo in Central Asia, based on the lessons learned from the past pursuit of multivector foreign policy doctrines.

Conclusion

The main argument made here is that both the US and Russia continue to favour their own short-/medium-term priorities towards Central Asia, rather than find cooperative ways to address the region's main security concerns. The US pattern of engagement illustrates this short-term interests approach, whereas Russia continues to be suspicious of the US presence in the region and is reluctant to cooperate with the US in addressing common concerns. Although the war efforts in Afghanistan could push both actors into a common effort, the inheritance of competition has hampered the good intentions of the reset policy. The lack of institutional frameworks for comprehensive consultation to take place has further limited cooperative efforts.

This context is today one of great urgency in making sure that Central Asia does not fall into a cycle of political instability, criminality and violence that could put an overwhelming strain on the fragile regimes in the region. History has taught us that the response by the ruling elites tends to reinforce a pattern of authoritarianism that could end up by further weakening these states. As the US prepares to leave Afghanistan, the trend will be for the forces operating in the region to move with more ease, posing renewed threats. Although Russia has claimed for itself a role of security guarantor, so far it has been reluctant to deploy forces either in the context of the bilateral agreements it has with some of the Central Asian states or of the CSTO. In this scenario Uzbekistan's role in regional stability will become crucial, and this might mean renewed tensions with its neighbours. This is of particular concern to Kyrgyzstan, whose political context is extremely vulnerable and which hosts a large Uzbek minority in the South.

What role the US will assign to its cooperation with Central Asia in a post-Afghanistan scenario and how much relations with Russia will normalise after the next round of elections in 2012 both in the US and in Russia, is a key question in Central Asian stability. As for Russia, it would be wise to acknowledge the limitations of its own strategy towards Central Asia and to design a long-term engagement aimed at the development and stabilisation of its southern borders.

Notes

The author would like to thank Professor Derek Averre for his comments on earlier drafts of this chapter. Naturally the usual disclaimer applies and the sole responsibility for the final outcome is mine alone.

1. The CST is a mutual defence alliance, establishing consultation and military assistance mechanisms in the event of an external attack on its members – Armenia, Belarus, Russia, Kazakhstan, Kyrgyzstan and Tajikistan. In May 2002, the Collective Security Treaty Organisation (CSTO) was established.

References

Akiner, Shirin (2001) *Tajikistan: Disintegration or Reconciliation?* (London: Royal Institute of International Affairs).

Allison, Roy (2001) 'Conclusion: Central Asian security in the regional and international context', in Roy Allison and Lena Jonson (eds), *Central Asian Security: The New International Context* (London: Royal Institute of International Affairs), pp. 247–68.

Anderson, Liam and Michael Beck (2000) 'U.S. political activism in Central Asia: the case of Kyrgyzstan and Uzbekistan', in Gary K. Bertsch et al. (eds),

Crossroads and Conflict: Security and Foreign Policy in the Caucasus and Central Asia (New York: Routledge), pp. 75–89.

Antonenko, Oksana (2001) 'Putin's gamble', *Survival*, vol. 43, no. 4, pp. 49–60.

Averre, Derek (2010) 'Triangulation or strangulation? The US, the EU and Russia in European security governance', paper presented at the University Association for Contemporary European Studies (UACES) 40th Annual Conference on 'Exchanging Ideas on Europe: Europe at a Crossroads', Bruges, 6–8 September.

Baev, Pavel K. (2004) 'Assessing Russia's cards: three petty games in Central Asia', *Cambridge Review of International Affairs*, vol. 17, no. 2, pp. 269–83.

Barry, Ellen (2009) 'Russia's neighbors resist wooing and bullying', *New York Times*, 2 July, available at: http://www.nytimes.com/2009/07/03/world/europe/03russia.html (accessed 20 September 2010).

Biden, Joseph R. (2009) Speech given on 7 February at the 45th Munich Security Conference, Munich, 6–8 February, available at: http://www.security conference.de/archive/konferenzen/rede.php?menu_2009=&menu_konferenz en=&sprache=en&id=238& (accessed 27 September 2010).

Blank, Stephan (2001) 'The United States and Central Asia', in Roy Allison and Lena Jonson (eds), *Central Asian Security: The New International Context* (London: Royal Institute of International Affairs), pp. 127–51.

Boucher, Richard A. (2006) Testimony by the Assistant Secretary for South and Central Asian Affairs at the US Congress, House of Representatives, 109th Congress, 2nd Session, 26 April, available at: http://commdocs.house.gov/committees/intlrel/hfa27230.000/hfa27230_0f.htm (accessed 29 January 2012).

Burghart, Dan (2007) 'The new nomads? American military presence in Central Asia', *China and Eurasia Forum Quarterly*, vol. 5, no. 2, pp. 5–19.

Buzan, Barry and Ole Waever (2003) *Regions and Powers: The Structure of International Security* (Cambridge: Cambridge University Press).

Cohen, Ariel (2010) 'Reset the Russian reset policy', *Wall Street Journal*, 10 August, available at: http://online.wsj.com/article/SB1000142405274870416490457420983022047918.html (accessed 26 September 2010).

Cooley, Alexander (2008) 'US bases and democratization in Central Asia', *Orbis*, vol. 52, no. 1, pp. 65–90.

Cooper, Helene (2009) 'Obama makes gains at UN on Iran and proliferation', *New York Times*, 23 September, available at: http://www.nytimes.com/2009/09/24/world/24prexy.html?scp=9&sq=Sanctions%20iran%20russia%20missile&st=cse (accessed 26 September 2010).

Cornell, Svante E. (2006) 'The narcotics threat in Greater Central Asia: from crime–terror nexus to state infiltration?', *China and Eurasia Forum Quarterly*, vol. 4, no. 1, pp. 37–67.

Cutler, Robert (2007) 'US–Russian strategic relations and the structuration of Central Asia', *Perspectives on Global Development and Technology*, vol. 6, nos 1–3, pp. 109–25.

de Haas, Marcel (2009) 'Medvedev's security policy: a provisional assessment', *Russian Analytical Digest*, no. 62, pp. 2–5.

Deyermond, Ruth (2009) 'Matrioshka hegemony? Multi-leveled hegemonic competition and security in post-Soviet Central Asia', *Review of International Studies*, vol. 35, no. 1, pp. 151–73.

EurasiaNet (2002) 'Russia to establish air base in Kyrgyzstan, deals blow to US strategic interests in Central Asia', 2 December, available at: http://

www.eurasianet.org/departments/insight/articles/eav120302.shtml (accessed 14 September 2010).

EurasiaNet (2005) 'Uzbekistan and Russia sign mutual defense pact', 14 November, available at: http://www.eurasianet.org/departments/insight/articles/eav111505.shtml (accessed 14 September 2010).

EurasiaNet (2009) 'Kyrgyzstan: Parliament to consider Bill closing American air base', 4 February, available at: http://www.eurasianet.org/departments/insightb/articles/eav020409a.shtml (accessed 12 April 2010).

Fenopetov, Vladimir (2006) 'The drug crime threat to countries located on the "Silk Road"', *China and Eurasia Forum Quarterly*, vol. 4, no. 1, pp. 5–13.

Foreign Policy Concept of the Russian Federation (1993) Reprinted in Andrei Melville and Tatiana Shakleina (eds), *Russian Foreign Policy in Transition: Concepts and Realities* (Budapest: Central European University (CEU) Press, 2005), pp. 27–64.

Foreign Policy Initiative (FPI) (2010) 'Evaluating the US–Russian "reset"', Foreign Policy Initiative, 22 June, available at: http://www.foreignpolicyi.org/node/19243 (accessed 28 September 2010).

Freire, Maria Raquel (2009) 'Russian policy in Central Asia: supporting, balancing, coercing, or imposing?', *Asian Perspective*, vol. 33, no. 2, pp. 125–49.

Freire, Maria Raquel and Licínia Simão (2008). 'As eleições presidenciais na Rússia: continuidade na mudança', Instituto Português de Relações Internacionais (IPRI), *IPRI Occasional Paper*, No. 32, March, available at: http://www.ipri.pt/publicacoes/working_paper/working_paper.php?idp=231 (accessed 26 September 2010).

Fried, Daniel (2005) Testimony by the Assistant Secretary, Bureau of European and Eurasian Affairs, at the US Congress, House of Representatives, 109th Congress, 1st Session, 27 October available at: http://Commdocs.house.gov/committees/intlrel/hfa24201.000/hfa24201_0f.htm (accessed 29 January 2012).

Garnett, Sherman W., Alexander Rahr and Koji Watanabe (2000) *The New Central Asia: In Search of Stability* (New York, Paris and Tokyo: The Trilateral Commission).

Giragosian, Richard (2004) 'The US military engagement in Central Asia and the Southern Caucasus: an overview', *Journal of Slavic Military Studies*, vol. 17, no. 1, pp. 43–77.

Gullette, David (2010) 'Kyrgyzstan: components of crisis', openDemocracy, 28 June, available at: http://www.opendemocracy.net/david-gullette/kyrgyzstan-components-of-crisis (accessed 3 September 2010).

Hill, Fiona (2001) 'Une stratégie incertaine: la politique des États-Unis dans le Caucase et en Asie centrale depuis 1991', *Politique Étrangère*, vol. 66, no. 1, pp. 95–108.

Hill, Fiona (2002) 'The United States and Russia in Central Asia: Uzbekistan, Tajikistan, Afghanistan, Pakistan, and Iran', *Brookings*, 15 August, available at: http://www.brookings.edu/speeches/2002/0815russia_hill.aspx (accessed 27 September 2010).

Hill, Fiona (2003) 'Central Asia and the Caucasus: the impact of the war on terrorism', in Adrian Karatnycky, Alexander J. Motyl and Amanda Schnetzer (eds), *Nations in Transit 2003* (Lanham, MD: Rowman and Littlefield), pp. 39–50.

Ikome, Francis and Dimpho Motsamai (2009) 'Moscow and Washington: "unclenching the fist" and "resetting the button"', *Global Insight*, No. 90, October (Pretoria: Institute for Global Dialogue), available at: http://www.igd.

org.za/downloads/global%20insight/Global%20Insight%2090-1.pdf (accessed 29 September 2010).

International Crisis Group (ICG) (2002a) *Central Asia: Border Disputes and Conflict Potential*, International Crisis Group, *Asia Report*, No. 33, 4 April (Osh/Brussels: International Crisis Group).

International Crisis Group (ICG) (2002b) *Central Asia: Water and Conflict*, International Crisis Group, *Asia Report*, No. 34, 30 May (Osh/Brussels: International Crisis Group).

International Crisis Group (ICG) (2005) *The Curse of Cotton: Central Asia's Destructive Monoculture*, International Crisis Group, *Asia Report*, No. 93, 28 February (Bishkek/Brussels: International Crisis Group).

Jackson, Nicole J. (2003) *Russian Foreign Policy and the CIS: Theories, Debates and Actions* (New York: Routledge).

Jafalian, Annie (2004) 'L'oléoduc Bakou–Ceyhan: paradoxes et cohérence de la stratégie américaine des pipelines', *Politique Étrangère*, no. 1, pp. 151–63.

Jolkver, Nikita (2009) 'Russia's security strategy considers new and old challenges', *DW-World.de Deutsche Welle*, 6 July, available at: http://www.dw-world. de/dw/article/0,,4459148,00.html (accessed 15 September 2010).

Jonson, Lena (2001) 'Russia and Central Asia', in Roy Allison and Lena Jonson (eds), *Central Asian Security: The New International Context* (London: Royal Institute of International Affairs), pp. 95–126.

Kanet, Roger E. (2008) 'The return of Imperial Russia: Russia and its neighbors', Program in Arms Control, Disarmament, and International Security (ACDIS), *ACDIS Occasional Paper*, September, available at: http://acdis.illinois. edu/assets/docs/309/TheReturnofImperialRussiaRussiaandItsNeighbors.pdf (accessed 13 May 2010).

Kanet, Roger E. (2010) 'Russia and the Greater Caspian Basin: withstanding the US challenge', in Maria Raquel Freire and Roger E. Kanet (eds), *Key Players and Regional Dynamics in Eurasia: The Return of the 'Great Game'* (New York: Palgrave Macmillan), pp. 81–102.

Kobrinskaya, Irina (2005) 'The CIS in Russian foreign policy: causes and effects', in Hanna Smith (ed.), *Russia and its Foreign Policy* (Saarijärvi: Kikimora Publications), pp. 77–92.

Laruelle, Marléne (2007) 'Asie Centrale: Le retour de la Russie', *Politique Internationale*, no. 115, electronic version, available at: http://www.politiquein ternationale.com/revue/read2.php?id_revue=115&id=630&content=texte (accessed 12 September 2010).

Laruelle, Marlène, et al. (eds) (2010) *China and India in Central Asia: A New 'Great Game'?* (New York: Palgrave Macmillan).

Lubin, Nancy (2004) 'Who's watching the watchdogs? Drug trafficking in Central Asia', in Dan Burghart and Theresa Sabonis-Helf (eds), *In the Tracks of Tamerlane: Central Asia's Path to the 21st Century* (Washington, DC: National Defense University, Center For Technology and National Security Policy, pp. 361–76.

Luong, Pauline Jones and Erika Weinthal (2002) 'New friends, new fears in Central Asia', *Foreign Affairs*, vol. 81, no. 2, pp. 61–70.

Maher, Heather (2010) 'Congressional panel told corruption allegations at Kyrgyz air base hurt US image', Radio Free Europe/Radio Liberty, 24 April, available at: http://www.rferl.org/content/Congressional_Panel_Told_Corruption_At_ Kyrgyz_Air_Base_Hurt_US_Image/2023292.html (accessed 20 September 2010).

Mankoff, Jeffrey (2009) 'The tricky US–Russia "Reset" button', *Council on Foreign Relations*, 18 February, available at: http://www.cfr.org/publication/18551/ tricky_usrussia_reset_button.html (accessed 20 September 2010).

Marat, Erica (2008) 'The changing dynamics of state–crime relations in Kyrgyzstan', *Central Asia Caucasus Institute Analyst*, 20 February, available at: http://www.cacianalyst.org/?q=node/4796 (accessed 20 September 2010).

Marat, Erica (2010) 'Bakiyev, the security structures, and the April 7 violence in Kyrgyzstan', *Central Asia Caucasus Institute Analyst*, 28 April, available at: http://www.cacianalyst.org/?q=node/5316 (accessed 20 September 2010).

Markedonov, Sergei (2010) 'Post-Soviet integration: does the CIS work?', open-Democracy, *oD Russia Post-Soviet World*, 13 January, available at: http://www. opendemocracy.net/od-russia/sergei-markedonov/post-soviet-integration-does-cis-work (accessed 31 August 2010).

National Security Strategy (2009) 'National Security Strategy of the Russian Federation until 2020', Decree of the President of the Russian Federation, Moscow, 12 May, no. 537, available at: http://www.scrf.gov.ru/documents/99. htmlhttp://www.scrf.gov.ru/documents/99.html (accessed 31 August 2010).

Nichol, Jim (2003) *Central Asia's New States: Political Developments and Implications for US Interests*, CRS Issue Brief for Congress, 18 May, available at: http://cnie. org/NLE/CRSreports/international (accessed 31 August 2010).

Olcott, Martha Brill (1999) 'Pipelines and pipe dreams: energy development and Caspian society', *Journal of International Affairs*, vol. 53, no. 1, pp. 305–23.

Plater-Zyberk, Henry (2009) 'US–Russia strategic relations: Obama and Biden visit Moscow, Tbilisi and Kiev – planed contradictions?', *Defense Academy of the United Kingdom, Research and Assessment Branch, Russian Series*, August, available at: http://www.da.mod.uk/colleges/arag/document-listings/.../09(10)%20HPZ2. pdf (accessed 31 August 2010).

Pomfret, Richard (2009) 'Central Asia and the global economic crisis', *EU Central Asia Monitoring (EUCAM)*, 7 June, pp. 1–5, available at: http://www.eucentral asia.eu/fileadmin/user_upload/PDF/Policy_Briefs/PB-7-eversion.pdf. (accessed 31 August 2010).

Pratt, Martin and Clive Schofield (1997) 'International boundaries, resources and environmental security in the Caspian Sea', in Gerald Blake et al. (eds), *International Boundaries and Environmental Security: Frameworks for Regional Cooperation* (London: Kluwer Law International), pp. 81–104.

Radio Free Europe/Radio Liberty (RFE/RL) (2004) 'Tajikistan: first permanent Russian military base opened', Radio Free Europe/Radio Liberty, 17 October, available at: http://www.rferl.org/content/article/1055375.htmlhttp://www. rferl.org/content/article/1055375.html (accessed 31 August 2010).

Rashid, Ahmed (1994) *The Resurgence of Central Asia: Islam or Nationalism?* (London: Zed Books).

Rashid, Ahmed (2002) *Jihad: Ascensão do Islão Militante na Ásia Central*, trans. by Freitas e Silva (Lisbon: Terramar).

Sakwa, Richard and Mark Webber (1999) 'The Commonwealth of Independent States, 1991–1998: stagnation and survival', *Europe–Asia Studies*, vol. 51, no. 3, pp. 379–415.

Stepanova, Ekaterina (2009) 'Does Russia want the West to succeed in Afghanistan?', (Program on New Approaches to Research and Security in Eurasia), PONARS Eurasia, *Policy Memo.*, No. 61, September (Washington, DC: George Washington University).

Stern, David L. (2009) 'Has Obama put human rights on the back burner?', *Global Post*, 14 August, available at: http://www.globalpost.com/dispatch/asia/090807/us-central-asia-policy?page=0,1 (accessed 28 September 2010).

Swanstrom, Niklas, Svante E. Cornell and Anara Tabishalieva (2005) 'A strategic conflict analysis of Central Asia with a focus on Kyrgyzstan and Tajikitan', Central Asia–Caucasus Institute and Silk Road Studies Program, Washington, DC, and Stockholm, June, available at: http://www.silkroadstudies.org/docs/publications/2005/SIDA_CA.pdf (accessed 28 September 2010).

Talbott, Strobe (1997) 'A farewell to Flashman: American policy in the Caucasus and Central Asia', Address at the Johns Hopkins School of Advanced International Studies by the US Deputy Secretary of State, Washington, DC, 21 July, available at: http://findarticles.com/p/articles/mi_m1584/is_n6_v8/ai_19715181/ (accessed 11 November 2011).

The Economist (2010) 'Troubled Tajikistan: where cure begets disease', *The Economist*, 23 September, available at: http://www.economist.com/blogs/asia-view/2010/09/troubled_tajikistan (accessed 28 September 2010).

Trenin, Dmitri (2007) 'Russia and Central Asia: interests, policies, and prospects', in Eugene Rumer, Dmitri Trenin and Huasheng Zhao, *Central Asia: Views from Washington, Moscow, and Beijing* (New York: M. E. Sharpe), pp. 75–136.

Tutubalina, Olga (2010) 'At least 23 soldiers killed in Tajikistan ambush', ABC News/Associated Press, 20 September, available at: http://www.abc.net.au/news/stories/2010/09/20/3016180.htm (accessed 28 September 2010).

US–Russia Bilateral Presidential Commission, website available at: http://www.state.gov/p/eur/ci/rs/usrussiabilat/index.htm (accessed 28 September 2010).

White House, The (2010) 'US–Russia relations: "Reset" Fact Sheet', 24 June, available at: http://www.whitehouse.gov/the-press-office/us-russia-relations-reset-fact-sheet (accessed 28 September 2010).

Wilhelmsen, Julie and Geir Flikke (2005) 'Evidence of Russia's Bush Doctrine in the CIS', *European Security*, vol. 14, no. 3, pp. 387–417.

Winchester, Lauren T. (2009) 'A unilateral US and a resurgent Russia: US–Russia relations, 2000–2008' (PhD thesis, Carnegie Mellon University, available at: http://repository.cmu.edu/cgi/viewcontent.cgi?article=1026&context=hsshonors (accessed 28 September 2010).

Wishnick, Elizabeth (2002) *Growing US Security Interests in Central Asia*, Report to the US Army War College, October (Carlisle, PA: Strategic Studies Institute, US Army War College).

Xing, Guangchend (2001) 'China and Central Asia', in Roy Allison and Lena Jonson (eds), *Central Asian Security: The New International Context* (London: Royal Institute of International Affairs), pp. 152–70.

8
Russia's Foreign Policy in Central Asia: From Yeltsin to Medvedev

Diana Digol

Introduction

Foreign policy-makers and scholars alike pay constant attention to Russia's foreign policy. To date several authors have attempted to identify phases in Russia's foreign policy. Hence Richard Sakwa (2008, 2009), reviewing the period from 1991 to 2008, identifies six main phases in Russian foreign policy since 1990: 'the emergence phase, before the abortive coup of August 1991'; 'the established phase: August to December 1991'; 'the romantic' phase, January 1992–February 1993; 'the reassertion phase, March 1993–December 1995'; 'competitive pragmatism, January 1996–99'; 'from new realism to New Cold War, 2000–08?' These phases are unequal in time and coincide with either a change of the Russian President or Minister of Foreign Affairs. Dmitri Trenin defines the period from 1992 to 2003 as 'integration into Western society'; the period from 2004 to 2008 as the 'self-affirmation period' or alternatively as the 'solitary voyage'; and the period from 2009 to the present as that of the 'country's modernisation' (Trenin, 2010). Vladimir Paramonov reviews Russian foreign policy in Central Asia over the period from 1992 to 2008 and divides it into three stages: 1992–95, 1996–99 and 2000–08 (Paramonov et al., 2009). This periodisation is also unequal in length, trying to capture for each period the changes in Russia's foreign policy towards Central Asia.

In this paper I argue that the period between 1991 and 2008 could be divided into two sub-periods that coincide with the presidencies of Boris Yeltsin and Vladimir Putin, 1990–2000 and 2000–08, respectively. I would further argue that in 2008, a new period in Russia's foreign policy started, which can already be associated with President Dmitri Medvedev. This periodisation is based on several criteria. First, it pays tribute to the individuals who were vested with the constitutional power to preside over Russia's foreign policy and who also assumed the responsibility, and often the blame, from domestic and international critics for its failures and successes. Second, this periodisation reveals different existing conditions, internationally and domestically, at the beginning of each president's first term. Third, this periodisation shows various foreign policy objectives and the means that were employed by three presidents to achieve them. Fourth, it also facilitates seeing the similarities in Russia's modern foreign policy from one period to another. Fifth, this division elucidates the differences in the foreign policy *styles* of the three presidents.

It would be wrong however to assume that these three periods were unrelated to each other – just the opposite. I argue that each of these periods was built on the previous period's failures and successes. Moreover a new period did not necessarily mean a comprehensive change in Russia's foreign policy, although each period had certain new features. I demonstrate that, overall, Russia's modern foreign policy from Yeltsin to Medvedev was simultaneously characterised both by continuity and by change. Continuity refers to the permanency of Russia's foreign policy interests and Russia's national ambitions; to the progressive complexity of Russia's foreign policy agenda, which both broadens and deepens its agenda; and to the continuous building up of the body of political documents that define Russian foreign policy. Continuity also refers to Russia's core foreign policy partners. Continuity refers to the lack of abrupt changes in Russia's foreign policy from one president to the next. Changes concern the progressive geographical extent of Russia's foreign policy interests and foreign policy vectors. Changes refer to the events that reshaped the international and domestic arena, and as a consequence impacted Russia's foreign policy. Changes refer to the change in Russia's standing on certain international issues. Change also refers to various individual styles of conducting foreign policy.

This chapter consists of three main parts. Each part is focused on Russia's foreign policy under one of the three presidents: Yeltsin, Putin or Medvedev. I start each section by providing an overall framework of Russia's foreign policy during the tenure of the given president, and then provide a synopsis of Russia's foreign policy in Central Asia within the same time period.

The Yeltsin period

The Yeltsin period occurred immediately after Russia proclaimed its independence from the Soviet Union in 1991.[1] Russia's survival as a state was of the utmost concern to Yeltsin. Domestically the disputed privatisation of Russia's state property and rampant criminalisation of Russia in the 1990s, separatist movements in Tatarstan and other parts of Russia, the Chechen War in 1994–96, the Russian constitutional crisis of 1993 and the shelling of Russia's White House, the presidential election in politically divided Russia in 1996, and the economic crisis of 1998, all posed a threat to Russia's integrity as a state, bringing Russia to the verge of civil war or state collapse (Perekrest, 2006). Internationally Russia was coping with the new reality of not being a winner in the Cold War,[2] of losing an immense swathe of territory, of no longer being a superpower, with a new division between non-Russian Europe and Russia that had moved significantly eastwards.

Yeltsin aimed at keeping the integrity of Russia; however he lacked a clear vision of the best policy for Russia to pursue in order to achieve this aim both domestically and internationally. No firm principles under-lay Russia's foreign policy. The first national concept of foreign policy would not be elaborated until 1993; the national security concept not until 1997 (Yeltsin, 1997); and when they were elaborated, they mainly served declaratory purposes, being elaborated mostly for domestic consumption rather than for the international community. Russia was in search of new objectives, both domestically and internationally. Yeltsin continued to take decisions often individually and then announce them publicly, catching Russian diplomats unawares.

Both domestic and international challenges were overwhelming. Russia was a weak state internally and internationally, politically, eco-nomically and financially, unable to exert any significant influence in the international arena, while at the same time being itself very vulnerable to external influences. This resulted in a hectic domestic policy and a chaotic foreign policy. The lack of efficient coordination, internal political struggles among Russia's political elite and the constant reshuffling of people in key positions were not conducive to a congruent foreign policy.[3] Hence Russia's foreign policy was shaped to a great degree by international events and international actors. Russia could not formulate an independent foreign policy, being largely reduced to a foreign policy recipient.

Throughout Yeltsin's presidency Russia pursued a univector foreign policy. In Yeltsin's early years Russia pursued a Euro-Atlanticist course in its foreign policy, seeking membership in Western organisations. This vector was visible in the destination and number of Yeltsin's international trips – most of them were to the West. Russia became a member of the Council of Europe in 1996; however its first membership application in 1995 was suspended from consideration by the Council on the grounds of human rights violations in Chechnya (Saari, 2006, p. 11). By 1998, Yeltsin had secured an invitation to Russia to join the informal but influential group of the seven most industrialised and powerful countries (G7). However it was not until 2002 that Russia would be allowed to participate in the finance ministers' meetings (Sakwa, 2008). Russia's initiative in 1994 to have the Commonwealth of Independent States (CIS) granted the status of a regional peacekeeping organisation at the UN was unsuccessful, and Russia's application for World Trade Organization (WTO) membership was blocked by the US (since 1993) (Curtis, 1996). Hence Yeltsin's struggle to integrate Russia rapidly into Western structures largely failed.

Furthermore Russia was unable to prevent the US/NATO bombing of Serbia,[4] which the US accidentally or specifically timed with then Prime Minister Yevgeny Primakov's expected official visit to the US to negotiate the next credit line (Glukhov, 2006). To Russia and the Russians this particular event – the bombing of Serbia – was one of utter humiliation and hence had numerous consequences. It caused a radical shift in the attitude towards the West, and to the US in particular. It also changed the political balance of forces in Russia, and thus caused a radical change in Russia's foreign policy from a pro-Western orientation towards the opposite.

Disillusioned with Russia's Western partners and hence with the Euro-Atlanticist orientation of his country's foreign policy, Yeltsin shifted his focus back to the 'Near Abroad' countries, simultaneously reinvigorating Russia's relations with its former Cold War allies in the Middle East and further away. He also declared the pursuit of a new foreign policy goal aimed at becoming an independent centre of power and reasserting Russia's role as a Eurasian power. However only by the end of the Yeltsin term was Russia able to restore control over basic state structures and show signs of economic recovery.

The Yeltsin period in Russia's foreign policy was characterised by a univector foreign policy, in constant search of objectives, characterised by a radical shift from a pro-Western – Euro-Atlanticist – vector towards a Eurasian vector. Progressive disillusionment with the Western partners' actions was in the background of many foreign policy decisions. Weak state structures, torn apart by internal political struggles and contradictions, and unclear decision-making made Russian foreign policy unpredictable. Overwhelming domestic and international challenges did not contribute to the elaboration of a congruent foreign policy, making it hectic and volatile. This determined the often emotional, inconsequential, chaotic and unpredictable style of Yeltsin's foreign policy, which overall was the weak foreign policy of a weak state, living in the shadow of its great past.

With the breakup of the Soviet Union, all Central Asian countries had become full-fledged independent states for the first time in modern history. This presented Russia, challenged domestically and internationally, with yet another challenge to formulate its foreign policy towards the Central Asian countries in new conditions.

This was the period when Russia considered these countries – the poorest republics in the Soviet Union, which had been on constant state subsidies, Muslim and thus viewed by the Russian leadership as less reliable than the Christian West – a burden to Russia, as it pursued a Euro-Atlanticist vector in its foreign policy in the hope of a fast economic recovery, while at the same time trying to maintain its territorial integrity.

Moreover each of the Central Asian states was willing to forge a distinctive relationship with Russia, conditioned by geographical proximity to Russia, China or Afghanistan, the size of the Russian minority on its territory, its endowment with various natural resources and its leaders' perception of the greatness of their own countries. Each Central Asian country was further willing to exercise its newly acquired sovereignty, while at the same time continuing to exploit the benefits of the previous relationship with Russia. Kazakhstan initiated a dispute with Russia on payments for the lease of the Baikonur space launching station, and since then periodic renegotiations on the level of payments for the lease have taken place (BBC News, 2002). Kyrgyzstan stopped sending gold to be processed in Russia (Olcott, 1996). Turkmenistan introduced entry visas for Russian citizens, seriously inconveniencing Russian businessmen maintaining their businesses with Turkmen partners. Furthermore Turkmenistan and Uzbekistan increased the price several times for gas exported to Russia. Tajikistan put forward demands for the withdrawal of Russian troops from its territory, but soon afterwards retracted these demands (Seifert, 2002).

This resulted in Russia's open disregard for the Central Asian countries, which were no longer treated even as 'junior brothers' but simply as 'abandoned children', or rather 'disenfranchised children'. The subsidies from Moscow were no longer delivered, products delivered from Central Asia were no longer paid for, military cooperation was reduced almost to zero, and so on. Various initiatives by Central Asian leaders as well as their appeals were neglected, refused or simply fell on deaf ears.

Russia did not develop a clear policy towards Central Asia during the Yeltsin years, nor did the Russian-led multilateral structures, such as the CIS. The CIS was more a 'paper' organisation than a functioning body, created to oversee the civilised divorce of the former Soviet republics. The Central Asian countries were not the focus of Moscow's attention either, since the region did not experience the rise of destructive nationalism that led to a pronounced anti-Russian policy and overall remained largely peaceful, unlike the situation in Moldova, Georgia, Armenia or Azerbaijan. This contributed to the further neglect of the Central Asian countries for several more years until the swing in Russia's pro-Western policy orientation occurred in the opposite direction, when once again Central Asian countries came back into focus for Russia.

However by then this was already a different Central Asia. There were five independent and sovereign countries engaged in an extraordinary effort in national and political self-identification intended to find their place in the international arena. Moreover several Central Asian countries, after undergoing a complex process of accelerated political change, consolidated their authoritarian regimes and strengthened their positions. By this time the Central Asian countries were already looking for partners elsewhere to solve their numerous problems: border instability, increasing Islamisation, inter- and intra-state tensions, and so on. Russia had lost the hegemonic position that it had enjoyed during the Soviet period. Russia had already lost its priority access to raw materials originating from Central Asia, such as gas and oil; Central Asian countries were actively negotiating alternative transit routes.

At the same time Russia became exposed to new threats originating from Central Asia. Tajikistan was going through a civil war, Uzbekistan faced the intensified anti-government activity of Islamist groups, including the Islamic Movement of Uzbekistan (IMU), both of which were risking destabilising the whole region. Russia's decreased military presence and involvement in Central Asia, coupled with a lack of alternative economic opportunities for its populations in these countries, gave rise to increased drug-trafficking from Afghanistan to Russia. General instability on the external border of the former Soviet Union and increased ethnic and nationalistic movements all over Central Asia provoked an extensive exodus of ethnic Russians from the Central Asian countries to Russia, an exodus that Russia could not accommodate.[5] The increased influence of radical Islam from Afghanistan that was spreading rapidly along the borders of the former Soviet Union and penetrating into the countries of Central Asia was seen by Russia as a threat to its own borders. In addition, a visa-free Russia was facing the arrival of labour migrants from Central Asia in search of economic opportunities.

These threats were the focus of Russia's interests in the region. Hence Russia's foreign policy was primarily oriented towards the political and security sector. Russia actively participated in negotiating a peace agreement to end the civil war in Tajikistan in 1997, and again assumed a joint patrol of the former Soviet Union border with Central Asian states. In the economic sector, Russia wanted to regain control over former Soviet resources in Central Asia. Thus Russia continued to exploit its position as a monopoly transit country for Central Asian gas and oil, in particular affecting Kazakhstan, Turkmenistan and Uzbekistan. Russia refused however to restart purchasing products originating from Central Asian countries, thereby causing the closure of several major industrial plants all over Central Asia, worsening the rate of unemployment and further increasing poverty. This policy was only partly attractive to Central Asian countries.

To sum up, on its return to Central Asia, Russia saw the Central Asian states already becoming foreign policy actors in their own right. In the wake of this Russia was unable to formulate the policy that was attractive to the Central Asian states, showing confusion over what constituted Russian interests in Central Asia: its own geopolitical interests, the protection of Russian minorities, energy resources, or other possible alternatives. Furthermore Russia lacked either the economic or military capacity required to continue to hold Central Asia and each of the region's individual states within its sphere of influence. Overall Yeltsin's foreign policy of neglect and of distancing Russia from the Central Asian republics was clearly a failure. The hegemonic role that Russia inherited from the Soviet Union was seriously weakened as a result of the almost decade-long neglect of Central Asia, a role that Russia might never ever fully regain.

The Putin period

The Putin period began in 2000 with his assumption of the presidential office after Yeltsin's largely unexpected resignation. The resurgence of Russia was Putin's most important concern. A certain degree of domestic stability had already been achieved.[6] The continuing war with Chechen rebels, the Beslan school hostage crisis and nearly concurrent terrorist attacks in Moscow, the disaster of the Russian *Kursk* nuclear submarine and several other events were destabilising factors for societal peace, but less so for Russia as a state. On the international scene the events that Russia strongly opposed but could not influence were still taking place: the suspension of Russia's voting rights in the Council of Europe Parliamentary Assembly in 2000 on the grounds of the renewal of hostilities in Chechnya, the 'colour revolutions' in Georgia in 2003,

Ukraine in 2004 and Kyrgyzstan in 2005, the US invasion of Iraq in 2003, the eastern expansion of NATO in 2004 and further US/NATO encouragement of Georgia's and Ukraine's bids for NATO membership, the independence of Kosovo in 2008 and so on. However favourable developments on the international oil market assured additional funds for the state budget that helped ease the most stringent domestic needs and increased the leverage of Russia in the international arena.

Russia was no longer a weak state, internally or externally, politically, economically or financially, and was thus already less vulnerable to external influences. Russia's gross domestic product (GDP) was soaring, making it the ninth largest economy in the world and the fifth largest in Europe. However it was not yet a strong state either. Hence Putin aimed to restore the political influence of Russia internationally and promoted its recognition as a 'great power' by the international community. This became Russia's foreign policy objective under President Putin.

Thus already at the beginning of his term Putin elaborated the National Security Concept (Putin, 2000b), followed by the Foreign Policy Concept (Putin, 2000a). This was the first serious attempt to present the foreign policy orientations and ideological considerations behind Russian policy, listing the challenges and discussing Russia's national interests. Furthermore Putin openly admitted that he considered the collapse of the Soviet Union as 'the greatest geopolitical catastrophe of the [twentieth] century' (BBC News, 2005). He stated that the territory of the former Soviet Union was in Russia's privileged sphere of influence, suggesting that Russia was willing to restore control over Ukraine, Belarus, the Caucasian republics and Central Asia. These statements that preceded Moscow's actions made Russia's foreign policy more predictable in the eyes of the international community.

To make Russia politically stronger and reassert its role as a 'great power', Putin also needed to make it economically and financially stronger. Helped by rising oil prices, Russia repaid the bulk of its debt to the Paris Club of Creditor Nations by 2006 and to the US by 2007. During Putin's presidency Russia's foreign reserves increased significantly, resulting in Russia's inclusion among the countries with the world's highest foreign currency reserves. Putin further made a point of paying off the country's massive Soviet-era debt and avoiding foreign borrowing during his eight-year presidency. Furthermore Putin capitalised the most on Russia's few but specific assets and maximised his leverage from Russia's energy supplies. He initiated a gradual move to increase the price of gas that Russia sold to former Soviet republics in order to bring it to market levels.

To help offset eventual oil market volatility, a Stabilisation Fund was created in 2004; the fund has also helped to prevent the ruble from appreciating. This further encouraged a significant inflow of foreign investments from many European investors attracted by cheaper land, labour and higher growth rates than in the rest of Europe. Russia's twenty-five top banks were listed among the Top 1000 banks of the world by *The Banker* (2006). These were the signs of Russia's eventual economic and financial recovery, which subsequently increased Russia's leverage in the international arena as well.

Russia's foreign policy was no longer univector. There were four discernable vectors in Putin's foreign policy: a 'Western' vector, a 'former Soviet Union' or 'Near Abroad' vector, a 'Cold War allies' vector (China, Syria, India, Iran and so on), and a 'new partners' vector (Brazil, Bolivia, Venezuela and so on). Hence Putin managed to establish and maintain good relations with Russia's core Western partners: US President George W. Bush, German Chancellor Gerhard Schröder, French President Jacques Chirac and Italian Prime Minister Silvio Berlusconi. In 2005, Putin and Schröder negotiated the construction of a major oil pipeline under the Baltic exclusively between Russia and Germany.[7] At the same time Putin made it clear that Russia no longer favoured a unipolar world, one dominated by the United States (BBC News, 2007; Putin, 2007). He clearly voiced Russia's preference for a multipolar world, in which Europeans, Russians, Chinese and others can act as a 'counterweight' to American power (Busvine, 2004). Moreover Putin saw Russia as an alternative power centre alongside America, Europe, China and others.

Russia as a 'great power' was seen by many Western partners as an unaffordable ambition of Russia, while neither Near Abroad partners nor former Cold War allies questioned this position. Thus Russia continued to reinvigorate the relationship with non-Western traditional partners, while maintaining the Western links. This is also the time when Russia started looking for new cooperation partners and began to promote non-Western alliances: with BRICs (Brazil, Russia, India and China), also known as the 'Big Four', and the Shanghai Cooperation Organisation (SCO).

To boost national self-confidence and further strengthen the image of a strong Russia, Moscow needed some international victories. Luckily, or through assistance, in 2007 Russia was chosen to host the 2014 Winter Olympics, and qualified for the Eurocup football semifinals, won the UEFA Cup and the Ice Hockey World Championship and a Eurovision song contest in Belgrade, all in 2008; the last mentioned led in the following year to Russia hosting the Eurovision song contest in Moscow.

Putin was a president of strong statements and many of them concerned the US. Thus in 2004, as a vocal opponent of the US invasion of Iraq without the sanction of the UN Security Council, he called it 'a great political error' and refused to recall the Russian Ambassador to Iraq and sever diplomatic relations with Iraq. In 2007, in what became known as the 'Munich Speech', Putin said that the 'United States has overstepped its borders in all spheres – economic, political and humanitarian, and has imposed itself on other states' and has gone 'from one conflict to another without achieving a full-fledged solution to any of them' (BBC News, 2007). In 2008, Putin accused the US of orchestrating the Georgian War (CNN, 2008; Digol, 2009).

His policy was also characterised by a degree of openness, at times not expected by the West. Hence to the surprise of many he welcomed the establishment of coalition forces military bases in Central Asia before and during the US-led invasion of Afghanistan in the wake of the September 11 attacks in the United States. For Russia it would have been preferable to keep the US out of the Central Asian republics, or at the very least to extract a commitment from Washington to withdraw from these bases as soon as there was no further immediate military purpose for them. However Russia could not disregard the US's status in the international arena and give up its relations with the core Western partner. Moreover Russia was willing to make justified concessions. However the US too changed its rhetoric about Chechen terrorists, acknowledging their links to the networks against which the US had declared a war on terror. At the same time Putin strongly opposed Washington's move to invade Iraq without the explicit sanction of the United Nations Security Council authorising the use of military force.

Russia's foreign policy under Putin was the policy of a state 'getting up from its knees', nurturing its great past and clearly seeing the objectives to be achieved. During Putin's presidency Russia strengthened its international position and formulated its foreign policy based on its national interests and self-perception as a great power. Learning the lessons of the recent past, Russia turned its attention back to its former allies and set out on a search for new partners, while maintaining the already existing partnership links with the West. Russia however could not fully prevent events of which it disapproved. Moreover economically, despite its recovery and the repayment of its debts, it still remained outside the most developed economies of the world. Overall however Putin was a cautious president, acting more like a rational manager of a country than a 'tsar', despite his strong statements. This made Putin's foreign policy more predictable in the eyes of the international community.

As regards Central Asia it was clear for Putin that this region was important in his foreign policy ambitions. Russia's recovered position in Central Asia was seen as instrumental in achieving Putin's foreign policy goals of Russia becoming an independent centre of power and of restoring its image and position as a 'great power'. Putin however no longer had the luxury of a monopoly of influence in the region that Yeltsin could have enjoyed in his early years. Hence Putin put forward a strategy aimed at increasing Russia's regional importance in Central Asia, employing a new policy mix of multilateralism and bilateralism (Putin, 2000a).

Russia accepted the Central Asian countries as independent and sovereign partners and gave a new impetus to its relations in all areas: political, security, military, economic and cultural. The historical ties existing from the time of the Soviet Union among the elites, but also among the populations of these countries, served as a fertile ground for this effort. The economic ties, especially Russia's predominant position regarding the transit routes for gas and oil exported from Central Asian states, added to the strength of mutual politico-economic dependency. Furthermore Russia as a destination country for Central Asian labour migration became the source of remittances, much needed by the Central Asian economies. Newly emerging concerns such as the danger of state disintegration both of Russia and of the Central Asian countries, the desire of the ruling elites to stay in power against the wave of the colour revolutions and increased terrorist activity added to the situation. Moreover Russia's interest in the energy resources of the Central Asian countries was of a different nature to that of China, the European Union and to a lesser extent of the US. The latter were pure importers of carbon resources, unlike both Russia and the energy-rich Central Asian countries.

Hence Russia reinforced its multilateral relations with Central Asia by reinvigorating or creating several regional cooperation frameworks. Within the politically oriented CIS – established in 1991 – Russia emphasised two seemingly effective projects: the creation of an economically oriented customs union with Kazakhstan and Belarus and the deepening of the militarily oriented Collective Security Treaty Organisation (CSTO, set up in 2002). Hence within the CSTO Russia initiated the creation of the Collective Rapid Reaction Force (CRRF), with the primary intention of conducting anti-terrorist operations, fighting transnational crime and drug trafficking and neutralising the effects of natural disasters. In addition, within the confidence-building oriented institutional structure of the SCO (created in 2001), Russia strengthened its relations, especially in the areas of security cooperation and energy policy coordination. Moreover in 2007, the CSTO signed an agreement with the SCO to engage in mutual cooperation on issues such as security, crime and drug trafficking (*Daily Times*, 2007). Parallel to this Russia succeeded in reconfiguring the Organization of Central Asian Cooperation (created in 1994) and the Organization for Democracy and Economic Development (GUAM Group) (Georgia, Ukraine, Uzbekistan, Azerbaijan and Moldova) (created in 2001), primarily oriented to exclude Russia from its cooperation frameworks. Russia's diplomatic efforts encouraged Uzbekistan[8] to leave the GUAM Group and join the CSTO and the economically oriented Eurasian Economic Community (EurAsEC; created in 2001). This reconfiguration of regional organisations in Central Asia could be counted as Russia's diplomatic success.[9] The Organization of Central Asian Cooperation ceased to exist through its absorption into the EurAsEC and GUAM has been seriously weakened by Uzbekistan's withdrawal, hence no Central Asian regional organisations remained of which Russia was not a member.[10] These steps locked Russia and all of the Central Asian states – with the exception of Turkmenistan – into a potentially positive-sum relationship.

Putin continued to view cooperation in political and security areas as the main focus of his foreign policy towards Central Asia. All of the Central Asian states were highly multinational; all of the titular populations had their brethren in the neighbouring countries, including Afghanistan. The kin-state policies of the previous decades were a subject of concern. Moreover some of the states, particularly Tajikistan and Kyrgyzstan, were weak and faced the danger of disintegration or collapse and relied on Russia's support for their survival as states. For its part, Russia was interested in a stable and peaceful Tajikistan as an outpost on the border with Afghanistan and China, in addition to Uzbekistan and Turkmenistan as outposts on the border with Afghanistan. Thus Russia renewed the training of Central Asian border guards and other military personnel, initiated joint military exercises with Central Asian partners within either the CSTO or the SCO, renewed the provision of military equipment at special prices or free of charge and established a military base in Kyrgyzstan and discussed opening others, acting both within multilateral frameworks and bilaterally.

There were however some noticeable developments in the economic sphere as well. To secure its continuing monopolistic position in the energy sector, Russia was no longer only interested in leasing its pipelines to Kazakhstan, Uzbekistan and Turkmenistan for the transport of gas and oil. Russia was now interested in preventing the construction of alternative transit pipeline routes that might bypass its territory, such as Nabucco, or where that was not possible to becoming a part in the deal. Energy was seen as a potent weapon, which could enable

Russia to develop into an energy superpower. Therefore most of Russia's investments went into the strategic energy sector. This earned Putin several rather sarcastic nicknames, including that of 'energy tsar' (Freedman and Brown, 2006).

To maintain the economic support provided to the Central Asian countries from the remittances of guest workers, Russia legalised the status of labour migrants in Russia. This was a significant step in Russian–Central Asian relations. While the Central Asian countries might export gas to a number of other countries and regions besides Russia, they can export their cheap labour only to Russia (*The Economist*, 2008b) or to each other (*The Economist*, 2008a; Kazantsev, 2008).

Russia controlled and exploited specific resources in the region. Still, having clear geographic, economic, social and cultural advantages as its legacy from the Russian and Soviet periods, Russia used them to nurture further interdependence between Moscow and the Central Asian countries. Central Asian leaders felt that Moscow was still more sensitive to their individual concerns than were Washington or Brussels. Hence Russia supported Uzbekistan in its intention to evict the American military airbase in 2005. Russia had the best intelligence sources on Central Asia, making it indispensable to any regional security measures. Moreover Russia had international diplomatic influence; hence Russia supported Kazakhstan's bid in 2007 for the Organization for Security and Co-operation in Europe (OSCE) chairmanship in 2010.

At the same time Russia was interested in specific resources in Central Asia: the energy resources of Kazakhstan, Uzbekistan and Turkmenistan; the Baikonur space launching station in Kazakhstan; metals and minerals in Uzbekistan and Kyrgyzstan; and the agricultural, mainly cotton, production of Uzbekistan. Moreover Russia was interested in Central Asia as a buffer zone for the protection of its southern border against the spread of radical Islam, terrorist intrusions and drug trafficking.

There were however some disagreements between Russia and individual states in Central Asia. Hence between Russia and Uzbekistan, there were several economic issues concerning Russian investments in Uzbekistan and Uzbekistani debts to Russia created in the 1990s. There was a notorious issue about the Rogun hydroplant construction carried out with Russian investments, but agreement between Uzbekistan and Tajikistan was needed before the dispute could be resolved (Cherniavsky, 2010). Furthermore Russia was interested in opening an airbase and getting control over one of the largest deposits of silver in the world located in Tajikistan (*Deutsche Welle*, 2010). Russia viewed with suspicion the continuing US military base in Kyrgyzstan. Turkmenistan kept increasing the price of its gas, while at the same time insisting on increased amounts to be transited through Russian pipelines. Russia enjoyed friendly relations with Kazakhstan; however Kazakhstan, faithful to its multivector foreign policy, continued to counterbalance relations with Russia with a significant increase in its cooperation with other partners, in the first instance with China.

Under Putin Russia partially restored its previously privileged position in the region, becoming the most actively engaged external actor in Central Asia. However Russia was no longer alone in the region. The US, EU, China, India and a number of neighbouring Muslim countries were increasing their diplomatic presence and offering financial support.[11] To ensure its own interests, Russia was receptive to the interests of individual Central Asian countries. Thus Russia practiced a new mix of multilateralism and bilateralism in its relations. The Putin period can be seen as a rationalisation of Russia's approach towards Central Asian states. Overall it was a policy of success in the region. There remained however some disagreements between Russia and the individual states of Central Asia.

The Medvedev period

In 2008, Medvedev was proclaimed the winner of the presidential elections in Russia. So started the Medvedev period. Although it is of course premature to list the *overall* characteristics of the Medvedev period, I argue here that it was already clear by the end of 2010 that the Medvedev period has not simply been a continuation of the Putin period: it is a distinctive period. Both domestically and internationally Russia enjoys relative stability.[12] Russia is nearing membership in the WTO (Golos Rossii, 2010). However Russia's economy is still resource-based and is less knowledge- and innovation-based, thereby keeping Russia off the list of the most developed economies. Thus the economic modernisation of Russia has had a pressing importance for Medvedev and is the focus of his foreign policy. Medvedev's goal has been to make Russia the world's fifth largest economy.

Medvedev made public a new version of the Foreign Policy Concept (Medvedev, 2008a) at the beginning of his term in 2008, the National Security Strategy in 2009 (Medvedev, 2009b) and a Military Doctrine in 2010 (Medvedev, 2010a). The content of these documents was not conceptually different from the documents adopted during Putin's period: the idea of making Russia a strong state and an independent centre of power remained at the core of all of these concepts. This speaks in favour of the 'continuity' argument. Where differences existed, they could be viewed as evolutionary developments conditioned by the changing international situation and thus as a fine-tuning of national interests.[13] However throughout these documents there is a clear emphasis on the economic vector; hence there are new sections in the National Security Concept, such as that concerning the rational use of nature, science and even of public health and culture (Medvedev, 2009b).

In addition, in his speech 'Russia Forward', Medvedev defined five strategic vectors for the *economic* modernisation of Russia that were aimed at transforming the Russian economy from a raw-material-dependent to a knowledge-based economy (Medvedev, 2009a). Yet another modification concerns the tasks assigned to diplomats. One of the three key objectives of Russian diplomacy should become the task of modernising Russia's economy. The other two are strengthening democratic and civil society institutions in Russia and fighting against organised crime (Medvedev, 2010b). Never before was Russian diplomacy charged with the task of employing foreign policy instruments for the economic modernisation of the country.

Nevertheless there has also been real progress in the political and security dimensions of Russia's foreign policy. One of the indisputable examples has been the eased tensions and revived relationship with Poland (Trenin, 2010). Putin's article in the Polish newspaper *Gazeta Wyborcza* and his visit to Gdansk to attend the ceremonies marking the outbreak of the Second World War, the Katyn Memorial jointly attended by Polish and Russian officials where Putin admitted and denounced Stalin's crimes, were themselves historic events (BBC News, 2009). This traditionally tense relationship immediately faced its most severe test to date both politically and publically with the crash of the Polish presidential plane and the tragic death of 87 members of the Polish elite. This tragedy, paradoxically, gave Russia and Poland yet another opportunity to reconnect and reconcile.

A more recent example was Medvedev's brief visit to the Kuril Islands – which Japan claims – in November 2010, marking the first visit of a Russian head of state to the disputed territories. This visit provoked a diplomatic storm between Russia and Japan, with the Japanese ambassador to Moscow being recalled. However three days later he resumed his duties in Moscow. Earlier that same year Russia signed an agreement with Ukraine to prolong Russia's lease of naval facilities for its Black Sea Fleet in the Crimea for a further twenty-five years beyond 2027.

Medvedev's presidency had already been significantly challenged when in the middle of the summer vacation period in August 2008, on the opening day of the Olympic Games in China, Georgia attacked the breakaway region of South Ossetia and Abkhazia aiming to 'restore' the territorial integrity so much needed for its aspired accession into NATO. Thousands of South Ossetians and Abkhazians tried to escape from the conflict zone by crossing the Russian border. After a ceasefire agreement signed four days after the outbreak of the conflict, both Abkhazia and South Ossetia declared their independence, which Russia subsequently recognised.[14] These events had numerous consequences. One of them has been the ongoing discussion about the significant change in Russia's foreign policy standing, giving priority to the 'self-determination of peoples' in the case of South Ossetia and Abkhazia, while previously sticking to the principle of 'territorial integrity', in particular in the case of Kosovo. Another one was the indefinite postponement of Georgia's membership in NATO.

Medvedev has also been a president of initiatives. The list of initiatives is already impressive only two-and-a-half years into his presidency. In September 2008, Medvedev discussed the issue of the protection of national interests in the Arctic (Medvedev, 2008c) and signed an Arctic Strategy of Russia (Medvedev, 2008b). In November 2009, he announced the proposal of a new legally binding European Security Treaty that would potentially replace outdated institutions such as NATO and the OSCE.[15] In October 2010, Prime Minister Putin made public Russia's Antarctic strategy (Putin, 2010). In November 2010, he proposed the creation of a European economic alliance, stretching from Vladivostok to Lisbon (Lenta.ru, 2010). Although these initiatives were not always announced and signed by President Medvedev, the initiatives and the respective documents do not contradict each other, but rather represent parts of the same picture.

Medvedev has also been responsive to the initiatives of others. US President Obama's move to 'reset' strained ties with the Kremlin was welcomed in Moscow. The agenda of 'reset' included security cooperation ranging from arms control to Afghanistan and Iran. Furthermore Medvedev accepted an invitation to attend the NATO summit in Lisbon and then agreed to cooperate with NATO on a missile defence shield and allow transport to travel both ways through Russian territory to support NATO's mission in Afghanistan (BBC News, 2010). If Putin had aimed at strengthening the position of Russia, Medvedev has aimed at strengthening the image of Russia as a cooperative and responsive partner.

These small but visible differences lead to the argument that Russia will in the near future confront a plurality of foreign policies. Hence Aleksandr Konovalov distinguishes between the foreign policy being promoted by Medvedev and Foreign Minister Sergei Lavrov, on one hand, and that promoted by Prime Minister Putin and Nikolai Patrushev, the current Secretary of Russia's Security Council, on the other hand. If Medvedev and Lavrov argue for a foreign policy aimed at attracting new technologies and solid investments in Russia's economy while at the same time decreasing military expenses, Putin and Patrushev put the emphasis on military security tasks, as argued by Konovalov (Konovalov, 2010). Roger McDermott, forecasting a 'seismic shift in Russian foreign policy' contemplated apparently by Medvedev and Lavrov, also forecast opposition from Putin and his team of foreign policy aides who represent a 'little foreign ministry' headed by Yuriy Ushakov (McDermott, 2010). There is also an argument that Russian foreign policy is fragmented and that foreign policy decision-making is not centralised – not only at the country level, but also within the Foreign Ministry itself.

These arguments seem to be an exaggeration, an attempt at magnifying the differences between Medvedev and Putin. Medvedev and Putin still remain a functioning tandem, guided by the national foreign policy interests of Russia. Sergei Lavrov, Russia's Foreign Minister since 2004, is still the Foreign Minister under Medvedev (as of December 2011), while Putin remains in power although he is only the Prime Minister, and Lavrov is likely to remain in power in one position or another regardless of the winner of the 2012 Russian presidential elections.

There is clearly a switch in emphasis from a foreign policy dominated by Russia's political agenda of claiming its place in the international arena to a foreign policy subordinated to domestic economic priorities – namely aimed at the internal economic modernisation of Russia: decreasing Russia's dependence on gas and oil revenues, modernising the economy and becoming a leader in a number of industrial production sectors. However this is an evolutionary step forward based on the Putin successes of strengthening the international role of Russia. At the same time I would not exclude the possibility – rather, I would expect – that in the remaining time of Medvedev's first term as president, there will appear additional features in Russia's foreign policy that characterise his period in power.

It is certainly too early to describe the Medvedev period comprehensively. I would argue however that it can already be characterised as a move towards continuity.[16] Hence in the Medvedev period so far there have been no sudden ruptures with the previous Putin period. There are already however some distinguishing features in Medvedev's foreign policy. Hence he clearly defines the next decades of Russia's foreign policy as being guided by the national interests of Russia's modernisation, economic in the first instance. Moreover Medvedev's foreign policy has been a policy in search of new cooperation frameworks in all foreign policy areas, from economics to military, security and politics. So Medvedev has aimed at modernising Russia and for this he has needed to promote the image of Russia as a cooperative partner.

Moreover Medvedev's foreign policy is that of a state firmly 'standing on its own two legs', but still hindered by deep-rooted issues of economic underdevelopment – an economic development that does not follow the much aspired to political status of a great power. As regards Medvedev's style, since the very beginning he created an impression of being a soft president. Indeed his style is that of soft initiatives, but not necessarily of soft actions, as the conflict in Georgia demonstrated. A lawyer by education, he also seems to emphasise the primacy of international law, as the ethnic riots in Kyrgyzstan in June 2010 have demonstrated. So far many of his speeches seem to have been prescriptive in character, maybe to a slightly greater degree than expected from a president. In sum Medvedev's policy could be characterised as innovative, proactive and responsive.

As it is too early to provide an overall summary of Russia's foreign policy in the middle of Medvedev's first term, it is equally impossible to characterise exhaustively and fully his foreign policy in Central Asia. However there are already certain visible trends that are likely to develop further. Under Medvedev Russia not only continued to maintain its presence in Central Asia, but increased its presence in a variety of ways. The main goal has been to reassert itself as a great Eurasian power. It is no longer an easy task, if it ever has been. Russia faces tough competition. In line with traditional global players, the US and lately the EU, there are new players, China, India and rich Muslim countries from neighbouring regions. Luckily for Russia, none of them alone is able yet to challenge the position of Russia, although a combination of them may well be in a position to do so.

In its relations with the Central Asian countries Russia emphasises both bilateral relations and multilateral cooperation. In bilateral cooperation each Central Asian country finally gained its own place on Russia's foreign policy agenda. Bilateral cooperation with Central Asian countries is constructed around cooperation in energy resources, in particular with Kazakhstan, Uzbekistan and Turkmenistan; in the area of state stability, in particular with Kyrgyzstan and Tajikistan; or in security issues, including a common protection of the region's borders, in particular with Uzbekistan and Tajikistan; and so on. In multilateral cooperation, Russia reasserts itself as a Eurasian power through cooperation in the CIS and seeks to contain China within the regional cooperation framework of the SCO. These efforts include further positioning the SCO as a complex regional structure to provide economic development and regional security to its members in addition to adopting rules to admit new members. There are talks about possibly broadening the SCO membership to countries such as Afghanistan, Turkmenistan and Iran. Moreover in 2008, Russia and China finally signed a border agreement paving the way for the return of 174 km^2 of territory to China (Li Xiaokun, 2008). Already now China has the propensity to become the region's leader. In such an unfavourable but not unlikely scenario Russia might be reduced to the role of China's junior partner – not to say little brother (Trenin, 2010).

Security issues feature prominently on the agenda of Russian–Central Asian relations. Russia is expected – and willing – to remain a guarantor of security in Central Asia, not only by the Central Asian countries, but also by the international community (Isamova, 2010). However the June 2010 ethnic riots in Kyrgyzstan seriously questioned Russia's ability to serve as a guarantor and showed Russia's overall unpreparedness to intervene effectively in intra-state conflicts, in particular in Central Asia. Furthermore these events not only questioned whether Russia still possesses the capabilities of a security guarantor, but also questioned Russia's capability as a regional leader. Some argue that the unknown possible reaction of China was the key factor behind Russia's non-intervention in events in Kyrgyzstan (Bhadrakumar, 2010).

At the same time, paradoxically, these events opened a new window of opportunity for Russia to recalibrate the regional security dynamics in its favour. First, in the aftermath of these events Russia initiated a move to change the CSTO's Charter in order to give the organisation extended powers to intervene in internal conflicts (CSTO, 2010). Second, Russia proceeded to intensify its efforts further in order to deepen its military footprint in Central Asia through a possible second military base in Osh, Kyrgyzstan and one in Tajikistan. Third, Tajikistani and Kyrgyzstani policy-makers voiced the idea of the necessity of direct bilateral security treaties with Russia as a better tool for security protection, as opposed to multilateral forums.

Another item on the security agenda aimed at ensuring Russian predominance in Central Asia is that for a more concerted effort to reduce regional US security influence. The results of the coalition forces' policy in Afghanistan played into the hands of Russia. Unprecedentedly Russia and the US for the first time had a common anti-drug operation in the Afghan provinces aimed at the destruction of drug-producing laboratories (English. news.cn, 2010).[17]

The shift from a political to an economic vector in Medvedev's foreign policy is less visible in Central Asia for obvious reasons. None of the countries identified by Medvedev as Russia's modernisation partners are in Central Asia (Medvedev, 2009a). However Central Asia possesses the resources needed for Russia's modernisation. Moreover there are many industrial plants in Central Asia that ceased to function after the breakup of the Soviet Union. Russia has expressed its interest in buying back these plants, starting with the military-industrial companies. Furthermore Russia is already involved in constructing roads and adjacent infrastructure, mainly however around its military troop stations, such as those in Kent, Kyrgyzstan. However in those line with Medvedev's proclaimed foreign policy goal of Russia's economic modernisation I expect that Russia will work to increase its hardware assets in Central Asia, such as roads, railways, pipelines and military infrastructure, by buying up Central Asian companies.

The Central Asian countries are often uneasy partners. Thus Uzbekistan left the EurAsEC once more in 2008 (Cherniavsky, 2010) and practically ceased to cooperate with the CSTO (Regnum.ru, 2010). Tajikistan deprived Russia of getting a share in the Rogun hydroplant project, despite years of Russia's mediation efforts in the construction negotiations with Tajikistan and Uzbekistan; of participating in an international tender to develop one of the world's largest silver deposits in northern Tajikistan; and of renting a military airfield at Aini, located near the Tajik capital (*Deutsche Welle*, 2010). Turkmenistan, with the support of Kazakhstan, put into operation a pipeline to China in 2009 and yet another pipeline to Iran in 2010 in an effort to diversify its gas export routes; both of these pipelines reduce Turkmenistan's and Kazakhstan's dependency on Russia as the pipelines do not cross the territory of Russia, nor is Russia a partner in the agreement. Kyrgyzstan, which accepted Russia's financial donations on the condition of evicting the Americans from its military base, has subsequently changed its mind, assigning a different status to what is de facto the same military base (Regnum.ru, 2010).

To sum up, the Medvedev period can already be seen as a continuation of the previous period, despite the numerous attempts by international and domestic analysts to forecast a fracture in the Putin–Medvedev tandem. Russia reasserts itself as a great power (even if currently an energy great power) and employs economic processes to reconstitute itself as the centre of Eurasia. Overall Russia's approach in Central Asia under Medvedev can be seen as self-interested but at the same time cooperative. Russian policy under Medvedev has been guided more by economic needs than was the case before; however defence calculations and Russia's own interests remain in the background of economic interests. Given a complex geopolitical situation, Medvedev is forced to pursue a cautious and conservative agenda in the region. To date Russia still remains the most actively engaged external actor in Central Asia, a position that Russia will strive to maintain.

Conclusion

In this chapter I have argued that Russia's foreign policy since the breakup of the Soviet Union can be divided into three periods, which I label by the name of the respective president. The reason for doing so is to identify and signify the person who was constitutionally vested with the presidential power over Russia's foreign policy, and also assumed the responsibility and through a lack of choice in the end, perhaps too the criticism for its subsequent successes and failures. Yet another reason is to demonstrate that each president's term was shaped by various domestic conditions and international events. This has conditioned different foreign policy objectives and the means employed to achieve them, while the personality of the president implied different foreign policy styles.

The three periods – those of Yeltsin, Putin and Medvedev – built upon one another. Thus in the past decade, Russia's foreign policy became more predictable and pragmatic and has been characterised by a high degree of continuity, as the last change in power has demonstrated. Overall Russia has witnessed a transition to a relatively balanced foreign policy course since Soviet times. Thus I argue that Russia's modern foreign policy is characterised by continuity.

This process was not linear however. Russia's post-communist foreign policy has been marked by some spectacular changes. Different presidents employed different strategies in concert with their perceptions of what is best for Russia. Hence Russia moved from a univector towards a multivector foreign policy; from foreign policy recipient towards an initiator of plenipotentiary foreign policy actions; from a heavily indebted state towards a state investor; and so on. In each period events occurred that did not have a precedent. Unlike Yeltsin both Putin and Medvedev built their foreign policy on the basis of the great Soviet/Russian past. Furthermore if under Putin the goal of foreign policy was to reestablish the role of Russia in global affairs, under Medvedev the shift has been towards the economic modernisation of the country with the help of its foreign policy. The actions of external actors, in particular of the US, played an important role in shaping Russia's foreign policy. Moreover I argue that the president had significant influence in shaping foreign policy during his term and thus each of these periods had specific features. The Yeltsin period was characterised by unpredictability, volatility and incoherence. The Putin period marked a move towards predictability and planning, with Russia's national identity being reformulated. Although it is a little premature to assert the defining characteristics of the Medvedev period, it does demonstrate signs of policy continuity as well as evolutionary developments. To sum up pragmatism, predictability and assertiveness of the Putin period replaced the initial incoherence of the Yeltsin years; and the Medvedev period has shown signs of continuity with the Putin period. Overall Russia's foreign policy has been characterised by both change and continuity.

In applying the periodisation of Russian policy to relations with Central Asia, I have noted that the Yeltsin period was characterised by a general neglect of Central Asia, which resulted in the loss of Russia's position in Central Asia inherited from Soviet times. The second period, that under Putin, was characterised by Russia's return to Central Asia and its search to regain its lost positions in all spheres, but primarily in the realms of politics and security. The Medvedev period has shown signs of continuity with the Putin period of reasserting Russia's position in Central Asia.

Will all of this be sufficient for Russia to reassert its position in Central Asia fully and successfully? There are solid preconditions that could help Russia to do so. First, the Central Asian countries do not challenge two of Russia's goals: its status as a great power and as a key player in the international community and Russia's Eurasian identity. Second, there is an impressive list of subjects on the agenda of their relations on which they see eye to eye: for example, their attitude to the colour revolutions, democratisation and human rights. Third, they share common major concerns about state instability, drug trafficking, Islamisation, terrorism and so on. Moreover the interests of Russia in Central Asia are to a great degree compatible with the interests of the Central Asian countries vis-à-vis Russia. Furthermore there is no strong resentment in Central Asia at the use of the Russian language in daily politics, business and life. Additionally Russia and a number of Central Asia states are exporters of energy resources to third countries, including Western countries. Yet another point is that both Russia and the Central Asian countries are notably interested in protecting their national minorities in each other's countries.

Still it is premature to give a definitive answer to the above question since there are many events with unknown outcomes that will certainly influence the future: the outcome of the coalition policy in Afghanistan and the 'winner' of the war there; the survival of individual states in Central Asia over the next decades; and the development of China and its economic and possibly territorial ambitions over Russian and Central Asian territories. Overall however the division into three periods according to the presidents of the country allows one to see the strategic vision of post-Soviet Russian foreign policy, at least at those times when there has been perceivable.

Notes

I would like to thank Wolfgang Zellner, Rustam Makhmudov, Roger E. Kanet and Maria Raquel Freire for their valuable comments on earlier drafts of this article.

1. This fact is itself interesting and adds to the argument of the incoherence of Russia's policy under Yeltsin. Already in 1992, Russia declared itself a legal successor to the Soviet Union.
2. This fact of not being the winners in the Cold War evinced little discussion since the whole of the Soviet generation had grown up with the national pride of being the winners in the Second World War. I share the idea that there was no winner in the Cold War, or at least that Russia was not a loser.
3. During Yeltsin's term in office, Russia had six prime ministers and three foreign ministers.
4. Serbia is a country that traces its close ties to Russia back to the nineteenth century.
5. About 2 million people emigrated from Central Asia during the Yeltsin period (Cummings, 2001).
6. Under Putin, Russia had fewer prime ministers and foreign ministers than Yeltsin. Putin had four prime ministers – one of them acting – and two foreign ministers.
7. Subsequently these negotiations landed Schröeder a job as a board chairman for this Russian–German gas pipeline.
8. Uzbekistan left the EurAsEC once again in 2008 (Cherniavsky, 2010).
9. RIA Novosti, 2009.
10. There were and are however some organisations in which all Central Asian countries are members while Russia is not, as, for example, the Organization of the Islamic Conference.
11. For a discussion of the expanded competition for influence faced by Russia in Central Asia see Freire and Kanet (2010).
12. Under Medvedev, Putin assumed the position of Prime Minister while Lavrov, who had previously been the Foreign Minister under Putin remained in his post.
13. Hence there were new sections in the National Security Concept: the rational use of nature, science and even of public health and culture (Medvedev, 2009b).
14. For discussions of the Russo-Georgian War, including both its background and implications, see the chapters in the present volume by Luke March and John B. Dunlop.

15. According to Lord Ismay, the first Secretary General of NATO, NATO was created 'to keep Americans in, Russians out and Germany down' (Ismay, 2001). Ironically the Medvedev proposal offers an alternative that can be phrased as 'kick Americans out, bring Russians back, push Germany up'.
16. *Preemstvennost* in Russian.
17. This successful operation was not bilateral, but trilateral, with the involvement of the Afghan army. It drew severe criticism of Afghan President Karzai.

References

BBC News (2002) 'World's largest launch facility', 12 May, available at: http://news.bbc.co.uk/2/hi/europe/1983026.stm (accessed 22 November 2010).

BBC News (2005) 'Putin deplores collapse of USSR', 25 April, available at: http://news.bbc.co.uk/2/hi/4480745.stm (accessed 22 November 2010).

BBC News (2007) 'Putin's speech: back to Cold War?', 7 February, available at: http://news.bbc.co.uk/2/hi/europe/6350847.stm (accessed 22 November 2010).

BBC News (2009) 'Polish, Russian press welcome Putin gesture', 1 September, available at: http://news.bbc.co.uk/2/hi/8232122.stm (accessed 22 November 2010).

BBC News (2010) 'Russia to work with NATO on missile defence shield', 20 November, available at: http://www.bbc.co.uk/news/world-europe-11803931 (accessed 22 November 2010).

Bhadrakumar, M. K. (2010) 'China plays it cool on Kyrgyzstan', *Asia Times online*, 20 April, available at: http://www.atimes.com/atimes/Central_Asia/LD20Ag01.html (accessed 22 November 2010).

Busvine, Douglas (2004) 'Russia's Putin calls US policy "dictatorial"', *Free Republic*, 3 December, available at: http://www.freerepublic.com/focus/f-news/ (accessed 20 November 2010).

Cherniavsky, Stanislav (2010) 'K vizitu Prezidenta Respubliki Uzbekistan I. Karimova v Rossiju', *Informacionnyj portal Moskovskogo gosudarstvennogo instituta mezhdunarodnyh otnoshenij MID Rossii*, available at: http://www.mgimo.ru/news/experts/document150667.phtml (accessed 22 November 2010).

CNN (2008) 'Putin accuses US of orchestrating Georgian War', 28 August, available at: http://www.cnn.com/2008/WORLD/europe/08/28/russia.georgia.cold.war/index.html (accessed 20 November 2010).

Collective Security Treaty Organisation (CSTO) (2010) 'CSTO meeting', Moscow, 10 December, available at: http://www.odkb.gov.ru/session_twelve/a.htm (accessed 12 December 2010).

Cummings, Sally N. (2001) 'Happier bedfellows? Russia and Central Asia under Putin', *Asian Affairs*, vol. 32, no. 2, pp. 142–52.

Curtis, Glenn E. (ed.) (1996) *Russia: A Country Study* (Washington, DC: Library of Congress, Federal Research Division).

Daily Times (2007) 'Security alliances led by Russia, China link up', 6 October, available at: http://www.cnn.com/2008/WORLD/europe/08/28/russia.georgia.cold.war/index.pk (accessed 20 November 2010).

Deutsche Welle (2010) 'V Tadzhikistane poliomielit schitajut politicheskoj bolezn'ju', 19 May.

Digol, Diana (2009) 'Right or wrong: debate in Russia on conflict in Georgia', *S+F (Sicherheit und Frieden/Security and Peace)*, vol. 2, pp. 112–20.

English.news.cn (2010) 'Kabul slams joint US–Russian anti-drug raid in Afghanistan', 1 November, available at: http://news.xinhuanet.com/english 2010/world/2010-11/01/c_13585941.htm (accessed 20 November 2010).

Freedman, Michael and Heidi Brown (2006) 'Energy Tsar', Forbes.com, 24 July, available at: http://www.forbes.com/forbes/2006/0724/094.html (accessed 10 February 2011).

Freire, Maria Raquel and Roger E. Kanet (eds) (2010) *Key Players and Regional Dynamics in Eurasia: The Return of the 'Great Game'* (Houndmills: Palgrave Macmillan).

Glukhov, Yuryi (2006) 'Kross po minnomu polju', Moscow, Sluzhba vneshney razvedki Rossiiskoi Federatsii, 17 November, available at: http://svr.gov.ru/ smi/2006/slovo20061117-n.htm (accessed 18 February 2011).

Golos Rossii (2010) 'Shuvalov: mezhdu Rossiey i ES bol'she net raznoglasiy po vstupleniyu RF v VTO', 24 November, available at: http://rus.ruvr.ru/2010/ 11/24/35578206.html (accessed 22 December 2010).

Isamova, Hulkar (2010) 'Kyrgyzstan asks Russia to help end ethnic clashes', Reuters, 12 June, available at: http://www.reuters.com/ (accessed 12 August 2010).

Ismay, Lord Hastings (2001) Cited in *Die Welt*, May 18, p. 8.

Kazantsev, Andrei (2008) 'Russian policy in Central Asia and the Caspian Sea Region', *Europe–Asia Studies*, vol. 60, no. 6, pp. 1073–88.

Konovalov, Alexandr (2010) 'V kol'ce druzei ili v ob'iatiiah vragov', *Ogonek*, 25 October.

Lenta.ru (2010) 'Putin predlozhil Evrope ekonomicheskiy al'yans ot Vladivostoka do Lissabona', 25 November, available at: http://www.lenta. ru/news/2010/11/25/wirtschaft/ (accessed 10 February 2011).

Li Xiaokun (2008) 'China, Russia sign border agreement', *China Daily*, 22 July, available at: http://www.chinadaily.com.cn/china/2008-07/22/content_ 6865847.htm (accessed 10 February 2011).

McDermott, Roger (2010) 'Kremlin contemplates a seismic shift in Russian foreign policy', *Eurasia Daily Monitor*, 19 May, vol. 7, no. 97.

Medvedev, Dmitry (2008a) 'The foreign policy concept of the Russian Federation', Moscow, Kremlin.ru, 12 July, available at: http://archive.kremlin.ru/eng/text/ docs/2008/07/204750.shtml (accessed 18 February 2011).

Medvedev, Dmitry (2008b) 'Osnovy gosudarstvennoy politiki Rossiyskoy Federatsii v Arktike na period do 2020 goda i dal'neyshuyu perspektivu', Moscow, scrf.gov.ru, 18 September, available at: http://www.scrf.gov.ru/docu-ments/98.html (accessed 18 February 2011).

Medvedev, Dmitry (2008c) 'Zasedanie Soveta Bezopasnosti "O zawite natsional' nykh interesov Rossii v Arktike"', Moscow, scrf.gov.ru, 17 September, available at: http://www.scrf.gov.ru/news/351.html (accessed 18 February 2011).

Medvedev, Dmitry (2009a) 'Dmitry Medvedev: Rossiya, vpered!', Gazeta.ru, 10 September, available at: http://www.gazeta.ru/comments/2009/09/10_a_ 3258568.shtml (accessed 18 February 2011).

Medvedev, Dmitry (2009b) 'O Strategii Natsional'noi Bezopasnosti Rossiiskoy Federatsii do 2020 goda', Moscow, scrf.gov.ru, 12 May, available at: http:// www.scrf.gov.ru/documents/99.html (accessed 18 February 2011).

Medvedev, Dmitry (2010a) 'Voennaya doktrina Rossiyskoy Federatsii', Moscow, Kremlin.ru, 5 February, available at: http://news.kremlin.ru/ref_notes/461 (accessed 18 February 2011).

Medvedev, Dmitry (2010b) 'Vystuplenie na soveshchanii s rossiyskimi poslami i postoyannymi predstavitelyami v mezhdunarodnyh organizatsiyah', Moscow, Kremlin.ru, 12 July, available at: http://www.president.kremlin.ru/ transcripts/8325 (accessed 18 February 2011).

Olcott, Martha Brill (1996) *Central Asia's New States: Independence, Foreign Policy, and Regional Security* (Washington, DC: United States Institute of Peace Press).

Paramonov, Vladimir, Aleksey Strokov and Oleg Stolpovski (2009) *Russia in Central Asia* (New York: Nova Science Publishers).

Perekrest, Vladimir (2006) 'Oktyabr' 1993 goda: Bol'shinstvo pogibshih – ne zashchitniki Belogo doma', *Izvestia*, 3 October, available at: http://www. izvestia.ru/special/article3097187/ (accessed 18 February 2011).

Putin, Vladimir (2000a) 'The Foreign Policy Concept of the Russian Federation', Moscow, Kremlin.ru, 12 July, available at: http://archive.kremlin.ru/eng/text/ docs/2008/07/204750.shtml (accessed 18 February 2011).

Putin, Vladimir (2000b) 'National Security Concept of the Russian Federation', Moscow, Mid.ru, available at: http://www.mid.ru/ns-osndoc.nsf/1e5f0de28fe77 fdcc32575d900298676/36aba64ac09f737fc32575d9002bbf31?OpenDocument (accessed 18 February 2011).

Putin, Vladimir (2007) 'Munich Speech', paper presented at the 43rd Munich Security Conference on 'Global Crisis – Global Responsibility', Munich, 9–11 February, available at: http://www.securityconference.de/Conference-2007. 268+M52087573ab0.0.html (accessed 1 October 2010).

Putin, Vladimir (2010) 'Strategiya razvitiya deyatel'nosti Rossiyskoy Federatsii v Antarktike na period do 2020 goda i na bolee otdalennuyu perspektivu', Moscow, Government of the Russian Federation, available at: http://www. government.ru/gov/results/12869/ (accessed 18 February 2011).

Regnum.ru (2010) 'Rossiya i ee sosedi v 2009 godu: vneshnepoliticheskie itogi', 14 January, available at: http://www.regnum.ru/news/1242230.html (accessed 1 November 2010).

RIA Novosti (2009) 'Voennaiay operatsia SSHA protiv Iraqa v 2003. Spravka' (Military operation of the USA in Iraq in 2003: summary), 20 March, available at: http://ria.ru/politics/20090320/165480935.html (accessed 1 October 2010).

Saari, Sinikukka (2006) 'Human rights cooperation between Russia and European intergovernmental organisations: a one-way transference of norms or a mutual process of adaptation?', Finnish Institute of International Affairs (FIIA) Working Paper, No. 54, available at: http://www.isn.ethz.ch/isn/Digital-Library/ Publications/Detail/?ots591=0c54e3b3-1e9c-be1e-2c24-a6a8c7060233&lng=en& id=19397 (accessed 18 February 2011).

Sakwa, Richard (2008) *Russian Politics and Society*, 6th edn (Abingdon: Routledge).

Sakwa, Richard (2009) *Power and Policy in Putin's Russia* (Abingdon: Routledge).

Seifert, Arne Clemens (2002) *Risiken der Transformation in Zentralasien. Das Beispiel Tadschikistan* (Hamburg: Deutschen Orient-Institut).

The Banker (2006) 'Top 1000 world banks', available at: http://www.thebanker. com/Top-1000-World-Banks (accessed 22 December 2010).

The Economist (2008a) 'After the boom', 389 (8604), p. 54.

The Economist (2008b) 'The incredible shrinking people', 389 (8608), pp. 12–14.

Trenin, Dmitri (2010) 'Rossiiskaia vneshniaia politika: perspektiva 2020', Moscow, Carnegie Moscow Center, Russia 2020: Scenarios for the Future, available at: http://russia-2020.org/2010/10/06/russian-foreign-policy-perspective-2020/ (accessed 1 November 2010).

Yeltsin, Boris (1997) National Security Concept of the Russian Federation, Moscow, Kremlin.ru, available at: http://document.kremlin.ru/doc.asp?ID=077218 (accessed 31 August 2010).

Part III
Energy in Russian–CIS Relations

9
Strategy, Security and Russian Resource Diplomacy

Matthew Sussex

Introduction

This chapter critically assesses Russian resource diplomacy as a core facet of its strategic policy. Whilst many excellent analyses of Russia's position as a producer nation exist in the burgeoning literature on energy security (Ebel and Menon, 2000; Nygren, 2007), the emphasis in current scholarship has focused significantly on security of supply. This is unsurprising given the current global power distribution, which sees a United States hegemon, a rising China and powerful European Union (EU) states in a potentially vulnerable position as client states of resource-rich nations. But dwelling on consumers in discussions on energy security overlooks important questions in relation to energy suppliers, especially those that seek to leverage their resources for maximum gain. Consequently in this chapter I ask whether Russia's choices in using its natural resources coercively, with particular attention to oil and gas, represents a sensible policy choice that advances Russian interests and helps it to achieve its strategic policy objectives.

Following on from this I examine what Russia's behaviour tells us about its policy goals and future ambitions. By analysing Russian resource diplomacy at the regional and global levels I find that the policy serves Russia's overriding determination to retain its great power status. In this respect it facilitates Moscow's local ambitions in terms of strategic geography, through buffer-zone politics and a geoeconomic policy of de facto empire maintenance. But I also suggest that at the global level Russia's behaviour is much more reminiscent of middle power diplomacy than that of the great power it continues to profess itself to be. The reasons for this are predominantly structural, stemming from Russia's loss of power and influence after the end of the Cold War.

Far from being an irrational attempt to secure influence, as some commentators might suggest (Blank, 2009), I argue that the use of energy as a muscular instrument of policy should not be surprising at all. This is because resource diplomacy, as part of an overall pattern in Russian strategy since the collapse of the USSR, is characteristic of significant continuity rather than change. As a result, it is incumbent upon other states, especially in the West, not to misunderstand Russian motivations or to perceive every regional demonstration of Russian interests as symbolic of a bellicose and aggressive global policy posture.

To make this argument the chapter proceeds as follows. First, I examine the global balance of power, in which Russia faces a number of hurdles to maintain its position – let alone become a leading state in any new or emerging multipolar order – before turning to consider Russia's immediate area of vital security interest: the former geopolitical space of the USSR. Second, I evaluate Russia's regional approach to resource diplomacy, with specific emphasis on the vital geostrategic Central Asian region. Third, I demonstrate that on the global level, Russian resource diplomacy is best interpreted as an instrument to maximise Russian gains from a position of weakness rather than strength. I conclude by offering some observations about the implications of a Russian strategy that appears neo-imperial in its local context, but is essentially attempting to 'punch above its weight' in Moscow's dealings with more powerful actors.

Russia and the global balance of power

In contemporary international politics material capabilities continue to act as both constraints and enablers for states. As it was during the Yeltsin period, Russian foreign policy under Putin and Medvedev remains determined by its power relative to others. In terms of purely 'hard' power it is customary to list the size of a state's economy as well as its military capabilities as key variables, not to mention physical size, population, natural resources and a variety of other demographic indicators from health and education levels to broader trends. However, as Hans Morgenthau argued, states need more than just power's empirical referents (Morgenthau, 1960, pp. 144–5). Rather they also need a way to harness power, to mobilise their populations effectively, and to show allies and enemies alike that they have capabilities that are credible and will be employed if necessary.

The centrality of power in understanding state behaviour can be seen in the Cold War, when major terms based on systemic factors relating to capabilities – such as 'superpower' and 'bipolarity' – were commonly used to describe the struggle between the USSR and the West. And it follows also that after the collapse of the USSR and the end of the Cold War, Russian foreign and security policy would face a fundamentally new set of constraints. Indeed on any indicator of power listed above, including raw territorial size and population, Russia declined radically after 1991. Between 1991 and 1999, Russia's economy lurched from one crisis to the next, with an overall gross domestic product (GDP) contraction over this period of 43 per cent (CIA, 1999). The sharp slump in Russian economic power began with the 'shock therapy' of January 1992, sponsored by then Acting Prime Minister Yegor Gaidar. During that year Russia's GDP fell by 15 per cent and inflation rose from the already very high rate of 93 per cent in 1991 to a staggering 1353 per cent (Bowker, 1997, p. 166). From 1992 until the end of 1995, the consumption of goods and services dropped by 33 per cent, and although the annual inflation rate was whittled down to 190 per cent by 1995, the budget deficit remained at 9 per cent of GDP (Gould-Davies and Woods, 1999). By 1997, the situation had marginally improved, with Organisation for Economic Co-operation and Development (OECD) reports putting the 1997 budget deficit at 6.8 per cent of GDP (Gould-Davies and Woods, 1999, p. 12); yet in other areas the Russian economy continued to struggle. In the realm of tax collection, for instance, Russia achieved only 65 per cent of its projected tax revenue goals for 1997. By 1999, Russia produced US$4,200 of GDP per head of population. In contrast the United States had roughly twice Russia's population, but nonetheless had a GDP per capita of US$33,900. Put more simply, in 1999 Russia produced less GDP per capita than Brazil, Gabon or Thailand, and only slightly outranked Botswana, China – with its population of over 1 billion people – and El Salvador.

In addition to economic weight, Russia's overall decline in military capabilities was a significant factor in the contraction of its power from 1991 to 1999. For example, even after Mikhail Gorbachev's unilateral pledge to cut 500,000 troops from Soviet armed forces, the USSR was still able to call upon some 3.5 million active service personnel. Following Yeltsin's demands in 1997 that Russia's armed forces be drawn down to reflect lessened international military threats as well as its inability to maintain a large standing army, Russia's armed forces shrank by 1999 to 1.2 million, including reservists and conscripts, dwindling later to around 850,000 active personnel. But the official rate of decline does not show the magnitude of the problems in Russia's military. In 1992, it was estimated that fully 75 to 80 per cent of Russian youths had successfully evaded military service (Grachev, 1993, p. 10), and the Defence Ministry stated during the same time that up to 270,000 officers would have to be cut from Russia's armed forces (Dawisha and Parrott, 1994, p. 243). Moreover government estimates in 1999 about the process of drafting some 150,000 conscripts every six months revealed that less than 10 per cent of Russian draft-age youth were inducted in each conscription period (*Nezavisimaya gazeta*, 1998, p. 1).

Russia therefore entered the new millennium with significantly less power than when it had started the previous decade. By the time of the *Kursk* nuclear submarine disaster, bombings in Moscow's Pushkin Square and the fires at Moscow's TV centre in August 2000, it was starkly clear that Russian power had deteriorated significantly. Despite claiming in his 'Millennium Manifesto' (Putin, 2000) that Russia remained a great power, Putin acknowledged that it would take fifteen years to catch up with Portugal and Spain, assuming an optimistic 8 per cent growth in annual GDP.

Nonetheless it is certainly true that Russia has experienced an almost equally dramatic turnaround in its fortunes since the beginning of the millennium, even though it still has far to go before it can unequivocally lay claim to great power status once again. By 2010, Russia ranked only seventy-one on the *Failed States Index* with an overall score of nearly 81 out of a possible 120. This placed it below the People's Republic of China (but still in the 'danger' category), and comparable to Mozambique, Serbia and Bosnia (*Failed States Index*, 2010). GDP per capita had risen to a much more healthy US$8000 in 2009, although it was surpassed on that measure by Libya and Lebanon (World Bank, 2009a). Health care funding only passed pre-1991 levels as recently as 2006, and in 2009 life expectancy for Russian males continued to lag a full eleven years behind that of the EU and the United States (RIA Novosti, 2010). In military expenditure Russia accounted for 3.3 per cent of the global total – about half of that of the People's Republic of China (PRC) – compared to the United States with some 45 per cent of world military spending (SIPRI, 2010). And whilst it was abundantly clear what Russia had lost in the period 1991–2000, it put much more effort into tapping its vast reserves of oil and natural gas. These became the drivers of a newly resurgent Russian economy, which saw construction and consumption of goods rise in turn.

The regional security order in the former USSR

Maintaining a stable regional security order in the former republics of the Soviet Union has been a core concern for successive Russian governments. This has been especially the case regarding potential threats in the Caspian region and in Central Asia. After Putin came to power the challenges of national and religious extremism, economic decay, illegal immigration and the trafficking of drugs were all identified in core Russian policy documents as major themes. Upon taking up the reins of the Russian presidency, Putin immediately signed a number of bilateral treaties with Central Asian states on issues ranging from military to economic cooperation. And prior to the official birth of the Shanghai Cooperation Organisation (SCO) in 2001, Putin promised during a meeting of the 'Shanghai Five' in Dushanbe to increase Russian military forces in Tajikistan and deter Islamic fundamentalism throughout the region.[1]

Yet even though the Russian economy has rebounded strongly, first under Putin and then under Medvedev since 2008, the perception of Russian weakness within its region has remained. In July 2009, in a now infamous interview with the *Wall Street Journal*, US Vice President Joe Biden remarked that Russia's leaders would eventually be forced to make hard compromises with the West on national security and noted that this would inevitably include Moscow loosening its grip on former Soviet republics (*Wall Street Journal*, 2009). Under the circumstances it is understandable that Russian responses to Biden's comments were somewhat less than enthusiastic, ranging from blistering critiques of the Vice President to bellicose reassertions of Russian power. Perhaps the most diplomatic response came from President Medvedev's aide Sergey Prikhodko, who merely referred to Biden's comments as 'perplexing' (MosNews.com, 2009).

What was instructive about Biden's remarks – and their aftermath – is that they neatly encapsulated a debate about security that has been ongoing since the fall of Mikhail Gorbachev, the termination of the 1922 treaty that established the USSR on 25 December 1991 and the emergence of a host of former Soviet satrapies as independent states. As this debate has developed, so too has a consensus on the importance of interpreting Russia's use of oil and gas as a coercive instrument of foreign policy – often referred to as resource diplomacy – in the context of current concerns over energy security, and also to assess the potential outcomes of that policy in relation to Russia's power prospects. On the one hand, the argument goes that Russia's future is bleak, marked by severe looming demographic challenges, a crumbling financial sector and a gradually stagnating economy. Faced with defaulting banks, a population implosion and an outdated resource-based economy that threatens to see Russia become little more than a raw materials appendage of China and the EU, this perspective holds that the West can act from a position of strength in negotiating down a future Russian sphere of influence in the former Soviet geopolitical space (Menon and Motyl, 2007). Yet, on the other hand, the reverse view can be found: that the Russian bear, reinvigorated by massive oil and gas exports, is creating energy dependencies in both Europe and Asia that will force the West and China to accommodate Russia's insistence on unrestricted freedom (Dibb, 2006).

Like most grand debates of its type, this one leaves many crucial questions unanswered. For instance, is it desirable for a potentially bellicose Russia to have a sphere of influence in the former USSR? Conversely, is it desirable to exacerbate Russian perceptions of marginalisation by forcing it to abandon a buffer zone? What types of popular attitudes, elite sentiments and policy preferences are emerging in the former Soviet space – in Kiev, in Tbilisi, in Tallinn and in Moscow – that give us a sense of how future security relations will develop? More broadly, what trends are evident in the previously coherent 'West' that may indicate a different policy landscape? And what added complications are posed by transnational challenges like organised crime, terrorism and corruption in an area riven by structural economic weaknesses, as well as ethnic and political discord?

The answers to these questions promise to help us understand what happens when empires collapse – and especially what happens in the aftermath of the USSR, which collapsed in a manner that was unfamiliar relative to other previous structural changes in international politics. This presents a problem for analysts since there is little with which to compare the end of the Cold War. While it was not a traditional 'war', it bore many hallmarks of major conflict: it resulted in the birth and death of states, produced structural change in international politics and hence was 'world-shaping'. In the past when international systems have changed there has been relative surety in identifying the nature of the coming order, regardless of whether this results in new power vacuums, new concentrations of power or new political alliances. Following the Second World War the European and Japanese imperial powers could not retain control over their possessions, whilst the US and USSR found themselves thrust to the forefront of international security by their relative superiority in material power. From this basis it was relatively easy to predict that the alliance of convenience formed to defeat Nazi Germany and Japanese expansionism would not last, and that a compact between America and the Soviet Union would also be unlikely. However, although the fall of the Soviet Union occurred relatively bloodlessly, the most important issues that emerged in 1989–91 remain unresolved some twenty years later. This includes even the basic new Russian 'project' of rediscovering a unifying national idea, which continues to encounter obstacles, amidst first NATO and then EU enlargement, a rising China, the rise to prominence of energy security, human rights debates and the integrative (but also fragmentary) impulses associated with globalisation.

At first glance the task of evaluating the shape of security politics in former Soviet space would appear straightforward. Adapting established principles of geopolitics dating back to Mackinder and notions of the 'heartland', one could begin with the giant Russian state as the major economic and military power and a focal point centred upon Moscow (Mackinder, 1904). This would traditionally be followed by a series of concentric circles, first enveloping Belarus and Ukraine as well as the Baltic states of Lithuania, Latvia and Estonia – not to mention Finland – then spreading outwards to encompass Eastern Europe to Russia's west, to Central Asia in the south, and finally to Central Europe, the Middle East and North East Asia.

Such a characterisation is deceptive. It oversimplifies the ability of Russia to secure its own territory, let alone those states in its notional sphere of influence. It also takes no account of the preferences of the Baltic countries or the Ukraine, which have sought firm security alliances with external actors to counterbalance Russian influence. Nor does it consider the interests of many of those powerful external forces, including the EU and the US; and its Western focus largely ignores North East Asia. Indeed, as constructivists would point out, there are a variety of alternative conceptions of Russia and its region, many of them proffered by Russian historians and writers themselves. They range from the notionally liberal and 'westernising' Russia to Eurasian ideational constructs that saw Russia occupying its own unique region. In contrast to the normatively pro-Western line articulated by Boris Yeltsin and his first foreign minister, Andrei Kozyrev, it has been well-documented that Putin and Medvedev have paid more attention to the latter vision of Russia's place in the world. Both of Russia's recent presidents have emphasised the unifying rule of Peter the Great, serving as the rationale for a Eurasian identity that enshrined Russia as a major force in global affairs.

Yet to concentrate on identity and ideas as criteria to define the former Soviet space is just as misleading as using geography alone. An arguably more accurate and sensible view of the former USSR is to meld strategic geography with considerations of material power, especially where economic opportunities lie alongside potent local and ethnic rivalries. As a round-table discussion in *International Affairs* (Moscow) indicated in 1998, international relations is less about control over territories, and more about the flow of information, in which 'realpolitik' was being replaced by 'real-economics' (*International Affairs* Round Table, 1998), and that the key to future prosperity lies in technological advancements. Unfortunately, though, Russia's economic crises of the 1990s have meant that these are the areas where Russia has been especially weak, given the inability of the Kremlin to oversee sustained investment in costly R&D programmes in the technical and defence sectors. In the new balance of power then the poor hand that was dealt to Russia after the collapse of the USSR has not been significantly strengthened by new realities, in spite of the benefits that have flowed from increased oil and gas sales. This is further complicated by the widening gap between the strategic priorities of Western energy consumers and Russia as a key producer nation.

Energy security and resource diplomacy: regional and global dimensions

Areas of divergent interest between Russia and the United States, not to mention Russia and many EU nations, on the issue of energy security and geoeconomics have exacerbated the already present divisions between East and West resulting from alterations in the global balance of power. The US National Intelligence Community posited in 2009 that the geopolitical implications of global economic dislocation represented the main security challenge facing the United States (Blair, 2009). In the report, which was written for the Senate Select Committee on Intelligence, the potential for future conflict based on economic turmoil was explicitly linked to the financial crises that heralded the Great Depression. And while the current global financial crisis appeared by 2010, the financial crisis had not produced an immediate global depression, as was initially feared, this is not to say that its effects were not keenly felt in the former Soviet territories, with the Baltic states all experiencing economic hardships, and the Ukraine suffering a bigger downward spiral in its economy than any other state in the world (World Bank, 2009b).

There is a clear and demonstrable link between economic crises and conflict, especially when vital strategic resources are at stake. For Russia and its immediate region this is compounded by the fact that numerous intersecting ethnic conflicts exist amongst historical protagonists. Hence the most significant geoeconomic challenges in the former Soviet area pertain directly to energy security, and in attempts at understanding the importance of the dynamics involved in the pursuit of energy security, a geoeconomic approach is logically most useful. This has already been noted in the National Intelligence Council's (NIC) *Global Trends 2025: A Transformed World*, which predicted a more entrenched Russian position in the former Soviet space:

> Russia, needing Caspian area natural gas in order to satisfy European and other contracts, is likely to be forceful in keeping Central Asian countries within Moscow's sphere, and, absent a non-Russia-controlled outlet, has a good chance of succeeding. (US National Intelligence Council, 2009, p. 55)

But it is here that the perspectives and preferences of powerful Western nations, including the US and prominent EU members, cloud the picture. This is because they perceive energy security from the opposite end of the supply-chain spectrum to Russia. For this reason Moscow's decision during the 'gas wars' of 2005 and 2006 to turn off the tap to the Ukraine amid (subsequently substantiated) accusations that Kiev had been siphoning off gas intended for European markets, and later on even to threaten to do so with its former close ally Belarus, raised the spectre in the West of unacceptable risk: namely being held hostage to Russian demands for spheres of influence. The culmination of the gas war in 2009, linked closely to the then upcoming Ukrainian presidential elections, saw shortages felt by some eighteen European client states for gas transiting Ukraine from Russia. When Viktor Yanukovych, Moscow's preferred candidate in the 2010 Ukrainian elections was victorious, it was instructive that the mood changed almost overnight. Putin even suggested a merger between Gazprom and the Ukrainian Naftogaz in May 2010. His proposal came a month after both the Ukrainian Parliament and the Russian State Duma had ratified a deal that saw Russia charge 30 per cent less for its gas exports to the Ukraine, whilst Kiev promised in turn not to reduce imports from Russia, and agreed to a 25-year extension of Moscow's lease over the area of Sevastopol in the Crimea that houses the Russian Black Sea Fleet (Wilson, 2010, p. 12).

The view that Russian gas entails potentially unacceptable risks is a persuasive one, especially since Putin and Medvedev, as a potential means of exerting leverage in other arenas of foreign policy, have identified the utility of promoting vulnerable overdependence on Russian energy. Such vulnerabilities in access to energy have been identified as challenges by Western states, but at the same time they have had little realistic option other than to diversify purchases away from future near total reliance on the Middle East. The logic of interdependence, which holds that mutual learning, trust and confidence-building stems from cooperation, has not been realised in the case of Russian energy policy, and this has been another area where the preferences of the West and Russia have been divergent. One should remember, though, that ensuring a secure supply of oil and gas remains a fundamental concern for Russia. It cannot afford to be shut out of global energy markets, given that energy is critical to its economic development.

In addition to gas, access to Russian oil is also a worrisome issue for the West. Maintaining a safe, secure and above all reliable supply of oil has been important in American foreign and defence policies for at least sixty years. During the 1950s under Harry S. Truman, the United States put significant efforts into Middle Eastern coalition-building, at least in part to shore up supplies of oil for itself and its allies in the looming bipolar confrontation with the Soviet Union, and to deny the USSR access to a strategically important region of the world. The Carter Doctrine, which stipulated that the US would respond to any attempt to gain control over the Persian Gulf with 'any means necessary, including military force', was the product of fears about interruptions to supply as a result of the Iranian Revolution, and then the Soviet invasion of Afghanistan (Yergin, 1991, p. 702). And, whilst in the first decade of the twenty-first century US policy has reiterated the need to 'drain America first' to avoid reliance on external suppliers, the Gulf States of Saudi Arabia, Iraq, the United Arab Emirates, Kuwait, Iran, Oman and Qatar remain critical to US and European interests. In total these states hold some 44 per cent of the world's proven oil reserves and one-third of the world's proven natural gas reserves.

One reason for this continued reliance is that US imports of oil have grown considerably (Shearman and Sussex, 2009). In the 1980s, imported oil accounted for only about 12 per cent of total US crude oil use. But by the year 2000, this had grown to 58 per cent and was continuing to increase (Art, 2004, p. 62). When Paul Wolfowitz was Under Secretary of Defence to Secretary Dick Cheney in the 1990s, he prepared a Defense Planning Guidance document for 1994–99, proposing that to 'preserve US and Western access to the region's oil' the US should remain the dominant power in South West Asia and the Middle East (Klare, 2008, p. 68). Likewise the 2001 National Energy Policy noted the importance of the former Soviet states in the Caspian to ameliorate US energy dependence on states in the Persian Gulf (National Energy Policy Development Group, 2001). And as the 2006 Silk Road Strategy Act stated, 'stability, democratic development [...] and rule of law in countries with valuable energy resources and infrastructure' were vital to 'safeguard US energy security' (US Senate, 2006). To this end, by 2010, USAID had provided over US$1.5 billion over fifteen years to fund health and education services in the five Central Asian former Soviet Republics (USAID, 2010).

Even prior to the collapse of the USSR, American companies had already begun investing in the Central Asian oil industry. In 1990, Chevron launched the joint Tengizchevroil venture in Kazakhstan's Tengiz oilfield, in a deal finalised in 1993 and representing – at the time – the largest single investment by an American oil company in the former USSR. In the Far East, companies like Texaco, Mobil, BP and Exxon all invested heavily in attempts to tap the estimated 700 million tons of oil and 2.5 trillion cubic metres of natural gas off Sakhalin Island. But Russia's renationalisation of its oil and gas industries, exemplified by the 'Yukos affair' that saw Yuganskneftegaz (Yukos's main subsidiary) liquidated to recoup alleged tax debts, signalled Russia's intention to lower the threshold for what it considered energy assets of strategic value. For the US this signalled a worrying trend, which meant that a dash to Russian energy would not necessarily be the reliable offset to Middle Eastern reliance. But by the time that the 2010 Quadrennial Defense Review (QDR) was published, it was routine to see references to the vital importance of oil from a variety of sources to meet the operational needs of the US armed forces (US Department of Defense, 2010).

Like the United States, China has also been aggressively seeking to diversify its sourcing of oil away from the Middle East, upon which it will shortly become 70 per cent dependent. This has seen increased activity by PRC state-owned enterprises in Central Asia. In particular, Chinese investment in Kazakhstan – as a potential competitor to Russia – rose to prominence in 1997, when the Chinese National Petroleum Company (CNPC) bought a 60 per cent stake in the Kazakh company controlling the Aktobe oilfields, and again in 2007 when the CNPC increased its share to 85 per cent (Chinese National Petroleum Company, 2010).

As the most fundamental strategic resource on the planet, energy is now regarded as much more than a simple commodity. The global realignments around competition for energy identified by academic authors like Michael T. Klare (2008, p. 7) are now also present in formal policy documents. As the NIC points out, Russia, as the world's largest producer of natural gas and with the globe's second reserves of oil, is clearly a major player in the geoeconomics of resource trading and transport (US National Intelligence Council, 2009, p. 44). While Vladimir Putin was president Russia became an energy superpower, and Russia has on occasion outstripped Saudi Arabia as the world's largest oil producer. The inability of the US and the West either to wean themselves off their addiction to oil or be able to become energy self-sufficient, means that the Caspian and the wider Eurasian region will remain a key factor in relations between the main powers. This is especially the case since countries like Georgia are vital transit countries for Caspian oil and gas, even though they lack large quantities of oil and gas themselves. It was this consideration, for instance, that was uppermost in the EU's recent emphasis on bypassing Russia to ensure a diversified base for energy transit routes (European Council, 2006). Similarly, US support for the BP-controlled Baku–Tbilisi–Ceyhan (BTC) pipeline carrying oil to Turkey via Georgia and Azerbaijan was premised on the fact that it did not run through either Iranian or Russian territory. As Bill Richards, the former energy secretary in the Clinton administration put it, the strategic significance of the BTC was that it helped prevent inroads by states that did not share US values (Klare, 2008, p. 155).

On a regional level Russia's energy strategy is closely linked to its ambitions for a sphere of influence in the Caspian and Central Asian regions, and Moscow has built larger military bases in both South Ossetia and on the Black Sea Coast in Abkhazia to accommodate that ambition. But the response from Russia on the global level of strategic interaction has been to reinforce its relationships with rising powers and primary energy producer states, especially after the 2008 war in Georgia. At the first BRIC (Brazil, Russia, India and China) summit in 2009, held in Moscow, energy security concerns were high on the agenda; and at the second meeting, held in Brazil during April 2010, the members reaffirmed their commitment to a polycentric, multipolar world order (Council on Foreign Relations, 2010). Outside the BRIC nations, Russia has keenly backed the G20 as a vehicle to give nations other than leading Western countries a greater say in world affairs. It has forged closer links with Venezuela, in particular, with joint naval exercises in the Caribbean, training flights by Tupolev bombers, and a meeting between Medvedev and President Hugo Chavez in November 2008 at which the prospects for a Russian airbase in Venezuela were discussed. More broadly the Russian government has considered reopening military bases in Cuba, and in October 2010 announced that it would move towards reopening a logistics base for its naval forces at the Vietnamese deep-water port of Cam Ranh Bay, after signing a deal that will permit Hanoi to purchase a fleet of *Kilo*-class diesel submarines. On the issue of gas cooperation, the relationship between Russia and Iran has intensified since January 2007, when a meeting between Igor Ivanov and Ayatollah Ali Khamenei yielded a suggestion for a cartel on gas cooperation, similar to OPEC in the oil production arena (Smith, 2007, p. 5). In fact in late 2008, Deputy Prime Minister Igor Sechin suggested that Russia might seek to join OPEC. He subsequently won Tehran's support for this possibility when Gholamhossein Nozarithe, the Iranian Oil Minister, endorsed the idea in March 2009.

Geoeconomics and energy are therefore critical motivating factors in Russia's regional foreign policy, but they also have implications for Russia's global strategic posture as well. Regionally the need has been to resist Western influence in the former Soviet states, where the Kremlin perceives a direct sphere of strategic influence. At the same time, Russia has resisted Western attempts to curtail its influence over a vital transit route for energy, which had become a cornerstone of its strategy for rebuilding national power. On the global level, geoeconomics and energy dovetail with Russia's desire to be an important player in a future multipolar world order. But does Russian resource diplomacy indicate a radical evolution – from the more accommodating face it sought to portray immediately after the collapse of the USSR – into a muscular and aggressive foreign and strategic policy, or is it more reflective of continuity? It is to this question that I now turn.

Strategic continuity: Russian resource diplomacy as a middle power strategy

It is tempting to regard Russian resource diplomacy as part of a complex strategy aimed at producing a new Russian empire to replace the USSR. But instead of viewing Russian strategic policy sliding gradually and inexorably towards neo-imperialism, the issue of resource diplomacy actually lends itself to a story of continuity rather than change. This manifests itself in several ways. First, since the end of the Cold War the primary determinants of Russian policy have been structural. After the collapse of the USSR, Russia (as the leading nation in the Soviet Union) lost a unifying national idea, but it also lost a significant amount of territory, as well as the ability to control it at times – as the wars in Chechnya demonstrated. It also suffered an immediate economic shock that led to further weakness and decline in the 1990s and to myriad internal social and cultural schisms. Thus Russian foreign policy has had less to do with remaining a great power; rather, it has been about preventing further haemorrhaging and then trying to recapture part of its old influence in a much less benign global order.

Second, on the regional level, even though Moscow has recently outpositioned Western efforts to encourage oil and gas source diversification in Central Asia, primarily by signing up former Soviet states to use Russian infrastructure for transit purposes. This was a feat that it accomplished particularly adroitly via the Caspian Pipeline Consortium (CPC) along an export route from Kazakhstan to the Black Sea. Yet Russia is nonetheless unable to exert lasting control over regional actors, many of which perceive Russia as a threat. It has been similarly unable to create a robust barrier against NATO enlargement, a body that Russia remains outside of without a vote or veto, and has largely abandoned using the gas tap as a threat to wealthy EU nations, with which it needs good relations and lasting investment. Institutional structures like the Collective Security Treaty Organisation (CSTO) remain weak and underdeveloped, and the SCO risks the prospect of a rising China relegating Russia to junior partner status.

The only way to break out of this geoeconomic pincer between East and West has been to adopt a diversified policy posture that seeks no firm allies or adversaries. In fact Russia has been playing precisely the same game as countries such as Kazakhstan and other former republics of the USSR, through what might be termed a 'multivector' foreign policy (Hanks, 2009) designed to preserve independence whilst simultaneously also allowing Moscow to reap the benefits garnered from relationships with more powerful actors. This is actually very similar to what many small and middle powers do when faced with uncomfortable external realities. The difference in the Russian case is that we have come to associate middle power diplomacy with progressive or constructive coalition-building. In much neoliberal scholarship it is axiomatic that middle powers routinely attempt to gain influence within multilateral institutions, leverage their strategic alliances and maximise their trade partnerships in order to enhance their relative positions in international politics. Yet as Russian policy demonstrates, adjusting to an uncertain place in the global power structure, and in a potentially hostile external environment, can in fact take the form of a hard power strategy.

At this point a sceptic may well ask whether there is much to be gained by splitting hairs over whether Russian behaviour is reflective of a great power or a middle power. But this is actually the point: given that relative capabilities continue to matter in international relations (and they matter much more, for instance, than approaches that focus on factors such as ideology and identity admit), the extent of material power that Russia possesses is either a vital enabler of strategic policy, permitting freedom of action or, alternatively, a constraint. In Russia's case raw natural resources represent precisely such a vehicle for power maximisation. Governments in such a position often label such strategies in ways that try to capture the language of enlightenment or innovation, stressing the need for 'active' or 'transformational' diplomacy and 'soft' or 'smart' power. Analysts of foreign policy, however, tend to prefer the rather more prosaic boxing analogy of middle powers 'punching above their weight'.

This last description fits neatly into the overall thrust of Russian foreign policy since the collapse of the USSR, in which energy security has come to play a leading role. This does not necessarily mean that its policy has altered fundamentally. There have been many occasions on which observers have identified a sea change in Russia's approach. These supposed grand shifts include the 'Friends with Everyone' policy of Andrei Kozyrev, which in fact was very similar to the 'common European home' espoused by Gorbachev as a component of New Political Thinking. Many analysts then leapt to conclude that the policy of multipolarism, coined when Yevgeny Primakov took over the Russian Ministry of Foreign Affairs (MFA) in the mid 1990s, was a fundamental break from the past, only to herald a new strategic partnership in the US–Russian rapprochement immediately after 9/11, when Vladimir Putin was the first foreign leader to call George W. Bush to offer support.[2] Soon after, though, bellicose Russian statements opposing the war in Iraq and at the Munich Security Conference in 2006, led to breathless pronouncements of a new Cold War. So too did the Medvedev Doctrine of 2008 that explicitly identified the former Soviet states as part of Russia's sphere of influence. And yet in 2009 and 2010, Medvedev's apparent openness to Barack Obama's effort to 'reset' relations with Russia has led to wary suggestions that perhaps Russian attitudes are changing once again.

Viewing Russian foreign and strategic policy in this way, as a series of episodes constantly veering between assertiveness and accommodation, is fundamentally incorrect. Doing so conflates the rhetorical level of policy pronouncements with their operational goals. By making the mistake of equating words with deeds it is easy to identify major shifts in policy, whether on specific issues pertaining to resources – such as former President Putin's renationalisation of the energy industry – or major issues of military security – like Russia's move to a virtual 'assured first use' nuclear doctrine.

In fact Russian strategic policy since the end of the Cold War has been remarkable for its continuity. At its heart, reflected in many official documents such as its Foreign Policy Concepts, Security Concepts and Military Blueprints have been surprisingly pragmatic realisations that the prospects for Russia are potentially grim, with the attendant identification of the economic situation as the main impediment to future Russian power. This is exemplified by the Russian Security Blueprint of 1997, which laid out the tasks for the rebuilding of Russian power in a remarkably frank fashion, especially compared to the aspirational language that often accompanies such documents in the West:

> Russia is lagging increasingly far behind developed countries in terms of science and technology. Dependence on imports of food, consumer goods, equipment and technologies is increasing. The external and internal state debt is growing. There is an exodus of skilled people from the sphere of material production and from the scientific sphere. The number of man-made emergencies is increasing [...] stratification of society is increasing, and the living standards of much of the population are declining. The level of crime and corruption is still high. The country's economic, scientific and demographic potential is declining. The markets and raw material infrastructure of Russian industry have shrunk [...] social accord has not been achieved, and the process of establishing a unifying national idea [...] has not been completed (Russian Federation National Security Blueprint, 1997, pp. 4–5).

The assertive nature of Russian resource diplomacy therefore fits neatly into the overall principles of multipolarism that were articulated by the Yeltsin government in 1996, and have been echoed in the 'five points' outlined in the Medvedev doctrine. The first element – respect for international law – emphasises the primacy of the state, in line with Moscow's determination that non-interference and states' rights remain as the key principles of international politics. Russia has been an enthusiastic participant in what Stephen Krasner (1999) refers to as the 'organised hypocrisy' of sovereignty, where states resist attempts by external actors to interfere in their own affairs, while keenly meddling in the affairs of others – so much so, in fact, that such behaviour has come to define Russia's dealings with the 'Near Abroad' of former communist countries. The second and third points – respectively, a desire for a multipolar world and the need to form diverse friendships to avoid isolation – are also reflected in Russian desires to sell oil and gas in Europe, to Japan and China, and within its immediate sphere of influence. The fourth and fifth aspects of the Medvedev doctrine, relating to preserving the dignity of Russians and maintaining a sphere of influence, was evidenced by the keenness with which Russia prosecuted the war against Georgia in 2008, using a legitimate argument about the human rights of ethnic Russians as a pretext to preserve its regional influence and to serve as a warning against further NATO enlargement. Just as importantly the ability to control oil and gas conduits featured prominently in that conflict.

Conclusion

What does the future hold then for the role of resource diplomacy in Russian foreign and strategic policy? Are we likely to see more attempts to exert pressure on actors with whom Moscow has a grievance? Or will Russia rein in its energy brinkmanship as the interdependencies it is developing with its clients, chief of which is the need for Russia to be regarded as a reliable supplier, become manifestly clearer? The analysis in this chapter suggests several conclusions. First, it should be recognised that Russia's use of oil and gas as coercive policy instruments may be geared around regional goals of de facto empire maintenance, but this does not mean that we should regard Russia's global approach as aggressive. In fact, as has been demonstrated above, it is much more reflective of a middle power strategy. In this respect, although cutting off gas supplies to Ukraine may seem the uninhibited actions of an energy superpower, in terms of the global balance of power it is actually a defensive posture, reflective of the changed material realities that Russia has experienced since the end of the Cold War.

Under such circumstances permitting interdependence with the West to dominate policy undercuts the logic behind multipolarism. On the contrary, its key benefit is in its flexibility and diversity, and in avoiding rather than facilitating a new set of regulatory institutional mechanisms. This means that we should not be optimistic about a compact on energy to develop between East and West, either in concrete multilateral terms or as a reinvigoration of the Helsinki process, as Putin himself has suggested. By the same token, we should expect Russia to continue to play divide-and-rule with its resource assets as it struggles to position itself between a number of large powers in Europe, North America and most especially Asia, all of which have burgeoning energy needs as well as a reluctance to become overly reliant on Middle Eastern sources.

This leads to a second conclusion: given the circumstances that Russia has experienced since the collapse of the USSR, the use of energy for strategic purposes actually makes eminent sense. Unlike great powers of the past or present, which have operated in stable security environments, projected their values regionally and globally and consolidated their national power projects, the challenge for Medvedev and Putin has been much more fundamental. The effective demodernisation of the Russian state under Yeltsin, the massive social and demographic challenges that Russia faces, the instability of the regional security order and the need to avoid becoming a raw materials appendage to either the rising East or a powerful West, have necessitated a policy that may appear alternately imperial or conciliatory, but is ultimately pragmatic. The sooner this is recognised in Western states, the sooner they will learn to deal with Moscow on an equally practical basis. At the very least, doing so will avoid a perpetual sense of puzzled disappointment.

Notes

1. The Shanghai 5 (China, Russia, Kazakhstan, Kyrgystan and Tajikistan) originally met in April 1996. After the Dushanbe meeting that led to the inclusion of Uzbekistan in 2001, the organisation was renamed the Shanghai Cooperation Organisation (SCO). An application by the US for observer status was rejected in 2006, whilst Iran, India and Pakistan have each suggested at various times that they would consider becoming full members of the SCO.
2. Russia in fact did much to support the US by facilitating access for its military personnel into former Soviet republics as part of its efforts to defeat the Taliban in the Afghan theatre.

References

Art, Robert J. (2004) *A Grand Strategy for America* (Ithaca, NY: Cornell University Press).

Blair, Dennis (2009) 'Annual threat assessment of the Intelligence Community for the Senate Select Committee on Intelligence', 12 February, available at: http://intelligence.senate.gov/090212/blair.pdf (accessed 5 January 2011).

Blank, Stephen (2009) 'Resetting the reset button: realism about Russia', Strategic Studies Institute, US Army War College, 2 December, available at: http://www.strategicstudiesinstitute.army.mil/pubs/display.cfm?pubID=956 (accessed 5 January 2011).

Bowker, Mike (1997) *Russian Foreign Policy and the End of the Cold War* (Aldershot: Dartmouth).

Central Intelligence Agency (CIA) (1999) *The World Factbook, 1999* (Washington, DC: Central Intelligence Agency), available at: http://www.odci.gov/cia/publications/factbook/rs.html (accessed 15 January 2011).

Chinese National Petroleum Company (CNPC) (2010) 'CNPC in Kazakhstan', available at: http://www.cnpc.com.cn/eng/cnpcworldwide/euro-asia/kazakhstan (accessed 12 May 2010).

Council on Foreign Relations (2010) 'BRIC Summit Joint Statement', available at: http://www.cfr.org/publication/21927/bric_summit_joint_statement_april_2010.html (accessed 5 January 2011).

Dawisha, Karen and Bruce Parrott (1994) *Russia and the New States of Eurasia: The Politics of Upheaval* (Cambridge: Cambridge University Press).

Dibb, Paul (2006) 'The bear is back', *American Interest*, vol. 2, no. 2, pp. 78–85, available at: http://www.the-american-interest.com/article.cfm?piece=187 (accessed 5 January 2011).

Ebel, Robert and Rajan Menon (eds) (2000) *Energy and Conflict in Central Asia and the Caucasus* (Lanham, MD: Rowman andLittlefield).

European Council (2006) 'An external policy to serve Europe's energy interests', May, available at: http://www.euractiv.com/29/images/External%20Policy%20 EUenergy%20_EN_tcm29-155777.pdf (accessed 5 January 2011).

Failed States Index (2010) *Foreign Policy Magazine Failed States Index, 2010*, available at: http://www.foreignpolicy.com/articles/2010/06/21/2010_failed_states_ index_interactive_map_and_rankings (accessed 5 January 2011).

Gould-Davies, Nigol and Naire Woods (1999) 'Russia and the IMF', *International Affairs*, vol. 75, no. 3, pp. 1–20.

Grachev, Pavel (1993) 'Interview with the Defence Minister', *Nezavisimaya Gazeta*, 8 June, p. 10.

Hanks, Reuls R. (2009) '"Multi-vector politics" and Kazakhstan's emerging role as a geo-strategic player in Central Asia', *Journal of Balkan and Near Eastern Studies*, vol. 11, no. 3, pp. 257–67.

International Affairs Round Table (1998) 'A multipolar world already exists', *International Affairs* (Moscow), vol. 44, no. 1, pp. 1–20.

Klare, Michael T. (2008) *Rising Powers, Sinking Planet: The New Geopolitics of Energy* (New York: Metropolitan Books).

Kotz, David and Fred Weir (1997) *Revolution from Above: The Demise of the Soviet System* (London: Routledge).

Krasner, Stephen (1999) *Sovereignty: Organised Hypocrisy* (Princeton, NJ: Princeton University Press).

Mackinder, Halford J. (1904) 'The geographical pivot of history', *Geographical Journal*, vol. 23, no. 4, pp. 421–37.

Menon, Rajan and Alexander J. Motyl (2007) 'The myth of Russian resurgence', *American Interest*, vol. 2, no. 4, pp. 96–101.

Morgenthau, Hans (1960) *Politics among Nations* (New York: Knopf).

MosNews.com (2009) 'Mixed message from US administration baffles Russia', MosNews.com, 26 July, available at: http://www.mosnews.com/politics/ 2009/07/26/usadmincriticism/ (accessed 5 January 2011).

National Energy Policy Development Group (2001) *National Energy Policy* (Washington, DC: US Government Printing Office), available at: http:// www.wtrg.com/EnergyReport/National-Energy-Policy.pdf (accessed 5 January 2011).

Nezavisimaya gazeta (1998) December 23, p. 1.

Nygren, Bertil (2007) 'Putin's attempts to subjugate Georgia: from sabre-rattling to the power of the purse', in Roger E. Kanet (ed.), *Russia: Re-emerging Great Power* (Houndmills: Palgrave Macmillan), pp. 107–23.

Putin, Vladimir V. (2000) 'Millennium Manifesto', in *Vital Speeches of the Day*, 9 July, available at: http://vsotd.com (accessed 10 January 2011).

RIA Novosti (2010) 'Putin says Russia needs major health reform', RIA Novosti, 20 April, available at: http://en.rian.ru/russia/20100420/158669620.html (accessed 27 January 2011).

Russian Federation National Security Blueprint (1997) *Rossiiskaya Gazeta*, 26 December, pp. 4–5.

Shearman, Peter and Matthew Sussex (2009) 'The roots of Russian conduct', *Small Wars and Insurgencies, Special Issue* on *Russia, Georgia and the West*, vol. 20, no. 2, pp. 251–75.

Smith, Mark A. (2007) 'Russian perceptions of the Iranian nuclear issue', Advanced Research and Assessment Group, Middle East Series, 07/33, Defence

Academy of the United Kingdom, October, available at: http://www.da.mod. uk/colleges/arag/document-listings/middle.../07(33)MAS.pdf (accessed 27 January 2011).

Stockholm International Peace Research Institute (SIPRI) (2010) *SIPRI Yearbook, 2010* (New York: Oxford University Press).

US Department of Defense (2010) *The Quadrennial Defense Review* (Washington, DC: US Government Printing Office).

US National Intelligence Council (NIC) (2009) *Global Trends 2025: A Transformed World* (Washington DC: US Government Printing Office), November, available at: http://www.cic.nyu.edu/internationalsecurity/docs/NIC_final.pdf (accessed 27 January 2011).

US Senate (2006) 'The Silk Road Strategy Act' (Washington, DC: US Government Printing Office), 4 May, available at: http://www.govtrack.us/congress/billtext. xpd?bill=s109-2749 (accessed 27 January 2011).

USAID (2010) 'Aid to the Central Asian republics', available at: http://www. centralasia.usaid.gov/page.php?page=article-566&from_t=default (accessed 14 May 2010).

Wall Street Journal (2009) 'Biden says weakened Russia will bend to the US', 25 July, available at: http://online.wsj.com/article/SB124848246032580581.html (accessed 10 January 2010).

Wedel, Janine (1998) *Collision and Collusion: The Strange Case of Western Aid to Eastern Europe, 1989–1998* (London: Macmillan).

Wilson, Andrew (2010) 'Tilting towards Russia?', *New York Times*, May 20.

World Bank (2009a) *World Development Indicators*, available at: http://data.world-bank.org/products/data-books/WDI-2009 (accessed 10 January 2010).

World Bank (2009b) 'World Bank worsens outlook for fall in Ukraine's GDP', Interfax News Agency, 7 April, available at: http://www.interfax.com.ua/eng/main/11681/ (accessed 27 January 2011).

Yeltsin, Boris (1997) 'On priority measures for reforming the Russian Federation Armed Forces and improving their structure', *Rossiskaya gazeta*, 19 July, p. 5.

Yergin, Daniel (1991) *The Prize: The Epic Quest for Oil, Money and Power* (London: Simon and Schuster).

10
Russian Resource Policies towards the CIS Countries

Bertil Nygren

Introduction

President Dmitri Medvedev is the third Russian president since the demise of the USSR in 1991. While the first began as a political hero and ended as a political wreck and the second began as a political hero and ended his terms still a hero, the third Russian president lacked a charismatic lure and his greatest asset was his predecessor's support and popularity. The second, Vladimir Putin, began a long journey in 2000 to rebuild what I refer to as 'Greater Russia', to recreate Russia as a great power, basically using 'soft power' means. The price was high: by the end of his second term, Putin had managed to split up the members of the Commonwealth of Independent States (CIS) into those that were more closely tied to Russia and those that were more or less in open conflict with Russia – not necessarily the same constellation as in the Yeltsin years. The inheritance left to Medvedev is strategically to counter the Western drift of some – especially Ukraine and Georgia – and instrumentally to use energy issues as a carrot and stick – cheaper or more expensive oil, gas and electricity. In this chapter I am concerned with how President Medvedev has handled the inheritance with respect to using energy politics, especially gas politics as a foreign policy instrument. My starting point is the status of the 'rebuilding' effort by the end of Putin's second presidential term, and I use primarily Putin's and Medvedev's gas politics to illustrate the mechanisms involved.[1]

The Western direction – Ukraine and Belarus: brutal resource politics

Ukraine

The Western – or European – direction is traditionally Russia's security and defence orientation, with strong traditions at least since the late seventeenth century and with three land invasions. In the last couple of decades the European direction has marred Russian decision-making also because of economic dependence issues, especially Russia's need for transit routes for oil and gas. By the time that Putin became President of Russia, the most serious political issues with Ukraine had already been resolved – those concerning the USSR's nuclear arsenal, the Crimea and the Black Sea Fleet. During Putin's presidency relations with Ukraine revolved around border issues, Ukraine's Western orientation, particularly Ukraine's possible NATO membership, gas export issues and Ukrainian elections. The border issue came to a head in late 2003 over the Tuzla islet but was peacefully resolved; the gas transit issue reached a peak in January 2006 and again under Medvedev in January 2009. Up to the Ukrainian presidential elections in early 2010, the Western orientation of Ukraine remained the most contentious issue in the relationship. Russian gas exports to Ukraine and to Europe via Ukraine is used as the prime example here of Russian resource policies vis-à-vis CIS countries – which has been by far the most brutal and explicit use of energy politics to deal with a recalcitrant neighbour. Ukraine's almost total dependency on Russian natural gas constitutes the background to the analysis as well as the fact that 80 per cent of Russian gas to Europe passes through Ukraine.

Although a problem in the relationship for a long time, gas-related issues became acute after the Ukrainian 'Orange Revolution', developing into the so-called 'gas wars'. The ultimate Russian goal was to take control of the gas pipeline network in Ukraine and particularly the gas transit pipeline system to Europe. The ultimate Ukrainian goal was to keep its ownership of the gas pipeline network intact, also as a lever against Russian price policies and possible political use of gas exports to Ukraine. The first so-called 'gas war' in January 2006 also came as a serious warning to Europe – the gas conflict between Russia and Ukraine was no bilateral affair. The positions were simple: Russia wanted a higher price for the gas distributed and sold to Ukraine, and at the same time required that the Russian gas passing through Ukraine did not disappear en route to Europe. The Russian and Ukranian presidents were directly involved and the first 'gas war' ended when they agreed to create an intermediary – RosUkrEnergo – based in Switzerland to handle gas relations. The decision was heavily criticised in Ukraine and within little more than a week, the Ukrainian government fell after severe domestic criticism of the gas deal.[2]

Payments of gas deliveries remained shaky, and an outstanding gas debt that had grown in the autumn of 2007 threatened to close the gas tap once again. This was successfully resolved and by the end of the year, as prices for 2008 were negotiated (in the vicinity of US$180 per 1000 cubic metres, a rise from $130 for 2007), a 'gas war' seemed to have been fully averted in January 2008.

Problems with payments seemed to be a more general phenomenon though, and in February 2008 Gazprom once again threatened to shut off the tap unless an outstanding debt of US$1.5 billion was paid. Putin and Ukrainian President Viktor Yushchenko personally had to negotiate an agreement. Since the debt was not paid by the end of February, Gazprom threatened to reduce gas supplies by 25 per cent on 3 March 2008. By that date Gazprom did indeed cut supplies by 25 per cent and later the same day by another 10 per cent, thus cutting by a total of 35 per cent. On 5 March, Russia resumed gas deliveries after the debt had been settled. A week later it turned out that Russia and Ukraine had finally had enough of the intermediary and signed an agreement to shut the intermediary out of the process and instead settle payments directly between the two states; a month later Russia and Ukraine also settled all previous gas debts. This haggling over prices for deliveries seemed purely economic and contained no obvious political aspect: the intermediary was the problem rather than the two state companies. Nevertheless it took two presidents to solve this purely economic deal.

In the autumn of 2008, with Medvedev in the Kremlin, price negotiations for 2009 were running into problems in talks between Prime Ministers Putin and Yulia Tymoshenko to establish a three-year transition period for gas price rises for Ukraine.[3] Gazprom had now hinted at a price for 2009 of some US$400, being in effect so-called 'European prices'. By late December, Gazprom made overt threats of sanctions if the US$2 billion gas debt for November and December was not paid and if no agreement for 2009 was signed. By now it was obvious that yet another 'gas war' was in the offing.[4] On New Year's Day 2009, the 'gas war' began when Gazprom simply cut off its gas supplies to Ukraine.

A repeat of the January 2006 'gas war' in which Europe would be freezing was now evident. The impact on Europe was being felt already by 2 January and Romania was the first to be seriously hurt with a drop of some 30 to 40 per cent in supplies on the second day of the 'war', while Hungary received some 25 per cent less gas. The next day the Czech Republic and Bulgaria also began to feel the cuts in deliveries. Gazprom promptly accused Ukraine of stealing gas, and on 5 January Putin ordered the closing of gas taps also for gas destined for Europe, since this gas was being stolen in Ukraine en route to Europe. Reactions in the EU were much more serious this time and EU member states met in Brussels to discuss the situation and there were calls for an immediate summit with Russia and Ukraine to resolve the conflict. Putin now explained that gas en route for Europe was to be rerouted.[5] By 6 January, gas was no longer being pumped to Bulgaria, Croatia, Turkey, Greece and Macedonia and only very little gas was being pumped to Austria, Hungary, Slovakia, the Czech Republic and Romania. This time Europe was the direct victim of the gas war between Russia and Ukraine.

The general Russian argument was that Gazprom simply wanted to be paid for its gas deliveries to Ukraine and that Ukraine was to blame for the freeze that East Europeans were experiencing because of gas thefts. Some analysts disbelieve the purely commercial argument and claim that there were also political undertones (Lavelle, 2009; Arnold, 2009a). The EU prepared to send observers and in a telephone call between President of the European Commission José Manuel Barroso and Putin, a preliminary deal was reached a few days later to turn the gas tap on again. On 13 January, Gazprom reopened the taps and gas began flowing in the pipelines.[6] On 19 January, the prime ministers of Russia and Ukraine, Putin and Tymoshenko, signed a ten-year agreement that Tymoshenko predicted would end the gas wars (RFE Russia, 19 January 2009). The price of the gas was very high – instead of the US$180 per 1000 cubic metres paid in late 2008, the price was now set at US$360 per 1000 cubic metres in the first quarter of 2009, thus being the double. In Ukraine citizens were outraged when they learned about the price.[7]

This time, as opposed to January 2006, the blame for the gas war and the plight of the East Europeans was put on both Russia and Ukraine (Closson and Perovic, 2009; RFE Russia, 8 January 2009). The gas war had been 'a lose–lose situation' (Lobjakas, 2009a), and although the gas supplier usually wins such conflicts in the short term, in the long term this was evidently not the case (Arnold, 2009b). For one thing the gas war could have led to a redrawing of gas pipeline maps in Europe. There were some other repercussions of the gas war as well. The Black Sea South Stream project that aimed at avoiding future gas stops in Ukraine was speeded up. More importantly, also in July, Turkey and four European states – Bulgaria, Romania, Hungary and Austria – signed a deal to begin building the Nabucco gas pipeline, which is generally seen as a way to diminish gas dependency on Russia since it will provide Caspian Sea gas without crossing Russian territory.

In the autumn of 2009, several Russian goodwill attempts followed, most likely as forerunners to the Ukrainian presidential elections to take place in early 2010. First, in September, Putin agreed to let Ukraine import less gas than agreed upon earlier. Second, Russia offered a loan to Ukraine to alleviate problems resulting from the financial crisis. Despite this, in November, the almost ritualistic Russian warnings to Europe of gas cuts to be made in the following January were heard once again (RFE Russia, 2 November 2009; Feifer, 2009). As with the previous year, Ukraine countered by saying that it had enough gas in store for the winter (RFE Russia, 6 November 2009). Further warnings followed through December, but on the last day of the year Russia announced that there would be no gas war this time (RFE Russia, 31 December 2009). Again this was a statement directly related to the upcoming Ukrainian presidential elections.

The outcome of the Ukrainian presidential elections with a new Russia-oriented president, Viktor Yanukovych, increased Russian hopes for better relations with Ukraine (Abdullaev, 2010; Granville, 2010; RFE Russia, 19 January 2010; Krainova, 2010). There was a definite feeling that there would be no more gas wars (Pirani, 2010). What followed was a well-directed reorientation of Ukraine's foreign policy that was to change the relationship with Russia altogether. In mid February of the same year, the new Ukrainian president announced that the Russian Black Sea Fleet may stay beyond 2017 (as the present agreement states). He noted that '[w]e have to return to a friendly strategic format of our relations and work for the benefit of both countries' (RFE Russia, 13 February 2010). A 'new page' in Russian–Ukrainian relations was promised during Yanukovych's first trip to Moscow after the elections – future relations would now become what they had never been under Yushchenko. Yanukovych even promised that Ukraine would not join NATO (Feifer, 2010a), and Russia invited Ukraine into the customs union with Belarus and Kazakhstan (Anishyuk, 2010).

In March and April 2010, a second stage in the Ukrainian reorientation showed who the winner really was, when Prime Ministers Putin and Mykola Azarov met in Moscow to discuss gas prices and Medvedev announced that Russia was considering new prices for Ukraine (RFE Russia, 16 April 2010). During the following week of 21 April 2010, Ukraine formally agreed to an extension of the Black Sea Fleet lease in the Crimea for another twenty-five years after 2017 – that is to say, to 2042 – in return for which Ukraine would get cheaper gas from Russia, a US$100 discount – the price was to be lowered from US$330 per 1000 cubic metres to US$230). Yanukovych called the agreement 'unprecedented in the history' of Ukrainian–Russian relations (RFE Russia, 21 April 2010;

Medetsky, 2010a; Golts, 2010).[8] The deal was signed later in April.[9] In an extra theatrical act somewhat later, Putin suggested that Gazprom and Naftogaz, the Ukrainian state gas company, should merge (RFE Russia, 30 April 2010). Yanukovych hesitated however. Such a merger would be similar to a rendezvous between a wolf and a sheep. Nevertheless the issue would not disappear from the agenda and Russia later sweetened the offer (Medetsky, 2010b; *Moscow Times*, 2010).

The Russian–Ukrainian relationship contained the most important conflict in the CIS region during Putin's second term, where the major issues ranged from Ukrainian NATO membership and general 'Westwardness' to the Crimea and the Russian Black Sea Fleet based there. This continued under Medvedev. The major resource instruments for Russia remained its gas tap. In this respect Medvedev continued in Putin's footsteps. For a short while the Georgian War and its repercussions in the CIS region strengthened Ukrainian opposition to Russia and made it more difficult for Medvedev to make any changes in the relationship. But the stage was set for a major shift in the 'balance of power' in the upcoming presidential elections in Ukraine, and Russia played its cards very well this time – there was no repeat of the scandalous interventions in the 2004 Ukrainian presidential elections. Indeed there was no need for this – the political leadership that took over in 2004 did not rule very well, leaving the Ukrainians few other alternatives than to vote in the very opposite direction: for a Russia-friendly president. The changes that followed in Ukrainian foreign policy were dramatic – a pro-Russian orientation instead of a Western-orientation, a no-NATO orientation and a continuation of the presence of a Russian naval base in the Crimea.[10] Cheaper gas was an immediate benefit to Ukraine. The control over Ukrainian gas pipeline networks, the ultimate Russian goal, was not yet achieved. In the near future however a solution – to Russia's benefit – is more than likely. Ukraine will get cheaper gas in exchange for the loss of control over its gas networks.

Belarus

During Yeltsin's last years, cooperation between Russia and Belarus had basically taken place within the framework of a possible Russia–Belarus Union when Belarus sought close relations with Russia and when Russia was fairly responsive to the idea. Putin put the issue of union between the two countries on the back burner, where it is still resting with no obvious sign of being revised.[11] The customs union idea, a much softer replacement of the Russia–Belarus Union, seemed to go nowhere for a long time but was finally signed in August 2010.

Much as with relations with Ukraine resource issues came to the fore under Putin. Gas transit issues to Europe were the main battleground, evidenced by the 'gas war' in 2004, when the Russian gas tap to Belarus was closed in response to Belarus's refusal to let Russia buy a controlling share in the Belarusian gas transit company. Russia used the price weapon, that is to say a large price increase for its gas exports to Belarus, in order to underline the seriousness of its stance on the matter. The gas war was only solved after a telephone conversation between Putin and President Alexander Lukashenka without a victory on the issue of control of the gas transit company.

The situation was repeated in early 2007, but literally a couple of minutes before the new year, in negotiations with Gazprom head, Aleksey Miller, Lukashenka gave in to Russia's demands and sold a 50 per cent share in Beltranshaz – over a period of four years – and thereby lost absolute control of the gas transit company, in exchange for a slow rise in prices, to reach the European level by 2011. A cold and difficult spring in 2007 taught Belarus the lesson of being an underling in the relationship and there was a continuing gas price row in the summer of 2007 with threats of cutting off gas deliveries unless gas debts were paid.[12]

The stage had thus basically been set before Medvedev entered the Kremlin: Lukashenka had been 'tamed', although he had not yet surrendered. When the world financial crisis of 2008 also struck Belarus, Lukashenka went to great lengths to humiliate himself in begging for loans and even asked the United States for a US$5 billion loan – which he did not receive – and then asked Medvedev for a US$3 billion loan in addition to the US$2 billion loan that had already been promised (RFE Russia, 22 December 2008). Russia did not provide the additional US$3 billion loan to Belarus. The basic reason was revenge: first, Belarus had approached Europe and the EU (after the EU had cancelled its travel restrictions on Lukashenka, initially imposed on him for breaching human rights); second, it had not recognised the two Georgian breakaway republics, Abkhazia and South Ossetia; and third, worst of all, it had not allowed Russian capital into Belarus (RFE Russia, 8 April 2009). In May 2009, Premier Putin refused to send Belarus another half-billion dollars after the first billion had already been handed over of the total US$2 billion promised half a year earlier, which of course further aggravated Lukashenka (RFE Russia, 29 May 2009). In addition, in June, Russia banned Belarus's exports of dairy products to Russia in the so-called 'milk war' followed by a 'meat war' later that summer.[13] The quarrels were toned down however and with the tenth anniversary of the Union approaching, Medvedev promised to help Belarus out of its current economic problems (RFE Russia, 10 December 2009).

Then in May 2010, Lukashenka made a strange offer to Russia: in exchange for cheaper gas prices it was offered full ownership of the Beltranshaz and some oil refineries. Russia turned the offer down however. The background was of course the increasing Belarusian difficulties in paying for Russian gas. In June, Belarus sent a crisis delegation to negotiate with Gazprom, which threatened to cut gas deliveries if gas debts – some US$250 million at the time – were not paid. The gas tap was indeed first shut by 15 per cent and the next day by 30 per cent. Lukashenka in turn ordered the closing of the gas transit via the Yamal gas pipeline to Europe. After a couple of days the gas debt was paid and the pipeline was opened again.[14] In many respects this gas war was more of an indicator of the bad relationship between the leaders than of a political struggle. Nevertheless the confrontation followed a familiar pattern: Russia demanded payments for gas deliveries and closed the tap, Belarus threatened transits for Europe, Belarus paid and blamed Russia for its not-very-comradely behaviour.

Oil was another, although different, problem in the relationship. Belarus has been able to buy cheap crude oil from Russia with low or no duties only to reexport its refined products back to Russia or to Europe at considerably higher prices. In late 2006, Russia introduced export duties on crude, in response to which Belarus raised the prices for oil transits – in the Druzhba pipeline – to Europe. Russian oil exporters then closed their oil tap and halted oil exports to Belarus – and thereby also to Europe – which caused a short 'oil war' in early 2007 and looked very much like the earlier gas war. In both cases Belarus used the 'transit tap', that is to say its power to close the tap for the transit of oil or gas to Europe in response to Russia's use of its price weapon. The oil war was solved only after a lengthy telephone conversation between Putin and Lukashenka, in which a compromise was reached. In the following year Russia searched for a new outlet for oil to Europe bypassing Belarus, at Primorsk in the north-east of the Finnish Bay, which would deprive Belarus of its economic leverage on Russia and thereby be fully in the hands of the Russian energy supplier – as a small consumer dealing with a large producer.[15]

In January 2010, a renewed and similar dispute over oil prices developed into a major row after Russia halted deliveries of crude oil to Belarus.[16] The background to this was that in 2009, Russia had introduced a customs duty on oil for Belarus – only about a third of the ordinary export duty for Europe. Europe was threatened by the cut-off, as it had been in 2007 – Russia pumps more than a million barrels a day through its Druzhba oil pipeline to Poland and Germany. In early January 2010, talks on oil prices in Moscow broke down but they were almost immediately resumed, this time by high-level Belarusian politicians. The oil flow to Europe did not seem to be affected on this occasion. The oil tap to Belarus was turned on and then off again as the negotiations continued. Later in January, Belarus responded by threatening to cut off electricity to Kaliningrad – Belarus demanded a fivefold increase in tariffs (RFE Russia, 22 January 2010). This was very much like the situation in the first gas war of 2004, when Belarus threatened to cut off gas deliveries to Kaliningrad. Nothing came of it though and Belarus had to give in to the tariffs.

As with Ukraine, gas had become a major resource instrument in Russian policies vis-à-vis Belarus. But unlike Ukraine, Belarus was forced to capitulate in the last gas war with Russia in 2007, which Putin won. The 'war booty' was the controlling share of the long yearned for Belarus gas transit network. Several remnants of that general conflict over prices and more deeply over the Belarus economy remained however and Medvedev continued the Russian policy of economically subjugating Belarus. Russia's end goal is most likely to gain control of important industrial assets in Belarus, while Lukashenka's end goal is to keep these assets out of Russian hands.[17] By the end of 2009, with Lukashenka ceasing his verbal attacks on Russia, the situation seemed to change for the better for a while, but in May 2010, it seemed that Belarus would not join the Customs Union.[18] In July, Belarus nevertheless signed up for the Union, thereby practically handing over custom issues to Russia. In the rather frivolous media treatment of Lukashenka afterwards, it seemed that Russia had finally had enough with Lukashenka and his rule and was looking for an alternative in the upcoming Belarusian presidential elections of early 2011 (Ryzhkov, 2010).

The southern direction – the Caucasus, Caspian and Central Asian Region: energy and dependency

Under Putin Russia reestablished more active relations with Central Asia and the Caucasus both as an attempt to meet the increasing threat from Islamic extremism and as an attempt to reestablish its economic preeminence in the region to counter increasing US and Chinese influence. The major Russian foreign policy instrument in the region remains military support and energy transit management, the former because of the porous borders within and outwards from Central Asia and the Caucasus, the latter as a necessary tool for securing income from the Central Asian and Caspian Sea states.

Energy issues have been the basic economic instrument by which Russia has exerted power over both exporting states – Azerbaijan, Kazakhstan, Uzbekistan and Turkmenistan – and those states that are poor and need access to energy supplies – Armenia, Kyrgyzstan and Tajikistan. The general trend has been for Russia to renew old pipelines and construct new export pipelines mainly from, and through, Kazakhstan, south to the Black Sea or north-west to Northern Europe. For the Caspian Sea export countries, the major aim has been to attempt constructing new pipelines under the Caspian Sea to Turkey via the Caucasus in order to avoid dependence on Russian transit pipelines. In the first half of the 2000s, Azerbaijan and Georgia were key players – with strong Western support – in constructing oil and gas pipelines through the Caucasus. Russia was also active: during Putin's term in office a gas pipeline from Russia to Turkey was built under the Black Sea and another gas pipeline under the Baltic Sea to Germany was proposed. In the late Putin presidency, a virtual gas cartel in Central Asia was established under Russian leadership to regulate and coordinate gas exports from Russia and Central Asia to Western markets. This confirmed Russia as the major transit country for all Central Asian gas to the West for the next decade – the indecisiveness of the EU with respect to the southern gas corridor (Nabucco) has so far benefitted Russia.

As for the energy exporting countries, Russia has basically controlled the 'transit tap'. Under Putin Azerbaijan has been a cooperative partner with respect to the Caspian Sea and its resources, and bilaterally electricity grids as well as the export of Azeri oil and gas to and via Russia have constituted important integrative measures. Some contentious issues have concerned Azeri oil and gas and its export to Russia and/or Europe via the so-called southern route – the BTC oil and BTE gas pipelines opened in 2006.

In the summer of 2008, the revival of the idea of a Caspian Sea pipeline to export Turkmen gas to Europe via Azerbaijan caused some excitement, and Medvedev suggested that Russia instead buy all of Azerbaijan's gas exports. A new gas pipeline from Azerbaijan to Russia was being discussed in March 2009, and in the summer it seemed that Russia had won the struggle over export gas routing when Russia was promised priority in the gas production of the second Shah Deniz Field (estimated at a cost of some US$10 billion). In July 2009, the EU Nabucco deal was finally signed, signifying the construction of the new pipeline, and Azerbaijan was expected to be one of the first to fill the pipeline.[19] On the one hand, in early 2010, there was an agreement on a fourfold increase of Azeri gas deliveries to Russia and by March the gas deliveries had already been doubled. On the other hand, the Azeri export routes for oil and gas through Georgia since 2006 have already diminished its dependence on Russia. Nothing fundamentally new has occurred under Medvedev, and today the big issue is what the Nabucco pipeline will mean to Azerbaijan: should the cross-Caspian gas pipeline materialise, Azerbaijan will become a major hub for Central Asian gas to Europe.

Turkmenistan

Turkmenistan is a crucial actor with respect to gas relations in the CIS region, especially since it competes with Russia over gas deliveries to Europe. The recent history of Russian–Turkmen gas relations is indicative of the changes that began in the mid 2000s and continue to this day. Ever since June 2006, when the principal and formal agreement on constructing the Nabucco gas pipeline from Central Asia via Turkey to Europe was signed – by Turkey, Austria, Hungary, Bulgaria and Romania – the question of the pipeline under the Caspian Sea has been debated. The construction of Nabucco is to be completed in 2012, with a total estimated cost of some US$6 billion and the European Investment Bank and European Bank for Reconstruction and Development as well as the World Bank will co-finance the project. The prospective Caspian Sea underwater pipeline would then link up with the existing BTE gas pipeline to Turkey and further on to Nabucco and Europe.

Not to upset Russia over the new plans for gas to Europe, Turkmenistan confirmed its honouring of the 2003 agreement to ship gas via Russia up to 2028 as well. Negotiations on an even bigger deal were already going on, and in May 2007 an agreement between Russia, Turkmenistan and Kazakhstan was signed, according to which a new gas pipeline would be constructed along the eastern shores of the Caspian Sea. Uzbekistan was also to be connected to the pipeline. Russia was also to invest heavily in gas production in Turkmenistan. In November of the same year the agreement was finalised and Gazprom at the same time enforced only a 50 per cent price increase (from US$100 to US$150 per cubic metre).[20] A long-time Turkmen desire was fulfilled a year later in March 2008, when Russia agreed to pay 'European prices' for gas delivered by Turkmenistan – and Uzbekistan and Kazakhstan – at the time US$210 per cubic metre. Russia now seemed to have won the race of the gas transit from Turkmenistan to Europe, but at a high economic cost.

The financial crisis in the autumn of 2008 lowered international gas prices and it was soon evident that the price level was too high for Russia. Conveniently in April 2009, a blast on the old Turkmen pipeline to Russia ceased all further gas deliveries and Turkmen accusations that the pipeline was intentionally blown up were certain to follow. Russia had asked for a 90 per cent reduction in gas deliveries due to the high price level of which Russia had already lost over a billion dollars in the first three months of 2009. This in turn renewed the Turkmen interest in joining the Nabucco pipeline project.[21] An attempt to mend fences between Russia and Turkmenistan in the autumn failed, and only in December 2009 was an agreement to restore gas deliveries to Russia signed. In the spring of 2010, with the renewed interest in Europe in the Nabucco pipeline, Russia attempted to court Turkmenistan in order to establish future gas deliveries. With the launching of the first major Russian oil and gas prospecting project in the Caspian Sea in May, Russia's courting of Turkmenistan went even further. Turkmenistan was intent on seeking alternative routes or export diversification however, and in August 2010 it seemed again as though it had succeeded both with respect to Nabucco and with a pipeline towards the east to Asia, with China helping out financially in both cases (Pannier, 2010).

Kazakhstan

In Kazakhstan there was towards the end of Putin's second administration an attempt to export oil also via Azerbaijan – shipped to Baku and then reloaded to the BTC pipeline – although this was but a small trickle as compared to the Kazakh oil flowing through Russia in the old and new pipelines. Russia was and remains for all practical purposes in charge of Kazakh oil export, especially since an agreement was concluded in May 2008 to double the throughput capacity of the CPC oil pipeline. Another major Russian involvement pointing in the same direction was directly tied to the Russian–Turkmen agreement of 2009 on a new gas pipeline that ran north along the eastern shores of the Caspian Sea, in which Kazakhstan committed itself to participate. As a consequence Turkmenistan, Kazakhstan and Uzbekistan abstained from signing the document on the Fifth Europe Energy Summit in 2009 that worked on the Nabucco solution.

Uzbekistan

In Uzbekistan after the reconciliation following Russia's support in the 2005 Andijon events and with its investments of US$2.5 billion, Russia was given gas exploration rights in the spring of 2007. A year later in the spring of 2008, several strategic energy projects were signed by Putin and Uzbekistan's president, Islam Karimov. With the Russia–Turkmen gas pipeline project, which Uzbekistan joined, Russia received yet a stronger hold on Uzbekistan.[22]

With respect to the poor and dependent countries of the Caspian Sea region, the Russian use of resource politics looks different. In the poor countries of Georgia, Armenia, Kyrgyzstan and Tajikistan, with no significant energy resources of their own, Russia has continued to be the major investor/builder/financer of energy-related projects and hydrocarbon prospecting. Russian resource politics here played out differently from the way that it had in the four hydrocarbon-rich countries of the Caspian Sea region.

Georgia

Georgia remains the major Russian headache in the Caucasus region. Apart from other power instruments, Putin also used resource politics in relations with Georgia. Until quite recently Georgia had been totally dependent on Russian gas and electricity supplies. In 2003, Georgia signed a twenty-five-year agreement in principle with Gazprom on gas deliveries, but because of popular resistance the agreement was never ratified in Georgia. Georgia did not allow Gazprom to take over the Georgian gas pipelines. In 2005, the Russian Duma proposed that Russia stop its 'gas socialism' and 'special treatment' – low pricing (RFE/RL Newsline, 11 July 2005) – and Gazprom announced that it would raise gas prices for 2006 (RFE/RL Newsline, 30 November 2005; Corwin, 2005). The sabotage of a gas pipeline in January 2006 closed the Russian gas pipeline to Georgia, and Russia was accused of sabotaging its own gas pipeline in order to take over the Georgian pipeline (RFE/RL Newsline, 24 January 2006; Petriashvili, 2006; Yasmann, 2006).[23] This takeover was indeed the Russian goal. Gas pricing continued to be an issue in the late autumn of 2006, when Gazprom suggested a price level of US$230 per 1000 cubic metres for 2007 – instead of the US$110 paid in 2006 – or a cheaper price in exchange for stakes in the Georgian energy sector. Georgia did not give in to the 'energy blackmail' and settled for the higher gas price (RFE/RL Newsline, 8 November 2006; RFE/RL Newsline, 27 December 2006). After 2006, Russia lost some of its gas resource levers, since it was no longer the sole gas supplier. Electricity too became a source of domestic conflict in 2003, when a subsidiary company of Russia's Unified Energy Systems (UES) acquired a majority share in the Georgian electricity distribution company. Since then the UES controls the electricity system of Georgia and owns 50 per cent of the Transenergy nuclear power plant and all of the Mtkvari power plant.[24] In 2005, UES bought another hydroelectric power station. Late into Putin's presidency Russia used 'trade wars' related to wine and mineral water and various trade barriers to bring pressure to bear against Georgia. Georgia remains sensitive to Russia's instrumental use of gas and other energy resources. Of course the 2008 war in Georgia has not changed this energy dependency on Russia.

Armenia

Russia's relations with Armenia have been solid and stable since 1991, although Armenia has been equally and strongly dependent on Russia, not least because of the Azeri and Turkish closing of their borders with Armenia, leaving only Georgia as a transit country for imports. Armenia too was severely hit by rising energy prices – which doubled between 2006 and 2008 to reach world market prices in 2011 – despite temporarily cheaper gas deliveries from Russia and a new gas pipeline from Iran. By the end of the Putin presidency, Armenia had become even more economically dependent on Russia. The 'assets for debts' policy also transferred many energy-related assets into Russian hands, especially hydropower and nuclear power stations. By 2006, the entire Armenian power distribution network was in Russian hands. In 2006, Russia used cheaper gas as a carrot and gave in to Armenian demands to lower the price of gas, which had been agreed on earlier, a rather evident politically based decision. Russia was to cash in the dividends later.

The new Armenian president since 2008, Serzh Sarkisian, knew that Armenia had to diversify its relations. The new Eastern Partnership Programme of the EU constituted a second opening for Armenia, which was in desperate need of assistance after the financial crisis in the autumn of 2008: a free trade deal was on the horizon. In addition the World Bank offered some US$800 million. Russia countered bids from the EU and World Bank with a loan of its own of some US$500 million. The old Metsamor nuclear energy plant, which generates some 40 per cent of Armenian electricity, was due to be decommissioned in 2017 and replaced by a US$5 billion nuclear plant to provide twice as much energy as the Metsamor plant. The plant was initially to be built by an Australian company but Russia later took over the construction. Furthermore and more to the point, in the autumn of 2009, it was announced that the expected quick rise in Russian gas prices would not be realised and that Armenia would have to pay less than the estimated US$200 in 2010. This too was effectively a politically based concession. Nothing fundamentally new occurred under Medvedev, although there have been some Armenian efforts to engage in new directions – Iran, the EU and Turkey – Armenia is in the firm grip of Russia.

Tajikistan

In Tajikistan, Russia under Putin has been quite active in the energy sector. Gazprom received licenses for the exploration of gas and oil resources in early 2007, but more importantly Russia completed the construction of the Roghun hydroelectric power plant. The long planned for Russian start of the Sangtuda-1 power plant, of which Russia owned over 75 per cent and had invested some US$500 million, was delayed, but came into production in early 2008. The Russian economic crisis in the autumn of 2008 had some repercussions on the financing and construction of the Roghun plant, and Tajikistan turned to the EU and NATO for help. In the summer of 2009, Medvedev and the Tajik president, Emomali Rahmon, opened the fourth facility of the Sangtuda-1 power plant that seemed to have the effect of normalising relations between the two countries once again.[25]

Kyrgystan

Kyrgyzstan is in an even worse situation than Tajikistan, with no real assets at all and being heavily dependent on Russia. Since 2001, the United States and Russia each have had an airbase there that have offered the Kyrgyz leadership some leverage, but as the 'revolutions' in 2005 and 2010 show, the inherently weak nature of the Kyrgyz state has prevented effective use even of that fairly insignificant leverage. The few economic assets that the country has are already in Russian hands, and the everlasting Kyrgyz energy debt to Russia has been compensated for by swaps or write-offs for assets. In the spring of 2009, as an extraordinary act of economic assistance to the crisis-stricken state, and probably also as a reward for the Kyrgyz attempt to close the US base in Kyrgyzstan, Russia offered a US$2 billion loan to Bishkek.[26]

Conclusion

There are today two categories of neighbouring CIS states with respect to Russian resource politics because of two different types of dependencies. Putin's policies were very different from those of his predecessor: gone is Russia's 'big brother' helping hand, now replaced by fairly heavy-handed capitalist arguments. Differences in these policies bilaterally are traceable to geopolitical, geoeconomic and geographical factors: while the Western border countries constitute a buffer zone in defence terms, they also constitute a transit area for the export of oil and gas from Russia that gives Ukraine and Belarus some leverage on Russia, since they control what I refer to as the 'transit tap' (Nygren, 2008b). This fact has been played out most evidently in the case of gas transits through Belarus and Ukraine to Europe. However Russia itself is a transit country for the most important hydrocarbon exports from the Caspian Sea region, best noticed in terms of Central Asian natural gas transits to Europe. In all bilateral relations, where applicable, the Putin administration has used a general policy of tying in the CIS countries closer to Russia by using its geographical and structural advantages. In this Russia has basically acted in order to rebuild what I refer to as 'Greater Russia'. So the question is: has Medvedev continued these strategies? And the answer is basically 'Yes, he has.'

The situation towards the western direction has dramatically changed recently. While relations with Ukraine were tense ever since the Orange Revolution, they have become much more relaxed as a result of the new Yanukovych presidency in Ukraine in 2010. Medvedev's policies remained the very same though – requiring heavy Ukrainian political concessions for economic benefits. Ukraine has so far managed to keep its gas transit network in domestic control, but handed over the Black Sea naval base to Russia for another twenty-five years and with a tacit promise not to seek NATO membership in exchange for cheaper gas. The struggle over the control of the gas transit networks continues. Other resource-related sectors are also liable to be taken over. Over the next years there is an obvious risk of what has been called a 'Finlandisation' of Ukraine (Asmus, 2010).

Relations with Belarus continue to be a mixture of real integration attempts and virtual takeovers. Russian attempts to take control of the most valuable Belarusian asset – the gas transit network – have basically been successful, despite Lukashenka's fierce resistance. Russia today controls 50 per cent of the Belarus gas transit company and it is likely that Belarus will sell the entire gas network to Russia in exchange for gas at Russian domestic prices. Should this succeed Belarus will have lost the only effective countermeasures against one-sided price hikes. In the longer term Belarus will most likely be overrun by Russian capital, much the same way as Ukraine has been, and the further integration of the three Slavic countries will then be entirely on Russian conditions. In other words Medvedev stood to gain from Putin's policies.

Russian relations with Central Asia and the Caucasus have involved more the direct use of energy resources to punish and reward states and their leaders. While security issues dominated in the late Yeltsin and early Putin years, later on in Putin's presidency economic issues came to the fore: Russia is today competing not only with the US but increasingly with China over influence in the chase after hydrocarbon resources. The southern direction of Russia's foreign policy has seen two different types of resource politics, one aimed at poor and dependent CIS states and another at energy exporting countries. The latter is the more interesting, since in the former Russia plays the role of the provider of energy and other economic resources to the poorest countries – Armenia, Georgia, Tajikistan and Kyrgyzstan – which are already stuck in the dependency trap.

For the four oil and gas exporting countries in the region – Azerbaijan, Kazakhstan, Uzbekistan and Turkmenistan – Russia has played its 'transit card' and made every attempt to keep them tied up by energy transfers to Europe, perhaps too firmly, since the energy exporting countries have at the same time attempted to break loose from this inconvenient embrace, with mixed results so far.[27] An actual Russia-led gas cartel is in the making and the only remaining salvation for the Caspian Sea states are the European Union-supported Nabucco pipeline project and the Chinese thirst for hydrocarbon energy. Only the Nabucco project, if successful in connecting gas pipelines across the Caspian Sea, could alleviate the situation of the four Caspian Sea export countries. At this time however the groundwork laid during Putin's second term still restricts outside competition – read United States and China – and Medvedev has had no reason to change Putin's successful domination policy of this region.

Energy issues, especially gas pipeline construction and gas transit routes, continued to develop after Putin left the Kremlin for the White House. The issues that took off in his second term developed further, and today it is obvious that Russia's having the previously evident upper hand in being a transit route for Central Asian gas to Europe is no longer that obvious: while Russia still has a dominance in Central Asia, there have also been several Russian concessions to producer countries in Central Asia and an acceptance of a direct Chinese role in building Central Asia's own pipelines eastwards to China and the involvement of others in building pipelines to South Asia. Turkmenistan is the case in point here, although both Kazakhstan and Uzbekistan play an important part in the second 'Great Game' as well. It has become evident that Russia intends to play the game more fairly and offered world market prices for previously extremely cheap gas. The winner in this new Great Game is still to be seen (Lourie, 2010). By and large Russia's standard policy of almost the whole of the last decade of using resource politics in its relations with the CIS countries has continued under Medvedev's presidency – to no one's surprise, since the architect of that strategy, Putin himself, remains the major power player in Russia.

Notes

1. For a comprehensive account of the development of Russia's CIS policies and the soft power instrument, see Nygren, 2008a and 2008b.
2. For contemporary analyses, see Abdullaev, 2006; Belton, 2006; and Maksymiuk, 2006. The intermediary joint company was heavily criticised and the general argument was to handle energy relations directly between the two states – both for practical negotiations and economic reasons. The intermediary made

as much as US$7 billion in 2006 alone on its middleman position (RFE/RL Newsline, 9 July 2007). The intermediary was also criticised in Russia and the need to get rid of the Swiss-based intermediary was strongly felt (RFE/RL Newsline, 17 October 2007). This discussion continued in early 2008, when Prime Minister Yulia Tymoshenko accused the intermediary of its murky and non-transparent businesses (RFE/RL Newsline, 14 January 2008).

3. In December, continued talks on the price for 2009 were also hampered by debt issues (some US$2 billion).

4. By referring to the large gas supplies stored in Ukraine, which would resist Russian gas cuts, Gazprom suggested that Ukraine would deal a blow to the European countries that would be without gas if the price issue was not solved (RFE Russia, 31 December 2008).

5. A strange statement given that there are no direct gas pipelines through Ukraine to Europe. Instead there are several pipelines, none of which is predestined for European consumers – all gas deliveries to Europe can be redirected to Ukrainian consumers as well.

6. The Ukrainian gas company immediately stated that it was blocking the gas for Europe because of the lack of so-called 'technical gas', suggesting problems with the technically outdated equipment. Thus gas did not reach Europe quite yet.

7. In an aftershock of the 'gas war', the Ukrainian gas company Naftogas and another gas company were raided as part of a criminal enquiry. For an analysis see Romanova, 2009; and Pannier, 2009.

8. Ukraine also needed the discount in order to receive International Monetary Fund (IMF) credit.

9. For an analysis see Feifer, 2010b.

10. For an analysis of the new Russia–Ukraine relationship, see Inozemtsev, 2010; and von Twickel, 2010.

11. The Union idea seemed dead, and prior to the new prime minister Putin's state visit to Belarus in May 2009, Lukashenka criticised Russia for its lack of interest in the ten-year-old project. Lukashenka's acceptance of the EU's Eastern Partnership Programme did not make Russia friendlier.

12. Furthermore a promised Russian stabilisation loan to Belarus was not effectuated. Only in December 2007, at a summit between Lukashenka and Putin did the two sign a memorandum on a stabilisation loan, and the loan was handed over in the spring of 2008.

13. Belarus answered by stricter customs control. After a few weeks Russia lifted the ban on milk. In July, a second round of the trade war occurred when Russia banned some meat imports from Belarus, and Belarus answered by closing a diesel pipeline to Latvia.

14. Belarus had by now wetted its appetite and demanded the immediate payment of some transit fees in an obvious attempt to save face.

15. Lukashenka used harsh words to condemn Russian energy trade policies under Putin, calling the Russian price increases 'barbaric actions' and referring to 'increasing imperial tones to Russian policy' (RFE/RL Newsline, 7 February 2007).

16. The amount of oil exported to Belarus – not the oil transited to Europe – and the major part of which is reexported after refining amounted to 14.5 million tons a year (RFE Russia, 8 January 2010).

17. Russia seems to have concluded that it will not be able to come to terms with Lukashenka, which can be seen, for example, in the fact that Medvedev and Lukashenka have not been able to reach any significant agreements at all during their frosty meetings. For example, when Medvedev and Lukashenka met at a summit in Sochi in August 2009, the extent to which the Putin–Lukashenka personal animosity had been contagious was obvious.
18. The suggested joint World Trade Organization (WTO) application had still not materialised.
19. For a discussion on the deal see Tully, 2009; and Lobjakas, 2009b.
20. In December, all three major players – Russia, Kazakhstan and Turkmenistan – signed the formal agreement amounting to 20 billion cubic metres (bcm) a year of gas transportation from Turkmenistan. There were also other significant pipeline deals made by the new Turkmen leadership. Agreement to build a pipeline to China was made in April 2006 to supply 30 bcm a year from 2009 for thirty years. In April 2008, still a third major gas pipeline deal was announced, this time via Afghanistan to Pakistan and India after talks that had lasted since 2002. The construction began in 2010 with a total cost of some US$7.5 billion. The ownership of the Caspian Sea gas fields themselves were still in dispute between Turkmenistan and Azerbaijan, but the new Turkmen leadership seemed willing to negotiate the issue.
21. It also renewed the issue of whether or not there would be sufficient gas to fill up the pipeline. The dispute over gas fields in the Caspian Sea between Turkmenistan and Azerbaijan broke out again.
22. In late 2008, as a consequence of the world financial crisis, Uzbekistan moved closer to Europe and once again distanced itself from Russia and threatened to leave the Russian-led economic bloc for the EU. The EU was openly striving for better relations and ended its sanctions against Uzbekistan in the autumn of 2009, which had been imposed because of the Andijon events.
23. Georgian President Mikheil Saakashvili himself blamed 'dark barbaric forces' for the sabotage (RFE/RL Newsline, 27 January 2006). For an analysis of the gas cut-off, see Giragosian, 2006; Petrishvili, 2006; and Latynina, 2006.
24. This caused the Georgian opposition to coin the famous phrase: '[t]his time [Russia is] using banks rather than tanks' (Georgian parliamentarian quoted in Khachatrian, 2003). In 2004, Georgian analysts debated whether or not Russia's new policies suggested 'keeping Tbilisi under its thumb by means of private sector investment into key sectors of the Georgian economy', the key methods of which were the attempts to take control of electricity distribution and gas deliveries (Areshidze, 2004).
25. In March, the World Bank announced its readiness to finance the Roghun plant.
26. Although Russia did not live up to the promise made. Some US$450 million had been received by the summer of 2009, among other things to finance the construction of a hydropower station. Russia officially protested in the autumn of 2009 that some of the money was used instead in commercial activities in Bishkek (*Eurasia Insight*, 16 February 2010; Djumataeva, 2010). This was in itself a precursor of the Russian unwillingness to defend the Kyrgyz president, Kurmanbek Bakiyev, in the summer of 2010 when Russia played a much more hesitant role and refused to take on the responsibility

of reordering the situation by offering peacekeepers. Instead its support for the new leadership was evident from the beginning.

27. The BTC and BTE oil and gas pipelines have solved some of the dependency problems for Georgia and Azerbaijan and provide at least an example of how export states could get out of the Russian grip. So far the Chinese oil and gas projects and pipelines have not been competing directly with Russia over exactly the same resources, but in the future they may very well do so, in which case the export countries of the Caspian Sea may be able to play the two off against each other for better conditions.

References

Abdullaev, Nabi (2006) 'Putin, Yushchenko defend gas deal', *Moscow Times*, 12 January, p. 1.

Abdullaev, Nabi (2010) 'Moscow prepares for better Kiev ties', *Moscow Times*, 15 January, available at: http://www.themoscowtimes.com/news/article/397456.html (accessed 13 September 2010).

Anishyuk, Alex (2010) 'Kiev invited to join Customs Union', *Moscow Times*, 9 March, available at: http://www.themoscowtimes.com/business/article/kiev-invited-to-join-customs-union/401163.html (accessed 13 September 2010).

Areshidze, Irakli (2004) 'Will Russian investment win Georgia's heart?' *Moscow Times*, 11 May, p. 8.

Arnold, Chloe (2009a) 'Barring "obstacles", Russia ready to resume gas shipments', RFE Russia, 12 January, available at: http://www.rferl.org/content/Russia_Says_Ukraine_Signs_New_Gas_Monitoring_Deal__/1368899.html (accessed 13 September 2010).

Arnold, Chloe (2009b) 'In short term, the one with the gas wins', RFE Russia, 23 January, available at: http://www.rferl.org/content/In_Short_Term_The_One_With_The_Gas_Wins/1374062.html (accessed 13 September 2010).

Asmus, Ronald D. (2010) 'Finlandization of Georgia and Ukraine', *Moscow Times*, 3 March, available at: http://www.themoscowtimes.com/opinion/article/finlandization-of-georgia-and-ukraine/400808.html (accessed 13 September 2010).

Belton, Catherine (2006) 'Rosukrenergo as winner in gas war', *Moscow Times*, 10 January, p. 1.

Closson, Stacy and Jeronim Perovic (2009) 'Hope won't keep Europe warm', RFE Russia, 8 January, available at: http://www.rferl.org/content/commentary_Hope_Wont_Keep_Europe_Warm/1367913.html (accessed 13 September 2010).

Corwin, Julie (2005) 'Georgia: Tbilisi, Kyiv seek energy alliance with West', *Eurasia Insight*, 18 December, available at: http://www.eurasianet.org/departments/insight/articles/pp121805.shtml (accessed 13 September 2010).

Djumataeva, Verena (2010) 'Moscow chills relations with Kyrgyzstan', RFE Russia, 23 February, available at: http://www.rferl.org/content/Moscow_Chills_Relations_With_Kyrgyzstan/1966393.html (accessed 13 September 2010).

Eurasia Insight (2010) 'Kyrgyzstan: Moscow withholding promised aid to Bishkek', 16 February, available at: http://www.eurasianet.org/departments/insightb/articles/eav021610.shtml (accessed 13 September 2010).

Feifer, Gregory (2009) 'Expert downplays fears over Ukraine–Russia gas crisis', RFE Russia, 4 November, available at: http://www.rferl.org/content/Experts_Downplay_Fears_Over_UkraineRussia_Gas_Crisis_/1869197.html (accessed 13 September 2010).

Feifer, Gregory (2010a) 'Ukraine promises "new page" in Moscow ties', RFE Russia, 5 March, available at: http://www.rferl.org/content/Ukrainian_President_Yanukovych_Visits_Russia/1975007.html (accessed 13 September 2010).

Feifer, Gregory (2010b) 'For Yanukovych, a fleet-footed dash to repair Russia divide', RFE Russia, 29 April, available at: http://www.rferl.org/content/For_Yanukovych_A_Fleet_Footed_Dash_To_Repair_Russia_Divide/2028075.html (accessed 13 September 2010).

Giragosian, Richard (2006) 'Gas cutoff highlights flaws in Georgia's National Security Concept', RFE/RL Newsline, End Note, 31 January, available at: http://www.rferl.org/content/article/1143564.html (accessed 13 September 2010).

Golts, Alexander (2010) 'Russia gets duped again', *Moscow Times*, 27 April, available at: http://www.themoscowtimes.com/opinion/article/russia-gets-duped-again/404838.html (accessed 13 September 2010).

Granville, Christopher (2010) 'Russia to the rescue', *Moscow Times*, 19 January, available at: http://www.themoscowtimes.com/opinion/article/397672.html (accessed 13 September 2010).

Inozemtsev, Vladislav (2010) 'Moscow's new best friend', *Moscow Times*, 5 May, available at: http://www.themoscowtimes.com/opinion/article/moscows-new-best-friend/405389.html (accessed 13 September 2010).

Khachatrian, Haroutiun (2003) 'Russian moves in Caucasus energy and power sectors could have geopolitical impact', *Eurasia Insight*, 25 September, available at: http://www.eurasianet.org/departments/business/articles/eav092503.shtml (accessed 13 September 2010).

Krainova, Natalya (2010) 'Russia's ambassador finally arrives in Kiev', *Moscow Times*, 26 January, available at: http://www.themoscowtimes.com/news/article/398180.html (accessed 13 September 2010).

Latynina, Yuliya (2006) 'Moscow and Tbilisi point fingers', *Moscow Times*, 1 February, p. 10.

Lavelle, Peter (2009) 'Gazprom simply wants to get paid', RFE Russia, 7 January, available at: http://www.rferl.org/content/Gazprom_Simply_Wants_To_Get_Paid/1367322.html (accessed 13 September 2010).

Lobjakas, Ahto (2009a) 'Will Russia lose its game of gas roulette?', RFE Russia, 17 January, available at: http://www.rferl.org/content/Will_Russia_Lose_Its_Game_of_Gas_Roulette__/1371191.html (accessed 13 September 2010).

Lobjakas, Ahto (2009b) 'EU Troika begins tour of South Caucasus', RFE Russia, 16 July, available at: http://www.rferl.org/content/EU_Troika_Begins_Tour_Of_South_Caucasus/1778503.html (accessed 13 September 2010).

Lourie, Richard (2010) 'The next round of the great game', *Moscow Times*, 11 May, available at: http://www.themoscowtimes.com/opinion/article/the-next-round-of-the-great-game/405652.html (accessed 13 September 2010).

Maksymiuk, Jan (2006) 'Terms of new Ukrainian gas deal unclear', RFE/RL Newsline, End Note, 6 February, available at: http://www.rferl.org/content/article/1143568.html (accessed 13 September 2010).

Medetsky, Anatoly (2010a) 'Deal struck on gas, Black Sea Fleet', *Moscow Times*, 22 April, available at: http://www.themoscowtimes.com/business/article/deal-struck-on-gas-black-sea-fleet/404501.html (accessed 13 September 2010).

Medetsky, Anatoly (2010b) 'Gazprom sweetens Naftogaz merger offer', *Moscow Times*, 28 June, available at: http://www.themoscowtimes.com/business/article/gazprom-sweetens-naftogaz-merger-offer/409170.html (accessed 13 September 2010).

Moscow Times (2010) 'Ukraine pushes for reduced gas price', 6 September, available at: http://www.themoscowtimes.com/business/article/ukraine-pushes-for-reduced-gas-price/414779.html (accessed 24 September 2010).

Nygren, Bertil (2008a) *The Re-building of Greater Russia: Putin's Foreign Policy towards the CIS Countries* (London and New York: Routledge).

Nygren, Bertil (2008b) 'Putin's use of natural gas to reintegrate the CIS region', *Problems of Post-Communism*, vol. 55, no. 4, pp. 3–15.

Pannier, Bruce (2009) 'Naftogaz raid raises concern about new round of gas war', RFE Russia, 5 March, available at: http://www.rferl.org/content/Naftohaz_Raid_Raises_Concern_About_New_Round_Of_Gas_War_/1504662.html (accessed 13 September 2010).

Pannier, Bruce (2010) 'Turkmenistan tips its hand on future energy exports', RFE/RL Russia, 22 August, available at: http://www.rferl.org/content/Turkmenistan_Tips_Its_Hand_On_Future_Energy_Exports/2134389.html (accessed 13 September 2010).

Petriashvili, Diana (2006) 'As Georgia loses gas, rancor at Russia on the rise', *Eurasia Insight*, 23 January, available at: http://www.eurasianet.org/departments/insight/articles/eav012306b.shtml (accessed 13 September 2010).

Pirani, Simon (2010) 'Preventing new gas wars', *Moscow Times*, 28 January, available at: http://www.themoscowtimes.com/opinion/article/398420.html (accessed 13 September 2010).

Putin, Vladimir (2008) Beginning of the Second Meeting of the Russian–Ukrainian Intergovernmental Commission, 12 February, available at: http://archive.kremlin.ru/eng/speeches/2008/02/12/2246_type82914_160016.shtml (accessed 13 September 2010).

RFE Russia may be accessed by date, available at: http://www.rferl.org/archive/Russia/latest/652/666.html (accessed various dates).

RFE/RL Newsline may be accessed by date, available at: http://www.rferl.org/archive/en-newsline/latest/683/683.html (accessed various dates).

Romanova, Olga (2009) 'Ukraine's leaders bite the bullet', RFE Russia, 5 March, available at: http://www.rferl.org/content/Ukraines_Leaders_Bite_The_Bullet/1504581.html (accessed 13 September 2010).

Ryzhkov, Vladimir (2010) 'Why the Kremlin is furious with Lukashenko', *Moscow Times*, 4 August, available at: http://www.themoscowtimes.com/opinion/article/why-the-kremlin-is-furious-with-lukashenko/411632.html (accessed 13 September 2010).

Trilling, David and Chinghiz Umeto (2010) 'Kyrgyzstan: is Putin punishing Bakiyev?', *Eurasia Insight*, 5 April, available at: http://www.eurasianet.org/departments/insight/articles/eav040610a.shtml (accessed 13 September 2010).

Tully, Andrew F. (2009) 'Is there enough Caspian gas, and political will, to make Nabucco a success', RFE Russia, 16 July, available at: http://www.rferl.

org/content/Is_There_Enough_Caspian_Gas_And_Political_Will_To_Make_
Nabucco_A_Success/1778164.html (accessed 13 September 2010).

von Twickel, Nikolaus (2010) 'Medvedev says rain "washed away" tensions with
Kiev', *Moscow Times*, 18 May, available at: http://www.themoscowtimes.com/
news/article/medvedev-says-rain-washed-away-tensions-with-kiev/406197.
html (accessed 13 September 2010).

Yasmann, Victor J. (2006) 'Is Georgian gas crisis evidence of Moscow's new energy
strategy?' *Eurasia Insight*, 24 January, available at: http://www.eurasianet.org/
departments/insight/articles/pp012405.shtml (accessed 13 September 2010).

11
Russia's Energy Policies in Eurasia: Empowerment or Entrapment?

Maria Raquel Freire

Introduction

This chapter examines the place of energy and energy diplomacy in Moscow's assessment of its national interest and in the implementation of its foreign policy. Looking at Russia's main policy options, it argues that Moscow has been pursuing the goal of internal consolidation as the basis for its external projection. This is visible in its multivectorial foreign policy where Russia seeks to affirm its interests in a wider area, with primacy being given to the post-Soviet space, in particular the Commonwealth of Independent States (CIS). Multipolarity has been defined as the key to the organisation of the international system where Russia wants to be treated as a major partner. In this context of reassertion the role of resource diplomacy has been central. Oil and gas as sources of substantial revenue have allowed the stabilisation of internal politics, the centralisation of power and the consolidation of the regime. Russia's power projection has to a great extent been the result of this consolidation, demonstrating the relevance attached by Russian leaders to the internal/external dichotomy:

> Russia possesses great energy resources – its territory contains 1/3 of the world natural gas reserves, 1/10 of oil reserves, 1/5 of coal reserves and 14% of uranium reserves – and a powerful fuel and energy complex, which is the basis of economic development and the instrument of carrying the internal and external policy. (Ministry of Energy of the Russian Federation, 2003, p. 2)

Energy has thus been used as a foreign policy tool aimed at enhancing Russia's leverage, particularly in Eurasia, an area that fits into its multivectorial foreign policy formula and where energy has gained increased relevance. In this setting Russia has been called a 'petrostate' with all of the implications of the term. And these point to problems of overdependence, control and corruption. In this way the energy has had a dual role in Russian politics: on the one hand, it has empowered Russia, not only internally but also regarding its positioning in the international system; on the other hand, Russia has been entrapped by complex dealings both at home and in its relations with other actors. In an interdependent context where Russia is simultaneously a producer, consumer and transit country of energy, variables such as reliability, price bargaining and unforeseen fluctuations in the control of production and transit routes are all central to resource diplomacy. These factors give energy the dual nature of constituting an added value or, rather, an added obstacle. Additionally, and in parallel to the fast growth that energy allowed in Russia for most of the 2000s, '[i]t is not Russia's strength that we should fear, but its weakness [Russia is threatened by a process of de-industrialisation, and at the same time faces a demographic time bomb]' (Annen, 2009, p. 9),[1] de-acceleration tendencies that have to be taken into account when analysing Russian foreign policy and regarding which energy diplomacy cannot do much.

Differentiated readings and perceptions about resource diplomacy also play a role. The West criticises Russia for seeking a 'divide and rule' approach, particularly visible in its relations with the European Union (EU), of pursuing a policy of pressuring CIS Western-oriented regimes, such as those of Ukraine and Georgia, and of controlling energy companies and not allowing market openness. Russia responds that its resource diplomacy does not mean using energy as a 'weapon', and that the increase in prices in world markets in the post-Soviet space directly responds to its business interests. Eurasia, as an area rich in fossil energy and from where much of Europe's energy supplies originate, has become a key region for Russian politics but also an area where the intersection of differentiated players with competing interests and leverages has rendered it added relevance.

In this context of change and interdependence, this chapter seeks to discuss the empowerment/entrapment relationship of resource diplomacy in Russian politics. This is visible both at the domestic and international levels, with internal disputes between a monopolistic approach to energy and private companies, along with the role of elites in seeking personal gains; and the energy geopolitics game, where Eurasia has been assuming a central place and where Russia wants to have a voice, or more than a voice – that is, the capacity to act and exert pressure for its own benefit.

The chapter concludes that as much as Russia is empowered by energy diplomacy, it is also entrapped by the complex network of interdependence that the energy grid has created. Its leverage over Eurasia is not as unlimited as Moscow would like it to be, with increasing challenges to Russia's influence coming from increasingly independent foreign policy orientations in some of these countries, such as Azerbaijan, Kazakhstan, Turkmenistan and Uzbekistan. In addition structural problems in Russia add to difficulties in managing a huge network of supplies, renovating and modernising it, along with a parallel effort at the diversification of its economic inputs and of dealing with a centralised political system that does not attract investment. The way forward should include the fostering of regional cooperation on the basis of energy interdependence, building on the producer/consumer/transit dynamics that demand coordination and could serve as a platform for the development of sustainable intra-regional cooperation mechanisms, starting with energy but spreading to other fundamental areas for development and growth in Eurasia.

Resource diplomacy in Russian politics

Russian politics have reflected possibilities and limitations in domestic and foreign terms in the effort to adapt and respond to a changing international setting. The legacies of an imperial past remain strong in Russia, where Moscow's perceptions about power, status and strategic considerations have been guiding its actions. A country of many contrasts, Russia has developed a unified policy based on an authoritarian style of rule. Sovereign democracy (Levgold, 2007) is now the defining course, and is based on a minimalist understanding of democracy translated as the holding of elections, and of the underlining of 'sovereign' as preventing attempts at involvement and interference in what Russia defines as internal matters. The control of the Duma by pro-Kremlin parties has been described as perverting the pluralism that the Assembly should represent (Allaman, 2004, p. 136), and constitutes a means of reinforcing the authoritarian path that has been followed.

Russian internal consolidation is understood as fundamental to an assertive foreign policy and to the affirmation of Russia's role as a great power. This rationale reflects the interlinkages between the internal and external dimensions in the formulation of foreign policy. This linkage is pursued in an asymmetrical way, since domestic consolidation has to precede international affirmation. Putin's words before the Federal

Assembly in April 2005, when he stated that the collapse of the Soviet Union was the major geopolitical catastrophe of the century, clearly demonstrated the desire to regain influence and status in the double logic of internal stabilisation and international projection. And the course of Russian politics seems to point towards this direction. In the words of Foreign Minister Sergei Lavrov, 'Russian foreign policy today is such that for the first time in its history, Russia is beginning to protect its national interest by using its competitive advantages', mainly energy geopolitics (RFE/RL, 2007; see also Shevtsova, 2005, p. 385; Goldman, 2008).

In this way it seems that the combination of domestic and international factors has made possible an affirmative tone both internally and regarding regional and international recognition of Russia's great power status. In fact Russian economic growth from the early 2000s remained at about 6 to 7 per cent per annum (*Russian Economic Reports*, 2001–08), with significant setbacks after the 2008 world financial crisis. The decline in energy prices had immediate consequences in an economy overly concentrated on oil and gas revenues:

> In the end, Russia's strength is garnered not from energy production, but rather from the wealth generated by windfall profits from high energy prices. While these profits are huge, they are also tenuous. They depend on continued high, and even rising, prices. And they depend on Russia's ability to sustain its production of oil and gas. Both the price of energy and the quantity of production are in question. (Gaddy et al., 2006, p. 4)

During Putin's presidency Russia emerged as the world's largest producer of natural gas, with an output totalling 607.4 billion cubic meters (bcm) in 2007, and as the number two oil producer after Saudi Arabia, with 9.98 million barrels per day (bbl/d) of output (Mankoff, 2009, p. 7). It seems that 'energy has provided the fuel for Russia's economic growth and has helped to stabilise Russia after the political chaos and economic turmoil of the 1990s. But the price of this stabilisation has been a decline in democracy and an economic development that disproportionately favours the raw materials sectors (Perovic, 2009, p. 8). Additionally the new Russian posture has generated concerns, since it has assumed a more assertive stance in its dealings with neighbouring countries, European governments and the United States (Saunders, 2008, p. 2).

The cuts in supplies have been an example of the pressure that Moscow applies on neighbouring countries such as Ukraine. The 'tap weapon' (Nygren, 2008, p. 13) seems however to be losing strength in tandem with the extent to which these neighbouring countries have to pay international prices for energy that they once received from Russia at subsidised prices. This is paralleled by a decline in Russia's influence over the governments of these countries: 'As they aptly say in Kiev, independence means no one is paying for you' (Trenin, 2008, p. 7). But the political variable also plays a dominant role. The new Ukrainian president's approach to relations with Moscow has already resulted in a more flexible approach, with favourable conditions for Russia in energy terms. This is exemplified by President Viktor Yanukovych negotiating cuts of 30 per cent in energy prices in exchange for an extension in the lease of the Black Sea Fleet beyond 2017. Moreover during Putin's visit in April 2010, the Russian prime minister suggested the possible merging of Gazprom with Ukraine's Naftogaz (RFE/RL, 2010d). Independently of the outcome, the symbolism of this proposal is self-evident. Additionally this deep change clearly demonstrates the relevance of the political elites in power in the energy diplomacy game.

This reflects a trend that has been characteristic of so-called 'petrostates', where power and business become closely interlinked, with a small political and business elite profiting from revenues. The results of such linkages include difficulties in defining a redistribution strategy, thereby deepening social inequality; the likelihood of corruption becoming endemic and state control prevailing, implying a monopolistic approach; and the basis of the economy becoming fragile due to overdependence on a specific sector that is much more volatile and sensitive to external developments, namely international pricing. 'The petrostate has no interest in modernisation but in preserving the natural resource economy. All these characteristics are increasingly typical of Russia' (Shevtsova, 2007, p. 132; see also Goldman, 2008).

Especially during the second term of Putin's presidency, this tendency became clear, with the centralisation of power gaining new contours. Various production-sharing agreements (PSAs) and joint ventures with foreign companies were cancelled, concessions and licenses to private Russian companies were withdrawn and there were cases of expropriation (Perovic, 2009, p. 9). According to Jeffrey Mankoff (2009, p. 9), Royal Dutch Shell was forced to cede its position in the Sakhalin-2 project; BP's concession in the Kovykta field was bought by Gazprom after the Kremlin threatened to withdraw BP's license; and a consortium of foreign owners sold its stake in the Vankor Field in East Siberia to Rosneft in 2003. In addition serious restraints were imposed on foreign companies operating in Russia, while private Russian companies also had to adjust and abide by the Kremlin's new rules:

> Gazprom produces 84 percent of Russia's gas, with the remainder split between independent firms (9 percent) and oil companies that produce gas as a by-product (7 percent). Since it acquired Yugansneftegaz from Yukos, Rosneft has been responsible for 21.56 percent of Russian oil production, and state firms' (including Rosneft) total share of Russian oil production has increased from just 6 percent in 2000 (when Putin became president) to 44 percent in 2008. The remaining private oil companies, moreover, are also closely connected with the state. These include LUKoil, whose chairman Vagit Alekperov long maintained close relations with Putin's Kremlin, and Surgutneftegaz, in which several leading Kremlin figures are rumored to be shareholders. (Mankoff, 2009, p. 9)

The instability that results as a consequence has a direct impact not only on delineating new projects, but also on the implementation of projects already agreed upon, since the need for stable and reliable conditions both in economic and legal terms is a prerequisite for such huge investments. In many cases projects are suspended, never finished; may have their names changed and eventually their direction, hampering the development of a consolidated supply network on the basis of a clear energy strategy that might be beneficial for both producers and consumers, including transit countries (Nies, 2008, p. 7).

The election of Dmitri Medvedev as President of Russia on 2 March 2008, meant continuity in Russian politics. The new Foreign Policy Concept published in June 2008 maintains the rationale of the previous document, released after Putin's succession to the presidency in 2000, and focuses on a multivectorial foreign policy, multipolarity and respect for international law. The document stresses the concept of a 'New Russia' and elaborates on its 'strong and respectful positions in the world community', underlining a positive reading of the place that Russia reassumed in the international system. But President Medvedev highlighted in a comment about the document what he understood to be persisting relics of the past:

> with the end of the Cold War the underlying reasons for most of bloc politics and bloc discipline simply disappeared. We simply do not need to return to that paternalistic system whereby some states decide for all the others. The behaviour of states in the international

arena is now much more varied and independent. But I would like to emphasise that this behaviour should not involve actions that constitute a violation of international law. (Medvedev, 2008)

Internally the power hierarchy remains strong. However and despite implying continuity with Putin's major foreign policy goals, Medvedev's proposal for modernisation of the Russian economy carries with it a new approach – a much needed change, expressed in the willingness to diversify investments and to develop other non-energy focused sectorial areas in order to overcome the over-concentration of the Russian economy in fossil energy resources. This dependence has rendered Russian economics vulnerable, demanding adjustments to avoid unexpected fluctuations in the prices of oil and gas, with direct consequences on the global performance of Russia's economy.

Simply put, '[i]n February 1999, the price for a barrel of Urals oil dropped to US$9. By the end of June 2008, a barrel of Urals was traded at over US$130 on the international spot market' (Perovic, 2009, p. 6). These variations in prices are fundamental to Russia's economy and politics, since its economic performance rests mainly on revenues from the energy sector. Consequently this political reorientation of attention towards other economic sectors is aimed at fortifying the foundations of Russian economics, demonstrating its centrality side by side with the recognition of its many limitations, and the Kremlin's understanding of the need for solid economic diversity as essential for a successful foreign policy.

In fact this alignment came to define the basis for the Russian response to the 2008 financial crisis that dragged the stock markets to historical lows, with losses in Russia approaching 70 per cent, exposing the economy's many frailties (Evans-Pritchard, 2008; Clover, 2009; RIA Novosti, 2009b). The fall in the prices of fossil resources resulting from a breakdown in demand, disinvestment in Russian markets and problems related to the payment of foreign debt, particularly at the industrial and corporate levels, have a direct and immediate impact on the economic–financial resources of the country. At the time Putin underlined the point that the budgetary problems of the country would not be solved at the cost of the citizens, seeking to reassure the population and the elite regarding the consequences of the crisis (Coalson, 2008; RIA Novosti, 2009a). Nevertheless the 'economic downturn that began in mid-2008 threatens to exacerbate this problem [the prospect of supply shortfalls] in the long term because Moscow now has less available capital to invest in new production' (Mankoff, 2009, p. 4). The signs of recovery from mid 2009 do not mean that there is sustainable growth based on economic diversification (Reuters, 2010). There is an urgent need in Russia for investment in existing and new energy infra-structures; however international and private Russian companies are reluctant to invest in risky and expensive projects without tax incentives and other contractual inducements to do so (Perovic, 2009, p. 7).

Despite the centrality of energy resources in Russian politics, Russia has not yet been able to craft an energy strategy setting priorities and identifying ways of managing production capacities, supply options and transit choices. Advances and setbacks in the definition of routes, the negotiation of investments and the choice of partners have been evidence of this lack of clear direction. 'Russia's economic condition and factional rivalry between elite actors plagued the successful formulation and implementation of an energy strategy' (Rangsimaporn, 2009, p. 79). This has been attributed to differences within the political and economic elites, as well as between the presidency and the government. Despite what is already being called 'conspiracy theories about conspiracy theories', there seems to be a prevailing impression that keeping a basis of understanding between different levels of governance is fundamental to stability (Whitmore, 2008). However it is interesting to note that Gleb Pavlovsky, the Director of the Foundation for Effective Politics, a pro-Kremlin organisation, asserts that any anti-leadership movements that might arise will come from within the elites:

> What is the 'pro-crisis' party discussing? The struggle over seriously reduced resources. When there was a lot of money, any faction in power could get a cut of the money flow [...]. But the rivers have become shallow and some people need a shake-up, which, on the one hand, will enable them to write off losses to the old regime and, on the other, to gain unrestricted access to the new one [...]. I repeat, if one is looking for sources of social protest in Russia, seek them in the corridors of power. (Pavolovsky, 2009)

It should be noted that the increasing trend in centralisation led by then President Putin pointed to a changed configuration in the energy market in Russia. In the post-Soviet period, 'the Russian authorities have shown economic muscle in several ways, but it is particularly within the energy sector that they have employed market power to reach strategic aims' (Kjærnet, 2009, p. 3). By the end of 2003, the centre of decision-making in energy-related matters was with the presidency, and the chairmen of the main companies were in tune with the Kremlin – recall that Yukos' chairman, Mikhail Khodorkovskii, was arrested for fraud and tax evasion in 2003. The statisation – nationalisation – of the energy business in Russia allows for the tight control of the decision-making process, but does not necessarily provide a clear direction for policy. It seems that:

> the assertive expansion of state control over the energy sector since mid-2003 has not been guided by a coherent ideology; instead, this forceful policy has been justified in a peculiar discourse that mixes the mantras of market economy, the maxims of quasi-Soviet dirigisme, and the expressive slang of 'shadow economy'. (Baev, 2008, p. 30)

In Russia's official energy strategy, the point is stated that 'energy security is the most important element in Russia's national security' and calls are made for the state to take an active role in the energy sector so as to protect the country from both internal and external threats (Mankoff, 2009, p. 4). This responds directly to the 'petrostate' concept and the statisation trend mentioned earlier. The document 'Russian Energy Strategy up to 2020' determines 'the ways of reaching a new quality of fuel and energy complex, the growth of competitive ability of its production and services on the world market', and assumes as strategic guidelines, 'energy safety, energy effectiveness, budget effectiveness and ecological energy security' (Ministry of Energy of the Russian Federation, 2003, p. 2):

> The new factor for the period up to 2020 will be the participation of Russia, as a large supplier of energy resources, in securing of the world energy safety. Forming of the common energy and energy and transport infrastructure in the regions of Europe and Asia, development of the international energy and transport systems, providing of the undiscriminatory transit of energy answer the strategic interests of Russia. In order to reach these aims, the state will foster the participation of Russian joint-stock companies in development and realization of the great international projects of transport of gas, oil and energy both in western and eastern lines. (Ministry of Energy of the Russian Federation, 2003, p. 12)

In November 2009, the Russian government approved a new 'National Energy Strategy Until 2030', that replaces the previous one and seeks to respond to a changed setting after the 2008 downturn. It mainly envisages raising the production of oil and gas while reducing Russian consumption of energy by investing in energy-efficient techniques (RIA Novosti, 2009c). This new document is a response to an unfavourable situation that resulted from the international financial crisis of

2008 that significantly affected the energy markets, including Russia's, as was noted above. The four main dimensions that the document refers to are: 'energy security; energy efficiency of the domestic economy; economic efficiency of the fuel energy complex; and ecological security of the fuel energy complex'. The language changed slightly from the previous version, from 'energy safety' to 'energy security', which is a stronger wording, and is more precise in its reference to 'efficiency' by connecting it to both the domestic context and the energy complex.

The new document is organised around two main scenarios. The first envisages a fast recovery of the economy until 2015; the second one is more cautious, working with a slower recovery track, up to 2020/2022 (Shadrina, 2009). In all, the new version seems notably careful in its scenario-setting, reflecting the international context where Russian energy politics are developed. Nevertheless Prime Minister Putin has remarked that the levels of consumption of fossil energy should remain high, since '[u]nfortunately, or fortunately, neither solar energy nor firewood nor dried manure will be able to replace hydrocarbons in the next 15 to 20 years' (Putin, 2010). As usual, Putin seeks to reassure the Russians about the prospects of recovery and the limited effects of the economic breakdown on their daily lives, even if 'Russian energy production remains imperilled by inefficiency, underinvestment, politicization, high taxes, and falling prices' (Mankoff, 2009, p. 8).

Internally Russia has been facing a number of difficulties: rich areas such as the Far East are very remote and cannot be readily accessed, rendering their exploitation very costly both technically and financially. The East Siberia–Pacific Ocean (ESPO) oil pipeline, inaugurated at the end of 2009 is part of the effort to overcome the difficulties in these inhospitable areas. In fact, and as cynical as it might seem, these rich areas have been suffering from energy shortages. This new oil pipeline, according to Transneft President Nikolai Tokarev, 'opens the way for the East Siberian oil to the perspective market of the Asia–Pacific region and to a great extent contributes to the strengthening of Russia's energy security' (RFE/RL, 2009), by assuring the diversification of consumers and allowing the exploitation of further reserves. This move reinforces the Russian diversification effort in order to reduce its dependency on European markets, even if to a small extent.

Nevertheless, and despite these developments, investment is much needed in order to secure the diversification of energy supply markets, to support projects with foreign investment in Russia, to develop new forms of international energy cooperation, and to create instruments of coordination of state policy regarding external trade regulation in the energy sector. However there has been no sufficient investment, the level of attractiveness of Russia as a market has been much limited by political and legislative measures, as already mentioned, in line with the 'petrostate' approaches, and the lack of strategy is definitely leaving Russian politics in such a central issue very much adrift (see Rangsimaporn, 2009, p. 83).

The geography of energy power

The Russian Federation is well placed in the geography of energy: not only does it have resources, but much of the existing infrastructure runs throughout the entire country. This has placed Russian resource diplomacy high on the agenda, with implications for its relationship with former Soviet states such as Ukraine, Moldova and Belarus, and further west, the EU; and to the east, including the southern Caucasus and Central Asia, and further east, China and Japan. However the balancing of interests and priorities along with real capabilities, has revealed many limitations to Russia's resource diplomacy.

Russia is a central player in the distribution of energy resources coming from Eurasia to Europe, although from the mid 2000s, its monopolistic advantage was circumvented by the construction of new pipeline infrastructures that bypass its territory, such as the Baku–Tbilisi–Ceyhan (BTC) pipeline inaugurated in 2006 that brings oil from the Caspian to Turkey, through Georgia and then to Europe. Some of the Central Asian republics have also been seeking the diversification of consumers, despite Russia remaining their major trading partner. Kazakhstan already has a pipeline that ships oil to China and there are Turkmenistan's gas flows to Iran. These alternatives are limited in capacity, therefore representing only a small percentage of resources that is nevertheless highly significant in terms of the independent stance assumed in the foreign policies of these countries. It is clearly a demonstration that Russian leverage in the post-Soviet space is not without limits.

In its search for primacy Russia has attempted to recover Soviet-era influence over what it describes as its natural area of influence and where its primary foreign policy interests are concentrated, the post-Soviet space. But using energy dependence as a form of pressure has not always served its purpose. The interruption of gas and oil supplies to Ukraine and Belarus, for example, with the direct impact this had on supplies to EU countries led to harsh criticisms of Russian actions, damaging its reputation and questioning its reliability as an energy supplier.

Moreover disruptions have also occurred due to Ukraine or Belarus not paying transit fees, rendering Moscow vulnerable to price-setting in these countries. For example, the June 2010 energy crisis between Russia and Belarus implied these two problems: on the one hand, Belarus was not complying with payments, leading Russia to diminish supplies; on the other hand, Belarus complained that Russia was not paying the due amount of transit fees and suspended gas supplies to Europe (RFE/RL, 2010b and 2010e). This row added to the distrust between Belarus and Russia (and Ukraine, especially prior to the election of Yanukovych in 2010, as well as the West in general, regarding Russia as a reliable energy supplier). The search for alternatives is a natural development that has consequences for Russia. Negotiations on new routes bypassing Russian territory, meaning ownership and/or control of pipeline infrastructure, demonstrate the increasing search for independence in the face of a Russia described as a non-reliable 'partner'.

However negotiations, agreements and the construction of new routes have not been simple processes, with successive postponements occurring due to financial constraints, inefficient strategic options and political disagreement. Nabucco's story is telling. Running through the southern corridor, its pipeline will bring gas from the Caspian through Turkey to Europe. Contradictory statements from the EU about financing have been delaying the process, which is now scheduled for construction to begin in late 2011 (Nabucco, 2010). But it is not just a financial matter, it is also very much a political issue. And the role of Russia has been fundamental in that Moscow tries to prevent any developments that hamper its interests, giving rise to feelings of vulnerability in the competition for control over production and transit routes.

In September 2010, Moscow signed an agreement with Baku assuring the doubling of gas imports to Russia, thereby strengthening Russia's energy capacity while undermining Nabucco's sources, essentially by adding pressure on the management of resource supplies (RFE/RL, 2010a). The bombardment of sections of the BTC at the time of the August 2008 armed hostilities between Russia and Georgia and the consequent disruption in supplies are also examples of how geostrategic factors might limit the potential of some projects. Moscow showed through this war, among other things, that energy politics related to the Caspian basin should not exclude its direct interests. Therefore new projects have been dealt with in a cautious manner in order to assure safety conditions and the reliability of supplies. Nevertheless the issue goes beyond safety and supply assurance, implying both price-setting, as mentioned, but also that the volume supplied suffices in pumping oil and gas into the existing and planned infrastructure.

Diversification policies are therefore constrained by financial and volume considerations, along with the logics of competition. When energy could constitute a resource that fosters cooperation and regional integration, as in Eurasia, it has been revealed to be more of an obstacle than an opportunity. In fact integration would logically be the solution to many of the problems that underlie energy issues, responding to the interdependence linkages that are clear in the current international energy setting. However regional integration processes in the post-Soviet space are usually regarded as pro-Russian or anti-Russian, leaving their existence difficult to sustain and hampering the delineation of new proposals. What could constitute a source of cohesion has exposed significant limitations (Freire, 2009).

These limitations are exemplified by the lack of solid integration mechanisms within the post-Soviet space as well as beyond it, as exemplified by EU–Russia energy relations. The lack of the ratification of the Energy Charter Treaty is a clear example of how finding the lowest common denominator for cooperation is delicate.[2] There have clearly been different understandings about the meaning of energy security. For some this means energy independence; others understand it as reliable and regular supplies; and yet others relate it to the role that they might play as 'rentier states' and to assuring their energy security on the basis of the materialisation of the transit of pipelines. These are in fact different ways of diminishing and/or controlling the level of uncertainty associated with access to energy resources. However it should be noted that the uncertainty issue is not just relevant to consumers, but also to suppliers who need to ensure reliable markets and safe transit routes:

> The present energy-supply situation between Russia and the EU is not quite one of mutually assured dependence. It is true that Moscow needs the money and the European states need the oil and gas. However, the bargaining positions are not symmetrical. In the critical gas market, Russia has an entrenched, state-owned monopoly exporter, Gazprom. Effectively, the Russian side is a single negotiating unit. On the EU side, various companies and governments act separately. (Hanson, 2009, p. 46)

The differences in the level of dependency between EU countries are substantial, and these do not facilitate a consensual approach. Whereas Portugal gets most of its energy (gas) from Algeria, Germany is very much dependent on Russian supplies. And this has enabled bilateral agreements, which are a response to immediate concerns, but do not necessarily contribute to the development of a coherent EU strategy towards Russia. The Nord Stream project – on which construction work began in April 2010 – linking Russia to Germany through the Baltic Sea bypasses the Baltic states, Ukraine and Poland, which have been very much critical of a gas project that they understand as increasing their vulnerability to Russia, while also hampering the finding of an EU integrated approach to energy concerns.

According to the EU understanding, Eurasian energy constitutes a valuable asset that could provide additional security for energy supplies in Europe. The more that the Eurasian countries are dependent on Russia, the more that the EU will also depend on Russia. Therefore a proactive approach is seen as an alternative to Russian control, eventually prompting further cooperation between the EU and Russia, in the context of more interdependence than dependency. This means that EU engagement should proceed in a cooperative manner and not to the exclusion of Moscow in order not to give rise to a sense of isolation or hostility. Russian policies in Eurasia are important for European energy security. The EU's Strategy for a New Partnership with Central Asia underlines the area's relevance for the Union, allowing for a diversification of trading partners and supply routes:

> The development of resources in oil and gas has significantly increased the role of Central Asian States as energy producers and transit countries. Increasing oil and gas exploitation will contribute to better world market supplies and will be conducive to diversification. Gas deliveries from the region are of special importance to the EU. (European Communities, 2009, p. 22)

The goal of fostering integration is present in the EU approach, although it raises questions regarding intra-regional competition, to which the role of Russia adds further complexity. The difficulties in the area demand from the EU a careful approach that enables the management of differences and the forwarding of innovative thinking on how to capitalise on the existing resources as a collective good, an approach that has been mostly absent in Central Asian energy dynamics.

To the east Russia has been attentive to the role and rise of China, and the furthering of cooperation within the Shanghai Cooperation Organisation (SCO) is illustrative of the double approach of cooperation and keeping a watchful eye on a potential competitor that Moscow pursues. China is a huge resource *demandeur*, and it has been seeking energy from Russia, but also from Iran and Kazakhstan (Atal, 2005, p. 101).

Within the SCO, China has agreed to the definition of an energy policy for Asia, the so-called 'Energy Club' resulting from a proposal by former President Putin in July 2007 (following an earlier Kazakh suggestion).

At the August 2007 SCO Summit, member states signed a 'Long-Term Agreement on Neighbourly Relations' that included an agreement on the creation of a 'unified energy market' and that underlined the relevance of energy resources as 'the basis for continued economic growth and security' (EurasiaNet, 2007). The central idea underlining the 'Energy Club' is ensuring greater energy security, including for major producers such as Russia, Kazakhstan and Uzbekistan and major consumers such as China and India. It is also expected to assist in the regulation of competition between these two giants for Central Asian energy resources (Freire, 2009). However the difficulties in rendering such a partnership effective have been many, resulting in serious limitations. And these go beyond the post-Soviet space.

Dealing with competing demands, such as those of China and Japan – from Angarsk in Eastern Siberia to Daqing in China or Nakhodka in Japan – has also revealed the frailties of Russian decision-making that demonstrates the lack of strategy due to the shifting from one project to another, depending on financial support and on the leverage power of the actors involved and the geopolitical international context:

> The decision on the oil pipeline route was made amidst rivalry over pipeline control between state monopoly Transneft and private Russian oil companies. The companies were frustrated that their increasing excess oil capacity could not be exported fast enough due to the limited and slow expansion of pipelines controlled by Transneft. Transneft disliked the idea that Yukos would possess its own oil pipelines, breaking Transneft's monopoly. Thus Transneft had a powerful ally in the Kremlin, who preferred to maintain state control over oil exports. Although Yukos intensified lobbying of the government against Transneft, Yukos' position had become highly untenable as the Kremlin charged Yukos of tax evasion and fraud. Khodorkovskii's arrest in October 2003 sealed the fate of Yukos control over the China route. (Rangsimaporn, 2009, p. 149)

The inauguration of the oil pipeline to China was hailed by Putin as an important step in bilateral relations and as strengthening the diversification approach with its emphasis on operations towards the eastern shores (RFE/RL, 2010c). According to Putin the decision had to be based on 'our own national interests', and that was how it was made, benefitting state control over energy deals. The concentration of power in the energy sector is evident in Russia's approach, which responds well to the 'petrostate' label. However centralisation and control do not necessarily mean gains and benefits, as has been shown.

Conclusion: oil and gas – the 'natural resource curse'?

The line between empowerment and entrapment in Russian energy policies is a tenuous one. Whereas energy has been the central pillar in Russian economic growth for the last ten years, its over-dependency on this sectoral dimension has rendered Moscow hostage to international market prices and to assessments of its engagement as a producer, consumer and transit country. Regional and international (mainly Western, but also Chinese) actors made up of the transit countries and consumer states of Russian energy supplies, have a cautious approach towards energy dealings with Russia. This is due to the latter's track record in supplying energy and when constructing new distribution networks and promoting new projects. These actors' understanding of Russia's actions is based on how Russia has by turns increased or cut off energy supplies and played with the consumers' dependence on these supplies. In the case of regional actors, the caution is also based on their own internal production problems and on the paucity of their financial conditions that does not enable them to make significant structural investments. This is what has effectively brought about the regional and international wariness in investments and dealings with Russia as an energy supplier. Russia has to deal with its geostrategic advantages and limitations in terms of energy, whereas it must also be able to reconcile differentiated interests and pursue a policy of reassurance in Eurasia as well as further afield. This is not an easy task.

Resource diplomacy has proven to be very complex. The difficulties of managing the differentiated and at times conflicting interests have not been given sufficient attention in discussions of Russian resource policy or of the implementation of regional cooperation on energy matters based on integrated policies and projects. Eurasia, as an area of strategic relevance, is a place where interested actors should not be competing against each other, but instead should be working jointly towards the promotion of a common good – that is, ensuring the safety and the reliability of energy production and its transit routes and supply of resources. But it is well known that it is difficult for all of the countries involved to make the endeavour to have a common political outlook. As mentioned, integration projects in post-Soviet space have been difficult to pursue. And even intra-regional cooperation on a smaller scale, such as for example between the countries in Central Asia, has become synonymous with disagreement. This fragile basis does not contribute to raising local leverage over Russia or to weakening Moscow's ability to use its advantage in energy resources unilaterally. An integrated approach involving the Central Asian states and Russia would require a mechanism for double-checking imbalances and assuring a more equitable sharing of benefits in terms of security, but also of investment. Despite the difficulties that this entails it would be a way to move forward.

Note

1. Second set of square brackets in source.
2. The Energy Charter Treaty was signed in December 1994 and came into force in April 1998. Russia notified the Energy Charter Secretariat into August 2009 that it did not intend to become a contracting party to the Treaty and to the Protocol on Energy Efficiency and Related Environmental Aspects (Delegation of the EU to Russia, 2010).

References

Allaman, Jacques (2004) *Vladimir Poutine et le Poutinisme* (Paris: L'Harmattan).

Annen, Niels (2009) 'Fearing a weak, embracing a strong Russia', *Is Russia Friend or Foe?*, Brussels Forum Paper Series, March (Washington, DC: German Marshall Fund of the United States).

Atal, Subodh (2005) 'The New Great Game', *National Interest*, no. 81, pp. 101–5.

Baev, Pavel K. (2008) *Russian Energy Policy and Military Power: Putin's Quest for Greatness*, Contemporary Security Studies (London: Routledge).

Clover, Charles (2009) 'Russian economy hit by 8.8% decline', *Financial Times*, 25 February.

Coalson, Robert (2008) 'Unified Russia Congress promises stability despite financial crisis', RFE/RL, 20 November, available at: http://www.rferl.org/Content/commentary_Unified_Russia_Congress_Stability_Despite_Financial_Crisis/1351291.html (accessed 5 January 2010).

Delegation of the EU to Russia (2010) 'Energy', European External Action Service (EEAS), available at: http://www.delrus.ec.europa.eu/en/p_217.htm (accessed 5 January 2010).

EurasiaNet (2007) 'Central Asia: SCO leaders focus on energy, security, cooperation', *Eurasia Insight*, 15 August, available at: http://www.eurasianet.org/departments/insight/articles/pp081607.shtml (accessed 5 January 2010).

European Communities (2009) 'The European Union and Central Asia: the new partnership in action', p. 22, available at: http://www.auswaertiges-amt.de/diplo/en/Europa/Aussenpolitik/Regionalabkommen/EU-CentralAsia-Strategy.pdf (accessed 15 January 2010).

Evans-Pritchard, Ambrose (2008) 'Russian default risk tops Iceland as crisis deepens', *Telegraph*, 24 October.

Freire, Maria Raquel (2009) 'Russian politics toward Central Asia: supporting, balancing, coercing or imposing?', *Asian Perspective*, vol. 33, no. 2, pp. 125–49.

Gaddy, Clifford et al. (2006) 'The Russian Federation', Brookings Foreign Policy Studies, Energy Security Series, October (Washington, DC: Brookings Institution).

Goldman, Marshall I. (2008) *Petrostate: Putin, Power and the New Russia* (Oxford: Oxford University Press).

Hanson, Philip (2009) 'The sustainability of Russia's energy power: implications for the Russian economy', in Jeronim Perovic, Robert W. Orttung and Andreas Wenger (eds), *Russian Energy Power and Foreign Relations: Implications for Conflict and Cooperation*, (Center for Security Studies) CSS Studies in Security and International Relations (London: Routledge), pp. 23–50.

Kjærnet, Heidi (2009) 'The energy dimension of Azerbaijani–Russian relations: maneuvering for Nagorno-Karabakh', *Russia's Energy Relations with its Caspian Neighbours*, Russian Analytical Digest 56/09 (Oslo: German Association for East European Studies; Bremen: Research Centre for East European Studies; and ETH Zurich: Center for Security Studies), pp. 2–5.

Levgold, Robert (ed.) (2007) *Russian Foreign Policy in the 21st Century and the Shadow of the Past* (New York: Columbia University Press).

Mankoff, Jeffrey (2009) 'Eurasian energy security', *Council Special Report*, No. 43 (New York: Council on Foreign Relations).

Medvedev, Dmitry (2008) 'Speech at the meeting with Russian Ambassadors and Permanent Representatives to International Organisations', Russian Foreign Ministry, Moscow, 15 July, available at: http://archive.kremlin.ru/eng/speeches/2008/07/15/1121_type82912type84779_204155.shtml (accessed 16 July 2010).

Ministry of Energy of the Russian Federation (2003) 'The summary of the energy strategy of Russia for the period of up to 2020', Moscow, 28 August, available at: http://ec.europa.eu/energy/russia/events/doc/2003_strategy_2020_en.pdf (accessed 16 July 2010).

Nabucco (2010) 'Timeline', Gasbridge between Asia and Europe, available at: http://www.nabucco-pipeline.com/portal/page/portal/en/pipeline/timeline_steps (accessed 16 July 2010).

Nies, Susanne (2008) 'Oil and gas delivery to Europe: an overview of existing and planned infrastructures', *Gouvernance Européenne et Géopolitique de l'Énergie*, No. 4 (Brussels: IFRI).

Nygren, Bertil (2008) 'Putin's use of natural gas to reintegrate the CIS region', *Problems of Post-Communism*, vol. 55, no. 4, pp. 3–15.

Pavolovsky, Glev cited in RFE/RL (2009) 'The power vertical: conspiracy theories about conspiracy theories', 9 March, available at: http://www.rferl.org/content/Conspiracies_About_Conspiracies/1506962.html (accessed 5 January 2010).

Perovic, Jeronim (2009) 'Introduction: Russian energy power: domestic and international dimensions', in Jeronim Perovic, Robert Orttung and Andreas Wenger (eds), *Russian Energy Power and Foreign Relations: Implications for Conflict and Cooperation*, CSS Studies in Security and International Relations (London: Routledge), pp. 1–20.

Putin, Vladimir (2010) Cited in 'Russian energy strategy based on growth of global demand – Putin', RIA Novosti, 10 February, available at: http://en.rian. ru/russia/20100210/157837247.html (accessed 2 July 2010).

Rangsimaporn, Paradorn (2009) *Russia as an Aspiring Great Power in East Asia*, St Antony's Series (Basingstoke: Palgrave Macmillan).

Reuters (2010) 'IMF sees modest Russian economic recovery in 2010', 14 December, available at: http://www.reuters.com/article/idUSN14139238 20091214 (accessed 16 July 2010).

RFE/RL (2007) 'Russia: Kremlin sees its foreign policy star on rise', 21 March.

RFE/RL (2009) 'Russia's Putin launches new Pacific oil terminal', 28 December.

RFE/RL (2010a) 'Azerbaijan to double gas exports to Russia', 3 September.

RFE/RL (2010b) 'Belarus threatens to cut Russian energy supplies to Europe', 25 June.

RFE/RL (2010c) 'Putin hails importance of oil pipeline to China', 29 August.

RFE/RL (2010d) 'Putin proposes merging Russian, Ukrainian state gas firms', 30 April.

RFE/RL (2010e) 'Russia resumes gas supplies to Russia', 24 June.

RIA Novosti (2009a) 'Economic crisis yet to peak – Putin', 27 February, available at: http://en.rian.ru/russia/20090227/120335257-print.html (accessed 5 January 2010).

RIA Novosti (2009b) 'Financial crisis wipes out two-thirds of richest Russians' Wealth', 11 February, available at: http://en.rian.ru/business/20090211/120088346-print.html (accessed 5 January 2010).

RIA Novosti (2009c) 'Russia adopts new energy strategy', 26 November, available at: http://en.rian.ru/russia/20091126/156995275.html (accessed 5 January 2010).

Russian Economic Reports (2001–10) Moscow Office of the World Bank, available at: http://web.worldbank.org/WBSITE/EXTERNAL/COUNTRIES/ECAEXT/ RUSSIANFEDERATIONEXTN/0,,contentMDK:20888536~menuPK:2445695~ pagePK:1497618~piPK:217854~theSitePK:305600,00.html (accessed 25 February 2011).

Saunders, Paul (2008) *Russian Energy and European Security: A Transatlantic Dialogue* (Washington, DC: Nixon Center).

Shadrina, Elena (2009) 'Russia's energy strategy up to 2030', Expert Comment, GeoPolitics in the High North, Norwegian Institute for Defense Studies, available at: http://www.geopoliticsnorth.org/index.php?option=com_ content&view=article&id=92:russias-energy-strategy-up-to-2030&catid=1: latest-news (accessed 16 July 2010).

Shevtsova, Lilia (2005) *Putin's Russia*, April (Washington, DC: Carnegie Endowment for International Peace).

Shevtsova, Lilia (2007) *Russia Lost in Transition: The Yeltsin and Putin Legacies*, October (Washington, DC: Carnegie Endowment for International Peace).

Trenin, Dmitri (2008) 'Thinking strategically about Russia', *Policy Brief*, December (Washington, DC: Carnegie Endowment for International Peace).

Whitmore, Brian (2008) 'Is Medvedev preparing Putin's return to the presidency?', RFE/RL, 11 November, available at: http://www.rferl.org/content/Is_Medvedev_ Preparing_Putins_Return_To_The_Presidency/1348061.html (accessed 5 January 2010).

12
Russian Energy Policy in the South Caucasus

Lilia A. Arakelyan and Roger E. Kanet

Introduction

It seemed that the Kremlin achieved the impossible over the seventy years of Soviet control of Eurasia: the heterogeneous populations of the region, who spoke 150 different languages and even more dialects and had very little in common with one another, were unified under the identical political institutions, participated in a single centrally planned economy and were educated in the same school system (Darden, 2009, p. 3). In short, the Soviet leadership made serious efforts to create a single nation-state based on a one-language-one-nation policy. This ideological position was so fully ingrained in the people's mentality that even after the disintegration of the USSR, some people from the former Soviet Union continue to call themselves 'Soviets' without any reference to their original nationality or ethnicity. Darden claims that this kind of standardisation of both the formal structures of the state and the informal organisation of everyday life within the USSR has been historically unprecedented. As a result the collapse of the Soviet Union left the fifteen republics in more or less similar economic conditions and without prior experience in dealing with international institutions (Darden, 2009).

When Mikhail Gorbachev called for democracy, *perestroika, glasnost'* and pluralism in 1985, he did not know that he was opening up Pandora's box. In his examination of the history of Armenia, Simon Payaslian argues that Gorbachev and his economic advisers sought to decentralise the Soviet system in a manner that would create and maintain a market-oriented environment for the purpose of making the socialist system more efficient. But they failed not only to improve the Soviet economic situation – which was not surprising, when one takes into account the economic stagnation in the country resulting from seventy years of a centralised economic system – but also to keep the Soviet Union intact (Payaslian, 2007, pp. 194–5). As soon as the non-Russian ethnic nations received the benefit of freedom of speech that was part of the Gorbachev reforms, they started to express the nationalistic and political feelings that had been suppressed for seven decades. Armine Ishkanian notes that, inspired by Gorbachev's *perestroika* and *glasnost'*, nationalist movements emerged in the late 1980s in Latvia, Lithuania, Estonia, Armenia, Ukraine and Georgia (Ishkanian, 2008, p. 114). Citizens in these countries created problems for the Soviet government through civil disobedience; they were basically fighting to bring freedom from the Soviet Union to their nations. There were very small 'civil disobedience' movements in Azerbaijan, Belarus and the Central Asian republics even after Gorbachev came to power. Ishkanian argues that all of the movements that emerged after *perestroika* began with calls for environmental and ecological policy reforms because this issue was tolerated in the Soviet Union.

Economic diversity in post-Soviet states

Despite the fact that the former Soviet republics had quite similar economic, political and social conditions, after 1991 the fifteen new states achieved different results in their economic growth and chose different paths in terms of the nature of their economic systems and of their membership in international economic institutions (Darden, 2009). Darden notes that the former Soviet states made their economic choices according to the type of framework that local leaderships have employed after the disintegration of the USSR. In this regard he identified three kinds of economic models within post-Soviet space: 'liberalism', 'Soviet integralism' and 'mercantilism'. On the one hand, liberals avoid intervening directly in economic activity and are prone to granting financial independence to individuals in order to promote market competition and free trade in their countries. Soviet integralists, on the other hand, inherited Soviet economic concepts and principles and favour quasi-monopolistic production over market competition and local cooperation over international cooperation as the key to economic growth. Finally, the mercantilists are strong proponents of so-called zero-sum games, by holding the view that the economic prosperity of their countries can be achieved at their neighbours' expense (Darden, 2009, pp. 14–15).[1] It is with this background in mind that we now turn to a discussion of the economic situation that has emerged in the three states in the Caucasus and of the relationship of these countries and their economies to the Russian Federation and to the place of energy in that relationship.

With the end of the Cold War the emergence of new actors in the international system came as a surprise not only for the West, but also for the former Soviet empire itself. The world identified Russia with the former Soviet Union; consequently the politics of Russia were largely viewed as the politics of the entire post-Soviet region. In fact, initially Russian leaders did not really take into account the geopolitical interests of the other former republics in their overall decision-making.[2] A full fifteen years after the fall of the Iron Curtain and the demise of the Soviet state then Russian president Vladimir Putin referred to these events as 'the greatest geopolitical catastrophe of the past century' (Lukyanov, 2010, p. 19). His speech sparked a strong reaction among politicians of the former Soviet states; they interpreted Putin's words not only as nostalgia for the former great power exercised by the USSR, but also as an expression of latent imperial ambitions.

Moreover, the new politics of the Russian Federation tended to support these fears: added to the periodic intervention in local political disputes during the Yeltsin years under the guise of peacekeeping (Kozhemiakin and Kanet, 1998), after the rise to political power of Vladimir Putin Russia increasingly tried to dominate all other actors in Eurasian space, including opposing the rise of effectively autonomous states within the region viewed as one of 'special Russian interest' by President Dmitri Medvedev. For instance, the extensive use of Russian military force in Chechnya (1994–2008), disagreements between Russia and neighbouring states over gas supplies at various times during the first decade of the current century, opposition to the so-called 'colour revolutions' in Georgia, Ukraine and Kyrgyzstan, and, finally, the invasion of Georgia by Russia during August 2008, were but a few of the events that provided evidence of efforts at renewed Russian dominance that also increased tensions between Russia and the West.[3]

Over the course of the two decades since the demise of the Soviet Union the South Caucasus and Central Asia have become regions of strategic interest for both the West and the East, including in the latter group both Russia and China, as well as India, Iran and Turkey (Freire and Kanet, 2010). When one emphasises the importance of the South Caucasus to Western interests, one must recognise that besides the fact that the region itself is rich in energy resources, it also provides Europe and the United States with direct access to Central Asian oil and gas supplies and an alternate route to some of the energy resources of the

Middle East. If Russia, as President Dmitri Medvedev noted in 2008, has always considered Eurasia as a region of Russian exclusive interests, the United States and the European Union (EU) member states neglected the South Caucasus until relatively recent times. Obviously, until the collapse of the Soviet Union at the end of 1991, the West had no real access to the region, which was an integral part of the USSR. During the Yeltsin presidency Russia virtually ignored the region, at least at the outset, while focusing its interest on expanding its relations with and integration into the capitalist West. It was during this period however that outside actors, beginning with the United States, began to establish direct relations with the new states of the region – in part, at least, in the hope of containing the future role of Russia in the region (Kanet, 2010).

In the remainder of this chapter we shall highlight the key role of energy in Russia's policies in the South Caucasus, as well as the Western attempts to reduce Russian economic and political influence in the region, in particular in the area of energy. We will briefly review Russian policy towards the three Transcaucasian countries, as well as the interstate relations among Armenia, Azerbaijan and Georgia. We will show that the three states of the South Caucasus are struggling to become truly independent actors within their own territory. However their intentions often conflict with the geopolitical interests of Russia, Turkey and Iran, three key and long-term players in the Caspian region, as well as with the strategic interests of both the EU and the United States, which have recently joined with other states in the revival of the 'Great Game' largely because of their dependence on external sources of energy.

A region of exclusive Russian interests

Surrounded by Russia to the north, Turkey to the south-west and Iran to the south-east, the South Caucasus not surprisingly has always been viewed as a territorial buffer that separated major competing empires, but that also linked Asia and the Middle East with Europe. Despite the rich and ancient cultures of the region, in the recent past the area first attracted the attention of the outside world because of several 'frozen conflicts' – those concerning Nagorno-Karabakh, Abkhazia and South Ossetia are the best known. Some analysts have compared the South Caucasus to the Balkans, pointing to the fact that belated Western intervention in the latter region, which is also characterised by a diverse, multiethnic population and had long been the source of discord between the East and West, has showed that the outside power cannot any longer tolerate ethnic-based conflict, especially in its own backyard. At the same time the Nagorno-Karabakh conflict has not received the same kind of attention, even from Russia, since nobody considers the South Caucasus as its own backyard (de Waal, 2010).

Russian involvement in the region dates from the annexation of the South Caucasus by the Russian Empire early in the nineteenth century. Eastern Georgia became part of the empire in 1801, while western Georgia was incorporated in 1804 (Curtis, 1994, p. 159). After the Turkmenchay Treaty, signed after Russia defeated Persia in 1828, eastern Armenia and most of today's Azerbaijan became part of the Russian Empire. One year after the Bolshevik Revolution of 1917, the short-lived Transcaucasian Democratic Federative Republic was formed, which included Armenia, Azerbaijan and Georgia. The Transcaucasian Federation did not last long, since its constituent states had their own nationalist interests and goals. Moreover much as the Tatar communist Mirsaid Sultan-Galiev (Mirsäyet Soltanğäliev) discovered in the 1920s when he failed in his push for a single integrated Muslim communist republic in Central Asia within the larger USSR, Stalin and those around him found it easier to control smaller political units within the Soviet 'federal' political system.

Some scholars from the region would argue that Moscow's policy in the South Caucasus throughout the Soviet period remained similar to that of Tsarist times and was based largely on Moscow maintaining control in order to benefit from the region's natural resources. Moreover some argue that even today Russian leaders are unable to forget their imperialistic past and are still attempting to control Caspian oil and gas production and delivery. For example, Pirog argues that 'Russia initially opposed western investment in Caspian Sea energy projects, insisted that oil from the region be transported through Russian territory to Black Sea ports, and argued for an equal sharing of Caspian Sea oil and gas' (Pirog, 2007, p. 12). Enayatollah Yazdani commented that Russia's efforts to control Caspian oil and gas production is merely an attempt to improve its own bargaining position with Western oil investors (Yazdani, 2006, p. 2). Besides Russia's continuing interest in the region, Turkey has indicated its economic interests in the South Caucasus; some in Ankara have also expressed their nationalistic dreams of influencing the Turkic states of Central Asia along with Azerbaijan towards a type of 'Pan-Turkism' (Areshev, 2010; Svarants, 2011; Jackson, 2010; Kudryasheva, 2009; and especially Mesbahi, 2010). Another regional actor, Iran, has also shown indications of its interest in the Greater Caspian region, including the South Caucasus. Besides its long history of control over much of the South Caucasus (Mesbahi, 2010), Iran has managed to preserve strong political and socioeconomic ties with Azerbaijan and Georgia, but also with Armenia – the latter, as one might recall, does not have diplomatic relations with either Azerbaijan or Turkey and must therefore carry on all of its foreign trade through Iran or Russia.

Energy relations are not the sole factor of importance in understanding the overall political and security situation in the South Caucasus. In addition longstanding ethnic conflicts, especially between Armenians and Azerbaijani, as well as political interdependence of the various actors in the region, are also of great importance. Russia, for example, has masterfully used the Nagorno-Karabakh conflict between Azerbaijan and Armenia in order to keep pro-Western Azerbaijan – more precisely its natural resources – under its control, while generally 'forgetting' the security promises that the Kremlin made to its faithful ally, Armenia (Muradyan, 2010). Moreover Moscow's attempts to maintain 'friendly' relations with both sides, the Armenians as well as the Azerbaijanis, not only irritates them, but could also lead to dangerous consequences such as fuelling the ongoing conflict. For example, both countries have accused Russia of supplying the other side with arms, a charge neither denied nor confirmed by the Russian state-run trading company, Rosoboronexport, despite the fact that there is the possibility of renewed fighting between Armenia and Azerbaijan since the latter cannot tolerate the loss of the Nagorno-Karabakh territory (Muradyan, 2010; Danielyan, 2011).

Energy as a Russian political weapon

At the very outset of the Putin presidency the new Russian government made clear its commitment to reestablishing itself as a major regional, even global, political actor. In addition to emphasising the need to reassert Moscow's effective internal control over the whole of Russian territory, President Putin focused on rebuilding Russia's influence, even control, within post-Soviet space as the first stage in the process of rebuilding Russia's international political position. For this purpose Russia's control over energy supplies and energy distribution networks became an especially important tool, used most visibly in the Russian Federation's relations with Belarus, Ukraine and Georgia (Nygren, 2008a).[4]

Control over energy became a central element in Russian foreign policy, more broadly not only because it represented an important tool in influencing decision-making in neighbouring countries, but also because of the West's – especially the United States' – attempts to reduce Russia's role in dominating energy flows to Europe from throughout all of Eurasia. Already in the 1990s, the Clinton administration had initiated efforts to develop alternative delivery routes to bring Central Asian gas to Europe that did not cross Russian territory and were not therefore likely to increase Russia's dominant role in supplying energy to Europe.

In the development of Moscow's relations with the three countries of the South Caucasus, the importance of control over energy differed significantly. In the years preceding the run-up to the Russian–Georgian War of August 2008, for example, Russian economic pressures on Georgia paralleled in many respects those that it brought to bear against Ukraine (Nygren, 2007) – and largely for similar reasons related to influencing both the domestic and foreign policy orientation of the country. After the Rose Revolution of 2003 reoriented Georgian politics towards more open political participation and more importantly towards full integration into NATO and the European Union, Russian relations with Georgia deteriorated appreciably. By the summer of 2008, Russian firms owned much of the internal energy distribution system in Georgia – ownership had been transferred in earlier years in order to cover Georgia's debts for energy imports from Russia. Yet Georgia, as we will see below, benefitted from Western efforts to construct alternative gas pipelines that avoided Russian territory and more generally from Western political and economic support. Moreover Azerbaijan, as an important energy producer and as a key participant in the development of alternative transportation routes from Central Asia to Europe, was largely able to avoid Russian economic pressures and to deal with Moscow from a position of some strength.

Because of its political and economic isolation and its geographical position, Armenia was in a much weaker position vis-à-vis Russia than were the other two states of the region. Given the unresolved conflict between Armenia and Azerbaijan over the status of Nagorno-Karabakh and other regions of western Azerbaijan still under Armenian control and the sour relationship between Armenia and Turkey that has its roots in the Armenian massacre of a century ago – both of which contribute to the closed borders between Armenia and both neighbouring Turkic states – the residual economic impact of the massive earthquake that devastated much of Armenia in 1988 and the absence of energy resources on Armenian territory, Armenia has been heavily dependent on Russia in the realms of both security and economics. Probably the major difference in the overall situation of Georgia and

Azerbaijan when compared with Armenia is the fact that to varying degrees the former have established growing ties with the European market into which they are being integrated (Woehrel, 2009).

At this point in our discussion we turn to the central question concerning the reasons that the South Caucasus has become an area of competition and discord between the West and the East. The answer clearly relates to energy, to the gas and oil reserves of Central Asia and the Caspian Sea region, even though, according to some Western analysts, the main objectives of European policy in the South Caucasus are security, and only secondarily energy, and economic factors (Meister, 2010).

In his analysis of the EU's policy in the South Caucasus, Stefan Meister states that Europe's failure to play an effective role in conflict resolution in the Caspian region resulted from the inability of EU member states to adapt to the change of the power balance in the region, in particular the rise of Azerbaijan's role and importance (Meister, 2010). As already mentioned the increase of Azerbaijan's role as an important energy supplier for Europe, thanks to the Baku–Tbilisi–Ceyhan (BTC) pipeline,[5] makes the South Caucasus an important region for the oil and gas supply to the European market. The BTC pipeline, which began supplying Europe with petroleum from Azerbaijan in May 2005, transports Caspian oil to the West bypassing Russia, a long-awaited event for the West. For European countries this and other planned oil and gas pipelines provide several important benefits. First, they expand the amount of oil and gas that can be imported into Europe, while simultaneously reducing the domination of the Russian Federation over the supplies of Eurasian oil and gas shipped to Europe. Until the opening of the BTC pipeline all oil and gas destined for Central and Western Europe, regardless of the country of origin throughout the entire region, flowed through Russian pipelines. Although Russia did not use this domination over energy supplies to pressure the countries of Western Europe, on various occasions it did use this dominance to pressure immediate neighbours, such as Belarus, Ukraine and Georgia.

The development of alternative supply routes to Europe has also been viewed by Caspian region producing states as a positive as well, since it expands both their economic and political options and strengthens their bargaining positions in their relations with Russia. So because of its geographic location as the non-Russian bridge between Central Asia and Europe and because of the energy resources of the Greater Caspian region, the South Caucasus has become an area of great interest to both Russia and the West. In the wake of the war between Russia and Georgia in August 2008 and the gas conflict between Russia and Ukraine in January 2009, the EU decided to formalise its relationship with some of the former Soviet republics. Thus the EU's Eastern Partnership, established in 2009, is supposed to accelerate collaboration between the EU and Belarus, Ukraine and Moldova, as well as with Azerbaijan, Armenia and Georgia, and to contribute to the economic and political development of these countries (Meister, 2010). Put differently the EU is attempting to find ways to influence former Soviet space beyond the areas already incorporated into the European Union itself. As one might have expected, Moscow's reaction towards the establishment of the Eastern Partnership has been quite negative, for it sees it as but another example of unwarranted Western meddling in areas of preeminent Russian interest. It is important to recognise that this is the political and security environment in which Western and Russian energy policy is being pursued in the South Caucasus.

The beginnings of the energy battle

It was not long ago when all Caspian oil was transported to the Western market via Russia's Black Sea terminal.[6] After the Soviet Union collapsed in late 1991, the former Soviet countries started to enter into the world market. At the beginning however Russia still played the key role in the energy projects of the post-Soviet states – Azerbaijan and Kazakhstan – because all of the oil and gas exports were transported through what had been the integrated Soviet pipeline network. This meant that oil or gas produced in Azerbaijan that was destined for the European market could only be delivered through pipelines that went through Russian territory. Already by the mid 1990s, the West – in particular the United States – concluded that, for various political and economic reasons, it was better to have direct access to the Caspian and Central Asian energy sources by bypassing Russia. With this decision the 'energy battle' began. Currently there are several potential oil transport routes from Central Asia and the Greater Caspian Basin to the Western market that bypass Russian territory: the Baku–Supsa and Baku–Tbilisi–Ceyhan (BTC) oil pipelines, along with the Baku–Tbilisi–Erzurum natural gas pipeline. Economists predict that Caspian oil production will increase to 1.5 billion barrels (29 billion tonnes) by the year 2015 (Tsagareishvili and Gvenetadze, 2009).

Unfortunately for the West the political situation in the South Caucasus is still unstable because of several frozen conflicts that have not been resolved for the last twenty years.[7] Moreover in the view of Stefan Meister (2010), the passivity of the EU over the past two decades in responding to the various conflicts in the South Caucasus allowed

Russia to continue to maintain its dominant position throughout the Caspian region (see also Karbuz, 2010). As Meister (2010) argues, Europe should use the opportunity of the recent Russia–Georgia conflict to try to secure the European presence in the South Caucasus. The geopolitical situation in the South Caucasus remains complex and even dangerous. Relations between Russia and Georgia are unstable, since Georgia has not accepted the secession of Abkhazia and South Ossetia. Relations between Armenia and Azerbaijan remain frozen over the issue of Karabakh; while Armenian–Turkish relations have fluctuated, but at the conflictual end of the spectrum. The outside observer can conclude that the EU and Russia should cooperate and try to solve these various 'frozen conflicts' in the region. But to date that has not occurred; moreover the growing competition between the EU and Russia to gain access to the Caspian energy sources and the Central Asia market are not likely to contribute to a mutual 'peacemaking initiative'. In the following pages we will discuss the extent to which Russian energy policy has affected the three countries of the South Caucasus.

As we have already noted, although, on the one hand, Russian President Dmitri Medvedev noted in 2008 that Eurasia, including the South Caucasus, is 'a region of Russia's special interest', that interest was shown only sporadically before the emergence of the presidency of Vladimir Putin in 2000. On the other hand, the United States and the EU member states neglected the South Caucasus until relatively recently as well, although NATO began to expand its involvement in the region already in the 1990s and the West began to push the construction of alternative pipeline projects at the same time. In the view of Margarita Assenova, 'the Organization for Security and Cooperation in Europe (OSCE) is limited because it is not able to deal in on-going conflicts' (Assenova, 2010). She elaborates that the South Caucasus and Central Asian regions have not received the attention that they require because of the obstacles that the OSCE experiences in Russia's self-declared sphere of influence. Moreover according to Assenova, 'The onset of the war with Georgia meant that the OSCE had failed in resolving conflicts within the European realm' (Assenova, 2010; see also Hopmann, 2010).

The establishment of differing economic institutions in the South Caucasus

Armenia

As we have already discussed briefly, the post-Soviet states took three different routes in managing their economic relations with other countries: the countries that favoured liberalist ideas entered the World Trade Organization (WTO). Others, which favoured participation in regional economic institutions over a market-oriented economy, so-called Soviet integralists, became members of the Commonwealth of Independent States (CIS). Finally, the last group chose the path that led toward autarky, with reliance on national institutions and the general closure of the economy by using high tariffs and inconvertible currencies (Darden, 2009, p. 51). Not all of the new states followed a single policy line. For example, Armenia, which has suffered from economic blockades by two of its neighbouring countries, went from liberalism to integralism and back again. As Darden argues, the Nagorno-Karabakh conflict was the main reason for the country to favour the liberal direction, since the integralist course was simply unavailable (Darden, 2009, p. 188). In other words Armenia's economic course after the fall of the Soviet Union was mainly determined by its security choices, albeit government officials wished to follow integralist policies. But according to Darden, 'the Karabakh question was so salient that it can be difficult even to identify the economic views of Armenian officials' (Darden, 2009, p. 185).

However, in comparison with the other post-Soviet states, one can conclude that Armenia, despite the fact that the economic and social crisis in the country in the early 1990s was particularly harsh – the Armenians survived with hot water and heating or electricity for only two hours a day during 1992–96 – has always had a liberal regime. On 21 September 1991, Armenia opened a complicated page in her history, when its first president, Levon Ter-Petrosian, one of the leaders of the 'Karabakhian movement' and a famous Armenian dissident who spent some time in a Soviet prison, proclaimed an independent democratic republic. While most were excited about the freedom they received with the new democratic status of Armenia, others in the nation – including former communists and professionals – were anxious about their future.

In addition, after Nagorno-Karabakh declared independence from Azerbaijan with the objective of becoming part of Armenia, the two neighbouring countries were involved in a bloody war that lasted for almost four years. The two alienated nations, which before had close ties as constituent republics of the Soviet Union, suffered significant losses. Indeed male emigration increased from Armenia because of the conflict. According to data presented in 1991–93 by the Aviation Ministry of the Republic of Armenia, the yearly balance of migration was estimated at 831,000 to 865,500 (Yeghiazaryan et al., 2003, p. 4). The male population aged 18–45 was leaving the country in order to escape war and mandatory military service, as well as because of the severe economic crisis that brought tremendous cuts in income for most of the population, the collapse of the energy supply and a sharp deterioration in living conditions.[8] Approximately 1 million Armenians were either unemployed or on involuntary forced leave by July 1993 (Dudwick, 1997, p. 237). In addition people received their salaries late and industrial workers received wages in the form of the goods that their factory produced rather than as cash. Nevertheless many workers preferred to work rather than leave, for the sake of socialising with friends and retaining access to public resources, information and professional contacts. Meanwhile prosperous Armenians, or those who had relatives abroad, were leaving the country, in most cases permanently, after the Soviet Union collapsed. Dudwick notes that about 10 per cent of the immigrants left as families and the rest were men between the ages of 18 and 60 (Dudwick, 1997, p. 241). During this time people left the country not only because of the economic crisis, but also because of the changes in the political system. According to Swedberg (2002):

> Preliminary census data, collected on October 10–19, 2001, indicated that 950,000 Armenians have emigrated since the Soviet collapse in 1991. According to the United Nations International Organization for Migration (IOM) Armenia has the highest rate of population outflow in the former Soviet Union. Nonetheless, the fact that the official population remained over 3 million came as a relief to many, considering the speculation that the number might have fallen below 2 million. (CIA, 2011)[9]

Armenia is one of the most industrialised countries among the post-Soviet states, although it lacks an internal natural resource base. During the years 1994–97, it was actively involved in CIS institutions. However with the election as president of Robert Kocharyan in 1997, Armenia chose a liberal policy orientation and became a member of the WTO in 2003. It was a rather compulsory choice, since to maintain close ties with other former Soviet states required shipments by heavy rail, which was impossible because of the Azerbaijani blockade but also because of the war in the Georgian region of Abkhazia (Darden, 2009, p. 189). Meanwhile, after the fall of the Soviet Union, Armenia maintained the highest level of economic relations with and dependence on the Russian Federation among the three Transcaucasian states because of its lack of natural gas and oil and its dependence on Russia for its energy supplies. Moreover, Armenia also continues to suffer from the unstable geopolitical situation resulting from the war with Azerbaijan and the ensuing blockade by Azerbaijan and Turkey, which greatly impacted the Armenian economy. Therefore Russian political and economic influence on Armenia cannot be underestimated. For example, the sole distributor and importer of Russian gas in Armenia is the Armenian–Russian firm, ArmRosgazprom, which was established in 1997. Gazprom holds 80 per cent of the company's stock, while only 20 per cent of the company's authorised capital belongs to the Armenian government. In return Russia continues to secure its military presence in the South Caucasus; for example, in August 2010, it signed a 49-year extension of an agreement providing Russia with military bases in Armenia. The latter will give Russia a chance to continue to play a key role in the South Caucasus region, despite the confrontation with Georgia and the pro-Western politics of Azerbaijan. In the meantime Armenia is trying to expand its involvement in the European market as well, but so far without much success because of its poor relations with Turkey and Azerbaijan, which provide the main routes for energy exports for the European market. Moreover because of the geopolitical situation in Armenia discussed above, Russia was able to participate in the Iranian–Armenian gas pipeline agreement.

In 2006, as part of Russia's policy of taking over energy-related assets in neighbouring countries to cover these countries' outstanding debts for past energy deliveries, Armenian officials announced that Gazprom would assume effective management control of the Iranian–Armenian gas pipeline. According to some experts this acquisition may indicate Russia's intent to block the use of Armenia as a pipeline route independent of Russian control. Some of the gas will be used to generate electricity for Iran and Georgia, but the remainder may satisfy all of Armenia's other consumption needs, removing its dependence on Russian gas transported via Georgia (Woehrel, 2009; Nygren, 2008b).

Despite the fact that Armenia has no substantial energy resources such as gas or oil, but because of its geopolitical location, Armenia is viewed as an area of interest both for the West and for Russia. Therefore Russia will continue to attempt to strengthen its influence in Armenia as part of its overall effort to influence, even control, the South Caucasus more generally – in particular in its ongoing effort to control energy flows to the West. Meanwhile the European Union continues to try to integrate Armenia into the European market, in part through its new Eastern Partnership Programme. Were Armenia able to resolve its important political differences with both Turkey and Azerbaijan, it would also likely be able to benefit from the construction of the planned Nabucco gas pipeline and other energy projects in the region.[10]

Azerbaijan

Azerbaijan is an important exporter of natural gas and oil and a crucial element in the transport corridor between Central Asia and Europe. According to *Oil and Gas Journal*, Azerbaijan's crude oil reserves were estimated at 7 billion barrels (approximately 50 billion tonnes) in January 2009 (US Energy Information Administration, 2009). The country has three major export pipelines (Map 12.1): BTC (the Baku–Tbilisi–Ceyhan pipeline system) runs 1110 miles from the Azeri–Chirag–Guneshli fields in the Caspian Sea, via Georgia to Ceyhan, the Mediterranean port of Turkey, and from there on to European markets. The BTC pipeline also transports Kazakhstani oil to the West. The Baku–Supsa pipeline system has an estimated capacity of 145,000 barrels per day (bbl/d) and runs 520 miles from Baku, Azerbaijan, to Supsa, Georgia, on the Black Sea. And, the third export route is the 830-miles-long Baku–Novorossiysk pipeline (northern route), which runs from the Sangachal terminal to the Black Sea. As we have already noted, the alternative export routes have provided the Azeris with the ability to resist Russian control over their exports to the West.

After the Soviet collapse members of the Azerbaijani government seemingly were more interested in personal enrichment than in the country's economic development. For example, the European Bank for Reconstruction and Development ranked Azerbaijan as the most corrupt country in the world in 1999 (Darden, 2009, p. 196). This has not been a revelation for those familiar with Azerbaijani history. Unlike Armenia and Georgia, where non-communist opposition groups came into power, the Kremlin once again appointed its own elites in Azerbaijan: Heidar Aliev, a former KGB officer and first secretary of the Azerbaijani Soviet Republic from 1969 to 1982, took office in June 1993. Indeed under his rule Azerbaijan had a reputation in the Soviet Union for being riddled with corruption. Aliev was also one of the closest friends of Leonid Brezhnev, and the latter was always given the most expensive gifts by Aliev on his multiple visits to the republic. According to Darden, from 1993 to 2000, Azerbaijan favoured different types of economic ideas: from integralist sentiments to vague liberal views. But unlike Eduard Shevardnadze in Georgia, Aliev never favoured Gorbachev's reforms and ruled Azerbaijan after the Soviet Union collapsed using the old communist style of 'divide and rule' (Darden, 2009, p. 197).

Nevertheless the main concern with the Caspian Sea resources is the ongoing legal dispute over the status of the sea: Russia, Kazakhstan, Iran, Turkmenistan and Azerbaijan all claim territorial rights over the Caspian Sea. Azerbaijan also participates in the Baku–Tbilisi–Erzurum pipeline

279

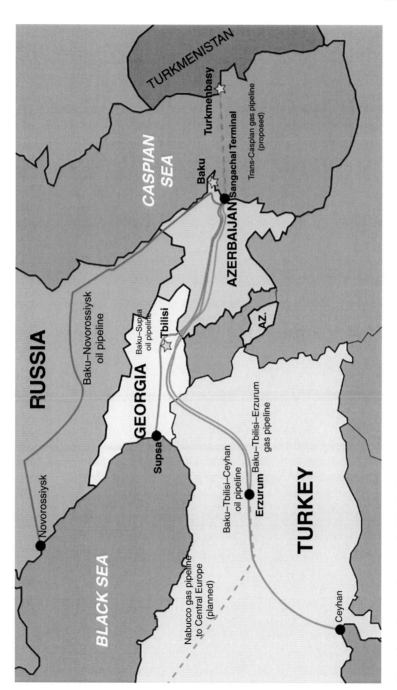

Map 12.1 Gas pipelines in the South Caucasus
Source: From Wikimedia Commons. Prepared by Thomas Blomberg, 10 August 2008.

project (BTE; which transports natural gas from the Shah-Deniz gas field in Azerbaijan to Turkey, and is involved in several other proposed pipeline projects, the most important of which is that which might construct the cross-Caspian pipeline. In sum Azerbaijan's natural gas and oil resources and its position as an important transit country help the EU to end its dependency on Russia as an energy transit corridor. It is for this reason that the development of 'the Southern Corridor required an extraordinary effort' that had to take into account complicated bilateral and multilateral relations among the Caspian states (Fitzpatrick, 2010). From the perspective of the Azerbaijanis, their situation enables them to play Russia and the EU against one another to some degree. They have been able, on the one hand, to sign a contract with Gazprom to sell an unspecified amount of gas to Russia, while, on the other hand, to participate in various energy projects aimed at bypassing Russia (Pannier, 2009; Svarants, 2011).

Georgia

For Moscow relations with Georgia have generated by far the most serious problems of the three South Caucasian countries over the past two decades. Georgia managed to maintain some cultural independence during the decades of the Soviet regime; consequently, Georgian nationalism was always an obstacle in its relationship with the Kremlin. However this strong ethnic identity of the Georgians did not affect its integration into the Soviet system in terms of political and economic interdependence (Curtis, 1994, p. 162). It was only at the end of the Soviet era that Georgian nationalism contributed to serious problems in its relations with the new Russian Federation. Nevertheless Georgia proclaimed its independence with a nationalist government, which favoured mercantilist economic views (Darden, 2009, p. 190). Hence a new independent republic became involved in several civil wars, with all of the economic and political consequences of the fighting. After former Soviet Foreign Minister and reformer Eduard Shevarnadze took office Georgia promptly chose a liberal course of economic development, which afterwards defined Georgia's economic policies (Curtis, 1994). As Darden has noted:

> Georgian economic policies follow closely the shifts in the ideas of the leadership, which were themselves the product of a highly contingent political struggle for control of the country. In terms of its foreign economic policy and institutional membership, Georgian policy appears to follow directly from the economic ideas of the

elite. Under Gamsakhurdia, the country pursued an autarkic path. The country practically ended shipments of goods to Russia and other post-Soviet countries through interstate contracts. Georgia, like the three Baltic states, initially refused to join the Commonwealth of Independent States and did not participate in its meetings or economic agreements. When Georgia finally did join the CIS in 1993, under Shevardnadze, it was not primarily for economic reasons. CIS membership was part of a deal that gave Shevardnadze's government the support of Russian-commanded CIS troops in the civil war he was fighting with Gamsakhurdia's forces and secured a ceasefire with the Abkhazian separatists. (Darden, 2009, p. 194)

Therefore it was only after the 'Rose Revolution' of 2003 that Georgian policy took a strongly pro-Western orientation, thereby contributing to a further deterioration in relations with Russia – to the point of actual military confrontation in the Georgia–Russia War of August 2008 (Woehrel, 2009).[11] As Bertil Nygren (2007, and 2008a, pp. 119–53) has pointed out, Russia first used a variety of economic levers, including those related to Georgia's dependence on Russia for energy, to influence Georgia's policy – especially its commitment to joining NATO. With the failure of these efforts, Moscow finally resorted to direct military intervention.

Despite its disastrous defeat in the August 2008 war with Russia, Georgia remains defiant vis-à-vis Russia. Obviously support from the United States is relevant. However Georgia is also fortunate to be a neighbour of oil- and gas-rich Azerbaijan and thus to be a transit state for several oil and gas pipeline projects that transit the energy from the South Caucasus to the European markets.

Conclusion

As we have maintained throughout this chapter, the three countries of the Transcaucasus – Armenia, Azerbaijan and Georgia – have had quite different relationships based on the degree of their economic dependence on Russia, especially for energy. This dependence has also been related to the type of economic system that the leaders selected to build their economies after the collapse of the USSR. After the Rose Revolution of 2003, the new leaders of Georgia opted to open up their economy to the global economic system, which meant establishing close economic, political and security ties with the European Union and NATO. This in turn brought them into increasing conflict with the

Russian Federation. Because of its wealth of energy resources and its location as a central player in the development of alternative energy transport to Europe that avoided Russian territory, Azerbaijan has also opted for an economic model that includes close collaboration with the global economy.

Armenia finds itself in conflict with its neighbours both to its immediate west and east, lacking domestic natural resources upon which to rebuild its economy. Throughout the post-Soviet period Armenia has been by far the most dependent of the three Caucasian countries on Russia, both for economic and security reasons and has generally pursued an economic policy that ties them to other post-Soviet members of the CIS.

Russia's position in the South Caucasus is generally a strong one. However the fact that Russia largely ignored the region in the 1990s and that other actors – from regional states such as Turkey and Iran to external ones such as the United States, the European Union and China – established themselves in various ways in the area, has resulted in a much more competitive position for Russia as it attempts to dominate the region. As we have seen, the central issue of interest to both Russia and the other state actors concerns control over the energy resources of the region. For Europe, direct access to the oil and gas resources of the Caspian region and the reduction of dependence on Russian control of these resources are an important policy concern (Kudryasheva, 2009).

Notes

1. Darden (2009, pp. 306–9) argues that a government's decision to join international trade institutions was rooted in its economic ideas. Therefore the countries where integralists had been in power for decades – Kazakhstan, Belarus, Tajikistan – were the drivers in this process. Meanwhile other post-Soviet states had an integralist faction in power for a certain period of time. Russia, for example, played a leading role in the 1990s in implementing an integralist policy in the region, but only during the period when integralists controlled the government in the country. However the countries where liberal governments had been in power tended to join the WTO: Kyrgyzstan (1998), Latvia (1999), Estonia (1999), Georgia (2000), Lithuania (2001), Moldova (2001) and Armenia (2003). Finally, while mercantilist ideas were less popular in the region than integralist and liberal views, some of the post-Soviet republics followed this course in the early 1990s: Ukraine, Moldova, Latvia, Lithuania and Georgia were ruled by mercantilist-oriented governments. In the meantime Turkmenistan and Uzbekistan became the typical bearers of mercantilist ideas, by pursuing an autarkic international strategy and rejecting active participation in CIS regional economic institutions and the WTO, closing their markets to imports in conjunction with controlling international exchange.

2. See the chapter in this volume by Diana Digol who discusses Moscow's initial ignoring of Central Asia before there was a shift in policy at the turn of the century. For a comprehensive assessment of Russian policy in the Caucasus and Central Asia in competition with other external actors see Freire and Kanet (2010); see also Ziegler (2010).
3. On Russia's relations with neighbouring states see Nygren (2008a).
4. Probably the most comprehensive treatment of Russia's use of energy as a political tool in relations with other post-Soviet states can be found in the work of Bertil Nygren (2008a, 2008b).
5. The Baku–Tbilisi–Ceyhan pipeline is the 1768-kilometer-long pipeline that transports Azerbaijani oil to the West through Georgia and Turkey, while bypassing Armenia. Russia and Armenia objected to the building of the pipeline, while the West played a major role in supporting the efforts of Turkey, Azerbaijan and Georgia to link the Caspian region and beyond to the European market.
6. Among the most important studies of oil and gas supplies from Russia and the Greater Caspian area to Europe, as well as the pipeline systems to bring the energy to Europe, are those by Ebel and Menon (2000); Mankoff (2009); Nies (2008, 2010); and Nygren (2008b).
7. This refers first and foremost to the dispute between Armenia and Azerbaijan over the territory of Nagorno-Karabakh and the corridor that connects it to Armenia proper. Although the disputes between Georgia and the secessionist provinces of Abkhazia and South Ossetia have seemingly been resolved by Russian military intervention, the long-term legal status of these areas remains in question.
8. For instance, gross domestic product (GDP) in 1993, the lowest point in the post-Soviet crisis, was 36.2 per cent of the GDP level of 1989, which could be considered as one of the most serious economic declines of any country in recent history (Yeghiazaryan et al., 2003).
9. The official Armenian population estimate is 2,967,975 (July 2011 estimate), with a population growth rate of −0.063 per cent, a birth rate of 12.85 per 1000, and a net migration rate of −3.76 migrant(s) per 1000 (CIA, 2011).
10. The Nabucco gas pipeline will link the eastern border of Turkey to Baumgartner in Austria, bypassing Russia. The construction of the pipeline will start in 2012 and the first gas will flow in 2015. The main suppliers of the gas will be Azerbaijan, Turkmenistan and Iraq, while the areas to receive the gas include Europe, as well as Egypt. Recently Richard Morningstar, Special Envoy of the United States Secretary of State for Eurasian Energy, stated during his visit in Istanbul, that Armenia can become a full participant in the region, if 'somehow an agreement is reached' (Kurd.net, 2010).
11. For detailed discussions of the Russian–Georgian relationship, including the outbreak of warfare, see the chapters in this volume by Luke March and John B. Dunlop.

References

Areshev, Andrei (2010) 'Turtsiya, Iran i Rossiya v Zakavkaz'e', *Geopolitika*, informatsionno-analiticheskiy portal, 26 October, available at: http://geopolitica.ru/Articles/1123/ (accessed 2 January 2011).

Assenova, Margarita (2010) 'Developing US strategy in the South Caucasus and Caspian Basin', paper presented at the Center for Strategic and International Studies and Institute for New Democracies (CSIS–IND) Conference on 'Passing the Torch of the OSCE Chairmanship', Washington, DC, 24 June, available at: http://csis.org/files/attachments/100624_caucasus.conference.summary_1.pdf (accessed 3 December 2011).

Central Intelligence Agency (CIA) (2011) *The World Factbook, Armenia 2011* (Washington, DC: Central Intelligence Agency), available at: https://www.cia.gov/library/publications/the-world-factbook/geos/am.html (accessed 20 November 2011).

Curtis, Glenn (ed.) (1994) *Armenia, Azerbaijan and Georgia Country Studies* (Washington, DC: Library of Congress).

Danielyan, Emil (2011) 'Russian leaders hail "strategic partnership" with Armenia, Azerbaijan', *Armenialiberty*, 4 January, available at: http://www.armtown.com/news/en/rfe/20110104/2266987/ (accessed 10 January 2011).

Darden, Keith A. (2009) *Economic Liberalism and its Rivals: The Formation of International Institutions among the Post-Soviet States* (Cambridge: Cambridge University Press).

de Waal, Tomas (2010) *The Caucasus: An Introduction* (Oxford: Oxford University Press).

Dudwick, Nora (1997) 'Out of the kitchen into the crossfire: women in independent Armenia', in Mary Buckley (ed.), *Post-Soviet Women: From the Baltic to Central Asia* (Cambridge: Cambridge University Press), pp. 235–49.

Ebel, Robert and Rajan Menon (eds) (2000) *Energy and Conflict in Central Asia and the Caucasus* (Lanham, MD, and New York: Rowman and Littlefield Publishers).

Fitzpatrick, Catherine (2010) 'EU seeks to broker tran-Caspian pipeline deal between Turkmenistan and Azerbaijan', EurasiaNet.org, 10 August, available at: http://www.eurasianet.org/node/61716 (accessed 5 December 2010).

Freire, Maria Raquel and Roger E. Kanet (eds) (2010) *Key Players and Regional Dynamics in Eurasia: The Return of the 'Great Game'* (Houndmills: Palgrave Macmillan).

Hopmann, P. Terrence (2010) 'Intergovernmental organisations and non-state actors, Russia and Eurasia: the OSCE', in Maria Raquel Freire and Roger E. Kanet (eds), *Key Players and Regional Dynamics in Eurasia: The Return of the 'Great Game'* (Houndmills: Palgrave Macmillan), pp. 238–70.

Ishkanian, Armine (2008) *Democracy Building and Civil Society in Post-Soviet Armenia* (Abingdon: Routledge).

Jackson, Alexander (2010) 'The Kyrgyzstan Crisis: a qualified success for Turkish diplomacy', *Caucasian Review of International Affairs*, vol. 4, no. 3, 24 June, available at: http://cria-online.org/CU_-_file_-_article_-_sid_-_94.html (accessed 10 December 2010).

Kanet, Roger E. (2010) 'Russia and the Greater Caspian Basin: withstanding the US challenge', in Maria Raquel Freire and Roger E. Kanet (eds), *Key Players and Regional Dynamics in Eurasia: The Return of the 'Great Game'* (Houndmills: Palgrave Macmillan), pp. 81–102.

Karbuz, Sohbet (2010) 'Losing the energy battle: how and why the US and EU need to engage the Black Sea region', *Journal of Energy Security*, July, available at: http://www.ensec.org/index.php?option=com_content&view=article&id=255:losing-the-battle-why-and-how-the-united-states-and-europe-need-to-engage-the-black-sea-region&catid=108:energysecuritycontent&Itemid=365 (accessed 6 December 2010).

Kozhemiakin, Alexander V. and Roger E. Kanet (1998) 'Russia as a regional peace-keeper', in Roger E. Kanet (ed.), *Resolving Regional Conflicts* (Champaign, IL: University of Illinois Press), pp. 225–39.

Kurd.net (2010). 'US welcomes Iraqi Kurdish gas in Europe-bound energy projects', Kurd.net, 3 October, available at: http://www.todayszaman.com/ news-223315-us-welcomes-kurdish-gas-in-europe-bound-energy-projects.html (accessed 19 November 2011).

Kudryasheva, Yulia (2009) 'Energeticheskaya politika Turtsii na postsovetskom-prostranstve', Informatsionno-Analiticheskiy Tsentr, February, available at: http://www.ia-centr.ru/expert/3839/ (accessed 5 December 2010).

Lukyanov, Fyodor (2010) 'Building a Great Europe', *Moscow Times*, October 26.

Mankoff, Jeffrey (2009) 'Eurasian energy security', *Council Special Report*, No. 43 (New York: Council on Foreign Relations), available at: http://www.cfrter-rorism.org/content/publications/attachments/Eurasia_CSR43.pdf (accessed 28 February 2011).

Meister, Stefan (2010) 'Recalibrating Germany's and EU's policy in the South Caucasus', in *Deutsche Gesellschaft für AuswärtigePolitik*, no. 2, pp. 1–16, available at: http://www.dgap.org/wp-content/uploads/2010/11/2010-02_DGAPana_Meister_gesamt.pdf (accessed 3 October 2010).

Mesbahi, Mohiaddin (2010) 'Eurasia between Russia, Turkey and Iran', in Maria Raquel Freire and Roger E. Kanet (eds), *Key Players and Regional Dynamics in Eurasia: The Return of the 'Great Game'* (Houndmills: Palgrave Macmillan), pp. 164–92.

Muradyan, Igor (2010) 'Rossiya i situatsiya na Kavkaze', *Lragir*, 11 December.

Nies, Susanne (2008) *Oil and Gas Delivery to Europe: An Overview of Existing and Planned Infrastructures* (Paris: Institut Français des Relations Internationales (IFRI)), available at: http://www.ifri.org/files/Energie/OilandGas_Nies.pdf (accessed 28 February 2011).

Nies, Susanne (2010) 'The EU-Russia energy relationship: European, Russian, common interests?', in Roger E. Kanet (ed.), *Russian Foreign Policy in the 21st Century* (Houndmills: Palgrave Macmillan), pp. 266–86.

Nygren, Bertil (2007) 'Putin's attempts to subjugate Georgia: from sabre-rattling to the power of the purse', in Roger E. Kanet (ed.), *Russia: Re-emerging Great power* (Houndmills: Palgrave Macmillan), pp. 107–23.

Nygren, Bertil (2008a) *The Rebuilding of Greater Russia: Putin's Foreign Policy toward the CIS Countries* (Abingdon: Routledge).

Nygren, Bertil (2008b) 'Putin's use of natural gas to reintegrate the CIS region', *Problems of Post-Communism*, vol. 55, no. 4, pp. 3–15.

Pannier, Bruce (2009) 'Germany's gas war? Nabucco versus South Stream and Schroeder vs. Fischer', Radio Free Europe/Radio Liberty, 3 July.

Payaslian, Simon (2007) *The History of Armenia: From the Origins to the Present* (New York: Palgrave Macmillan).

Pirog, Robert (2007) 'Russian oil and gas challenges', Congressional Research Service (CRS) Report for Congress (Washington, DC: Congressional Research Service), available at: http://www.fas.org/sgp/crs/row/RL33212.pdf (accessed 5 February 2011).

Svarants, Aleksandr (2011) 'Rossiiskaya energeticheskaya politika i problema Nagornogo-Karabakha', *NoevKovcheg*, no. 1 (160), January, available at: http:// noev-kovcheg.ru/mag/2011-01/2319.html (accessed 4 January 2011).

Swedberg, Jeffrey (2002) 'Armenian census numbers spark debate but are good news for president', Central Asia–Caucasus Institute, *Analyst*, 27 March, available at: http://www.cacianalyst.org/?q=node/140/, (accessed 15 November 2011).

Tsagareishvili, Paata and Gogita Gvenetadze (2009) 'New Caspian oil production will bypass Russia', in *iStockAnalyst*, 26 January, available at: http://www.istock analyst.com/article/viewiStockNews/articleid/3071249 (accessed 10 February 2011).

US Energy Information Administration, Independent Statistics and Analysis (2009) 'Azerbaijan, Country Analysis Briefs', October, available at: www.eia. doe.gov (accessed 3 December 2010).

Woehrel, Steven (2009) 'Russian energy policy towards neighboring countries', Congressional Research Service (CRS) Report for Congress, 2 September (Washington, DC: Congressional Research Service), available at: http://www. fas.org/sgp/crs/row/RL34261.pdf (accessed 29 September 2010).

Yazdani, Enayatollah (2006) 'Competetition over the Caspian oil routes: oilers and gamers perspectives', *Alternatives*, vol. 5, nos 1–2, pp. 1–64, available at: http://www.alternativesjournal.net/volume5/number1%262/yazdani.pdf (accessed 2 March 2011).

Yeghiazaryan, Armen, Vahram Avanesian and Nelson Shahnazaryan (2003) *How to Reverse Immigration* (Yerevan: Ameria CJSC).

Ziegler, Charles E. (2010) 'Russia, Central Asia and the Caucasus after the Georgia conflict', in Roger E. Kanet (ed.), *Russian Foreign Policy in the 21st Century* (Houndmills: Palgrave Macmillan), pp. 155–78.

Conclusion: Russia and its Near Neighbours

Maria Raquel Freire and Roger E. Kanet

Shifts in Russian foreign policy have accompanied the process of transition from the Soviet to the post-Soviet domestic order. From a close engagement with the West in the early 1990s, which brought disillusionment regarding the level of both the West's and Russia's commitment to the transition effort, policy evolved towards a new format that is more inclusive, pragmatic and assertive. The Commonwealth of Independent States (CIS) was soon defined as an area of 'special interest', and the Western dimension in Russian politics was balanced by the inclusion of an Eastern dimension, with China and India gaining primacy. While recognising the importance of the shift in Russian interest from the West to the East and keeping in mind that Russian relations with the East are often aimed at balancing current difficulties in relations with the West, we have focused in this volume on Russian policies towards its neighbourhood and on the interplay between Russia and the West in this region, which is the aspect of Western engagement in this area that has been of most concern to Russian policy.

In fact both the United States and Russia continue to view the world largely within a Westphalian framework of absolute sovereignty and the central importance of their ability to act in what they view as the 'national interest' unencumbered by external restrictions. In the past decade, especially since the revival of Russian capabilities and self-confidence under former President Putin, this Russian concern about reestablishing their role in what they once termed the 'Near Abroad', a term that is still in current usage, has on various occasions pitted a Russia determined to reassert its great power status against a United States just as strongly committed to maintaining a dominant – or hegemonic – position in the international system, a positioning that has implications for the nature of relations between more powerful states and their weaker neighbours.

This book analyses Russian foreign policy in a context where Russia has reemerged as a major player in the post-Soviet area. The emergence of centralised domestic governance, along with high revenues from oil and gas, allowed stabilisation at home and constituted a solid basis for an enhanced foreign policy. As has been made clear on many occasions at the highest level, by both Prime Minister Putin and President Medvedev, a resurgent Russia is no longer willing to brook the expansion of Western – that is to say, both NATO and EU – involvement in what Moscow considers its areas of 'privileged interest'. These have been defined essentially as those portions of post-Soviet space, where the CIS has not been capable of aggregating these states in a unifying institutional framework under the command of Russia.

In fact the CIS has grown increasingly divided and over time the differences between the states party to the organisation have underlined its heterogeneous nature, including the differences in the sense of identity and the ways in which those differences have impacted policy. An expression of this trend can be seen in the differentiated courses that these states have been following, depending in part on their own domestic resource bases that have resulted in increasingly independent foreign policies that play off the involvement of external actors. The 'colour revolutions' that swept across Ukraine, Georgia and Kyrgyzstan raised fears in Russia about Western-fuelled movements promoting fundamental changes in the policies of these states, which was understood in Russia as contrary to its interests. Ukraine and Georgia were particularly difficult cases. Their turn towards the West meant a challenge to Russia's reengagement in the CIS that questioned its capability to attract and influence the newly independent states.

The discussion about NATO's further enlargement towards the east, in the context of Western engagement in the post-Soviet space, generated vehement opposition in Russia and demanded a different response from the Russian authorities than those of the past. Vladimir Putin's toughened discourse, which President Medvedev has continued, reinforced the Russian vision of an unbalanced order. Russia's leadership is committed to a multipolar world order in which it exercises clear influence. For Moscow, Western involvement or interference in its neighbouring areas represented a challenge to Russia's national interests. The US decision to pursue a policy of de facto containment of Russia beginning already by the mid 1990s, reinforced Moscow's concerns for security and for its future role in areas adjacent to Russian territory that it viewed as crucial to Russia's long-term interests. The war in Georgia in the summer of 2008 demonstrated well the level of conflict that was reached between Russia and Georgia, but it also showed Russian opposition to Western involvement in an area where Russia wants to play the dominant role. The post-Georgia developments, with the 'reset policy' allowing a changed tone in policies in both Russia and the US, set the stage for a strengthened dialogue that constitutes a window of opportunity for defining a new basis for cooperation. However the change to a more favourable context in Russian relations with the West did not modify Russian assertive policies in its neighbourhood.

In this setting the contributors to this volume make clear the importance to Russian foreign policy of the reassertion of Russian interests and involvement throughout post-Soviet space, as well as the degree to which that involvement has run up against opposition from neighbouring states. They analyse current trends and bring new insights to 'common places', challenging some of the more traditional, realist-based, perspectives and approaches. The study of the determinants of Russian foreign policy is based on an understanding that foreign policy results from a merger between domestic and international dynamics and that issues traditionally embedded in a realist perspective, such as the definition of the national interest or even understandings about national identity, can be read through different lenses with an added contribution to the debate. In this way the approach to power discussed in this volume seeks to go beyond traditional readings, unpacking the many variables that assist in explaining the Russian path towards an assertive foreign policy.

In order to detail the analysis more effectively, the final part of the volume includes the study of energy policies and how the coincidence or not of policies and practices in this fundamental domain play out in Russian foreign policy. The authors concur that the reassertion of Russian policy objectives in its neighbouring area, despite limitations, has brought added leeway for the pursuit of Russian influence. What is innovative about the approach to Russian foreign policy presented here derives from the fact that this study is not tightly wedded to the equation of influence and power but, rather, is based on a conceptual framework that includes the analysis of non-material variables, including assessments of the meaning of 'national interest' and 'national identity' that are at the very core of policy-shaping and policy-making.

Index

Abkhazia
  and August 2008 war, 18, 26, 52,
    63, 76–8, 95, 189, 276, 281
  and Russia, 28, 72, 214, 229, 268
Afghanistan
  and NATO, 131, 189
  and Russian interests, 151, 155,
    158, 164, 183, 189
  and Russian–US cooperation, 165–8
  and security issues, 5, 30, 32, 51,
    140, 152, 156, 179
  and US, 110, 153–5, 163, 192, 212
Armenia
  and Eastern Partnership, 120, 273
  and energy, 232, 235–6, 238
  and Iran, 270
  and Russia, 179, 265–6, 268, 270–2,
    281
  conflict of with Azerbaijan, 270–80
Azerbaijan, 266, 282
  and Eastern Partnership, 120, 273
  and energy, 160, 214, 232, 239,
    272–3, 278–80
  and Nagorno-Karabakh, 271, 274–5,
    277
  and Russia, 179, 185, 232–4, 248,
    268–70

Bakiev, Kurmanbek, 157, 167
Baku–Tbilisi–Ceyhan pipeline (BTC),
    232, 234, 256, 273
  and Azerbaijan's policy, 272, 278
  and Georgia War, 257
  US support for, 214
Belarus, 160, 223
  and Eastern Partnership, 120, 124,
    273
  and NATO, 131
  and Russia, 30, 66, 181, 184, 209,
    227–30, 238, 256, 270–2
  gas war against, 211, 229–31, 256–7
Berdymukhammedov, Gurbanguly,
    121

Biden, Joseph, 5, 207
  speech of, 165

Central Asia
  and EU Strategy for a New
    Partnership, 259
  and Russia, 9–10, 119, 174–94, 207,
    214, 232, 262
  and SCO, 124, 192
  and Turkey, 269
  and US, 9–10, 30, 131, 152–3, 189
  and US–Russia relationship, 153–5,
    158–67
  as a region, 8
  as a security complex, 154–8
  colonial typology of, 119–20
  external actors in, 140, 184–5, 211,
    266–7
  in Chinese core policy strategy, 120,
    193
  oil industry and gas resources of,
    213–14, 232–9, 259–60,
    271–4
Chechnya, 2, 45–6, 48–52, 56, 110,
    118–19, 122, 142, 162, 177,
    180, 215, 267
Collective Security Treaty
    Organisation (CSTO),
    131, 139–41, 145, 163,
    184–5, 192–3, 216, 231,
    239
Commonwealth of Independent
    States (CIS), 112, 157, 177
  conflict resolution in, 161, 228
  establishment of, 160, 184
  integration process, 8, 30, 50, 73,
    275
  intra-CIS politics of, 157, 161, 233,
    275–6, 281, 288
  Russian politics and, 161, 177, 191,
    223–4, 228, 237–9, 243, 281,
    287
  Western criticism, 247